SAVING WILD TIGERS
1900-2000

THE ESSENTIAL WRITINGS

Saving Wild Tigers

This is the rarest picture in the world of a complete family of tigers, including the resident male.

Published by
PERMANENT BLACK
D-28 Oxford Apartments,
11, I.P. Extension,
Delhi 110092

Distributed by
Orient Blackswan P. Ltd.
Bangalore Bhubaneshwar
Calcutta Chennai
Ernakulam Cuwahati
Hyderabad Lucknow
Mumbai New Delhi Patna

First published 2001
First paperback printing 2006
Second impression 2011
ISBN 81-7824-150-1

Typeset by Eleven Arts, Delhi
Printed by Sapra Brothers,
Delhi 110 092

Saving Wild Tigers
1900–2000

The Essential Writings

edited by
VALMIK THAPAR

permanent black

For

Sanjna

Contents

ACKNOWLEDGEMENTS

The idea of doing a book on 'Saving Wild Tigers' came from a discussion with Rukun Advani and from that moment it was a process of ferreting out the right article or essay to give a feel of the last hundred years of the tiger. Many people have helped and I have to thank first of all Peter Smith of ESSO India for his continued commitment to saving wild tigers, and for this book. Mahesh Rangarajan was a great help as a sounding board on the events of the last century. And then there are all the amazing contributors, their publishers, and some authors' offspring, who have permitted me to use their remarkable writings for this volume. Some of these articles have been shorn of academic material—such as footnotes, cross-references, and learned bibliographical data—which were not relevant to the more general purposes of the present book. However, I have nowhere modified, altered or impaired the essays I have used, except in that minimal way.

I thank Sanjna Kapoor for the use of her cover picture, Uttara Mendiratta for helping on the computer, Anuradha Roy for her help on the manuscript and Neelima Rao for the design.

New Delhi
September 2000

VALMIK THAPAR

Valmik

Thapar

Introduction

There is no greater delight than to turn over leaves from the past, to imagine the richness of the natural world and the kind of men who fought to keep it alive. It has been a fascinating exercise to put together this volume of essays on tigers. What emerges is a startling array of people who wrote with passion and zeal about their concerns and their view of the future. This book is a sketch of a century of tiger conservation and I believe it is our understanding of what happened to the tiger in the last century that will enable us to deal with the tiger crisis of this century.

1900–1935: It all started at the turn of the last century with Sainthill Eardley-Wilmot writing about the vanishing wilderness of India. He scans the state of the world's timber and then comes to India and states emphatically that it is the state of the forest that protects the water supply of the country. E.P. Stebbing, by 1920, was one of India's first great protectionists and a man who spoke out for change in the law and governance. He believed that developments in the rifle would destroy India's wildlife—he talks of the closure of tracts of forests, of creating a series of permanent sanctuaries, and he analyses the law in great detail with a view to bringing in amendments. In the same period as Stebbing, F.W. Champion arrived as a tireless campaigner for wildlife. He only used the camera and never the gun—he was passionately opposed to the use of motor cars for shooting and wanted them banned from reserved forests. He wanted to limit gun licences. He had seen enough of death through the years of the First World War and wanted peace, especially with animals. Champion lives around the same time as Corbett and both worked on conservation issues. The writings of both men are remarkable and, as Mahesh Rangarajan puts it, 'Both Corbett and Champion stood out as harbingers of change. Writing about nature and life in the forest gained a wider audience than ever before.'

Jim Corbett realised earliest that the blame for creating the man-eating tiger lay with bullet injuries from hunters. He, with Champion, was the first to befriend the tiger—to fight for the tiger's cause and its gentle nature. Corbett argues on the tiger's behalf, he fights for its survival because the tiger is a true 'gentleman'. His appeal touches the soul of anyone who has worked with tigers.

Both Corbett and Champion left India in the end to live in East Africa.

These must have been strange times for conservationists. Mahesh Rangarajan, in his forthcoming book, *India's Wildlife History: An Introduction* (Permanent Black, 2001), states: 'In sheer numbers, over 80,000 tigers, more than 150,000 leopards and 200,000 wolves were slaughtered in a period of 50 years from 1875 to 1925.' Can you even imagine how much prey existed—in their millions—since their slaughter each year must have been tens of thousands? This butchery of wildlife had its impact on people. This is the time that S.H. Prater, Curator of the Bombay Natural History Society, made his appeal for the protection of wildlife and strict conservation measures. He must have been a witness to the slaughter of the first part of the century. A remarkable period for writings on saving tigers, this must have been triggered by the revulsion people felt at the slaughter. Stanley Jepson also wrote in the late 1930s about the need for protecting the fast depleting wildlife of the country.

1940–1990: Then comes 'the great gap,' from 1940 to 1960 in the writings on saving wild tigers or dealing with conservation issues. We gained Independence and in these twenty years the tiger and wildlife of India came closest to decimation at the hands of man. I think the reason for this gap is the turmoil of those times. The beginning of the Second World War in 1939 resulted in enormous pressures on Indian forests for timber in the early 1940s. Contractors moved in and large tracts of forest were cut down. They had guns, they hunted on a large scale. Few accurate records exist of the slaughter that took place. The wood was sent even to Burma and beyond for building all that the British required. The forest service was fully occupied in this task. The Independence movement was at its peak and soon after Independence the new nation was settling down to its rhythms.

In this post-Independence period the focus completely shifted to growing more food and large tracts of forest land were converted for agriculture. A series of river-valley projects sprung up in tiger habitats. Some of the best tiger habitat of the terai was cleared to settle refugees from Pakistan. While all this habitat devastation took place the elite took to more sophisticated guns and tougher vehicles like jeeps to make inroads into the forest and shoot thousands of tigers and other game. It was a free-for-all. The British had left but the Indian elite was on a binge to shoot tigers. Shikar companies sprang up everywhere, enticing hunters from all over the world to the killing game. Thousands of tigers died each year: we cannot provide exact numbers because our record-keeping in those early years of Independence was abysmal. Even though the first Indian Inspector General of Forests, M.D. Chaturvedi, spearheaded the beginning of wildlife preservation and was responsible for constituting the Indian Board for Wildlife in 1952, it was in vain. The period between 1950 and 1960 remains one of the worst decades for tigers and the wilderness.

The horror of the decade triggered a flurry of conservation writing in the 1960s but for twenty years India had suffered enormous losses to her natural heritage. By the late 1950s for many conservationists the situation must have again appeared dreadful in terms of the tiger's survival. This was the moment for the birth of serious tiger conservation. Then in 1964 E.P. Gee came out to strike a critical note for conservation in *The Wildlife of India*. Gee had battled to save tigers in the 1950s and spoken against those forest officers who felt that a forest officer was not fit to take charge of a division till he had shot his tiger. Gee was convinced that if this continued, there would be no tigers left in India. As a member of the 1952 Indian Board for Wildlife he played an important role in those early years. This was also when Richard Perry produced his treatise on the tigers of the world—he predicted that only a few hundred tigers would be alive at the end of the century. He felt that in the early 1960s India had 4000 tigers and was losing them at the rate of 400 each year! As Perry was writing his book, the first scientific study was being conducted on tigers in Kanha, Madhya Pradesh, by George Schaller, who in a way has been the great guru of all present-day tiger-wallahs. Even Gee met him and was inspired by his work in the field.

There was a great flurry of writing in the 1960s and the 1970s about tigers and their fate. It was the first time science was injected into tiger conservation. Foresters started to speak out for the tiger. The intensity of the debate led first to the ban on tiger shooting and then to the Wildlife Protection Act. Arjan Singh in Dudhwa, Charles McDougal in Nepal, S.P. Shahi in Bihar, K. Sankhala in Delhi, and M. Krishnan in South India wrote on the protection of tigers and the wilderness of India. Though K. Sankhala's book *Tiger* came late, he talks of the birth of Project Tiger around now. As the first Director of Project Tiger, he was really worried about the skin trade—he writes about the critical years of the late 1960s and early 1970s, just before the birth of Project Tiger. After the birth of Project Tiger Sankhala remained devoted to tigers.

Charles McDougal worked in Nepal and in 1977 he went to the extent of saying that at the end of the century the world's tigers would probably all be in cages. It is remarkable that most of the tiger-watchers of the last century did not foresee the survival of the tiger in the wild beyond 1999! It was at this moment that Mel Sunquist started his first radio-collaring of tigers in Nepal to learn more about their lives. This was a vital step forward in the use of science for conservation. Arjan Singh was the remarkable character of those times. Obsessed with tigers, he was the first person in the world to introduce a captive-born tigress, Tara, into the terai forests of Dudhwa. He too was convinced that Dudhwa would not have tigers left in the wild at the turn of the century—but they still do. In a way, all these people in the 1970s played a vital role in ensuring that India would go into the twenty-first century with some tigers in the wild.

S.P. Shahi, in 1977, discussed threadbare the problems of governance and administration and the bleak future of our wilderness. In the light of what we face today it is a fascinating essay, for it depicts the remarkable force of political will in those challenging times. Even today we have a lot to learn from it. At this juncture came M. Krishnan with a review of the first three years of Project Tiger—he was more hopeful than Shahi about the future. Krishnan's life had been full of wildlife and his greatest pleasure came from watching wild animals. For fifty years he wrote about wildlife and served on endless committees of the government hoping to resolve some of the problems.

The 1970s were taken up by 'Saving the Tiger' articles from all over the world: those years must have been fascinating. Guy Mountfort describes the excitement of the times and scans the world of tigers to see how they stand. He played a vital role in starting the process of saving wild tigers in the 1970s. Soon after came John Seidensticker's 'Bearing Witness' which described the process of extinction in a subspecies in Indonesia, the Javan tiger. Seidensticker's association with the tiger in Nepal, India and Bangladesh, as well as other places, is very deep. His contribution to understanding wild tigers has been enormous.

1990–2000: At the end of the 1980s Peter Jackson wrote of the problems and solutions to tiger conservation. He had spent many decades in India and travelled extensively across tiger habitat worldwide. Again, he is a man whose entire life is entangled with the tiger's. By the early 1990s Alan Rabinowitz made a statement of fact about the state of Thailand and it's booming market in wildlife derivatives. Then came Geoffrey Ward's touching exposé on the tiger massacres of India and, like most of us, he believed that the tiger would be virtually extinct at the turn of the century. His account woke the world up to the tiger's plight. John Seidensticker came back in 1996 to talk of tigers and the necessity of saving them while Ullas Karanth, with fervour and optimism, wrote a very pertinent piece on conservation. Over the decade, Karanth played a critical role, injecting conservation with concentrated doses of science.

In 1999 an exciting conference, Tiger 2000, took place in London Zoo and I have used a chunk of papers presented at that meeting to summarise the end of a century of tiger conservation. My personal favourite among these is Alan Rabinowitz and his view of the status of wild tigers in Indo-China—but Siberia and its strategies were equally vital to what was happening. The great anti-poaching operation launched there probably prevented the extinction of the Siberian tiger. R.S. Chundawat's ongoing study of tiger ecology in Panna, Madhya Pradesh, reveals a set of critical problems that requires urgent attention in the present century. One of the last statements in this book comes from P.K. Sen, present

Director, Project Tiger in the Ministry of Environment and Forests. It is a frank look at the severity of the crisis that engulfs India.

Individuals save tigers. This book contains writings by some of the greatest champions of the tiger in the world. There were other legendary figures whose writings I have either not been able to use or who did not write about tigers but played vital roles in keeping the wilderness alive: Dunbar Brander, Sanderson, Forsyth, Lydekker, Burton, Fateh Singh Rathore, S.R. Chowdhury, S. Deb Roy, K.M. Chinnappa, Brijendra Singh and so many more. Then there are some like Rajendra Singh of Tarun Bharat Sangh and Dr G.S. Rathore of Prakratik Society who, against all odds, have worked with local communities to protect tigers and wildlife. There are scores of people who did not know how to read and write among the forest staff but of course their sacrifices for the tiger have been remarkable. Many, like Badhyaya, Laddu, Ramu, and others whose names are not even known, laid their lives down for the tiger's. They all played a vital role.

What is remarkable is that most of us over the past hundred years believed that there wouldn't be a tiger alive in the wild at the turn of the century. We were proved wrong: 2000–3000 tigers still live in India and 5000–7000 live in the world. That is a remarkable achievement in itself. By engaging in this huge battle we do keep delaying the inevitable and that is why some of the people included in this book seem so vital. Saving wild tigers is among the most exciting and challenging tasks confronting us, and I hope the next century sustains the same commitment to the tiger as the last one.

Sainthill

Eardley-Wilmot

Of Forests and Foresters

Sainthill Eardley-Wilmot was, at the turn of the nineteenth century, Inspector General of Forests with the Government of India. He was obsessed with forestry and, in those early years of the forest service, provoked many new conservation initiatives.

A hunting camp in a forest. Several dead tigers await skinning. The twentieth century started with the massacre of tigers throughout India and camps such as this were to be found all over the subcontinent's forests.

The forests of India, vast as they are, will have but little effect in solving the difficulty that is already beginning to be felt in supplying the demand for timber in the British Isles, because they have first to meet the demands of a yet vaster population. They will continue to yield teak and ornamental woods, because India cannot yet fully utilise these expensive products; and there will be an increasing supply of lac, tanning material, and other forest products, available for export, as the exploitation of the forests continues to develop. There may also spring up in the future other industries of some magnitude, such as the manufacture of paper pulp and tannin extracts, but this will probably not take place until the prices of these commodities rise; for it is impossible at present to compete against the advantages possessed by factories in other countries which are located in the midst of dense coniferous forests, or in virgin mangrove swamps, that are both treated on the system of clear felling, often without any provision for a marketable regrowth, when in India much larger areas would have to be worked over in the search for material of suitable quality, and arrangements made for effective natural reproduction.

In the difficulties that are likely to be experienced from a shortage of the timber-supply of the world, England would be well advised to remember the old adage about self-help; for she will get but little from outside, as yearly those countries become fewer that possess enough timber for export as well as for home consumption. As population and prosperity progress, so does also the demand for forest products, so that even those countries that now possess a surplus stock may not in the future have enough even for their own requirements. In some European countries, where there are large areas of both public and private forests that have been under scientific management for centuries, the demand of the population for timber is already in excess of supply, while both to the east and to the west of these islands difficulties before unknown are beginning to make themselves felt. For instance, the combined forest area of France and Germany and Switzerland approaches

'Conclusion' from *Forest Life and Sport in India* by Sainthill Eardley-Wilmot (London, 1911). Retitled.

some 100,000 square miles, yet each of these countries imports timber from abroad, and can better afford to do so by reason of the profit derived from the careful management of their own forests. Denmark, Italy, Spain, and Portugal, are in a worse plight; for their forests neither yield sufficient produce for the inhabitants, nor, apparently, any large revenue to the State.

Russia, Scandinavia, and Austria-Hungary are still exporters of timber, but the amount that will continue to be available from thence must depend on the demands of the population of these countries, and on the answer to the question whether the forest capital, or only the interest therefrom is now being used; while the price of the material that these countries export will rise if it should happen that those nearer the source of supply than England have in the future a larger use for the surplus available. For instance, Continental countries absorb the excess forest harvest of Austria and Hungary, and will probably intercept that of Russia and Scandinavia as soon as any pressing need for it arises; and thus England might easily occupy a worse position in the timber market in the future than she does at present.

In America the needs of the future have been recognised, and within a comparatively few years a State Forest Department has been created, with the intention of supplying later on the needs of the population; but trees do not grow in a day, and if the Americans want Canadian timber they can get it cheaper than we can. In the East, Japan is an instance of a country that has foreseen the importance of forest conservation, and is taking steps to make it effective; while China has hitherto paid little attention to the matter, so that now there are places of which it is said that, so great is the scarcity of wood, there is neither fuel for the living nor coffins for the dead.

All these countries are forced to maintain forests to protect the water-supply and to prevent erosion in the hills, and in proportion to the timely recognition of these indirect benefits, has been that of the direct benefits that have been conferred by the forests. England, on the other hand, is in a position to ignore to some extent the indirect influences of the forest, and will certainly suffer in the future from the absence of the direct benefits they confer; for she has preferred to place entire dependence upon the forest resources of other countries, although she has before her eyes examples of how State forestry not only aids in meeting an ever-increasing industrial demand, but, while bringing profit to the Treasury, also provides remunerative employment to the inhabitants of the country. In the case of an European war, the starvation, not only of the timber market, but also of all those traders that depend on forest material, either in its raw or converted form, would probably deal a severe blow to very many important industrial concerns in England.

The arguments that are adduced against the introduction of State forestry in England appear to be, chiefly, that it will not pay, and that, if it does, a long period must be passed before any return is received on the capital expended. The first objection is based on the current price of timber, which will probably rise in the future much more rapidly than it has in the past, and, moreover, it takes only cash returns into consideration, leaving out others that may become of equal or even greater importance; the second is based on the assumption that it is not the duty of a Government to make provision for the future welfare of the nation; and both appear to have their foundation in errors, either commercial or political.

Meanwhile India has prepared for the future as regards the direct benefits the forests afford to its population, and is commencing to understand that their indirect influences may also affect the industrial progress of the country, not only as regards agriculture, which is, of course, of paramount interest, but also as regards those manufactures for which only the raw material is at present exported. With regard to the former, the yearly yield of five million tons of timber as fuel, of two hundred millions of bamboos, of half a million sterling of minor produce, as well as the grazing afforded to thirteen million cattle, shows what the local demand is at present; and to this may be added produce amounting in value to a quarter of a million sterling that is given freely away to the people. The forest, however, is not exploited even for the amount of produce it can supply at present, nor probably for a tithe of what it could supply if a larger demand justified the expense of more extensive working; but that demand will come in time with the increase of population, and with the construction of railways and their feeder roads that provide cheap and sure carriage; for without such communications the moving of material bulky in proportion to its value must always be hindered by an expenditure incommensurate with the probable profit on its delivery.

The object of State forestry in India is therefore to supply the requirements of its population in forest products, to protect the water-supply of the country, and to afford help in its industrial development. As is the case in European countries, the forest management should, as it always has, result in profit, but this profit should be subsidiary to the main object in view; it should be a consequence of, and not a reason for, a forest policy. The financial success of State forestry as a whole is now assured in India, but even so it is not possible that the forests of each district should produce a profit until they have been so organised as to discount the ill-treatment of the past; and it is certain that, at the introduction of scientific forestry in any locality, reasonable liberality in expenditure pays far more in the results attained than rigid economy merely for the sake of saving, and equally is it sure that any system that restricts expenditure in a fixed proportion to the revenue of the past years must result in limiting the expansion of the income of the future. The estimates of reliable and experienced experts are vain if it is insisted on that an increased revenue should precede an increased expenditure; nor is this believed to be the mode of business adopted by progressive commercial firms in any country in the world.

The growing importance of forestry in India has demanded a proportionate increase in professional knowledge and in the strength of establishments. It has been shown how during the past few years these matters have received practical consideration involving somewhat expensive improvements in conditions of service and recruitment. There remains one other, perhaps the most important, attribute of the Forest Officer that should be fostered, and that is enthusiasm, a virtue that may spread by contagion through all classes, from the jungle savage to the head of the Government. Without enthusiasm persuasion and personal influence are ineffective, but enthusiasm is difficult without contentment.

Of all the Indian public services, the Forest Department acknowledges no superior in loyalty to its employers and in self-abnegation, however trying the conditions of the work. All the more is it a pity that there should have existed an almost chronic state of agitation for concessions to this Service. Such a state is probably not peculiar to one department of the Uncovenanted Services more than to another, and the concessions that have been granted from time to time during the past generation prove that agitation has been based on legitimate demands. There can be no disloyalty in the presentation of such demands by men who in early youth have signed a lifelong contract; the regret is rather that the demands were not conceded as a voluntary gift, whereby generosity would have been imputed instead of pressure from difficulty of recruitment.

But there remains yet opportunity for a trial of what may be termed original munificence, by removing some remnants of the ancient Uncovenanted Service rules that appear to be either obnoxious or unsuitable to present conditions. For instance, differentiation between the age of retirement of Englishmen recruited from the same public schools, colleges and Universities of England; and limitation of the pension of certain branches of the public Service to a small maximum sum, ignoring either length of service or amount of salary, and thus fixing the pension at a much lower sum than can be earned by Englishmen who serve the Empire either at home or in the colonies. Were such concessions made, the time and talent freed from the public Service, by obviating the necessity of the preparation of arguments that shall insure the ultimate success of organised protest, would be a considerable asset in any department that has already more than its full tale of work to perform, without taking into consideration the gain in the harmonious relations of employer and employed.

Finally, as to sport in India, in so far as the forest is concerned, the time has already arrived when bitterness and jealousies are not uncommon, as a perusal of correspondence in the daily press will show. And this is but natural when the Government has been forced to interfere to protect from promiscuous slaughter the interesting fauna of the country. At present no one can shoot in Government forests without first purchasing a licence that defines the area placed at the sportsman's disposal, the number and kind of animals he may kill, and the close seasons that have been fixed; and in the midst of the eager applications for these licences, the Forest Officer may find himself entirely cut off from sport in the area under his charge, or be afraid to fire a shot, lest he should be encroaching on territory leased to another. So much is this the case that more than one Forest Officer has laid aside gun and rifle entirely, so as to have a freer hand in the issue of licences and in the decision of disputes that may arise amongst others—a distinctly humorous result of game laws that add to the duties of the forester that of gamekeeper, and deprive him of one of the most popular incentives to a forester's career.

As a rule, the man who passes his life amongst the big game attacks it in his youth, with the ferocity born of primeval instincts and of novelty. As he grows older he becomes more merciful, till at last intimate acquaintance conduces to sympathetic affection. He may still feel his blood boil with the excitement of a tiger-hunt, for here is a pastime that never stales with its monotony, provided that man and tiger meet with some pretence of equality; but, for the rest, the wild beasts afford a companionship that is fully recognised in the feeling of solitude experienced when living in a forest devoid of animal life. To read by day on the ground the circumstances and occupations of his neighbours, to interpret by night the cries that tell of their passions and dangers, supplies that added interest which brings vigour to the continuous labour of the forester. For that labour he will find his reward in the generous response of the forest to his fostering care, and in results that will endure for generations after he has completed the short work of a lifetime.

E.P.
Stebbing

Game Sanctuaries and Game Protection in India

E.P. Stebbing spent sixteen fascinating years at the turn of the last century in the forests of India as an officer of the Indian Forest Service. He believed there was an unique opportunity for forest officers to study Indian animal life, and he was among the first vocal protectors of the forest service.

Old engraving of a tiger coming across hunters on foot. Stebbing was among the earliest fighters for inviolate areas of wildlife. While his colleagues collected trophies, he wrote in favour of strict laws to keep India's wilderness alive.

All sportsmen who have studied the question [of wildlife protection] at all closely will readily agree that it is not possible for a country, for any of the countries of the world, to continue indefinitely to provide either sport or commercial products unless some measure of protection is extended to the animals which yield them. Our own islands form an apt illustration. Had not a vigorous protection been afforded to the animals combined with the formation of extensive sanctuaries—the New Forest and Forest of Dean were Royal Sanctuaries in olden times—some of our formerly existing wild animals would have been exterminated at a far earlier date than was the case; and nowadays all sport necessitates the closest protection, combined with artificial rearing, to maintain the required head per area. And the bulk of the animal life so reared and protected, deer, birds and fish, is sold for human consumption after it has been shot or captured.

It might have been thought that a country so extensive as India would not have required that protection should be extended to its fauna for many a long year to come. Yet a perusal of the incidents and deductions contained in the previous pages will, I think, prove that this is by no means the case.

I propose, therefore, to lay down the rifle and consider the beautiful jungles of India from the point of view of the steps which appear necessary to ensure the maintenance of the game and fauna generally, in the threefold interests of its health-giving capacity and enjoyment to the hard-worked Anglo-Indian, in the interests of its revenue-producing possibilities, and in those of zoological science.

During the past decade or so it has become increasingly evident to the keen sportsman in india, to the man who is not alone animated by the mere desire to kill, that the game of the country is in many parts in serious danger of disappearing owing amongst other causes to the extraordinary developments in modern sporting rifles, to the greater facilities in communications and to the increasing numbers of those out to kill. With many others—it would be invidious to mention names since there must be many with whom I am

Extract from *The Diary of a Sportsman Naturalist in India* by E.P. Stebbing (London, 1920).

unacquainted—I have given this question careful study for some years. As a result of observations carried out personally, and enquiries made in many parts of India, I have been gradually led to the conclusion that it is not only the game animals that are in jeopardy, but the fauna as a whole and especially that very interesting portion of it which was its home in the jungles and great forests. Under the orderly and systematic conservation of the forests by the Forest Department it has become evident that a proportion of the shyer members of the fauna, those who require large areas of *untouched* primeval forest to dwell in, must without adequate protection inevitably disappear. Now this is an important matter, and admittedly opens out a very large question; but it is one, I think, which is not beyond the scope and power of the Government of India to grapple with aided by the advice of its scientific experts, combined with the help which the true sportsmen in the country will be only too ready to offer. And it has its economic side, a not unimportant one. This aspect of the question, which it is probable will require similar consideration and treatment in America, Africa and elsewhere, will be considered later. We will at present confine ourselves to the protection of game animals.

The most natural way to afford an asylum to animals which are in danger of extinction from overshooting, is by the closure of tracts of country of varying size to all shooting in order to allow them unrestricted rest to breed and increase in numbers. In this manner the recognised Game Sanctuary came into being and such exist in India, America, Africa and elsewhere.

In India we are only in the initial stages of this form of protection, and much yet remains to be done. By the placing of the statutes of the 'Wild Birds and Animals Protection Act of 1912,' to be dealt with shortly, the Government of India practically placed the whole responsibility for the protection of the game in the country in the hands of the Local Governments.

If it is desired to obtain some idea of the abundance of game animals in India in the past, one has only to read some of the sporting chronicles of old-time shikaris. What a glorious shikar country it was in the days of yore and what a royal time our fathers and grandfathers had of it!

To mention but a few of these classic volumes: Forsyth's *Highlands of Central India*, Sterndale's *Seonee or Camp Life in the Satpuras*, Sanderson's *Thirteen Year's Sport among the Wild Beasts of India*, Simpson's *Sport in Eastern Bengal*, Kinloch's *Large Game Shooting in Thibet, the Himalaya, and Central India*, Colonel Fire Cookson's *Tiger Shooting in the Dun and Alwar*, Baker's *Wild Beasts and their Ways*, Pollock's *Sports in British Burma*, Pollock and Thom's *Wild Sports of Burma and Assam*, Pollock's *Sporting Days in Southern India*, etc., and, a more recent and admirable volume, Eardley Wilmot's *Forest Life and Sport in India*. One and all of these stirring reminiscences convey in language which there is no mistaking that up to a score or so of years ago India was a paradise *par excellence* for the sportsman. What then, when we contrast present conditions, do these fascinating volumes teach us—inevitably tell us? That the game of India is on the decrease, on a very rapid decrease, and that the good old days of yore are gone never to return.

That the modern rifle has to some extent been responsible for the present state of affairs is beyond cavil—its accuracy and also the cheapness with which the more roughly made forms can be purchased. The native shikari has now to some extent replaced the old blunderbuss of his father's days by a breech-loader, and when possessed of such, kills an infinitely larger head of game in the year as a consequence. The weapon itself costs 45 rupees only, but it is doubtless the price of cartridges which merciful prevents the breech-loader from coming into as general use amongst this class of men as would otherwise be the case.

But the startling decrease which the head of game existing in India has undergone during the last two or three decades cannot be attributed only to the improved accuracy of the weapons with which the modern-day sportsman is armed. The opening out of the country and the consequent restriction of the animals is also largely responsible. It is now some years since the buffalo disappeared from the United Province forests—about the nineties of last century or thereabouts. Bengal and Assam, e.g., the Western Duars, no longer contain sufficiently extensive jungles to harbour rhinoceros and buffalo. The great increase in the number of sportsmen who visit the jungles annually on sport intent, an increase brought about chiefly by the greatly improved communications owing to railway and road development, has also been a great factor in the case, and motor-cars will intensify it. The two other important factors are the native armed shikari and that curse of the country, the unarmed poacher. It is probable that there are—because the trade is now a more paying one—an infinitely greater number of competent native shikaris in existence; I write 'competent' in the sense merely to express their power to *kill* game. The vast majority of these men are poachers pure and simple, as were their fathers and fathers' fathers before them. Formerly, however, owing to their antiquated low-power weapons, the damage they were capable of doing was of a negligible quantity: nowadays it is far otherwise, and the methods to be put in force to deal with them form one of the most difficult problems those responsible for the upkeep of the game in the forests, and country generally, have to solve.

The plea ever placed in the forefront by such men is that the guns are required to protect the villagers' crops, and this plausible excuse has been accepted in the past by Local Government after Local Government; and we can quite see the difficulties that have confronted the latter, and still do so, in a settlement of the question. It cannot, however, be said to have been ever satisfactorily or fairly faced, and this inaction on the part of the central authority has checkmated the efforts of many a Collector and Forest Officer in his attempts to keep down the number of (poaching) guns in a district. A sympathetic Government was always too eager to listen to the tales of destruction of crops, and the District Officer, without local knowledge, preferred to err on the side of liberality, and so readily granted licences to applicants.

We all know the way these licensed gun-holders go to work. A machan (platform) is built on a known deer-run on the edge of the forest and just without its boundary, if not inside, with the connivance of the Forest Guard. The shikari occupies his post in the late afternoon—he is no respecter of a close season or of sex or age—and by sunrise next day several bucks and hinds may be lying round the machan; the skins, horns, should there be any of the latter, and the flesh are taken off to the bazaar, where a ready sale is found for them throughout the country. The meat is sold locally, the skins and horns being bought by middlemen for export. It was a common thing to see on the platform at wayside stations near forest areas piles of skins and horns booked, and openly booked, in defiance of all rules and regulations, to some large centre.

I would not be understood to say that it is the native shikari alone who acts in this way. It is an open secret that the native soldier of shikar-loving propensities, as also his British brother, will act in an exactly similar manner when occasion offers. Once, however, this matter is properly faced, the latter class of offenders can easily be coped with. For the non-military native offender a licence to protect his crops should be given only after careful personal enquiry on the ground by the District Officer. Also the sale of venison in the open market should be made a criminal offence.

The whole crux of the position is, of course, the necessity for regulating the number of animals killed, so as to prevent deterioration or extermination of the game. The European has generally been considered to be more destructive than the native of the larger animals, gaur, rhinoceros, buffalo. But even this is doubtful, when the poaching proclivities of the native are taken into account. In any event rules and the proper control and management of shooting-grounds can control the European. The native is, however, not so easily dealt with. In order, therefore, to arrest the slaughter which takes place ostensibly to protect crops, some special measures are necessary. Wherever it can be proved that game is no longer destructive, the licences should be cancelled and the weapons called in. In other cases where destruction is still being done the guns must be retained. Since, however, these weapons are given merely for the protection of the crops, they should be restricted to that purpose and be rendered unfit for any other. This can be easily done by cutting down the gun-barrel to eighteen inches or two feet.

There remains the unarmed poacher. To date this man and his methods appear to have escaped all notice. And yet the part he has played in the past and is playing at present is bringing about a serious decrease in the game—and other animals—which is at least as great if not greater than the rest of the above-mentioned causes put together. The Government to date has never considered this side of the question. And yet this is the conviction held, I believe, by many well-known authorities, such as, e.g., Mr. Douglas Dewar, I.C.S., P. Wyndham, I.C.S., P.H. Clutterbuck, I.F.S., and W.F. Perrée, I.F.S. I have detailed in the previous chapter some of the poacher's methods, the diabolic barbarity and inhuman cruelty of which is beyond credence. There can be little doubt that with this record before one, and but a tithe of the practices in force throughout the country have been mentioned, the poacher must be put down if game animals are to be afforded adequate protection.

It may be admitted, so far as the sportsman is concerned, that the steps taken to protect game have considerably improved the position. Local Governments throughout the country have revised their Game Rules, and in some cases have ordered the formation of Game Sanctuaries in addition to limiting the number of head of game to be shot in a district or block of forest to a definite numbers per year. Further, in certain provinces sportsmen are only allowed to kill individually a certain head of each different species of animal, thus eliminating the worst feature of the old-time sportsmen—the butcher, whose boast was not the size of the trophies he obtained so much as the *number* of animals he had killed. For the departures thus made throughout the country I think a due meed of credit should be accorded to the Nilgiri Game Association. Inaugurated about 1885, this Association has now for years not only protected the game of the Plateau which the sportsmen and the Todas between them were surely exterminating, but has enabled an increase to be maintained and recorded. The annual reports of the Association point to a satisfactory increase in the head of ibex or saddlebacks (*Hemitragus hylocrius*) and the sambar (*Cervus unicolor*). For some years past the number of such to be shot by each sportsman has been regulated under the authority of the Association, directly supported by Government. The departure thus initiated in the distant Southern Plateau was followed in the far North when the game of Kashmir was threatened with extinction owing to the annually recurring large influx of sportsmen who visited the Fair Vale. Game Protection in Kashmir now forms a separate Department of the State, and one which has fully achieved under its able head the objects anticipated from its inauguration.

The late enlightened ruler of Chamba State also took up the question, and prohibited all shooting except on passes issued on his own authority.

Whilst such laudable commencements were thus made to preserve the game of areas which, owing to their peculiarly favourable climatic conditions for the European sportsman, were threatened with extinction, the Local Governments in India for long remained apathetic in the matter. Game Rules were in existence for the Forest Reserve of the country, but they related chiefly to a close season, the latter in some cases only applicable to the females, and the same was the case for the open country, where the rules usually related to birds only. These regulations were, however, openly broken, and the penalties in existence were practically rarely put into force, except by some exceptionally energetic officer; and even then an appeal was often upheld and the orders passed reversed.

At length, however, the apathy that hung over this question gave place to some show of interest, which was followed by activity on the part of the Government of India, galvanised into activity by the outcry, increasing in intensity each year, that the game of the country was doomed and that but a few years separated it from extinction. Local Administrations were addressed on the subject of the Rules and Regulations in force in their Presidencies and Provinces under the Forest and other Acts, and as to the steps necessary to be taken to prevent the extinction of the several heads of game, excluding carnivora. This led to many separate enquiries being undertaken throughout the country, to a prolific correspondence in the Press, of which desultory rumblings are still heard, and to many improvements being initiated in the Shooting and Game Rules throughout India. I am aware that I am laying myself open to serious attack in thus stating the case, but it is maintained that any and every rule that is made with the idea of *protecting* the game of a country is a step in the right direction, and therefore advantageous both to the sportsman and the game itself, however hard it may seem to fall on a particular body of individuals or on a particular individual.

What was required was to fix the close seasons definitely, and the Government of India have now, as we shall see, promulgated an Act to give power to fix a close season for different kinds of animals.

It must be remembered that the old-time rulers in India were the *de facto* owners of all the forests and waste lands of the country, including all the animal inhabitants thereof. The Government of India are the present owners, and have, therefore, every right to safeguard this valuable property. They have done so in the case of the forests. But they have been slow to realise the value of the animals and the fact that a very reasonable profit can be made out of this valuable asset.

The native of India has never made any claim to the ownership of game animals (mammals) or birds, since he has never possessed it. He only asks that his crops should be protected against their depredations, and legislation which will do this will never be resented.

That steps have been taken in the right direction is all to the credit of the Administration, but a study of the present position renders it obvious that many of the difficulties have not as yet been faced by the authorities. I propose to allude to these in the succeeding sections. It will first, however, be necessary to consider what the Game Sanctuary really is and what its formation aims at.

The Game Sanctuary

The idea of the Game Sanctuary was a natural outcome of the indiscriminate slaughter to which wild animals have at all times and in all countries been subjected by man. So long as it was man imperfectly armed against the animal with its natural sagacity or fierceness to protect it, conditions were equal, or in favour of the animal, and there was no reason for intervention. From the day, however, of the introduction of the breech-loader and the repeater and a whole host of perfectly built weapons of every kind, enabling man to kill with comparative ease and certainty, the odds were against the animal and the question of affording some degree of protection to the game of a country became of paramount importance; and, curiously enough, the question became most vital in the more uncivilised, uninhabited, and wilder portions of the globe. Such shooting grounds were open to one and all, just as for centuries the shooting in India had been open, with the result that the modern rifle soon threatened the extinction of all game. That modern conditions have rendered this quite feasible the two well-known and oft-quoted instances afforded by the practically extinct American bison and the extinct quagga of South Africa sufficiently illustrate.

In India we have come within measurable distance of exterminating the rhinoceros (*Rhinoceros unicornis*), which, together with the elephant and the gaur or Indian bison (*Bos gaurus*), would without protection probably soon disappear from the jungles which have known them for so long.

With a view to affording a certain protection to animals of this kind and of giving a rest to species which have been heavily thinned in a district by indiscriminate shooting in the past or by anthrax, drought, etc., the idea of the Game Sanctuary was introduced into India (and in other parts of the world) and has been accepted in many parts of the country. The Sanctuary consists of a block of country, either of forest or grassland, etc., depending upon the nature of the animal to which Sanctuary is required to be given; the area has rough boundaries such as roads, fire lines, nullahs, etc., assigned to it, and no shooting of any kind is allowed in it if it is a Sanctuary pure and simple; or the shooting of carnivora may be permitted, or of these and of everything else save certain specified animals.

Sanctuaries may be formed in two ways:

I. *The area is automatically closed and reopened for certain definite periods of years.* II. *The area is closed until the head of game has become satisfactory, and the shooting on the area is then regulated, no further closing taking place, save in exceptional circumstances.*

I. *THE SANCTUARY IS AUTOMATICALLY CLOSED AND REOPENED FOR A DEFINITE PERIOD OF YEARS.*

The Sanctuary is notified for a period of years: this period would naturally be variable, but it is of importance, I think, that it should not be placed at too great a length, or the animals in the Sanctuary, so long immune from danger, would on the reopening of the area be so unused to the sportsman that they would be shot down in a very short space of time. Probably the period during which a block of forest is closed to all shooting should never exceed, at the most, three years. Sir John Hewett, when Lieut. Governor of the United Provinces, held the opinion that a period of five years for a Sanctuary was too long. He thought that the ground of the Sanctuary should be changed every two or three years, probably the former, and that the animals would soon learn where the Sanctuary was. He also agreed that before opening a Sanctuary to sportsmen the area should be *beaten* through so as to distribute and disperse the game, and not have them collected together Noah's-ark-fashion on a large scale for the first permit-holder who enters to shoot down with ease.

Whilst, however, this system of opening and closing areas to shooting is best adapted to some localities and to certain classes of game, it is quite inadequate for the satisfactory protection of others. In many parts of India I would favour the second suggestion as being by far the most satisfactory in the long run and in some cases essential.

II. *THE AREA IS CLOSED UNTIL THE HEAD OF GAME HAS BECOME SATISFACTORY, AND THE SHOOTING ON THE AREA IS THEN DEFINITELY REGULATED, NO FURTHER PERIODS OF CLOSURE BEING ENFORCED SAVE IN EXCEPTIONAL CIRCUMSTANCES.*

The length of time a Sanctuary should be in existence is of very considerable importance, and to a certain extent is intimately dependent upon a knowledge of the habits of the animals for which the Sanctuary is formed. The period of closure to be effective must depend:

1. On the condition of the head of game of the area when the Sanctuary is first formed.

2. *On the nature of the animal,* e.g., the rhinoceros, with a period of gestation of two years and a period of fifteen years before it reaches maturity, would require practically permanent closure of its haunts to produce any appreciable result, as has, in effect, been carried out in Goalpara in Assam.

The procedure followed should usually be determined by the condition of the head of game on an area. There would be no question of fixing a definite period for the Sanctuary in the first instance. When the requisite effect on the game had resulted from its formation, careful and efficient rules and management should be sufficient to keep up the head of game, and it would not be necessary to continue the rigid exclusion of sportsmen. It would be sufficient to limit *the number of each species* to be shot *each year,* as is done in many parts of the Central Provinces. When the limit had been reached the shooting of the species in that locality would cease for the year.

Once a sufficient head of game has been established in a locality, it is questionable whether regulated shooting each year would not have a better effect than the alternative proposal of closure for a term followed by a period of unrestricted shooting. It would certainly minimise the chance of the animals becoming too tame.

It may be of interest to give as an instance the procedure in the Central Provinces.

As a whole, the Central Provinces may be considered to be one of the most advanced regions so far as game protection is concerned. The shooting regulations provide that areas or blocks of forests may be closed to shooting *absolutely* for purposes of forest management or as *sanctuaries* for the protection of game, other than carnivora, for the destruction of which special permits may be issued. The list of closed forests or blocks is prepared each year in October by the Conservators and is published in the Central Provinces Gazette, and copies are hung up in the offices of the Deputy Commissioner and Forest Officer.

It will thus be obvious that the Game Sanctuaries in the Central Provinces are formed automatically by the closing alternatively of different forests or blocks of forest yearly. As a matter of fact, however, most of the present Sanctuaries, though in many instances reduced in size, have been Game Sanctuaries since 1902, though a few others have been added later. It would be better if these areas were closed for periods of not more or less than three years. Of course, in the case of areas reserved for purposes of forest management it is possible that they are closed for a considerable period of years, but nothing is said on this score in the rules nor as to the length of time blocks are closed for purely sanctuary purposes.

In addition to automatic closure and opening of blocks there are other most valuable restrictions for the preservation of game, and I believe that I am correct in stating that this procedure is now applied to most of the blocks, instead of automatically closing and opening them. In any particular block or series of blocks only a certain head of any particular species may be shot. As soon as this number has been reached, that species is closed to shooting for the year. This rule might well be introduced elsewhere in the country. The permit of each sportsman is endorsed with the number of head he may shoot, e.g., one bison, one sambar, two chital, four other deer, and carnivora *ad. lib., provided the maximum number of head of the species allowable to be shot in the year has not been already reached.* This latter information is supplied to the sportsman either by the divisional officer or by the Range offices in the area for which his permit is made out. Were not this latter provision in force, one sportsman might shoot the whole number of, say, barasingha (*Cervus duvauceli*) permissible for the year and thus close this particular animal to succeeding rifles for the rest of the season—a somewhat unfair and onerous restriction.

The size of a Sanctuary must, of course, entirely depend on local conditions and on the nature of the animals to be protected. Such animals as the rhinoceros or gaur, which are of an extremely shy disposition and are given to roaming considerable distances, would require an area of considerable dimensions, whereas chital (*Cervus axis*) and hogdeer (*Cervus porcinus*) would require a comparatively small one.

Pheasants, again, would not require large areas, and the same applies to the hill sheep and goats—a nullah or certain nullahs being proscribed as closed to shooting, as, in fact, is done in Kashmir.

Game Sanctuaries may then be of several kinds:

1. Entirely closed to all shooting.
2. Closed to beating only.
3. Closed to the shooting of certain species of game.
4. Closed to shooting of all game, save noxious ones, carnivora, pig, etc.

The question of enforcing the Sanctuary law against shooting is one of some difficulty. In Reserved Forests it is comparatively easy, since all shooting without special passes in such areas is forbidden and the granting of these would be stopped for Sanctuaries. Outside, however, the matter is by no means so simple, and the people of the country, particularly the shooting element, will require a careful education if they are to understand and respect the Sanctuary, should it be formed in Government Waste Land. It will be necessary to fully explain the uses of Sanctuaries, and the reason for closing the areas as soon as attempts have been made to form them.

At present anyone may enter on land, which is not reserved forest, and shoot. To alter this would at once curtail what is a prescriptive right, and this is the main obstacle to the introduction of a Game Law. Rich and poor alike enjoy this privilege, and although the occupier may in time come to learn that shooting rents can add to his income, or reserve his waste land for his own shooting and close it to the general public, as is done in some cases in the Dun below the Mussoorie Hills, it will be difficult to introduce restrictions on areas in which shooting is practically a right in all but name.

It is, we fear, hardly to be expected that the question of the formation of Sanctuaries and their closing will be received without opposition throughout the country, even amongst the Europeans, but I am of opinion that the matter is one of such great importance that the outcry of the few interested people opposed from personal motives to their formation on Government Land, both Reserve Forest and Waste Land, should not be allowed to blind the public generally to their immense value. It is conceivable that the Zemindar and large landed private proprietors would in course of time follow an example so set when its value had made itself apparent to them.

The policing of the Sanctuary is a matter requiring some consideration. It may prove comparatively easy to check illicit shooting both on the part of the European and native, although even this is not a facile matter in the case of Sanctuaries of large size in remote localities. The question of dealing with the poacher pure and simple who goes to work without firearms is even a more difficult problem, whose importance, as we have seen, has as yet been scarcely realised by either the Supreme or Local Governments.

THE INDIAN WILD BIRDS AND ANIMALS PROTECTION ACT OF 1912

This Act was passed on 18th September 1912. It is entitled—'An Act of make better provision for the protection and preservation of certain Wild Birds and Animals.'

Its clauses are as follows:

Short title and extent. 1. (1) This Act, may be called the Wild Birds and Animals Protection Act, 1912; and

(2) It extends to the whole of British India, including British Baluchistan, the Sonthal Parganas, and the Pargana of Spiti.

Application of Act. 2. (1) This Act applies, in the first instance, to the birds and animals specified in the Schedule, when in their wild state.

(2) The Local Government may, by notification in the local official Gazette, apply the provisions of this Act to any kind of wild bird or animal, other than specified in the Schedule, which, in its opinion, it is desirable to protect or preserve.

3. *Close time*. The Local Government may, by notification in the local Gazette, declare the whole year or any part thereof to be a close time throughout the whole or any part of its territories for any kind of wild bird or animal to which this Act applies, or for female or immature wild birds or animals of such kind; and, subject to the provisions hereinafter contained, during such close time, and within the areas specified in such notification, it shall be unlawful—

(*a*) To capture any such bird or animal, or to kill any such bird or animal which has not been captured before the commencement of such close time;

(*b*) To sell or buy, or offer to sell or buy or to possess, any such bird or animal which has not been captured or killed before the commencement of such close time, or the flesh thereof:

(*c*) If any plumage has been taken from any such bird captured or killed during such close time, to sell or buy, or to offer to sell or buy, or to possess, such plumage.

Penalties. 4. (1) Whoever does, or attempts to do, any act in contravention of Section 3, shall be punishable with fine which may extend to fifty rupees.

(2) Whoever, having already been convicted of an offence under this Section, is again convicted thereunder shall, on every subsequent conviction, be punishable with imprisonment for a term which may extend to one month, or with fine, which may extend to one hundred rupees, or with both.

Confiscation. 5. (1) When any person is convicted of an offence punishable under this Act, the convicting Magistrate may direct that any bird or animal in respect of which such offence has been committed, or the flesh or any other part of such bird or animal, shall be confiscated.

(2) Such confiscation may be in addition to the other punishment provided by Section 4 for such offence.

Cognizance of offences. 6. No Court inferior to that of a Presidency Magistrate or a Magistrate of the second class shall try an offence against this Act.

Power to grant exemption. 7. Where the Local Government is of opinion that, in the interests of scientific research, such a course is desirable, it may grant to any person a licence, subject to such restrictions and conditions as it may impose, entitling the holder thereof to do any act which is by Section 3 declared to be unlawful.

Savings. 8. Nothing in this Act shall be deemed to apply to the capture or killing of a wild animal by any person in defence of himself or any other person, or to the capture or killing of any wild bird or animal in *bona fide* defence of property.

Repeal of Act of 1887. 9. The Wild Birds Protection Act, 1887, is hereby repealed.

The Schedule

(i) Bustards, ducks, floricans, jungle fowl, partridges, pea-fowl, pheasants, pigeons, quail, sand-grouse, painted snipe, spur-fowl, woodcock, herons, egrets, rollers and kingfishers.

(ii) Antelopes, asses, bison, buffalos, deer, gazelles, goats, hares, oxen, rhinoceroses and sheep.

Some Reflections on the Act

It will be of interest to consider in some slight detail several of the provisions of this Act. The Provincial Rules in force when it was passed comprised the Arms Act, Forest Act and Fisheries Act. The new Act extends to all India with the exception of Burma, and, of course, the Native States. Some of these latter are, however, already doing excellent work in Game protection and others will doubtless follow any firm lead set them by the Imperial Government.

In many respects the present Act is a great improvement on the draft one. Instead of being confined to 'game' animals and then endeavouring to define 'game', 'large' animal, and 'specified kind' of animal it contents itself with the title 'Wild Birds and Animals

Act.' The title, zoologically, is unfortunate, since the word 'animal' comprises the whole of the fauna. If only birds and beasts are understood the title should have been 'birds and mammals.' I use the word 'animal' to include the fauna as a whole. Section 2 (1) of the Act makes it applicable to certain classes of animals and birds specified in the Schedule, but with the saving clause, 2 (2) that the Local Government may by notification in the local Gazette apply the provisions of the Act to any kind of Wild Bird or Animal, other than those specified in the Schedule which, in its opinion, it is desirable to preserve. Thus in this respect the onus is put upon the shoulders of the Local Government. This is also the case with reference to the 'close seasons.' The responsibility of declaring a close season either for a part or the whole of the year for any species—'Kind of wild bird or animal,' as the Act puts it—to which the Act applies is laid on the Local Authority.

The Schedule is the weak part of section 2 (1). It would have been far better either to have drawn it out in a more detailed form or to have omitted it altogether, the Local Government being empowered in clause 2 (2) to enumerate a list of birds and animals which might be exempted from the protection of the Act from time to time, when their numbers had become excessive or for other specified reason. The periods of such exemption to be limited to a certain maximum, an extension of which period would require the sanction of the Government of India.

But even better than this would, I think, have been the preparation of a list of the fauna by groups and its inclusion in the Act. This, of course, can be done by Local Governments and it is a step which, I believe, it being undertaken in some Provinces. On this question I made the following remarks in my paper read in 1911:

'If the drafters of the Act were to apply to any Zoologist in the country who has a practical working and sporting knowledge of the game life of India they could be furnished with detailed lists of animals both large and small; and by 'animals' I here mean 'mammals' classified, say, into some such groups as, e.g.—

'(*a*) *Carnivora.* Each species in the country to be quoted.

'(*b*) *Herbivora.* Each species in the country to be quoted.

'The various deer, antelope, goats and sheep are all perfectly well known, and the preparation of lists detailing each animal by name is an absolutely easy matter.

'(*c*) *Rodentia.* Including the hares, porcupines, etc., the total extinction of which from a sporting point of view is far from desirable.

'(*d*) *A General Group* which may be made to include the rest of the *Mammalia.* This would allow protection to be extended, should it be deemed necessary from the point of view of *the preservation of the species* in the case of rare species now perhaps being exterminated for the value of their fur or for other reasons, to animals not at present included in the sportsman's category of Game.

'Turning to the Birds. There is no distinction made between migratory birds and non-migratory birds, and no mention made at all of *Insectivorous* Birds, and yet the distinction is one of enormous value in a great agricultural country like India, where the benefit the cultivators must derive annually from insectivorous birds is quite incalculable.

'I suggest that the Birds be sharply defined into groups and the names of all the game birds and of all the chief insectivorous birds be definitely given in the Act. This likewise is a matter of the greatest simplicity, since there would be no difficulty in drawing up such lists.'

Similarly in section 3 it would have been preferable had the Act definitely laid down with the authority of the Supreme Government behind it that the breeding seasons for all animals and birds should be a *close time* and made Local Governments responsible that the breeding seasons for each species were definitely ascertained in their several jurisdictions and notified in their Gazettes. Not only would this have been more satisfactory in the interests of the preservation of all game animals, but it would have been a valuable aid to an extension of our knowledge of the life histories of many of the rarer animals and birds, since in order to render possible the working of the Act it would have been necessary to undertake such investigations throughout the country. Also it would have afforded certain protection to animals and birds other than 'game' ones which run the chance of being neglected under present conditions.

The extension of this close or breeding season to a longer period for specified reasons could have then been safely left in the hands of the Local Authority. From the zoological and scientific point of view the Act of 1912 fails in not having officially and authoritatively recognised the breeding season in the interests of the fauna as a whole as a close time, power being given to the Local Government to proscribe within a certain defined area and for a certain definite period any species which was becoming noxious to the community.

Further, it would have been better had the Act (sec. 3) distinctly prohibited the killing of immature animals and birds, empowering Local Governments to notify exceptions in the case of dangerous carnivora, etc., when and only when considered necessary. If the Act is really intended, as we have no doubt that it is, to ensure the preservation of the fauna as a whole throughout the country certain definite prohibitory clauses laid down in the Act with the Authority of the Governor-General in Council behind them would surely be more likely to achieve the object arrived at than by placing the onus of enacting such clauses on the respective Local Administrations.

In sub-sections 3 (*b*) and (*c*) which concern themselves with the sale of animals and birds or parts of them killed in the close season, we should have liked to see skins and horns especially enumerated. This would have checked their sale in the close seasons; for the local officers would be acquainted with these seasons for the fauna of their own Province and Districts, and would be responsible for seeing the Act obeyed.

It is true that Local Governments have now framed Rules under sections 2 and 3, but this does not necessarily ensure such continuity of action as would have been secured had the Government of India taken the responsibility upon themselves.

There remains the poacher who, without possessing firearms, certainly outrivals in his power for cold-blooded slaughter the whole of the armed community. Neither the Government of India nor the Local Governments have yet attempted to deal with him. Clauses 2 and 3 do not really touch him. As the chapter on poaching shows to some slight extent, his operations can only be described as devilish in their inhuman ingenuity. To the average officer, whether magistrate or forest, they are unknown. Even if a District official has some cursory knowledge that the native is a skilled poacher he in most instances has no specific acquaintance with the methods, the common methods, in force in his district and he will never have seen them put in force practically. The Government of India and the various Local Governments are, we may feel sure, unaware of their existence, or surely some effort would have been made to put an end to practices which involve appalling torture to the wretched animals thus done to death.

It may be suggested that what is required is the preparation of a schedule for each Province, detailing the various poaching contrivances in force in the Province, drawn up district by district. The schedule should be hung up in the offices of the Magistrates and Forest Officers and their subordinates, and a thorough acquaintance with it be exacted from all officers. Further, an annual return should be called for detailing the number of offences under each of the various poaching methods in force prosecuted in each district and the sentences imposed in each case.

The preparation of such schedules should present no difficulties. Some of the European officers of the Local Governments and many of the native officials would be able to give such information. By whatever means they are drawn up there can be little doubt of their urgent need.

In this connexion the 1912 Act would appear to require amendment, and severe penalties [need to] be enacted on the perpetrators of the cold-blooded and diabolical butchery of inoffensive animals which annually takes place throughout the country all the year round. For these men are no respecters of seasons nor of age or sex. Male and female, old and young, all are treated with the same terrible callousness. A man working a lame horse is taken up by the police in England and fined by a magistrate. And rightly so. And yet far greater barbarities are perpetrated daily in India without notice.

It is very necessary to stop the slaughter at present carried out by the native shikari, soldier and poacher during the close seasons, the proceeds of which slaughter in flesh, skins and horns finds a ready sale in the bazaars. Stop this traffic and you bring to an end one of the great incentives to kill.

Sub-sections 4 (1) and (2) deal with penalties. In a country like India it has always seemed to me that there should be two scales of fines. Fifty or a hundred rupees should be a sufficient deterrent to the poaching native shikari. But would it stop the more wealthy European shikari who, for instance, wanted to be able to say that he had shot a bison and sooner than go back empty-handed would risk the penalty and shoot a female? I had an instance of this kind of thing in Chota Nagpur myself. A wealthy so-called sportsman came up with a permit to shoot and seated in a machan had the animals in the forest driven past him and shot a cow bison and a three-week-old calf! The penalty did not stop him and he hoped by bluffing to be allowed to keep his spoils even if he had to pay the, to him, small fine.

Section 5 empowers the magistrate to confiscate all illicit spoils captured and should be fearlessly and unwaveringly put in force.

Section 7 empowers a Local Government to permit in the interests of scientific research a departure from the rules in force both in and out of the close season for any specified animal or bird or classes of such. A short decade ago this would have been hailed, and rightly hailed, as an example of broad-minded statesmanship. Now, however, the permission will require to be jealously watched; for the last few years have witnessed startling developments as a result of the grant of such permissions. In fact so delicate has this question become that we would rather that the Supreme Government had kept this power in their own hands. Latter-day so-called scientific expeditions for the purpose of adding specimens to great Museums, to provide cinematograph films for alleged educational purposes, and so forth, have entirely altered the aspect of this question. For in some instances these so-called scientific missions have simply become glorified slaughter and butcher expeditions financed by a wealthy man in the name of science. The old-time butcher has not disappeared. He still exists, and with modern rifles his power for slaughter as we have seen is infinitely more terrible. But he is held in check by modern restrictions. He is unable to kill indiscriminately as he wants to. If he is wealthy he endeavours to get over the difficulty by fitting out a scientific (*sic*) expedition and so evades the law. Events move so fast nowadays that what would have been a perfectly safe clause a score of years ago, in fact a clause marking a distinct progress by the Supreme Government in its recognition of the claims of science, has now become a danger to the very aims and objects of the Act. Such a permit should never be allowed to take effect in any Game Sanctuary and the permission to kill in the name of Science should be retained by the Supreme Government. Glorified slaughter is not scientific research nor is it so considered by the great Museums in whose name it is sometimes carried out. If such expeditions are necessary it should always be possible to lay down definitely the number of head of each species which may be shot or trapped, specifying age, sex, etc. Every museum will agree to such a restriction, and the wealthy butcher, whose chief aim is to have a free hand in the forests, to remain unhampered by restrictions and to kill everything that gets up, would be kept in check.

Further, in the case of cinema films, the cold-blooded cruelty to trapped animals one sees depicted in these films—baiting the poor beasts to make them show their 'points,' trussing them up in most diabolical ways, etc.,—should be absolutely prohibited and met by severe punishment.

Section 8 deals with the old question of granting licences to protect crops. The making of rules in this respect must, of course, be left to Local Governments. This is obvious. The question is now, I understand, being treated with a more enlightened knowledge than has been displayed in the past. In the interests of the hard-working ryot, a man of few joys, all that can possibly be done for his protection should be carried out. But the village shikari who lives by his gun should be discouraged. And the poacher should be put down with a firm hand.

The 1912 Act makes no mention of the granting of rewards for the slaughter of noxious animals or birds. This is a departure in the right direction. The matter can be safely left in the hands of the Local Governments and such grants should be made with discrimination and discretion. In my paper already alluded to I made the following remarks on this subject:

'I am of opinion that Game rewards in general should be abolished and that no provision on the subject should be included in the Game Act.

'It would be quite within the power of the Local Government to issue rewards for the destruction of a particular species which is on the increase and becoming a danger either to public life or property or to the sporting interests of a particular area of country.

'Also, save in exceptional cases, e.g., rogue elephants and man-eaters, I would abolish the giving of a reward for *every* tiger, leopard, wild goat or wolf slain.

'Where any of these animals were becoming a pest or scourge to the community or endangering the head of game of other species in any locality, the Local Government should notify or empower its officers to notify a reward or scale of rewards to remain in force until the danger is past and the balance of power between man and animal or animal and animal is once more normal. The rewards on the proscribed animals should then be taken off.

'Every shooting season nowadays sees an army of eager sportsmen competing for blocks and shooting-permits, and surely the giving of the old-time reward for a tiger is quite unnecessary. I would leave the grant of rewards or offer of rewards to the discretion of the District Officer or Forest Officer. They would when necessary proclaim such and such an animal to be a man-eater or cattle-lifter of notoriety and would fix a reward upon the animal, procuring, if considered necessary, the sanction of the Commissioner or Conservator to their doing so. Why Government should nowadays pay a reward of from Rupees 20 to R. 50 for a tiger which may be a pure game-eater and rarely if ever touches a cow (and there are numbers of such) is beyond comprehension. Sportsmen will not slack off if the rewards are withdrawn. Many a District official would be only too delighted if they would! Once a man-eater or a noted cattle-lifter is proclaimed, then make it worth the sportsmen's while to collect [or] to tackle him by giving straight off a large reward commencing at R. 200 and going rapidly up to R. 500. It would be a far more satisfactory way of working the reward system both from the point of view of the cultivator, the man who lives on the soil, and that of the sportsman; and, I think, would probably be less costly to Government.

'Or rewards might be offered only for tigers in a district or parts of a district where a noted man-eater or cattle-lifter has made his home. For every tiger killed in this area a suitable reward might be given, say, Rs. 50, with the larger reward to be paid to the sportsman who bagged the particular man-eater or cattle-lifter proscribed.

This would probably be the best method, since it would tempt sportsmen to have a try for the man-eater, knowing that they would receive a certain reward for each tiger killed, even if they should not be lucky enough to kill the proscribed beast.'

Lastly, the New Act omits all special mentions of separate rules with respect to the pursuit, killing or capture of game by non-commissioned officers or·soldiers of the Army. Only the Supreme Government possesses the necessary authority and power to grapple with such a question. No Local Administration has power to override military regulations or permits granted to the Military by the Supreme Government, nor can such non-commissioned officers and men be brought within the jurisdiction of the civil courts as long as they are in the enjoyment of special privileges, such, e.g., as those enjoyed by the Gurkha Regiments. True the Act section 4 (1) applies the penalties to everyone, but in the absence of any direct clause this cannot obviously be made to apply to military individuals safeguarded by special privileges. How are such privileges to be reconciled with the 1912 Act? On this subject I made the following remarks in my paper and they appear to be still applicable:

'Allowing that it is necessary to make separate rules for the Army ("this was the case in the draft Act; the Act as passed omitted all mention of such rules") I think that the Act should specifically lay down that permits may not be given for parties of more than, say, four to six men from a cantonment to go out *together* to shoot in any area. At present it is well known that at times parties of from fifteen to twenty or more men go out into a block of forest and drive the game systematically into a *cul-de-sac* and then slaughter the animals in numbers. The Gurkha is particularly addicted to this form of 'sport' during the rainy season, when in the parts of the country where they are cantoned it is generally impossible for the European to go near the Terai forest owing to its great unhealthiness. Parties of military men should be small and the number of head they may shoot should be distinctly laid down on the permit, and penalties be enforced if this number is exceeded.

'I think the Game Act might embody some such definite ruling for the whole country.'

In past years but scant attention has been paid to the severe attacks of a disease having kindred affinities to anthrax which appears at intervals and takes a heavy toll of the head of game (such as bison [gaur], buffalo, sambar, etc.) on the area it affects.

Further, in years of severe drought the mortality amongst the wild animals of the country affected is often very heavy, and in the past this factor has received no consideration from the authorities in the interests of the wild game.

It may be suggested that in the wake of such calamities a very careful and detailed inspection of the area or areas affected should be undertaken, with the object of ascertaining which species have suffered and to what extent. Until such survey has been carried out, no shooting-permits should be issued for the area or areas. After the survey the species which have suffered severely should be notified, as also the area affected, and this area should be entirely closed to the shooting of those particular species for such period as will ensure their multiplication to the number of head it is required to maintain on the area. In closing such area the notifiction should distinctly state the reason for the closure. No true sportsman would be found to cavil at such a procedure.

And now to turn for a moment, in conclusion, to the question of the sportsman—the outside sportsman, not the District official—and the rules under which he can enjoy sport in a District.

The rules under which the District official enjoys sport in his District are, it would appear, quite fair in most if not all Provinces.

I think, however, that the outside sportsman has often a justifiable complaint, though more often than not he goes the wrong way to work in making it, and so puts himself out of court.

The whole matter really turns, and must always turn, on the number of individuals of a particular species it is permissible to shoot in a given area. This number can only be fixed by the District Officers on the spot. There can be no cavil against this, as they are, or ought to be, the best judges on the question.

In fact, as matters in game protection at present stand, and in the absence of a separate Game Protection establishment, there can be no appeal from their decision.

Probably the best and most elastic method for the outside

sportsman is to give him a block or blocks, depending on what is available on receipt of his application, and to enter on his permit the number of individuals of any one species he may shoot and the number of different species. This number would, of course, vary according to the length of time for which the permit was issued, but would never exceed a fixed maximum for each species. So far so good.

But it will doubtless soon be found necessary to definitely limit the number of head of a species to be shot in any one area in a year, as is done, in fact, in the Central Provinces. It is in this limitation that complaints arise and causes for friction come in.

For instance, supposing twelve sambar may be shot in any particular block. A military man, whose leave season will not open before the 15th April, applies for and is allotted a block. He arrives to find the maximum annual number of the animal it is permitted to kill already reached and is debarred from shooting that particular species. It is quite conceivable that he might find more than one species in the same condition. In fact the total number of head of a particular species might be easily shot off by the civilian element in the first couple of months of the open season, the animal becoming then *de facto* closed to shooting for the rest of the open season.

This is where the shoe pinches the heel of the military man very hard, as also, of course, that of his civil brother when shooting on areas outside of his own jurisdiction. To remedy a state of affairs which is undoubtedly a real grievance, it may be suggested that the number of individual to be shot in a particular block or area in any one year should be allotted in a fixed proportion *throughout each month of the open or shooting season* for that animal, say, two or three or four per month, according to the total number notified as shootable during the season, any balance remaining from any one or more months being, of course, carried forward and distributed throughout the remaining months of that shooting season.

This would give the hot-weather sportsmen, both military and civil, who in pursuit of their favourite pastime are ready to put up with many and decided discomforts, an equal chance with their civil brother who is not so tied during the cold weather. The suggestion is made simply with the idea of giving a fair chance to all.

But I would suggest a further step. I would allot a certain proportion of the head of a particular species to be shot in an area to the local District officials, the balance going to the outside sportsman. The District officials could be left to make their own arrangements as to when their proportion of head was to be shot, but I think that in the case of the outside sportsman the number to be shot should be allotted throughout the shooting months, so as to give an equal chance to all the block-holders.

No reflection is intended on the District officials by any of these suggestions. They are made only in the interests of that particular quality all Englishmen pride themselves in possessing—Fair Play.

The Preservation of the Indian Land Fauna as a Whole: The Permanent Sanctuary

... I now propose to deal briefly with the Sanctuary regarded from the aspect of the preservation of the fauna of a particular area or country as a whole. A Sanctuary formed for such a purpose requires to have a permanent character. In other words, the area should be permanently closed to shooting and to all and every interruption to the ordinary habits of life of the species to be preserved.

It will be obvious at once that Sanctuaries of this nature and their management will differ widely in different parts of the world. In some cases the only prescriptions would probably relate to shooting, poaching, egg collection, and so forth. It would be unnecessary to close the areas entirely to man. In others, however, it is certain that some of the larger and shyer animals and birds, and, I believe, certain classes of insects and so forth, can only be preserved from inevitable extinction if Permanent Sanctuaries of considerable extent are maintained, solely with the object of safeguarding the species for which they are created. In Sanctuaries of this class it will not be merely sufficient to forbid shooting. It will be necessary to close them to man altogether, to leave them, in other words, in their primeval condition, to forbid the building of roads or railways through their fastnesses, to prevent the Forest Department from converting the areas into well-ordered blocks of forest managed for commercial purposes; in fact to prevent in them all and every act of man. In every case throughout the world such Sanctuaries will require to be under supervision, but such supervision should be entirely confined to a police supervision to prevent poaching, collecting, and any entrance by man into the area.

In a previous chapter I alluded to the Presidential Address delivered by Dr. P. Chalmers Mitchell, F.R.S., Secretary of the Zoological Society, in London, before the British Association at Dundee in 1912.

Dr. Chalmers Mitchell was the first, I believe, to enunciate this theory of a Sanctuary for the preservation, not merely of animals whose protection from extinction was considered necessary either from their sporting or economic value, but of the fauna as a whole.

He quite correctly pointed out that my paper, read before the Zoological Society in November, 1911, only dealt with the former aspects of the question.

After discussing the position of Europe in respect of the diminution or extinction of animals which were abundant in the past the author comes to India.

'India contains,' he says, 'the richest, the most varied, and, from many points of view, the most interesting part of the Asiatic fauna. Notwithstanding the teeming human population it has supported from time immemorial, the extent of its area, its dense forests and jungles, its magnificent series of river valleys, mountains and hills have preserved until recent times a fauna rich in individuals and species.'

After pointing out that the books of sportsmen show how abundant game animals were forty years ago, he continues:

'The one-horned rhinoceros has been nearly exterminated in Northern India and Assam. The magnificent gaur, one of the most splendid of living creatures, has been almost killed off throughout the limits of its range—Southern India and the Malay Peninsula. Bears and Wolves, wild dogs and leopards, are persecuted remorselessly. Deer and antelope have been reduced to numbers that alarm even the most thoughtless sportsmen and wild sheep and goats are being driven to the utmost limits of their range.'

After alluding to the diminution of animals in other countries, and especially game animals and those killed for economic reasons, the author continues:

'And to us who are Zoologists, the vast destruction of invertebrate life, the sweeping out, as forests are cleared and the soil tilled, of innumerable species that are not even named or described is a real calamity. I do not wish to appeal to sentiment. Man is worth many sparrows; he is worth all the animal population of the globe, and if there were not room for both, the animals must go. I will pass no judgment on those who find the keenest pleasure of life in gratifying the primeval instinct of sport. I will admit that there is no better destiny for the lovely plumes of a rare bird than to enhance the beauty of a beautiful woman. ... But I do not admit the right of the present generation to careless indifference or to wanton destruction. Each generation is the guardian of the existing resources of the world; it has come into a great inheritance, but only as a trustee. We are learning to preserve the relics of early civilisations, and the rude remains of man's primitive arts and crafts. Every civilised nation spends great sums on painting and sculpture, on libraries and museums. Living animals are of older lineage, more perfect craftsmanship, and greater beauty than any of the creations of man. And although we value the work of our forefathers, we do not doubt but that the generations yet unborn will produce their own artists and writers, who may equal or surpass the artists and writers of the past. But there is no resurrection or recovery of an extinct species, and it is not merely that here and there one species out of many is threatened, but that whole general families, and orders are in danger.'

The late Lord Salisbury was one of the first British statesmen to take up the question of the preservation of wild animals. Lord Salisbury had been a former President of the British Association. In 1889 he arranged for a convention of the Great Powers interested in Africa to consider the question of the protection to be afforded to what some unscientific members of the Civil Service designated as the 'Wild Animals, Birds and Fish' (a nomenclature which has been continued in subsequent Game Acts) of Africa. This convention did some good pioneer work, but its deliberations were confined to the preservation of animals of sporting and economic value only. And this rather narrow outlook has governed the operations of the Great Powers and local administrators in the wilder and tropical portions of the globe to the present day. The preservation of game has always been the main factor underlying the action taken. The economic value of the fauna has only received a cursory attention; and the question of the preservation of the fauna as a whole has scarcely received any countenance. It may be admitted, however, that the pioneer work done has been of the highest value.

In alluding to the work in this connection which has been done by the Government in India Dr. Chalmers Mitchell added: 'The fact remains that India, a country which still contains a considerable remnant of one of the richest faunas of the world, and which also is probably more efficiently under the control of a highly educated body of permanent officials, central and local, than any other country in the world, has no provision for the protection of its fauna simply as animals.'

In 1909 Lord Crewe, then Secretary of State for the Colonies, received a deputation arranged by the Society for the Preservation of the Wild Fauna of the Empire. One of the questions discussed was that of changes in the locality of reserves. Such changes were, I think, made or became necessary owing to the opening-up of the country by railways, extension of agriculture, and so forth.

It was pointed out, by Dr. Mitchell I think, that a change of one piece of land for another, even if both were of equal area, might be satisfactory in affording the protection desired for certain animals, either of sporting or economic value, but from a zoological point of view, in the interests of the preservation of the fauna as a whole of the locality, might prove the reverse of satisfactory. This is a view I have long held. Primeval forests and lands which have never been interfered with by man may contain, undoubtedly do contain, many small forms of animal life which can only live under such conditions. Alter these conditions and they will be exterminated once and for all. This is necessarily a point upon which the trained zoologist alone can speak with any certainty; but if that zoologist has had the good fortune to spend a number of years studying the tropical and semi-tropical forests and lands on the grounds his opinion is at least worthy of careful consideration.

There still remains, then, the problem of carrying the preservation of animals the one stage further to include the whole fauna—in a word, the formation of Fauna Sanctuaries. Their creation so as to include some of the most interesting of the fauna is still possible in India, e.g., in that fascinating tract stretching from Assam down into Burma.

I am so entirely in sympathy with Dr. Mitchell's opinions on this question that I will quote his concluding remarks before the Association.

'There are in all the great continents large tracts almost empty of resident population, which still contain vegetation almost undisturbed by the ravages of man and which still harbour a multitude of small animals, and could afford space for the larger and better-known animals. These tracts have not yet been brought under cultivation, and are rarely traversed except by the sportsman, the explorer, and the prospector. On these there should be established, in all the characteristic faunistic areas, reservations which should not be merely temporary recuperating grounds for harassed game, but absolute Sanctuaries. Under no condition should they be opened to the sportsman. No gun should be fired, no animal slaughtered or captured save by the direct authority of the wardens of the Sanctuaries, for the removal of noxious individuals, the controlling of species that were increasing beyond reason, the extirpation of diseased or unhealthy animals. The obvious examples are not the game reserves of the Old World, but the National Parks of the New World and of Australasia. In the United States, for instance, there are now the Yellowstone National Park with over two million acres, the Yosemite in California with nearly a million acres, the Grand Cañon Game Preserve, with two million acres, the Mount Olympus National Monument in Washington with over half a million acres, as well as a number of smaller reserves for special purposes, and a chain of coastal areas all round the shores for the preservation of birds. In Canada, in Alberta, there are the Rocky Mountains Park, the Yoho Park, Glacier Park, and Jasper Park, together extending to over nine million acres, whilst in British Columbia there are smaller Sanctuaries. These, so far as laws can make them, are inalienable and inviolable Sanctuaries for wild animals. We ought to have similar Sanctuaries in every country of the world, national parks secured for all time against all the changes and chances of the nations by international agreement. In the older and more settled countries the areas selected unfortunately must be determined by various considerations, of which faunistic value cannot be the most important. But certainly in Africa and in large parts of Asia, it would still be possible that they should be selected in the first place for their faunistic value. The scheme for them should be drawn up by an international commission of experts in the geographical distribution of animals, and the winter and summer haunts of migratory birds should be taken into consideration. It is for zoologists to lead the way, by laying down what is required to preserve for all time the most representative and most complete series of surviving species without any reference to the extrinsic value of the animals. And it then will be the duty of the nations, jointly and severally, to arrange that the requirements laid down by the experts shall be complied with.'

To the thoughtful man this lucid exposition of the case places the whole problem in a nutshell.

I think the concluding extract from Dr. Chalmers Mitchell's paper is one of the highest importance both in its wider sense and in the more confined one as regards India.

Sanctuaries such as above sketched are the only possible method of saving from extinction the rhinoceros, bison or gaur, and buffalo, to take three of the best-known of the big game animals requiring protection in India. But these Sanctuaries require to be left in their state of primeval forest. They cannot be treated as commercial forests managed from a revenue-making point of view by the Forest Department. The most scientific arrangements for opening and closing the blocks of forest as they come up in rotation for felling and other operations will not avail to make such areas true Sanctuaries. I have an idea that some of the areas in America and Canada alluded to above by Dr. Chalmers Mitchell are Sanctuaries which it is proposed to treat as revenue-giving forests. If this is the case they will not remain Sanctuaries for a certain proportion of the fauna they at present contain.

There can be little doubt that as it is with some of the shyer mammals so must it be with a proportion of other forms of animals life living in the forests.

They can be preserved from extinction in an area of primeval forest left untouched by man and maintained in its *original condition*. Amongst insects it is, I think, probable that some of the forest members of the longicorn, buprestid, brenthid and bark-boring beetles (*Scolytida*), to mention but four families, many species of which are still probably unknown to science, will disappear with the cleaning up of the forests and their systematic management by the Forest Department.

My point is that I am in complete agreement with Dr. Mitchell in his contention that the Sanctuary, the large, permanent Sanctuary, should not be regarded merely as a harbour for animals of game or economic interest, but that it should be formed in the interests of the fauna as a whole. I would, however, add to this the rider that in the case of the large Sanctuaries required to preserve from extinction animals either of a naturally roving disposition or of very shy habits the prohibition to entry should not be confined to the sportsman alone or to man generally outside the officials connected with the area. But further, that it should be recognised that in order to realise the objects aimed at it should be rigidly laid down that no working of any kind can take place within the Permanent Sanctuary. That in other words a Permanent Sanctuary does not fall within the boundaries of any area worked by Government officials, either for profit or other reasons, on behalf of the Government. Officials would be appointed to supervise the Sanctuary, but their duties would be confined to policing the area in order that the objects for which it was created might be realised to the full.

Colonel A.I.R. Glasfurd

Various Musings

Colonel A.I.R. Glasfurd served in the Indian Army and travelled widely through India's forests as a hunter pursuing sport. He arrived in India in his teens as a Second Lieutenant and traversed the country over the early twentieth century, writing all the while about the wilderness.

Finding the tiger on elephant-back was among the favourite pastimes of British India at the end of the nineteenth century. Among the Indian royalty, huge records for tiger shooting were amassed. From 1875 to 1925 India lost at least 100,000 wild tigers.

Tiger-shooting off elephants (which are more often than not 'cadged' from native potentates), may be the only way of dealing with the giant grass-coverts of the Terai, etc., and provide very jolly, sociable parties, but cannot be compared for true value with lone-hand shikar, with the subaltern's well-earned prize. Any fat, breathless man can shoot a tiger off elephant-back if he happens to hold his gun straight. The real performers here are the people who trained the elephants and personally directed the locating and driving of the tiger. 'All 'untin' is good; but some is better nor others,' a matter of personal predilection; some prefer the quiet working of hedgerows and rough with a clever spaniel, or stealing along the wood's edge at evening with a rabbit-rifle, to a big rise of the most cleverly-managed pheasants.

As to the ethics of using a motor-car in connection with sport, I have little to add to the remarks already made except that the vast majority of those who take an unfair advantage by artificial means well know what they are doing. On the other hand, it is amusing to hear people who enjoy special advantages for shikar, or those who cadge or command the use of elephants, inveighing against, say, the use of a Ford car; for, when it comes to comparisons, the Ford might in a way be described as the other man's rather inferior elephant. And I do not remember ever having heard the use of an elephant dubbed unfair.

One of my strongest objections to the car in India is that the saddle seems to be going out of use in favour of lolling over a steering-wheel, very much on the same principle that elephant-back is easier business than Shanks' mare ...

... I would suggest, however, that the lack of a proper ordinance may be due more largely to the fact that India groans increasingly under an incubus of paper, pens, and ink, reports and pigeon-holes, and that probably there is a horror of adding yet another department of State, although such has long since been introduced by practically every other big-game country.

As things are at present, or were when I left India, seven years ago,

Extract from *Musings of an Old Shikari: Reflections on Life and Sport in Jungle India* (London, 1928).

this playing at 'game-keeping' falls on the District and the Forest Officer; and although I have no doubt at all that in some cases it is willingly put up with—for fairly obvious reasons—it must, generally speaking, prove a nuisance and lead to unpleasantness; while, remembering India, I doubt that the additional work carries additional pay. Most Forest Officers must detest having to cater by order for the sport of wire-pullers.

Since criticism, to be useful, should be constructive, the following rough suggestions are made, with a hint that the Game Ordinances of Kenya and Tanganyika would repay study; and those who are interested will probably acknowledge that something of the sort would go far towards ensuring a proper state of affairs—decreased friction, better game-keeping, and prevention of the native wile that delights in setting white men at loggerheads. Considering that, *inter alia,* there is revenue in it, it is inconceivable that such an asset has been so long neglected:

A general Game Ordinance, including limitations and penalties, for all India—with special clauses for localities and conditions differing from the normal.

Scale of annual licence fees:

For British and Indian servants and ex-servants of the Crown, and for *bona fide* British and Indian residents, Rs. 10 for small game, and Rs. 60 for big game (the greater to include the less).

For British visitors the above to be multiplied by 20, and for foreign visitors by 50.

Licence-holders to be entitled to shoot, anywhere in British India, big game within one specified area at a time, with a time-limit for each, on the general of first-come-first-served, personal presence to be obligatory.

Transport, supplies, and native co-operation to be on a strictly public footing of ordinary supply and demand, divorced from local official imprimatur, favour, or disfavour.

The Game Department to be directly under the Government of India, separate from other branches, in no way subject to District, Divisional, or Provincial control, and with its own Wardens to administer the Game Laws.

Sale of 'trophies' to be made a penal offence in or out of India.

In India game sanctuaries would not answer unless watched continually by a white man, my experience being that they provide fine opportunities for native poaching while keeping the sahib away—the latter, when one comes to consider the matter, being the best unofficial gamekeeper.

As to limitations, a couple of tigers for every completed or current year of Indian service is surely enough for any man. It is considerably more than the average keen shikari totals. This restriction would give the 'small' man more opportunity of sharing in sport, and put an end to selfish arithmetical methods of those too advantageously placed.

To represent the normal tiger as destructive vermin, the plague of the country-side, 'cuts little ice' with those who know. I am also sceptical of the annual figures representing humans killed by tigers. Moreover, the tiger has his definite place in Nature's scheme, and keeps down the rapidly multiplying numbers of crop-destroyers such as pig and deer. When I hear the multi-tiger man enlarging on the need of 'keeping down tigers' I always wonder what he does with his skins. What *is* one to do with even fifty tiger-skins? Where is he or his relatives and friends going to put them all? *I take it that no true shikari ever contemplates that foul crime, the turning of trophies into money.*

F.W. Champion

Preserving Wildlife in the United Provinces

F.W. Champion worked in the Indian Forest Service and was based in the United Provinces. He was one of those rare people who, instead of a gun, used a camera. His commitment to tiger protection inspired, among others, Jim Corbett.

F.W. Champion: this picture of his was taken with a camera device and trip wire. His own photographs of those times are superb. Each picture could take days and nights of tremendous effort. Champion was painstaking with detail.

One among the numerous striking results of the Great War has been an awakening all over the world to the fact that wild animals are tending to become less and less in numbers in many countries, and often species that were common a few decades ago are being, or actually have been, entirely exterminated. Most of us who went through the War saw far too much of killing ever to want to see any more; and the natural reaction has been that a new spirit of sympathy with wild creatures has become firmly established in many countries. Wild life protection societies are springing up here and there, particularly in America and England, and the Society for the Protection of the Fauna of the Empire is doing great work in trying to preserve the wonderful fauna of the British Empire from further wanton destruction. An enthusiastic branch of this Society has been started in India and a very good work is being done, but unfortunately it is not receiving so much support from Indians as could be desired. Indians, many of whom are prohibited by their religion from taking life, should be the very first to support such a Society and a number are already whole-heartedly doing so, but real mass support has yet to be received. This I believe to be very largely due to lack of knowledge of the aims and objects of such a society, and insufficient propaganda, and I am confident that much greater support will be received in future as a result of the great efforts now being made by the Bombay Natural History Society and the various local branches of the Society for the Preservation of the Fauna of the Empire, which all who have the slightest interest in wild animals should join without a day's further delay. After all, once a species of wild animal has been exterminated, no money, no Society, no human agency can bring that species back to the world, and delay in helping those who are doing their best to save species already threatened with extermination may mean that help, tardily given, is given too late.

F.W. Champion was Deputy Conservator of Forests in the UP when he wrote this, in the early 1930s. Published in the *Journal of the Bombay Natural History Society*, vol. 37 (1934).

Position of Wild Life

The present position in the United Provinces is perhaps not quite so bad as in some other parts of India, owing to the presence of a very sympathetic government, an influential Forest Department, and great land-holders, all of whom have always remembered that, within limits, wild creatures have just as much right to exist as the human race. The position inside reserved forests and in certain large estates, which is fairly satisfactory, will be discussed later in this article, but first the present state of affairs in the ordinary districts will be considered. It is the conditions in these ordinary districts composing 80 per cent or more of the whole Province, which are causing so much worry to those who are interested in wild life. Frankly the position is appalling. The vast increase in gun-licenses which has taken place within recent years, combined with the greatly improved means of transport, has caused a drain on the wild life of the districts such as can end only in the almost complete destruction of any kind of wild creature considered to be worth powder and shot. Laws do exist imposing close seasons, but these laws often are not, and cannot be, observed in present-day conditions. Deputy Commissioners and Superintendents of Police in some cases do their utmost, but they are so over-worked nowadays with political and economical troubles that, however keen they may be, they literally have neither the time nor the energy to try to enforce unpopular laws, which, by comparison with present-day troubles, possibly do not seem very important. Further the responsible officers in a district are very few in number and it is quite impossible for them to stop bribery among their often low-paid subordinates. A rupee or two or a piece of meat is quite sufficient temptation to an underpaid *chowkidar* not to report an offence under a Wild Animals' Protection Act, particularly as it is often extremely difficult to prove such an offence, and, even if proved, a subordinate magistrate will generally let off the offender with a purely nominal fine. It therefore seems that, in the present state of the country, any Act enforcing close seasons outside Reserved Forests, however well it may be conceived, is worth little more than the paper on which it is written. In actual fact special efforts are now being made in Hamirpur and Meerut districts to protect sambar and chital; but it is not known to the writer how far such efforts are proving successful. Animals like black-buck and chital and game-birds, both in the plains and particularly the hills, are literally being wiped out at an increasingly rapid rate and one wonders if there will be anything left except monkeys and jackals after another two or three decades. There is one bright spot, however, and that is that non-game birds at least are not harried to the same extent as in England because the egg-collector is scarce, and the average Indian boy, unlike his English confrere, does not amuse himself by collecting vast numbers of birds' eggs, only to throw them away in most cases as soon as the boy begins to grow up. Taken as a whole there is no doubt whatever but that the position in these plains districts of the United Provinces is just about as bad as it could be, but one must always remember that these areas are very densely populated and that really there is not very much room for any considerable numbers of the larger game animals, which must tend to interfere with the cultivator and his crops. In any case leopards are found in many places, since they are prolific breeders and very difficult to keep in check, and even if more adequate protection were given to the game animals in cultivated districts, it is probable that their numbers would still be kept down by a corresponding increase in the numbers of leopards.

Sufficient has now been written to show that the position in the cultivated districts is very unsatisfactory, but that increasing population in already heavily populated areas, combined with the present political and economic distress, makes it very difficult to make practical suggestions for improving matters. What can be done is for large land-holders in sparsely populated districts to preserve restricted areas really efficiently and noble examples of what a great help to the wild life of a country such measures can prove to be is to be found in the great swamp-deer preserves of Oudh, notably those of the Maharani Saheba of Singahi and of Captain Lionel Hearsey. The former of these has been under careful protection for many years and an area of perhaps 20 square miles now contains several thousand head of these magnificent deer. A few are shot annually, but the number destroyed is almost certainly less than the natural increase and these public-spirited benefactors can justifiably feel that, so long as they maintain their present standard of efficient preservation, there is no fear of the swamp-deer following the already long list of fine animals which have been exterminated from the United Provinces.

Reserved Forests

Now the position of wild animals in the Reserved Forests, of which the writer, being a Forest Officer, has perhaps a specialised knowledge, will be considered. Firstly the writer would state most emphatically that United Provinces forest officers as a class are, and always have been, extremely sympathetic towards wild animals. Few are really heavy killers and quite a number do not shoot animals at all, beyond their requirements for food for themselves or their camp followers. An odd individual here and there both in the present day and in the past, has possibly let his sporting instincts drive him into becoming a really heavy killer, but the amount of slaughter done by the average forest officer in these Provinces is conspicuously small. It sometimes happens that disgruntled sportsmen state that Forest Officers are selfish or destroy more animals than all other classes put together; but these statements are most emphatically untrue and generally have an inner history, which reveals the accuser as having some personal grudge against an individual Forest Officer, which leads him to make general insinuations which are totally unfounded. None could be keener on the preservation of wild life than the present writer, and, if he thought that his brother officers were indifferent to the preservation of wild animals, he would not hesitate to say so. The writer believes that it would be a great mistake to remove the wild animals inside Reserved Forests from the protection of the Forest Department and place them in charge of a separate Game Department. The present system is working very well and such action would be regarded as a slur on Forest Officers and would alienate the all-important sympathy of the powerful Forest Department.

The United Provinces reserved forests are not very extensive and they are all under the personal supervision of divisional forest officers. Poaching does occur to a limited extent, particularly during the monsoon when the forests have to be deserted owing to their unhealthiness, and from motor cars, but such poaching is not very extensive and every effort is made to keep it in check. Elaborate rules, which are constantly being amended, do exist for the issue for shooting licenses, for the enforcement of close seasons, and for helping any species which is tending to become scarce. These rules may not be perfect—no rules ever are—but at least their object is to provide shooting for all who apply in the right way, and at the same time to preserve the wild animals in perpetuity without letting them increase to such an extent as to become a nuisance to forest management or to surrounding villagers. Species that, for any particular reason, need help are entirely protected, examples being wild elephants for many years and sambar in Lansdowne division since an attack of rinderpest in 1927; and senior forest officers are always ready to listen sympathetically to applications for protecting particular animals in particular tracts. Even tigers now have a close season and are not allowed to be shot by artificial light. Some may argue that it is a wrong policy to protect tigers, but at least such protection shows that forest officers consider that even tigers have the right to live in their own jungles.

On the other hand some wild animals, such as deer, do seriously interfere with the management and revenue of valuable forests, and the forest officer cannot allow deer to increase to an excessive extent. In some cases, particularly where the balance of nature has been upset by the excessive destruction of carnivora, deer have become a positive pest, and it has proved necessary to reduce their numbers. Or again, the proportion of hinds may have become excessive, with consequent deterioration in the size of the stage, so that some of the hinds have had to be shot off; but such destruction is stopped as soon as the position becomes normal once again. It is true that individual forest officers, keen silviculturists who have found all their efforts at improving the forests ruined, have occasionally advocated the total destruction of deer; but it is not the general opinion that such drastic measures are required and interesting experiments are now in progress by which considerable areas, in which plantations or efforts at obtaining natural regeneration of valuable trees are in progress, are entirely closed with game-proof fencing, which keeps out the deer. Such fences are somewhat expensive in initial cost, but they can be moved from place to place as required and are probably the best solution for managing forests both in the interest of the forester and also of the indigenous wild life.

It is sometimes stated that, even in the reserved forests, wild animals are much scarcer than they used to be. The writer cannot speak for thirty or forty years ago since the old records are not clear and he was not in India at that time; but, even if the head of game had diminished, it is possible that the numbers were excessive in the past or that the memories of those who claim that animals are disappearing are a little at fault. After all, most of us tend to think of the 'good old times', although it is possible that those times were not quite so good as they now appear in perspective. An effort has been made to collect figures of animals shot in the past with those shot nowadays for comparison, but records of thirty or forty years ago do not give the information required. The following are the conclusions that the writer draws from the figures that are available:

(a) Taken as a whole the head of game shot recently has generally not shown any marked decrease, except in the mountain reserved forests, where control is not so easy.

(b) Tigers appear to have increased and marked decreases seem to have taken place in the numbers of nilgai, kakar, wild-dog and black-buck. The decreases are partly due to serious floods and rinderpest epidemics, and are probably natural fluctuations which will right themselves in time. Wild-dogs have decreased owing to the large reward paid for their destruction.

(c) The decreases in the number of some animals shot recently are due to the removal of rewards as a measure of economy.

(d) It must always be remembered, however, that the number of animals inside Reserved Forests is probably being artificially swelled by the influx of refugees from the appalling conditions at present prevailing outside. This influx will decrease as animals outside become exterminated. Also modern rifles are so good and shooting with the help of a motor-car is so easy, that probably a greater proportion of the existing animal population is shot annually nowadays than was the case in the past.

(e) The Forest Department watches these lists carefully and takes action whenever such action appears to be required.

(f) The general impression of senior forest-officers is that, although there have been considerable fluctuations in particular areas, the game in the United Provinces Reserved Forests as a whole has not markedly decreased during the last 25 years, except in the high hill forests.

To summarise, the present position of wild animals inside the Reserved Forests of the plains and foot-hills of the United Provinces does not give cause for serious anxiety, except for the ever-increasing use of that arch enemy of the wild animals—the motor car. The numbers of wild animals in the mountain reserved forests appear definitely to be decreasing. The position in some zemindari estates is good and in others poorer; and the position in the ordinary districts is almost hopeless.

Some Suggestions

The writer would make the following suggestions to help the present state of affairs:

(a) *Public opinion.* This is by far the most important of all methods of wild life conservation and without it, all efforts to preserve wild creatures will prove abortive. Good work is already being done by propaganda and by lectures but much more remains to be done. Good illustrated books help greatly and the formation of sanctuaries and national parks, where the general public can see wild animals in their natural state, would all help. Major Corbett as local Secretary of the United Provinces branch of the Preservation of the Fauna of the Empire Society is doing a lot to assist in this work.

(b) *Laws.* It is much easier in the present state of India to pass a law than to see it enforced, but the writer would greatly like to see laws passed on the following points:

1. *Sale of shikar meat, trophics, etc.* It is of vital importance that a law be passed at an early date totally forbidding the sale of any portion of a wild animal, with certain definite exceptions. Such exceptions would be the dropped horns of deer, and the hides of deer where numbers have to be reduced. Special licences should be issued in such cases and such licences, liable to cancellation at any moment, should be under the personal control of the Divisional Forest Officers, where reserved forests are anywhere near, or under Deputy Commissioners where there are no Forest Officers. The sale of any shikar trophy should be entirely and absolutely prohibited. Such a law, properly enforced, would finish the professional

poacher, and would end the nefarious dealings of certain taxidermists who sell shikar trophies to those 'sportsmen' who are incapable of bagging anything themselves.

2. *Limitation of gun licences.* This is very difficult in the present political state of the country, but at least greater efforts could be made to differentiate between game licences and licences for the protection of the crops, person, property or display. Gun licences for the protection of crops should insist that barrels should be sawn-off short, as such licences are very largely applied for when the real object is poaching.

3. *Motor cars (and also carts and tongas).* The shooting of any wild animal from, or within, say, 400 yards of a motor-car, cart or tonga, either by day or by night, should be made an offence liable to prosecution. The writer personally would like to stop motor cars altogether from entering Reserved Forests, or, where this cannot be done, he would like to place check-chowkies at the entrances and exits of such roads, the cost to be covered by a small wheel-tax. Fire-arms would either have to be deposited at such chowkies or would be scaled, so that they could not be used while inside the forests. The excuse of requiring fire-arms for protection en route should not be accepted, as passengers in motor-cars very rarely need protection from wild animals except possibly from occasional rogue elephants or man-eaters. Luckily recent economies have resulted in the abandoning of some of the motor-roads in the Reserved Forests of the United Provinces. The writer would like to see them all abandoned! The old time shikari or Forest Officer managed perfectly well without them, and they tend only too often to make his modern successor slap-dash and lazy.

4. *Protection of rare stragglers.* It occasionally happens that a rare animal, such as a rhinoceros, strays into Reserved Forests from Nepal or elsewhere. Such animals should be rigidly protected with a fine of, say, Rs. 2,000, or imprisonment, for their destruction. The excuse that 'If I don't shoot it, someone else will' should never be accepted in such cases. The recent law passed in Bengal for the protection of the rhinoceros, should be extended to the whole of India.

5. *Rewards.* The writer considers that Government rewards for destroying wild animals should be given far more sparingly than in

the past. Luckily, recent economies have resulted in a great reduction in the rewards offered, and it is sincerely to be hoped that such reduction will be permanent. Rewards in the past have encouraged poachers and have sometimes caused an upset in the balance of nature where they were misapplied. They are really quite unnecessary except for man-eaters and notoriously destructive creatures such as porcupines.

It has been suggested that details of breeding-seasons of various animals should be appended to this article. Inside Reserved Forests every effort is made to protect wild creatures during their breeding seasons and nothing more can be done. Outside Reserved Forests, as already explained in this article, the position is such that protection can very doubtfully be enforced. Hence such an addition to an article which is already too long seems unnecessary, but the writer can supply a list of breeding seasons, so far as they are known, to anyone who is specially interested in the matter.

Since writing the above I have been reconsidering the question and have read up a certain amount of literature on the subject. On the whole I have little to add to what I wrote before except that I am not so certain as I was that the head of game inside the United Provinces' reserved forests is not decreasing. I was posted to N. Kheri Division in 1921 and I returned there again in 1931. Although still a good place for animals in 1931, I would estimate that there had been at least a 25 per cent decrease in nearly all species during that decade. The reasons for this reduction I would put down to *(a)* Motor-cars making shooting far easier than it used to be, *(b)* the destruction of game in the adjoining areas outside the forests resulting in a smaller influx and greater damage to animals straying outside.

I am now in Bahraich division in Oudh which has a reputation of being a good game division. I have now been here for 5 months and so far I have found game of all kinds to be rather scarce although I hear that more animals come in from Nepal in the hot weather. The reasons for this apparent decrease are the same as in Kheri, i.e., motor-cars and destruction of animals outside the forests, combined with increased poaching along and near the Nepal border.

I have recently heard from Col. A. E. Wood, I.M.S.—a keen supporter of the Darjeeling Natural History Society—that in his earlier days Lachiwala in Dehra Dun division used to be a 'veritable paradise' for wild animals. I am well acquainted with Lachiwala and I can only say that it is very far from being an animal paradise nowadays. It is more a 'paradise' for motor-picnickers from Dehra Dun City and Cantonment!

On the whole I am afraid that there is a distinct doubt that the game inside the reserved forests—particularly in Oudh, where motors now penetrate to every corner—is so plentiful as it was, although the recent position does not give rise to the same anxiety as is the case with other areas not under the control of the Forest Department.

Jim Corbett

Why Tigers Become Man-Eaters

Jim Corbett started his professional life as a railwayman and soon became a master of jungle craft, focusing himself entirely on tigers. His exploits are internationally renowned through his 'man-eating tiger' stories, but he loved the forest and its denizens and was a great champion for the cause of saving tigers.

An old engraving, signifying the plight of a tiger when it was surrounded by scores of elephants and then hammered by bullets. Many escaped with bullet injuries which turned them into vicious man-eaters.

A man-eating tiger is a tiger that has been compelled, through stress of circumstances beyond its control, to adopt a diet alien to it. The stress of circumstances is, in nine times out of ten, wounds, and in the tenth case old age.[1] The wound that has caused a particular tiger to take to man-eating might be the result of a carelessly fired shot and failure to follow up and recover the wounded animal, or be the result of the tiger having lost his temper when killing a porcupine. Human beings are not the natural prey of tigers, and it is only when tigers have been incapacitated through wounds or old age that, in order to live, they are compelled to take to a diet of human flesh.

A tiger when killing its natural prey, which it does either by stalking or lying in wait for it, depends for the success of its attack on its speed and, to a lesser extent, on the condition of its teeth and claws. When, therefore, a tiger is suffering from one or more painful wounds, or when its teeth are missing or defective and its claws worn down, and it is unable to catch the animals it has been accustomed to eating, it is driven by necessity to killing human beings. The changeover from animal to human flesh is, I believe, in most cases accidental. As an illustration of what I mean by 'accidental' I quote the case of the Mukteswar man-eating tigress. This tigress, a comparatively young animal, in an encounter with a porcupine, lost an eye and got some fifty quills, varying in length from one to nine inches, embedded in the arm and under the pad of her right foreleg. Several of these quills after striking a bone had doubled back in the form of a U, the point and the broken-off end being quite close together. Suppurating sores formed where she endeavoured to extract the quills with her teeth, and while she was lying up in a thick patch of grass, starving and licking her wounds, a woman selected this particular patch of grass

Extract from *Carpet Sahib* by Martin Booth (London, 1986). Originally written by Corbett in the early 1930s.

[1]Since Corbett wrote this, there has been established an eleventh case. It is that of the tiger dispossessed of his natural environment either by human habitation or, in the case of successful tiger reserves, increasing numbers of tigers in an inadequate territorial area and which, forced to exist in a locality in which natural food is in very short supply [or totally absent] takes to killing domestic stock or humans—Martin Booth.

to cut as fodder for her cattle. At first the tigress took no notice, but when the woman had cut the grass right up to where she was lying the tigress struck once, the blow crushing the woman's skull. Death was instantaneous, for, when found the following day, she was grasping her sickle with her hand and holding a tuft of grass, which she was about to cut when struck, with the other. Leaving the woman lying where she had fallen, the tigress limped off for a distance of over a mile and took refuge in a little hollow under a fallen tree. Two days later a man came to chip firewood off this fallen tree, and the tigress who was lying on the far side killed him. The man fell across the tree, and as he had removed his coat and shirt, and the tigress had clawed his back when killing him, it is possible that the smell of the blood trickling down his body as he hung across the bole of the tree first gave her the idea that he was something that she could satisfy her hunger with. However that may be, before leaving him she ate a small portion from his back. A day later she killed her third victim deliberately, and without having received any provocation. Thereafter she became an established man-eater and had killed twenty-four people before she was finally accounted for.

A tiger on a fresh kill, or a wounded tiger, or a tigress with small cubs, will occasionally kill human beings who disturb them; but these tigers cannot by any stretch of the imagination be termed man-eaters, though they are often so called. Personally, I would give a tiger the benefit of the doubt once, and once again, before classing it as a man-eater, and whenever possible I would subject the alleged victim to a post-mortem before letting the kill go down on the records as the kill of a tiger or a leopard, as the case might be. This subject of post-mortems of human beings alleged to have been killed by either tigers or leopards or, in the plains, by wolves or hyenas, is of great importance, for, though I refrain from giving instances, I know of cases where deaths have wrongly been ascribed to carnivora.

It is a popular fallacy that *all* man-eaters are old and mangy, the mange being attributed to the excess of salt in human flesh. I am not competent to give any opinion on the relative quantity of salt in human or animal flesh; but I can, and do, assert that a diet of human flesh, so far from having an injurious effect on the coat of man-eaters, has quite the opposite effect, for all the man-eaters I have seen have had remarkably fine coats.

Another popular belief in connection with man-eaters is that the cubs of these animals automatically become man-eaters. This is quite a reasonable supposition; but it is not borne out by actual facts, and the reason why the cubs of a man-eater do not themselves become man-eaters, is that human beings are not the natural prey of tigers, or of leopards.

A cub will eat whatever its mother provides, and I have even known of tiger cubs assisting their mothers to kill human beings; but I do not know of a single instance of a cub, after it had left the protection of its parent, or after that parent had been killed, taking to killing human beings.

In the case of human beings killed by carnivora, the doubt is often expressed as to whether the animal responsible for the kill is a tiger or leopard. As a general rule—to which I have seen no exceptions—tigers are responsible for all kills that take place in daylight, and leopards are responsible for all kills that take place in the dark. Both animals are semi-nocturnal forest-dwellers, have much the same habits, employ similar methods of killing, and are both capable of carrying their human victims for long distances. It would be natural, therefore, to expect them to hunt at the same hours; and that they do not do so is due to the difference in courage of the two animals. When a tiger becomes a man-eater it loses all fear of human beings and, as human beings move about more freely in the day than they do at night, it is able to secure its victims during daylight hours and there is no necessity for it to visit their habitations at night. A leopard, on the other hand, even after it has killed scores of human beings, never loses its fear of man; and as it is unwilling to face up to human beings in daylight, it secures its victims when they are moving about at night, or by breaking into their houses at night. Owing to these characteristics of the two animals, namely, that one loses its fear of human beings and kills in the daylight, while the other retains its fear and kills in the dark, man-eating tigers are easier to shoot than man-eating leopards.

The frequency with which a man-eating tiger kills depends on

(a) the supply of natural food in the area in which it is operating; (b) the nature of the disability which has caused it to become a man-eater; and (c) whether it is a male or a female with cubs.

Those of us who lack the opportunity of forming our own opinion on any particular subject are apt to accept the opinions of others, and in no case is this more apparent than in the case of tigers—here I do not refer to man-eaters in particular, but to tigers in general. The author who first used the words 'as cruel as a tiger' and 'as bloodthirsty as a tiger', when attempting to emphasise the evil character of the villain of his piece, not only showed a lamentable ignorance of the animal he defamed, but coined phrases which have come into universal circulation, and which are mainly responsible for the wrong opinion of tigers held by all except that very small proportion of the public who have the opportunity of forming their own opinions.

When I see the expression 'as cruel as a tiger' and 'as bloodthirsty as a tiger' in print, I think of a small boy armed with an old muzzle-loading gun—the right barrel of which was split for six inches of its length, and the stock and barrels of which were kept from falling apart by lashings of brass wire—wandering through the jungles of the *terai* and *bhabar* in the days when there were ten tigers to every one that now survives; sleeping anywhere he happened to be when night came on, with a small fire to give him company and warmth; wakened at intervals by the calling of tigers, sometimes in the distance, at other times near at hand; throwing another stick on the fire and turning over and continuing his interrupted sleep without one thought of unease; knowing from his own short experience and from what others, who like himself had spent their days in the jungles, had told him, that a tiger, unless molested, would do him no harm; or during daylight hours avoiding any tiger he saw, and when that was not possible, standing perfectly still until it had passed and gone, before continuing on his way. And I think of him on one occasion stalking half a dozen jungle fowl that were feeding in the open, and on creeping up to a plum bush and standing up to peer over, the bush heaving and a tiger walking out on the far side and, on clearing the bush, turning round and looking at the boy with an expression on its face which said as clearly as any words, 'Hello, kid, what the hell are you doing here?' and, receiving no answer, turning around and walking away very slowly without once looking back. And then again I think of the tens of thousands of men, women, and children who, while working in the forests or cutting grass or collecting dry sticks pass day after day close to where tigers are lying up and who, when they return safely to their homes, do not even know that they have been under the observation of this so-called 'cruel' and 'bloodthirsty' animal.

Half a century has rolled by since the day the tiger walked out of the plum bush, the latter thirty-two years of which have been spent in the more or less regular pursuit of man-eaters; and though sights have been seen which would have caused a stone to weep, I have not seen a case where a tiger has been deliberately cruel or where it has been bloodthirsty to the extent that it has killed, without provocation, more than it has needed to satisfy its hunger or the hunger of its cubs.

A tiger's function in the scheme of things is to help maintain the balance in nature and if, on rare occasions, when driven by dire necessity, he kills a human being or when his natural food has been exterminated by man he kills two per cent of the cattle he is alleged to have killed, it is not fair that for these acts a whole species should be branded as being cruel and bloodthirsty.

Sportsmen are admittedly conservative, the reason being that it has taken them years to form their opinions, and as each individual has a different point of view, it is only natural that opinions should differ on minor, or even in some cases on major, points, and for this reason I do not flatter myself that all the opinions I have expressed will meet with universal agreement.

There is, however, one point on which I am convinced all sportsmen—no matter whether their viewpoint has been a platform on a tree, the back of an elephant or their own feet—will agree with me, and that is, that the tiger is a large-hearted gentleman with boundless courage and that when he is exterminated—as exterminated he will be unless public opinion rallies to his support—India will be the poorer by having lost the finest of her fauna ...

WILDLIFE IN THE VILLAGE: AN APPEAL*

It was a small village of some 16 ploughs differing in no respect from hundreds of similar villages, scattered throughout the length of the tract along the Bhabar. Originally the village had been surrounded by tree jungle intercepted with grass, and in this virgin jungle lived all the numerous denizens of the wild. To protect their crops the villagers erected thorn fences round their fields. As an additional safeguard a member of the depressed class was encouraged to settle in the village whose duty it was to watch the crops at night and see they were not damaged by stray cattle or wild animals. Owing to the abundance of game tigers did not interfere with the village cattle and I cannot remember a single case of cow or bullock having been killed by a tiger. In the course of time, a great change took place not only in the villagers themselves but also in the jungle surrounding the village. Hindus who formerly looked upon the taking of life as against their religious principles were now clamouring for gun licences and were competing with each other in the indiscriminate slaughter of game. As profits from the sale of game increased field work was neglected and land began to go out of cultivation. Simultaneously, lantana, introduced into Haldwani as a pot plant, started to kill out the grass and basonta until the village was surrounded with a dense growth of this obnoxious weed. Government now stepped in and at great expense built a pucca wall all round the village. The building of this wall freed the villagers from the necessity of erecting fences and watching their crops and gave them more time to devote to the killing of game. This heavy and unrestricted shooting of deer had the inevitable consequence of disturbing the balance in nature with the result that tigers and leopards, that had hitherto lived on game, were now forced to live on the village cattle. One morning in May of the present year [1932] I arrived in the village and pitched my tent in a little clearing just outside the cultivated land. News of my arrival soon spread through the village and in a short time a dozen men were squatting in front of my tent. One and all had the same tale to tell. A tiger had taken up its quarters in the lantana and in the course of two years, had killed 150 head of cattle and unless it was

*Extracted from *Review of the Week* (Nainital, 1932).

destroyed the village would have to be abandoned. While the men were pouring out their tale of woe I observed a pair of vultures circling low over a narrow stretch of lantana running between the village wall and the public road. The two vultures were soon joined by others; so picking up a rifle I set off to investigate. Progress through the lantana was difficult but with the aid of a good hunting knife a way was eventually cut and the remains of a horse killed the previous day found. There were plenty of pug marks round the kill, little of which remained, and it was easy to locate the tiger from his low continuous growling but impossible to see him in the dense cover. Returning to the road which was only 40 yards from the kill and little used at this time of the year, I concealed myself behind a bush in the hope that the tiger would follow me to see if I had left the locality, quite a natural thing for it to do. Half an hour later the tiger walked out on to the road and gave me an easy shot as he stood facing me. That evening after I had skinned the tiger—he was a very old animal and I took four old bullets and nine pellets of buck-shot out of him—I called the villagers together and made an appeal to them on behalf of the few remaining deer in the jungle. On the opposite side of the village from my camp, irrigation water had been allowed to flow into the jungle. Over this water machans had been built in the trees and in these machans men sat through the heat of the day, and all night on moon-lit nights, and shot down animals that came to drink. There was no other water within miles and if a thirst-maddened animal avoided one machan, it fell victim to the man in the next. I told the villagers that God had given water free for all, and that it was a shameful thing for man to sit over the water God had provided and shoot his creatures when they came to drink. To do this was to lower themselves below a corpse-eating hyaena, for even he, the lowest of all creation, did not lie in wait to kill defenceless animals while they were drinking. The men listened to me in silence and when I had done, said they had not looked at the matter in this light, and they promised that they would take down the machans they had erected and in future would not molest the animals that came to the vicinity of the village to drink. I stayed in the locality several weeks, taking bird and animal pictures, and am glad to say the men kept their promise. I believe that much of the slaughter of deer that is daily taking place throughout the length and breadth of the Bhabar and Terai would cease if an appeal was made to the better feelings of men. I do not exaggerate the damage that is being done to our fauna by shooting over water.

Let me give you but one instance. An acquaintance of mine living in a village in the Bhabar adjoining my own, in one hot season, over one small pool of water shot, with a single barrel muzzle-loading gun, 60 head of cheetal and sambar which he sold in a near-by bazaar at the rate of Rs. 5 per cheetal and Rs. 10 per sambar. It is no exaggeration to say that the banks of every little stream and every pool of water in the vicinity of Bhabar villages are soaked with the blood of animals that never took toll of a single blade of the villagers' crops. I assert without fear of contradiction that for every shot fired on cultivated land from guns provided for crop protection, a hundred shots are fired in the jungle over water. Pigs and nilgai are the only wild animals that damage the crops in the Bhabar to any extent, and to keep them out of cultivated land Government has expended lakhs of rupees in building pucca walls. It is asserted that in recent years tigers have increased. With this assertion I do not agree. It is a fact that more cattle are being killed every year; this is not due to the tigers having increased but due to the balance of nature having been disturbed by the unrestricted slaughter of game, and also to some extent to tigers having been driven out of their natural haunts where they were seldom or never seen by man, by the activities of the Forest Department. A country's fauna is a sacred trust, and I appeal to you not to betray your trust. Shooting over water, shooting over salt-licks, natural and artificial, shooting birds in the close season and when roosting at night, encouraging permit-holders to shoot hinds, fencing off of large areas of forest and the extermination by the Forest Department of all game within these areas, making of unnecessary motor tracks through the forest and shooting from motor cars, absence of sanctuaries and the burning of the forests by the Forest Department and by villagers at a time when the forests are full of young life are all combining to one end—the extermination of our fauna. If we do not bestir ourselves now, it will be to our discredit that the fauna of our province was exterminated in our generation and under our very eyes, while we looked on and never raised a finger to prevent it.

Stanley Jepson

An Appeal for the Preservation of Wild Life

Stanley Jepson was in the army before and till soon after the First World War. Later he became Editor of *The Illustrated Weekly of India.* He was an avid sportsman and hunter in the 1930s.

Stanley Jepson poses with dead tiger, wife and motor car. The combined technology of gun and motor car, as well as the building of new roads, devastated the tiger population. Debates raged in the 1920s about the use of cars to hunt.

There is nothing selfish or incongruous in the idea of sportsmen taking up the preservation of wild life. They are in the best position to do so and in India and Africa have always supported these movements—people who spend leisure hours in the jungle soon become very keen on the preservation of the wild.

Were the Taj Mahal at Agra to be allowed to fall into ruins, or to be destroyed by vandals, a cry of indignation would arise from north to south and east to west of the Indian Empire and of the world. But—the hand of man could re-create this structure. Yet several equally beautiful works of the Creator, rare species in the rich and varied fauna of India, are threatened with complete extinction and the hand of no man can re-create them. No howl of indignation arises. As the years go by, people seem to grow apathetic to the need for some action to preserve India's fauna for posterity.

There is little need here to recapitulate the evidence which is available on all sides. Trained observers have described the position province by province and the observations of these forest officers have been published from time to time. Some of these observers have gone so far as to say that species of animals, such as the Indian antelope (blackbuck), etc., which frequent non-forest areas, are doomed to extinction, and that practically nothing can be done to save them. Already their numbers are only a small proportion of what they were ten or twenty years ago.

Few people who have any personal knowledge of how game is wantonly slaughtered in the jungles of India will refuse to agree that protective measures are long overdue. In those days of cheap rifles and cheaper guns, India should take to heart the lesson of South Africa, whose gameless veldts are now a sorry contrast to what they were some decades ago when many kinds of big game were abundant. Mr. F.W. Champion, the Deputy Conservator of the United Provinces, describes the position in ordinary non-forest areas—comprising eighty per cent of the Province—as 'appalling.' He says the vast increase in gun licences in recent years, combined with improved transport, has caused a drain on the wild life of the

Extract from *Big Game Encounters*, edited by Stanley Jepson (London, 1936).

United Provinces which 'can only end in complete destruction.' Inside United Provinces Reserved Forests he finds the position generally satisfactory, though with marked decreases in the numbers of certain animals.

Any action taken is bound to vary in accordance with local provincial conditions, which are so different in various provinces that one standardized ordinance for India would be unworkable. Take the case of tigers. Suggestions have been made for elaborate rules for the protection of tigers in particular. But this might be undesirable in some parts of India where nature's balance of game has been disturbed, and the tiger finds it too difficult to get his food out of the forest, whereupon he turns to cattle-lifting or even to the easiest quarry of all—man himself. General Burton in his recent *Book of the Tiger* tells of parts of India many years ago where it was doubtful at one time whether man could survive because of the depredations of the king of the jungle. Had it not been for the efforts of European sportsmen in killing off tigers, large areas of cultivated land would have been reclaimed by the law of the jungle. Forest officials have to consider very carefully this question of 'balance of game.' In her ruthless and seemingly cruel manner, Nature seems to have provided 'dangerous game' like panthers and tigers to keep down herds of deer and other grazing animals, which if unthinned would become an unbearable nuisance to the cultivator and his crops. The tiger will kill every four or five days, so that the number of animals taken by even one tiger in the course of a year is considerable. Wild pig alone are estimated to cause scores of rupees worth of damage each year in India, and for weeks before harvest the wretched cultivator has to sleep out all night to guard his crops against the attacks of these and other animals.

In her tigers, elephants, bison and buffaloes India has an economic asset, but one cannot avoid the conclusion she does not make the best of it financially. We allow the shooting of what is called dangerous game—tiger, panther, bear, etc.—without limit, whereas other countries make the sportsman pay according to his bag, the revenue to go to the game warden's guards for policing purposes. This innovation would also put an end to the cruel and senseless slaughter by wealthy people who try to set up records in tiger shooting in some areas. Generally speaking, the tiger needs further protection. An idea of the extent to which the tiger has been exterminated may be gained by reading old books like *Forty Years among the Wild Animals of India*, by Hicks, who was asked how many tigers he had shot. 'I kept count up to 200, then stopped,' he replied. 'It may be 400, or more or less, I don't know.' That was more than half a century ago, when tigers were a great menace in forest areas and even threatened to drive out man from cultivable areas. But the contrast with conditions today is a startling one.

Writing in *The Field* recently, Col. C.H. Stockley described how he had just visited the Kala Chitta Range of hills in the Punjab, near Campbellpur, in order to secure photographs of the oorial and wild sheep. I knew these blocks immediately after the War when they were full of game, and a day's hard work would reveal many fine heads. Sometimes as many as twenty or thirty rams could be seen in the course of a morning in the best block. Col. Stockley observed that there were very few animals at all, and he could hardly get any photographs. On the other hand, when he visited a piece of *zemindari* ground which was looked after by a keen Indian sportsman (in his own interests), he found plenty of oorial, and got some fine photographs. This story is typical of what is going on in many parts of India, where lack of interest and a policy of *laissez faire* have considerably reduced the numbers of certain animals.

It is only fair to add that one or two forest officers who have examined the problem (notably those who have contributed articles to the series invited by the Bombay Natural History Society), have reported that *in certain forest areas*, game of most kinds is as plentiful as it was twenty years ago. It is, of course, on the borders of forest areas, especially where there are good roads, and where there are cities for the sale of game, that the most striking contrasts are observable.

Mr. H.J.C. Millett, a Khandesh (Bombay) Forest Officer of keen observation, has given me an instance of the difficulty of detecting offences. He points out that in his area there is one guard to detect offences that may be committed over 6,000 acres of reserved forest area—obviously an impossible task. Mr. Millett states that in the last ten or twelve years, the decrease of big game and especially of sambhur in East Khandesh is fully 50 per cent—though he cannot state the reason with any certainty. The four main reasons he gave me in order of priority were: 1. epidemics; 2. poaching; 3. motor-car; 4. crop protection firearms—a pretty fair analysis probably. He thinks that animals requiring special protection are Indian antelope (blackbuck), sambhur (particularly against poaching), and tiger—the latter because the balance of nature is being disturbed and pig and nilgai increasing. He advocates one tiger per annum per licence.

Another contributor to *The Field* recently stated that a Delhi contractor informed him that by receiving thirty-six hours' notice he could guarantee a supply up to 2,000 partridges, etc. These would be probably obtained through the co-operation of certain jungle tribes, and the quantities show that regular organisations must exist. The same author ascertained that the average daily supply of game birds for Delhi was 500, so that this will give some conception of the drain on bird life. Similar markets near sources of supply exist in the case of venison, and near big cities a profitable trade has been built up, especially now that cold storage is so easy.

There are, of course, many kinds of animals, especially those of nocturnal habit, which are well able to look after themselves even in the face of all the present tendencies of attrition. These include panthers, and in a recent letter to the writer, Mr. F.W. Prideaux said that his own experience is that panthers, in the C.P. at any rate, are still as numerous as they were twenty years ago. This is also the experience of many forest officers in other provinces, for the panther is well able to look after himself. Under the same heading one might put elephants in Southern India, which do not attract the *average* sportsman, and which at times become so numerous as to constitute a danger to life and property.

Among the indirect causes of this state of affairs, one is bound to place public indifference high on the list. The destruction of priceless works of art such as old temples or magnificent buildings would not be tolerated by public opinion, but it is curious that in India of all places, where animal life is often sacrosanct to an extraordinary degree, the extirpation of her fauna continues without any public outcry. Its conservation is a national task, and the first step must be the awakening of the public conscience in this matter.

Among the more direct factors bearing on the present situation may be placed the commercialisation of shikar, i.e. the legalised trade in things like venison, game birds, hides and horns. In this respect the experiences of other countries point a moral to India. It has been estimated that it would have taken much longer for South Africa to denude herself of game if people had shot, poached, netted, snared, etc., solely for their own requirements; but as soon as hides and dried meat secured a market value, then it paid unscrupulous people to organise a trade, and extermination rapidly followed. Many Indian forest tribes are very clever at snaring, netting, etc., and though it is extremely difficult for the Forest Department to stop them carrying this on in certain areas, it should be easy to remove the markets by illegalising or controlling such sales. Incidentally, the Forest Department can do little or nothing for the protection of the species, whose natural habit is outside the boundaries of protected forests. The problem has been the same in all countries. Once the trade in horns, skins and meat has been developed, an unremitting toll has been taken day by day, week by week, of game of both sexes until it has been exterminated or driven away to more peaceful areas. This sort of slaughter is carried on by rifles, by old guns, by sitting over the animals' only water or salt licks, and by traps. It will continue while the trade flourishes—even if a Forest Guard could be stationed in each village. It attacks animal life at the fountain head, destroying females, and even young. It is the acme of cruelty. The only way to stop it would be to prohibit such trade in horn trophies, in pelts of wild animals, and game meat—to illegalise sales.

Closely allied to the foregoing causes is poaching, though frequently the poacher acts on his own for himself and his friends. It has always been very difficult to deal with this problem. It is easy to pass laws, but very difficult to enforce them in the remote areas where the poacher works. The hungry villager, living in forest areas, may be surrounded by game, and for generations he has learned how to beat, how to net, and how to kill, by bow and arrow and other means. He regards this perquisite almost as a right in some cases, and certain tribes even go so far as to steal the tiger's dinner and remove his kill.

That poaching has increased of recent years is ascribed by many to the increase in what are known as crop protection guns. The primary object of these weapons is that the cultivator may protect his crops against the depredations of things like pig, nilgai, cheetal, sambhur, etc. This appears quite a sound scheme—almost a necessity for the cultivator. But the strange fact is that such weapons are not used for their intended purposes. They come in very handy for supplying people with meat, hides, etc. Cartridges are not cheap for the villager, and even if the intention is that the villager should lessen the number of pig which certainly do great damage, it is as well to remember that the *average* villager is no match for the wily boar leader of the herd of pig; and his efforts at reducing the size of the herd with his blunderbuss are often useless. Several forest officials have told the writer that they have seldom heard of a crop protection gun being used to protect crops; and one or two have said that too often such licences are given as rewards without any regard to the real needs of the cultivator. It is but natural to conclude that the majority of the game animals which are being ruthlessly slaughtered all over India with 'crop protection' guns are females and young.

Villagers' firearms need special thought, and for genuine crop protection guns might be issued by Provincial Governments which could be short barrelled, and might well be withdrawn when crops are not standing; and, equally well, licences might be cancelled unless the licensees could prove that they have killed pig during the year. W. Burns, formerly Director of Agriculture in the Bombay Presidency, sent me some pertinent points about the villagers' problem. Naturally he is concerned with the point of view of the cultivator, and he is fully aware of the very heavy damage done by pig in the course of a year—he estimates this at about half a million sterling for Bombay Presidency. He and his shikar officer have organised gun clubs in order to keep down pig in a scientific way, particularly in sugar-cane areas. Wild pig breed like rats, and mere noise will not scare them away at nights. He therefore believes that it is necessary to kill pigs, especially females at the time of gestation. If pigs are not really scared away, he says, the unfortunate villager has to sit up and watch his crops all night, and is subject to fatigue and malaria—anyone who knows Indian rural areas can vouch for this statement.

It is also open to question whether Government should not allow under suitable provision, the hunting by bow and arrow or trapping, etc., of a certain amount of game by those jungle tribes who have done so for many centuries and who look upon this as providing part of their normal food supply. Such official sanction might go far to put an end to surreptitious poaching with firearms.

While analysing the causes of game diminution, the inevitable progress of cultivation, and what may be called the advance of civilisation generally, should be remembered. Such progress necessitates the opening out of forest areas.

There are, of course, other but less permanent natural causes of reduction in forest fauna, such as outbreaks of disease like rinderpest, foot and mouth disease, large forest fires, droughts, etc. Under this heading one might also include the disturbance through the hand of man of the 'Balance of Nature.' For instance, if there are too many tigers or panthers in a certain forest, game such as cheetal, sambhur, pig, etc., will be entirely depleted. Remove the carnivora altogether and pig, deer, nilgai, etc., may become so numerous as to constitute a nuisance if there is no check on them. Red dog also come under this heading. They hunt and kill many animals.

While indicting the village poacher, one cannot let sportsmen go guiltless. Nowadays, the canons of shikar have been lowered to such an extent that it is difficult to assess the weight of this factor. People go out in cars along forest roads and shoot headlight-dazzled deer, etc., in a most cruel manner. What satisfaction they can derive from such slaughter is difficult to conceive. Even in the daytime the use of the motor car to approach game is so unsporting that several writers, including Mr. F.W. Champion, have advocated that a new game ordinance should prohibit the use of cars in this connection. It is debatable whether the Government of India in any new game ordinance should not entirely prohibit shooting by artificial light except in the cases of tiger or panther proscribed as a menace. The real sportsman can be the jungle's best gamekeeper because his movements reveal to him what is going on, and news of existing conditions is brought back to the town or city. Sportsmen rarely live permanently in the haunts of game, and their movements are easily controllable, especially in the East where an inescapable publicity dogs their footsteps.

Action indicated to ensure conservation of wild life is obvious when many of the above causes are examined. For instance, statutory measures might include a revision of the Arms Act, the illegalising of traffic in venison, hides, horns, etc., the prohibition of shooting by artificial light except in certain cases and some action to prevent the abuse of motor cars in the realm of sport. The present game licences might also be revised to afford a further measure of protection to tigers, which are at present classed as vermin. It would be quite reasonable to ask a visiting sportsman to pay more for his second, third, fourth tiger, etc., if he wants the luxury—often unsporting—of a big total.

Then there arises the question of game sanctuaries. The formation of these on lines which have proved so successful in many countries should surely commend itself to the Government of India without delay. Mr. Dunbar Brander has mentioned in the *Bombay Natural History Society's Journal* one very suitable area in the Central Provinces, and other places might be selected within motorable distances of Bombay, Calcutta, Delhi, etc. Thus, visitors would have an opportunity of seeing wild life in its natural surroundings. Such sanctuaries would be under a separate Game Department with a warden in charge, and shooting would, of course, be permanently forbidden. Or Government might sanction a *local* increase in the F.D. staff for the especial purpose of protecting the sanctuary.

There is ample information available about game sanctuaries in other countries. In Canada, New Zealand, Australia, and the Union of South Africa large areas have been reserved which offer security and shelter to wild life. Other countries have rapidly followed these Empire examples. Switzerland has her national park amid Alpine splendour. Italy and Spain have established similar areas. Sweden surpasses all Continental countries with her fourteen national parks. Finland, Austria, Poland and Czecho-Slovakia have such districts. Belgium has in the Congo that great sanctuary the Parc National Albert, created by royal decree in 1925, and proving so successful that four years later its area was increased tenfold. An example to India has been set by Travancore State where the Maharajah is personally interesting himself in the formation of a large sanctuary on the shores of Periyar Lake to give a sure refuge to the elephant, bison and other species which are about there. There may be nervousness about the financial liabilities in setting up a game sanctuary. This aspect rightly demands careful study. But there is encouragement in the history of the Kruger National Park in South Africa. This covers over 8,000 square miles of territory, and contains the best collection of wild animals anywhere in the world, while its 500 miles of motor road bring tourists and photographers from all parts. The Park fully justifies its existence by increasing revenues to the State.

Such sanctuaries, however, should be run on scientific game-keeping lines, with *effective supervision*; otherwise experience has shown that they may merely encourage quiet poaching in out-of-the-way forests. When nalas have been closed in Upper Kashmir and Ladakh in order to increase the number of markhor and ibex, the authorities have at times had a rude surprise on reopening them to sportsmen after some years—one or two nalas were found to be completely devoid of big game. The same experience occurred once in Sind, where an effort was made to preserve the Sind ibex through closing certain areas—with the final result that the ibex disappeared from those areas.

One of the main benefits such sanctuaries would give would be the arousing of public opinion to the value of India's rich and varied fauna. It is surely an anachronism that while most other countries have big game sanctuaries, India with her fine religious traditions which give protection to animal life, and with a selection of wild animals amazing in its numbers and variety, was until recently doing nothing to arouse public opinion on this point.

S.H.

Prater

The Wild Animals of the Indian Empire

S.H. Prater is a household name among conservationists for his work in the 1930s as a curator with the Bombay Natural History Society. His best-known work is *The Book of Indian Animals,* which sells regularly even today.

When S. H. Prater wrote of the wildlife of the Indian Empire it was being fast converted into trophies for hunters. Few knew what lay ahead for tigers and India's wildlife; few believed that anything would be alive in the twenty-first century.

What other Nations are Doing to Preserve Wild Life

It is interesting and instructive for us in India to know what other nations are doing to preserve wild life.

The movement for the protection of Nature had its origin barely 50 years ago. It is the European nations and the American people who set an example to the World as to what could and ought to be done to preserve wild life within their lands. In the United States of America, the rapid development of the country, the spread of agriculture and industry threatened the destruction of its indigenous fauna. The tragedy was averted by establishing great national Parks or Reserves which not only give inviolable sanctuary to wild animals, but also offer the people an added attraction because of their scenic beauty, their historical, geographical or archaeological interest.

These National Parks provide the means by which the clash of interests between man and the Animal is obviated; whereby security is found for the creature without imposing undue restraint upon human progress. The idea gained ground because of the people's approval. Today, in the United States, there are no less than 40 great National Parks covering more than 3 million acres of land set aside for the protection of wild life.

This magnificent effort for the protection of nature has its parallel in the British Empire, so rich in the varied aspects of its wild life. In Canada, in New Zealand, Australia and the Union of South Africa great reserves have been created which give shelter and security to the wild life of these lands. The Kruger National Park in South Africa is the largest in the British Empire if not in the world. It covers over 8,000 square miles of territory. No park in the world contains a more marvellous assemblage of wild animals. Quite apart from the protection given to the wild life of the country, this magnificent park fully justifies its existence by way of the yearly increasing revenues it brings to the State. The effort for the conservation of wild life has

An Address given by Mr. S.H. Prater, M.L.C., C.M.Z.S., the Bombay Natural History Society's Curator, at the Jubilee Meeting of the Society held in Bombay on the 10th of August 1933. Extracted from *The Wild Animals of the Indian Empire* by S.H. Prater (Bombay, 1933).

been equally splendid in Canada. Here again the public response evoked by the numerous National Parks within the Dominion has resulted in bringing in a great amount of money into the country. These measures have been taken by a race of people who are keenly concerned in the progress and development of their countries and nevertheless realise the advantage of making provision to safeguard their wild life from destruction.

Within the last twenty years other nations have followed the example set by the Anglo-Saxon peoples. Switzerland has established her splendid national park amid the scenic grandeurs of the Engadine. Italy and Spain have created similar sanctuaries. Sweden surpasses all Continental countries with her fourteen national parks. Finland and Austria have established numerous reserves for the protection of wild animals. Poland and Czecho-Slovakia have created a common park on their frontiers in the region of Tatara and thus incidentally, in a common desire for the protection of Nature, they have found a happy solution of a vexed territorial problem. Belgium, if not the first in the field, has been equally energetic. The great wild life sanctuary in the Belgian Congo, known as the Pare National Albert, was created by Royal Decree in 1925 and by 1929 increased tenfold in area. Five hundred thousand acres of mountain and forest have been set apart for the protection of African wild life, This great reserve is open to the students of the world and in the years to come it will prove of inestimable value to scientists and to all who love Nature and are interested in it.

The cause of conservation has been advanced also by various International Conferences the last of which was held in Paris in 1930. In 1900, the British Government convened a conference in London of the representatives of the Powers which resulted in the London Convention for the Preservation of Animals, Birds and Fish in Africa. It was signed by the Plenipotentiaries of Great Britain, France, Germany, Belgium, Italy, Spain and Portugal, and is described as the Magna Charta of wild life in Africa. In 1913 an International Conference for the Protection of Nature was held at Berne at which seventeen Governments were represented. The principal conclusion of this Conference was the decision to establish a central organisation to deal with the question of Wild Life

Preservation on an international basis. The war made this impossible and it was not till 1928 that the recommendations of the Berne Conference were given effect. A central Bureau, designed to develop as the pivot of an international movement for the protection of wild life was established at Brussels. It is known as the 'International Office for the Protection of Nature'.

Similarly, within the British Empire, the London Conference resulted in the foundation of the Society for the Preservation of the Fauna of the Empire, which has given a great impetus to the movement in England and the Colonies and has now for many years exercised its great influence in the promotion of all forms of wild life protection. Reference must also be made to the American Committee for International Wild Life Protection, representing a unity of the large museums in the United States and to the Dutch Society for International Wild Life Protection.

It will be seen from what has been written that in all civilized countries there is a general recognition of the need for concerted and practical measures to stop the forces of destruction which threaten wild life in all parts of the world. There is in India, too, the gravest need for such concerted action.

THE PROBLEM OF WILD LIFE PROTECTION IN INDIA

We have endeavoured to show how great an asset to our country is its wild life and to give the many reasons why we should do everything for its protection. But for the protection given to the Lion in Junaghad State and the Great Indian Rhinoceros in Nepal and Assam these two interesting animals would have been exterminated long ago. The cheetah or Hunting Leopard, once common in Central India, is now almost extinct in the wild state. The Lesser One-horned Rhinoceros and the Asiatic Two-horned Rhinoceros, once said to be common in the grass jungles of Assam and the Sundarbans have been practically exterminated in these areas. In many districts wild animals have been totally wiped out. In others, where they were once common, they are now hopelessly depleted. One does not wish to overdraw the picture. There are parts of India where the position of wild life is still satisfactory though insecure. But equally, there are extensive areas where conditions are so appalling that, if left unchecked, they must lead to the complete destruction of all the larger wild creatures which live in them. There is yet another point which must be stressed. Any scheme for the Protection of Wild Life would be incomplete without due provision for the protection of our Birds. Quite apart from a sentimental value, birds render incalculable service to Man. While certain species may damage crops, such harm as is done by birds is overwhelmingly offset by the benefits we derive from them. Without their protection, our crops, our orchards, our food supply would be devoured or destroyed by hordes of ravaging insects. Birds are the principal agency that controls the bewildering multiplication of insect life which, if unchecked, would overwhelm all life on this planet. Birds by reason of their predominating insect food are an indispensable balancing force in Nature. The abundant bird life of this country is one of its valuable possessions. Those who appreciate its value, cannot but strive for its conservation.

If we accept this principle of Conservation as it is now accepted by almost all civilised countries, what methods must we employ to give it effect? It is obvious in a country like India, where conditions in different provinces vary so greatly, the methods of conservation must also vary, but it is necessary to arrive at some understanding of the broad principles which underlie the problem. The land may be classified for this purpose into three main categories: urban lands, agricultural lands and forest and waste lands.

Agriculture and Wild Life Protection

As far as our wild life is concerned, one cannot expect its preservation in urban lands. Nevertheless, we believe that it is time that measures should be taken for the protection of birds in urban areas. Areas actually under the control of Municipalities or local Boards could be made, with advantage, Bird Sanctuaries, where the killing of birds should be forbidden. There is need to put an end to the wanton destruction of familiar birds which takes place in the immediate vicinity of towns.

The second category—land under cultivation—provides at once the opportunity for a clash between the interests of Man and the Animal. There are two main reasons for this. Firstly, the areas under cultivation in India are extending and will continue to extend to meet the needs of a rapidly increasing population. This has increased by 35 million within the last decade! The need of increasing the available sources of food supply can be met only by the continued absorption of waste lands or forest—the natural domain of wild life. Secondly, there is the equally imperative need of protecting these cultivated areas from wild animals. The depredations of wild animals present one of the most serious handicaps the ryot has to face. In addition to loss of cattle, there is the damage done to crops and, not uncommonly, loss of human life. Therefore, whatever the views of the protectionist, this much is clear. Human progress must continue and in the clash of interests between Man and the Animal human effort must not suffer. But this problem has been faced by other countries. Cannot a reasonable effort be made to face it in our own? That an intensive development of the agricultural resources of a country may accompany a sane and adequate policy for the conservation of its wild life is shown by the measures taken to this end by all progressive nations.

If our wild life is to find protection at all, it must find it somewhere in our forests. It is often claimed that the proximity of forests to agriculture makes them a constant source of harassment to the cultivator. If this argument is pushed to its logical conclusion, the only remedy would be to remove such protection as is now given to wild animals in our forests, for it would not be possible to remove this menace entirely, until all the large wild animals in them were killed, died of wounds or were exterminated over large areas because of their inability to breed. Surely our goal is not the total extermination of our wild life—which is what must inevitably happen unless some form of protection is given to it within its natural domain. While it is essential that the cultivator should have reasonable latitude to defend his property, it is equally essential that there should be certain areas or reserves where the shooting of animals is regulated and where the laws for their protection are rigidly enforced. Such reserves exist—roughly about one-third of British India and Burma consist of Reserved Forest—but, while we have extensive forests to shelter and laws to protect it, our wild life is everywhere on the decrease. The time has surely come when it is necessary for us to review the position and to take such measures as are necessary to give real protection to the wild life of the country. It is the opinion of some that these great State-owned forests, where laws now operate for the protection of animals, are and must continue to remain the natural sanctuaries of wild life in this country and that they would adequately fulfil the purpose of protection if they were effectively warded. The correctness of this view depends entirely on actual conditions in a particular Province. The extent and nature of the forests, their accessibility, the density of the population and the extent to which cultivation surrounds them are factors which must influence the issue. It may be found that in certain Provinces the establishment of a national park or reserve, in specially selected areas, will provide the only means of giving adequate protection to wild life without hampering agricultural development. It is certain that the creation of such a reserve or national park would give a special status to it, and thus facilitate the passing of special laws made applicable to such an area. Further, the actual selection and declaration as a National Park of certain definite areas would have the practical effect of forcing on the attention of successive generations of officials the importance of saving these areas from any danger of disafforestation and of taking all practical measures for the preservation of the wild animals found within them.

The Need for a Special Organisation to Protect Wild Life

Whether our reserve forests remain the principal sanctuaries for wild life in this country or whether in some of the Provinces the purpose is affected by establishing national parks, there is need for a real organisation whose sole concern will be the protection of wild animals in these preserves. Our efforts to protect wild life have failed mainly *because of the haphazard methods we employ, the lack of any co-ordinate policy and the lack of any real protective agency to carry that policy into effect.* The Forest Department which ordinarily administers the Forest laws has multifarious duties to perform and, while the Forest Officer had discharged this trust to the best of his ability, he cannot give the question his personal attention, nor can he find time, except in a general way, to control the protection of wild life in our forests. Experience of other countries has shown the need of a separate and distinct organisation whose sole concern is the protection of wild life in the areas in which it operates.

Further, the existing laws, as now applicable in many of our Provinces, are obsolete. Naturally, their primary purpose is the protection of the forest rather than its wild life. These laws require consolidation and bringing up to modern standards of conservation. No better guide to our Provincial Governments seeking to amend their game laws exists than the recently issued report of the Wild Life Commission in Malaya. Volume II of this Report gives the general principles of conservation. It shows how these principles may be embodied in an Act and indicates new administrative methods, based on actual experience and on the laws of other countries. With modifications, where necessary, it will serve as a model for Protective Legislation in India.

Lastly there is the all-important question of making adequate financial provision for carrying out the work of conservation.

In these days of depression, when most Governments are faced with deficit budgets, the apportioning of money for this purpose must be a matter of difficulty but, unless and until suitable financial provision is made by the State for the conservation of wild life within its borders, the effort cannot succeed. This much is clear. Our present haphazard methods have failed. The experience of other countries indicates the system that should replace them. The effective introduction of this system depends upon money being provided to work it. In the United States and in other countries the problem of financing the work of conservation has been helped by the creation of special funds.

The recent Wild Life Commission in Malaya, which made a careful study of this aspect of the problem, strongly urges the creation of such a fund to be termed the *Wild Life Fund* and to be used solely for the purpose of conservation. The idea is that all fees which could be collected under Wild Life Enactments, including any licenses or fees for riverine fishing, as well as revenues from all sporting arms licenses, permits, duties on arms (sporting) and ammunition (sporting) should be credited to the Wild Life Fund. If any of these fees are collected by another department, then the cost of collection should be borne by the Wild Life Fund. It is the only means by which financial provision can be made expressly for the purpose of conservation. It is the only means by which the money devoted to this purpose will have a definite relation to the revenue derived by the State from wild life sources and which, therefore, can be expended with every justification upon the conservation of these sources. It is the only way to ensure an equitable system of conservation; the only way in which a properly organised department can be stabilised. It is the solution advocated in other countries and one which is equally applicable to any country which undertakes the conservation of wild life on sound lines. If the idea of creating a Wild Life Fund is not acceptable and, if we are yet serious in our intention to do what is possible for the conservation of wild life in India, then we must replace the Wild Life Fund by an alternative policy, which will ensure the allocation of sufficient money to meet the requirements of adequate conservation. It is so easy to refuse a constructive policy and then put nothing in its place. The necessity for conservation being clear, the importance of an adequate financial policy to support it cannot be ignored.

So much for the broad outlines of the problem. They resolve themselves as we have seen into the formulation of a co-ordinate policy for the protection of wild life in India, into the selection of suitable areas where our wild life can be protected without undue detriment to human interests, the creation of a special agency for carrying out the work of protection and finally, a revision, wherever necessary, of such laws as exist in order to help these agencies to carry out their task effectively.

We have indicated what other countries are doing for the protection of wild life but it must be apparent that the measures which they have taken, whether initiated by acts of Government or by private enterprise must owe their success to the support of public opinion. There is need for the creation of sane public opinion on the subject of wild life protection in India. At present, such opinion hardly exists and even if it does, in some quarters it may be antagonistic. This is mainly because people do not know, nor has any attempt been made to teach them something of the beauty, the interest and the value of the magnificent fauna of this country. In most western countries there is a wealth of cheap and popular literature dealing with the natural history of those lands. In India such literature as exists, is either unintelligible to the average reader or sold at a price beyond popular reach. Again, in most western countries, Nature Study teaching is a serious part of the earlier stages of the school curriculum. While its main object is to develop the child's powers of observation, it creates a love of Nature and a sense of companionship with life out of doors. It is true that in India feeble attempts are made from time to time to introduce Nature Study teaching into our Primary and Secondary schools. But often such teaching as is given, deals with pine trees and acorns, with polar bears and robin redbreasts, and has little or no relation to the child's own environment.

E.P.

Gee

The Wildlife of India

E.P. Gee was a great naturalist and wildlife photographer. He was a member of the Indian Board of Wildlife from its inception in 1952. Jawaharlal Nehru described him as 'one of the best-known authorities in India on the subject.'

The author was a great fighter for India's wildlife in the 1950s. He was a tea planter in Assam at a time when Assam's flood-plains and grasslands teemed with wildlife.

His picture of the Gaur was made into one of the first wildlife stamps of Independent India.

It may seem strange that the task of wild life preservation is entrusted to the Forest Departments in India, and that there are no separate wild life departments. When this problem came up in 1952 it was decided to entrust this work to the Forest Departments of the various States because nearly all the wild life and sanctuaries of this country happen to be in the forests and other lands which are under the jurisdiction of the Forest Departments. To create another department to preserve wild life would lead to overlapping and unnecessary duplicating of work, and in any case it would be difficult to find the trained personnel for another department.

So the Officers and Subordinate Staff of the Forest Department in India are entrusted with the task of preserving the fauna as well as the forests, and for this purpose there are Wild Life Divisions and special personnel within the Forest Departments, under the Chief Conservators of Forests, to deal with wild life matters.

... In the long history and culture of India, there is something of a tradition of nature conservation. Consider the measures described in the treatise on Statecraft called the *Artha Shastra*, attributed to Kautilya about 300 BC, where certain forests 'with game beasts open to all' were specially protected.

In these protected forests there was strict supervision and certain mammals, birds and fish were fully protected. If these animals became vicious, they were 'to be entrapped or killed outside the sanctuary, so as not to disturb the rest. The extraction of timber, burning of charcoal, collection of grass, fuel and leaves, the cutting of cane and bamboo, trapping for fur skins and tooth and bone were all totally prohibited.' Such forests were called *Abhayaranya*, and in some measure can claim to be the forerunners of the national parks of the modern era.

Much later, under British rule, attempts were made in the various Provinces to preserve game, mainly in order to ensure the continuance of big and small game shooting. With the same object in view, an even greater amount of preservation was done by rulers of many of the princely states.

Extract from *The Wild Life of India* by E.P. Gee (London, 1964).

At the dawn of Independence in 1947, however, much of this good work was undone by the ordinary people who, suddenly realising that it was now they who owned the animals, often went out into the wild places and massacred whatever they could find. I have been told the story of how a jeep-load of hunters sallied forth in old Jaipur state and shot between seventy and eighty sambar in one night. Only one young one could be brought home to eat.

It was five years after Independence before the Government of India could start to devote time to the task of wild life preservation; the Indian Board for Wild Life [IBWL] was constituted in November 1952.

Under the Constitution of India, 'wild life' is a State and not a Central subject. The Central and its advisory Indian Board for Wild Life can only recommend, co-ordinate and encourage: all the actual work of legislation, implementation and general wild life preservation has to be done by the States themselves.

The weakness of this set-up is that some States move forward at a slower rate than other States, depending chiefly on the amount of personal interest and energy displayed by the Forest Minister and the Chief Conservator of Forests of a State at any given time. The Wild Life Boards of the States are powerless and can only advise—if and when they are called on to do so. This is why India's small band of wild life enthusiasts, which includes Salim Ali, Dharmakumarsinhji, Krishnan and others (including myself), is continually trying to enlist the support of the public by way of articles in the Press and other means.

This kind of set-up also explains why some States have upgraded their best sanctuaries to the status of national parks, while some really good sanctuaries in other States have not yet become national parks. The IBWL at the Centre is endeavouring to ensure that only those sanctuaries, which are of real national value to the whole of India and to the rest of the world, should be constituted as national parks.

Since 1952 a great effort has been made both at the Centre and in the States to conserve the rapidly diminishing wild life, but this has not been enough to keep up with the continual and alarming increase in human population.

This increase is by far the greatest threat to wild animals, involving as it does the cutting of forests, the cultivation of land for food, and grazing by domestic stock. After all, 1.27 million square miles which include sparse desert areas, the high Himalayas, and rain forests in the north-east, are populated by more than 440 million people—most of whom are under-educated and under-nourished. The problem of preservation in India is therefore very different from that in Africa, Europe or America, where the main danger comes from 'sportsmen'. Bona fide sportsmen in India have, indeed, contributed a great deal to our knowledge of natural history and, indirectly, to game preservation. (These must not be confused with poachers, who recklessly and, alas, increasingly—slaughter the country's edible animals.)

Clearly the needs of human beings must come first. In the new India of today large-scale industrial development is taking place so that the standard of living will be raised. But material progress is not an end in itself: sources of spiritual enjoyment such as the beauties of nature must be safeguarded.

In highly industrialised countries more and more people are turning to wild and unspoilt countryside for rest and recreation; and more and more tourists will visit India to see her scenic beauties and wild life. In fact tourism is already becoming an important industry in India and a valuable foreign exchange earner.

Large national parks as in North America and Africa are not feasible in this over-crowded country, but at least all the small sanctuaries and parks should be strictly maintained, and some new ones created.

As I see it, there can be no doubt that, at the present rate of cutting vegetation, overgrazing by domestic stock and killing of wild animals in India, by the time public opinion can rally in support of wise conservation of wild life there will be practically nothing left to conserve. There will be very little wild life left by the year AD 2000, only thirty-six years from now, except in zoological gardens.

The first to go will, generally speaking, be the larger mammals and birds, especially those which are edible. Smaller mammals and birds, particularly the latter which can escape by flying, will be the last to disappear.

Imagine the year 2000, with the only wild life consisting of those creatures which can adapt themselves easily to thickly populated areas, such as jackals, rats, mice, vultures, pariah and Brahminy kites, crows and sparrows!

How the inhabitants of the future India would miss the lovely sight of a snowy-white cattle egret gracefully alighting on the back of a rhino placidly grazing among the flowering reeds and grasses of Kaziranga! What would the Gir Forest be like if, bereft of its stunted trees, there were no noble lions and lionesses with their cubs to enrich our lives? Can one imagine Bandipur without its magnificent 'bison', or Periyar without its lordly elephants, or Kanha without its elegant swamp deer? Or Bharatpur without its wonderful congregation of breeding water birds?

If the spectacular tiger, the proud peacock and all the other splendid denizens of the forests and grasslands were to cease to exist, then how dull life would be!

All this can and will happen, unless proper conservation measures can be taken in good time before it is too late. Of course it is not only an Indian but also a world problem, for which the World Wildlife Fund has been started in western countries. In many parts of the world careful planning is being done to ensure the survival of wild life and wild places for future generations.

I am not altogether pessimistic about the future. Much is being done, although very much more is necessary.

If nature conservation could be considered important in India as long ago as 300 BC and 242 BC, it should surely be accepted as a first priority necessity at the present time. The existence of a sound nature and wild life conservation organisation in a country is a reliable indication of the stage of a country's progress and development. There is a very good chance that the leaders, planners and people of India will see the 'writing on the wall', and that they will not fail today in their duty of preserving the country's heritage of forests and fauna for those of tomorrow.

Richard Perry

The World of the Tiger

Richard Perry delved deep into the world of the tiger, and the literature available on the subject, during the middle of the last century. He travelled widely within all the tiger areas of Asia.

By the 1960s the world of the tiger had turned into a living hell. Skulls, skins and trophies piled up in hunters' homes as hunters competed for bigger records and larger trophies. India's record of 11,000 tiger trophies was held by the Maharaja of Surguja.

We must examine in more detail the world distribution of tigers, noting that their numbers from Trans-Caucasia across the two thousand miles of central Asia to the Altai seem never to have been in any way comparable to those south and east of the Himalayas.

Not much more than a hundred years ago the tiger's range in Trans-Caucasia extended as far west of the Caspian as Ararat and exceptionally Tiflis, with the tropical low-lands and foothills of Azerbaijan as headquarters as recently as the early nineteen-thirties. It is possible that an occasional straggler may still reach Azerbaijan from Iran; and despite this century's intensification of agriculture and hunting in Iran it is estimated that there are still between eighty and one hundred tigers in the Mazandarn and Boujnourd districts south-east of the Caspian, where they were extensively trapped early last century and exhibited in wild-beast shows throughout Persia.

Eastwards across central Asia, with their northern boundary running from Bogaz Bay on the Caspian to Lake Balkhash and the Altai mountains, the various races of tigers were localised in pockets far apart; but wherever there were large enough reed-jungles around the lakes and oases, or forests in the mountains, there were tigers which, like those in Iran, were longer-haired and less distinctively but more densely striped than Indian tigers, and possibly smaller on the average.

The largest of these colonies was in the reed-jungles of the Oxus, where it delta'd into the Aral Sea; though tigers were also to be found along the whole length of the Oxus as far as the frontiers of Darwaz under the Pamirs, where they were especially numerous in the two hundred square miles of the Urtai and Tugai forests, home of the Bokhara deer. A hundred and fifty years ago the emperor Timur hunted tigers in the marshes and woods around Bokhara, where the waters of the Zarafshan ran to waste in the sandhills; and in 1907 Carruthers heard a tiger killing a pig in the Makhan Kul catchment to the east of Bokhara; but tigers have not been seen near Bokhara itself for more than a hundred years. The Aral tigers proved very

Extract from *The World of the Tiger* by Richard Perry (London, 1964).

troublesome to a Russian survey expedition one midwinter last century, and Russian officers used to hunt them from Tashkent; but for some decades now there have been no breeding tigers anywhere in the area, and reports of an occasional one wandering in from the south Caspian to hunt pigs in the marshes of the Oxus must be considered doubtful. This is also true of Afghanistan, where there were formerly some tigers in the forested north-west of the country above Herat.

Lake Balkhash, with its numerous reed-jungles, was another stronghold of tigers; and there, as we have seen, their range extended upwards to four thousand feet where the cork forests thinned out; while in the summer, when the low country was waterlogged after the freezing winter, and swarming with mosquitoes, they went up to the tamarisk and thallophyte country at eight thousand feet. There were tigers eastwards to the reed-jungles and dense forests of Dzungaria, home of the ubiquitous wild boar, roe-deer and a variety of wapiti resembling the Yarkand stag; and at four or five thousand feet among the thick spruce scrub of the upper Ili river.

Although there was no regular hunting of tigers in central Asia, farmers and shepherds took toll of them in winter with the poisoned carcasses of sheep and goats, and steppe fires destroyed their reed-bed haunts. Writing in 1908, Carruthers considered that the tigers of central Asia were in danger of becoming extinct, and this has finally proved to be the case in Russian territories within the past five or ten years, and probably also in their old Sinkiang haunts around Lop-Nor and in the Altai. There are historic records of tigers almost as far north as Novosibirsk, roughly midway between Lake Balkhash and Lake Baykal; and there are old Chinese records of tigers in the hills above the Koko-Nor salt-plains in the Nan Shan and in the Munni-ula hills of Inner Mongolia on the most northerly bulge of the Yellow or Hwang river, forming a link between Sinkiang and the Chinese hinterland.

Tigers were formerly distributed all over China, and some 2,500 years ago captive tigers may have been hunting wild horses in China, for tomb tiles from Loyang depict a tiger, apparently wearing a collar; and Marco Polo refers to the Grand Khan Kublai hunting deer, wild cattle, boars and bears with 'striped lions'. In time they came to be isolated in pockets by the destruction of the forests and reed-jungles and the spread of cultivation accompanying the human population explosion from the Hwang river. In the north of China they were hunted to the verge of extinction for their valuable winter pelts and especially the quack properties of their organs. In south China it was not the spread of human population that was the direct cause in reducing their numbers, but the deforestation of virtually all the coastal mountain ranges in the unending search for fuel by peasant and townsman alike. This resulted in all the tigers, together with leopards, serow and wapiti, being driven inland. Thirty years ago tigers were relatively common in south China, especially in the rocky gorges of Fukien, where they were numerous; and were occasionally visiting Hong Kong's new territories. Today however, tigers are found only in Yunnan on the borders of Burma and Viet-Nam; in the mountains of Heilung Kiang and Kirin in Chinese Manchuria; and until quite recently in Fukien; west of Shanghai and along the Yangtse into Szechwan and north of Peiping. Those of Heilung Kiang link up with the last remaining Ussurian colonies in Russian Manchuria of Khabarovsk and Primorie, and those of Kirin with the very few (if any still remain) in the wooded mountains of north Korea, where they swarmed last century. At that time tiger skins were not only much valued by Korean chiefs, but as many as a hundred and fifty skins a year were exported as tribute to China or Japan; but tigers were already becoming scarce in Korea in Yankovsky's day, and are not historically known to have penetrated as far south as Seoul, where the country was always very heavily populated.

Formerly the Manchurian tiger's domain covered an equilateral triangle with its base on the Sea of Japan, from north Korea and the Maritime Territory, heavily forested with spruce and pine, to the mouth of the Amur and the Island of Sakhalin; and its apex north and south of Chita in the Yablonovvy mountains, some two hundred miles east of Lake Baykal—which a single tigress reached from Ussuria around 1875. In the north the range followed the approximate line of the Amur and Shilka rivers, and in the south this large, long-furred race may have inter-bred with the small south China race around Peiping and the Hwang river. The Manchurian race seldom wandered far inland from the north bank of the Amur, though during the Russo-Japanese war of 1905 some were driven almost as far north as Yakutsk on the Lena, more than five hundred miles from the Amur. Though often hunted in the marshes and the wooded valleys of the foothills, their main haunts were in the dense cedar forests, among the precipitous crags, rocks, caves and ravines from two to four thousand feet in the mountains.

For decades these Manchurian tigers were persecuted by professional hunters: Chinese, Russian, Tartar and Korean. Aramliev's aboriginal hunter from north of the Amur shot from one to six adult tigers every year for nearly fifty years, and until 1918 they were also shot by Russian officers stationed at Vladivostock. Between 1912 and 1914 eighty-three tiger cubs under two years old were captured in Russian Manchuria; but by 1920 adults were becoming extremely difficult to shoot, and by 1956 or earlier the only tigers remaining on Russian territory in the whole of central Asia were estimated to number fifty-eight in Khabarovsk and Primorie; though in 1959 this figure was revised upwards to ninety-one, and they are now strictly protected, with a limited licence only for the capture of cubs for zoos.

If any country was, and perhaps still is, more densely populated with tigers than India, it was the southern half of Indo-China, where Défosse, Millet, Monestrol and Bazé shot and trapped many hundreds of tigers. There, three hours out from Saigon and the rubber plantations, begins a dense jungle as impenetrable as any in the world; though there are also vast savannahs of grass and reeds as high as an elephant, and these are the main hunting grounds of tigers until the game are driven out by the fires of the dry season.

In Thailand, with its strong Buddhist antagonism to the taking of any form of life, tigers are still to be found in all jungles, becoming especially numerous in the mountain ranges stretching down the spine of Malaya from Thailand and Burma. Tigers multiplied in Malaya during the Japanese occupation, and are still to be found throughout the country, with the exception of Penang and Singapore, from the cool forests of the lowlands, where their pugs are often seen on the coastal beaches or the hardening mudflats of the mangrove swamps, to the highest places in the mountains. Locke made a rough calculation, on the basis of one tiger to every ten square miles in the average jungle, and one to seventeen square miles overall, that in the nineteen-fifties there were a minimum of three thousand tigers in Malaya. Today, forests are being extensively felled in Malaya, and the tiger population has no doubt been drastically reduced.

Although a crossing to Singapore Island presented no difficulties to such powerful swimmers as tigers, they appear to have been very scarce on that island in the earlier half of the nineteenth century, though by 1843 they had become a scourge to the Chinese coolies, and continued to be so for the next twenty years or so.

A century ago tigers were very common throughout Indonesia, and by the nineteen-twenties Ledboar, the most prolific hunter in those islands, had shot one hundred from ground pits near kills; but by 1961 there were no tigers in the islands off Java, and they had disappeared almost entirely from the mainland, being restricted to the palms and pandanus wilderness in southern parts of the Island. Today it is possible that the half-dozen tigers in the large game reserve of Udjung-Kulon are the last in Java; while on Bali they may be extinct. In Sumatra, however, where there are still abundant jungles, in contrast to the immense areas under cultivation in Java, tigers are still numerous and widely distributed. They were never found east of Bali, because between that island and the next, Lombok, lies that very ancient deep-water channel, twenty miles wide, which has presented an impassable barrier to very many animals seeking to disperse west from Australasia or east from India and Ceylon—and which tigers never reached over the original land-bridge.

Burton, contradicting earlier authorities, showed that there were frequent references to tigers in India in Buddhist books dating back nearly 2,500 years. The Sanskrit word for tiger, for example, was *Vyaghra* (and *citra-vyaghra,* spotted tiger, for leopard). In Hindi, a language of Sanskrit origin, a tiger is *bagh* or *wagh,* with which may be compared *waghderh,* tiger-valley; *waghdo* or *wagholi,* the place of the tiger; and *wagnak,* tiger-claws or a Maratha weapon with steel claws. He showed also that the tiger's presence in India could be dated back a further 2,500 years by the discovery of seals, engraved with tiger figures, in the ruins of the buried city of Mohengro-Daro [*sic*] in the valley of the Indus—one seal depicting a man in a tree angrily apostrophising a tiger walking below. Some of these seals were identical with others found in Babylonia's Sumer and Edom, and linked perhaps with Alexander's retreat through Baluchistan and the south of Persia. This route, Burton suggested, might also have been that followed by tigers extending their range from India to their westerly outposts around the Caspian Sea. But the Caspian region is much more likely to have been reached by way of Sinkiang and Lake Balkhash from Manchuria and north China, or possibly direct from central Siberia. There is in fact complete continuity in distribution and racial characters between Chinese and Indian tigers, but discontinuity in both respects between the tigers of west India and those of Iran. There are regional vacuums between India and Trans-Caucasia, with no records of tigers ever having inhabited Baluchistan, Lower Sind, Kutch and the desert parts of Rajasthan; and although once abundant in the Indus reed-beds—the last one was shot in 1886—they have always been scarce in Upper Sind and west Punjab.

By the eighteen-sixties or seventies tigers had been exterminated in many parts of India, and greatly reduced in numbers in other parts, with such notable exceptions as the Narbada and the Bombay Presidency, the Terai and the Sundarbans; and by the early years of this century they were almost extinct in the Punjab. The lapse of shooting during the First World War permitted a substantial increase in numbers over the next decade, and in one week in 1921 Wardrop was able to shoot seven adult tigers from the same tree in a nullah in one of the Native States in the north of India. Since 1930, however, there has been a steady contraction of tiger jungles, though tigers are still generally distributed throughout the Peninsula—except in the south where they have been almost exterminated by poachers and armed villagers—and up into the Himalayas, where they are numerous in Nepal and all along the forested foothills to Lower Kashmir. Wide-scale concessions to safari organisers in Nepal may however alter this situation drastically during the next few years. It is generally believed that today there are less than four thousand tigers in India, and that rather more than ten per cent of these are being killed annually. This is itself is not a critical toll; but it could obviously very easily become so, and by the end of this century a truly wild tiger may be a rarity in India.

We end as we began. The present world population of tigers is perhaps 15,000, perhaps rather more. Therefore, one might think, *Panthera tigris* is in no immediate danger of extinction; but only a super-optimist would expect more than a few hundred wild tigers to be alive by the end of this century. National Parks on their present scale—and this is especially true of Asia—have hardly begun to touch the problems of wild life conservation, and are in any case entirely at the mercy of political, national and tribal pressures. We have very little time left in which to find the final solution to this world-wide twentieth-century conflict between human and animal populations. One suspects that in the end it will probably be solved in a manner disastrous for both men and animals; but we must continue trying to solve it humanely.

George
Schaller

The Deer and the Tiger

George B. Schaller is among the most renowned wildlife biologists in the world. He has studied lions, tigers, gorillas, pandas, snow leopards and several other species. His book *The Deer and the Tiger* is a bible for all tiger-wallahs.

George Schaller at work in the early 1960s, Kanha National Park, Madhya Pradesh. He was the first scientist to record the tiger's natural behaviour. His work in Kanha is still inspirational for tiger conservationists.

India is remarkable for the variety of its large mammals, a richness in species exceeded by few countries in the world. From the rain forest of Assam to the snows of the Himalayas and the deserts of Rajasthan, from the deciduous forests of the central highlands to the mangrove swamps of the Sunderbans, India presents a great diversity of vegetation types, each with its unique faunal assemblage. The immense sweep of the Himalayas harbour sheep such as the bharal and urial as well as wild goats—the markhor, tahr, and ibex; and there are takin and goat antelopes such as the serow. Snow leopards stalk musk deer in the rocky gorges, and black bears prowl the forested slopes. Many of these species belong to the palaearctic faunal region, and the mountains represent the most southerly part of their range in India. The peninsula has its own distinctive mammals, with some, such as the blackbuck, nilgai, and chital, being almost wholly confined to it. The thorn forests and other open habitats are or were the home of the Asiatic lion, cheetah, Indian gazelle, and others; the grass jungles of the Gangetic basin hold wild buffalo, barasingha, hog deer, and the great Indian rhinoceros; the forests harbour elephant, sloth bear, leopard, gaur, barking deer, sambar, pig, and the unique four-horned antelope. And many of the forests contain the tiger, an animal which perhaps more than any other over the years has become the symbol of India's wildlife heritage.

The Western world was largely unaware of the variety and abundance of the mammals in India until the nineteenth century, although the four principal Vedas (2000–1500 B.C.) mention the tiger, lion, wild pig, and twenty-seven others (Rao, 1957) and the Mogul emperors from the thirteenth to the sixteenth century were famous as hunters. Akbar the Great is said to have kept one thousand trained cheetahs with which to hunt antelope, and his successor Jehangir shot, among other animals, a total of 889 nilgai (Ali, 1927). With the advent of British rule, and particularly after the consolidation of the whole country following the mutiny of

'Introduction' and 'Conclusion' from *The Deer and the Tiger: A Study of Wild Life in India* by George Schaller (Chicago, 1967). The author-date bracketed references relate to Schaller's bibliography, which readers may wish to pursue by referring to his classic study.

1857, many hunters penetrated all parts of the country. Books by Rice (1857), Shakespear (1860), Baker (1890), Forsyth (1889), and Kinloch (1892), among others, give a vivid picture of the great herds of hoofed animals and the numerous large predators that occurred even in the parts heavily populated by man. Jerdon (1874) reported herds of blackbuck in the Punjab numbering ten thousand animals; 'travelling through almost any district, you will come across them, sometimes in large herds, and herd after herd' (Aflalo, 1904). Rhinoceros and wild buffalo still existed at the foot of the Himalayas, and 'swamp-deer, hog deer, sambhur, and other cervine species, herd together in the tall grateful cover of the friendly jungle grass—and wild pig, porcupine, wild fowl, game fowl, and other animals, dear to the sportsman, are to be met with in incredible numbers' (Inglis, 1892).

These herds are no more. The cheetah is extinct in India, the last ones having been shot in 1951 (Talbot, 1960). The great Indian rhinoceros, which was hunted in the Indus valley by the Moguls as late as 1519 (Rao, 1957), survives only in a few isolated sanctuaries in India and Nepal. The population of the Kashmir stag has been reduced to fewer than two hundred fifty individuals (Gee, 1962*a*). The Asiatic lion, once found throughout the dry open forests north of the Narmada River, now occurs only in the Gir Forest of Gujarat, where fewer than three hundred animals remain (Gee 1962*a*). probably no more than two thousand wild buffalo exist in scattered remnants (Daniel, pers. comm.). Of the 'herds of thousands' of barasingha seen by Pollock and Thom (1900) in Assam and Bhutan only some four thousand survive in the country and in the world. Where Forsyth (1889) observed herds of blackbuck 'which must have numbered a thousand or more individuals', none are now seen and this species once so abundant is reaching a critical stage in its survival. The other large mammals—the Indian gazelle, nilgai, chital, gaur, and so forth—which were exceedingly common have all declined drastically in number. The ubiquitous tiger has become scarce in most parts of the country. The Himalayan fauna has suffered a similar fate (Dang, 1964*a,b*). What has been the cause for the decline?

Direct shooting has been an important factor in the decrease of wildlife. Many British civil servants were inveterate hunters, as were the maharajas, for whom it was a major form of recreation. Animals of any age and sex were bagged indiscriminately. Hunting was not just a sport but a symbol of status, the criterion for the latter being the number of animals, especially tiger, shot. In Cooch Behar (1908) the caption on one photograph reads: 'A record day's bag of bison—3 bulls and 8 cows'; books by Rice (1857), Shakespear (1860), and Smythies (1942) contain representative descriptions of this type of hunting. By the end of the past century the decline had accelerated to such an extent that some hunters grew concerned. The rhinoceros was gone from most of its former haunts, and the lion was nearly exterminated, although one was shot in central Madhya Pradesh as late as 1851. (Forsyth, 1889). Russell (1900), after bagging twenty-four blackbuck in one outing, noted the general scarcity of the species in the area. Baldwin (1877) wrote: 'In former years tigers were doubtless a scourge, now they are becoming rare even in the wooded parts of the country, where in days of yore they abounded, and where once a dozen could be shot by a party in the hot weather with but little difficulty, two or three now will only be bagged over the same ground, and these not without great exertion and perseverance.' Attempts were made to regulate the shooting, with acts for the preservation of animals being passed in 1887, 1912, and 1935. The Nilgiris Game Association was founded in 1877 and the Bombay Natural History Society in 1885, both designed to promote the conservation of wildlife. A number of reserves were established, prominent among them the Banjar Valley Reserve, Corbett National Park, and Kaziranga Sanctuary. However, the decline of the wildlife continued, and Champion (1953) wrote in 1934: 'Animals like blackbuck and chital and game-birds, both in the plains and particularly the hills, are literally being wiped out at an increasingly rapid rate and one wonders if there will be anything left except monkeys and jackals after another two or three decades.' Yet in spite of the apparent apathy with which the government viewed the protection of the large mammals (Stebbing, 1912), and the great amount of damage done by army personnel during the Second World War, India retained a considerable amount of its wildlife until 1947.

Independence ushered in a period of destruction that could almost be compared to the slaughter on the American prairies in the 1880s. Rejecting shooting regulations as a form of colonial repression and released from restraint, Indians shot down wildlife everywhere, including sanctuaries and private estates. As a result of food shortages the government initiated a national drive to protect crops from the depredation of wild animals, and guns were issued freely to farmers, an action which literally doomed almost all animals near cultivation. For instance, G. Singh, Conservator of Forest in Punjab, wrote to me in 1964: 'Blackbuck was found in large number in central and southern parts of the Punjab state until 15 years ago. Then it was treated as a crop pest and killed in large numbers. This resulted in virtual extermination of the species.' A new type of hunter emerged, too, a motorized one who drove in jeeps along forest roads at night and shot at any eyes that reflected the beam of his light. For about five years the destruction continued unabated. In 1951 Bombay state passed the Wild Animals and Wild Birds Protection Act; in 1952 the Indian Board for Wildlife was formed and in 1958 the Wild Life Preservation Society of India. Conditions improved slowly with each state government making serious attempts to preserve its fauna and to strengthen the existing shooting regulations. A number of fine but small reserves were established. But enforcement against poaching on the local level remained inadequate, with the result that the wildlife continued in its decline.

Coupled with the outright destruction of wildlife by shooting was the indirect method of eliminating the habitat. As late as the sixteenth century, rhinoceros, elephant, buffalo, and other animals characteristic of fairly moist conditions occurred in parts of western India that are now covered with dry thorn scrub (Rao, 1957), indicating a rapid dessication of the habitat undoubtedly caused by misuse of the land by man (Puri, 1960). Chinese pilgrims in A.D. 600 talked of the dark jungles in the Gangetic basin, and even three centuries ago large areas of Uttar Pradesh were still covered with virgin forest (Robertson, 1936). Today, the heavily populated Gangetic basin retains sizable patches of forest only at the base of the Himalayas, areas that were uninhabitable earlier because of malaria. Tremendous tracts of grass and reeds in the valley of the Brahmaputra River were put under the plow, and Kaziranga Sanctuary remains as one of the few remnants of a habitat that once covered thousands of square miles. Forests were cleared throughout India for cultivation, and the timber was cut for use in railroad construction. After Independence the drive for more food and the unchecked increase in the population resulted in the cultivation of most marginal land. The natural vegetation cover of India is forest, but less than a quarter of the country is still covered with it.

A great scourge of India's land is the vast numbers of domestic animals which are undernourished, diseased, and unproductive, yet are permitted to exist for religious reasons. The plains of West Bengal, for instance, had in 1961 a human population of 1,031 per square mile and a cattle and buffalo population of 351 per square mile. The animals received only one third of their estimated daily nutritional requirements, and annual mortality due to disease was about 15 per cent (Anon., 1962). India had an estimated 204 million cattle and buffalos and 94 million goats and sheep in 1956, of which 21 million of the former and 13 million of the latter grazed exclusively in the forests (Venkataramany, 1961). Livestock is permitted to graze with-out restrictions in virtually all forests and most sanctuaries, and serious damage to the vegetation culminating in widespread erosion is common particularly in the thorn and deciduous forests. The carrying capacity of many forest areas and other uncultivated lands is so far exceeded by livestock alone that a substantial amount of wildlife could not support itself even if it were protected from shooting.

Livestock diseases, especially rinderpest and foot-and-mouth disease, also affect the wild ruminants. There are numerous records of gaur, chital, and others contracting diseases from cattle and dying in large numbers, whole populations having been wiped out in this manner (Brander, 1923, Ali, 1953). The health of domestic and wild hoofed animals is mainly a function of the quality of the range, and animals in poor condition as a result of malnutrition become highly susceptible to parasites and disease, making the problems of range condition and disease inseparable.

In one hundred years the combination of land clearing, uncontrolled slaughter, habitat destruction by livestock, and disease have reduced one of the world's great wildlife populations to a small remnant. Yet in spite of a realization that wildlife represents the country's fastest vanishing asset, no detailed studies of any kind have been attempted on the large mammals. Published information consists for the most part of incidental observations collected in the course of shooting the animal, the majority of books, even the better ones like Forsyth (1889), Sanderson (1912), and Champion (1927), presenting only general life history notes. Articles in the *Journal of the Bombay Natural History Society, the Journal of the Bengal Natural History Society,* and others are either cursory or consist of notes and anecdotes of unusual encounters. The books on Indian mammals—Jerdon (1874), Sterndale (1884), Blandford (188–91), Lydekker (1924), Prater (1948)—although providing useful summaries, do little more than repeat the information first published in the books by hunters. By far the best single book on Indian wildlife is by Brander (1923), who, though occasionally in error, presents a good deal of accurate data. E.P. Gee is virtually the only person in India who has in recent years consistently gone into the field and published first-hand accounts of certain mammals, particularly of the threatened ones like the Indian rhinoceros and Kashmir stag (Gee, 1953; 1962*a,b;* 1963), and he has also been the major voice in drawing international attention to the plight of the wildlife. His book *The Wild Life of India* presents a useful introduction to the animals and his work. So far even the most rudimentary forms of ecological research, such as making accurate annual censuses and determining rates of reproduction and mortality, have yet to find a place in the plans of the state forest departments and the Zoological Survey of India, the two governmental services with direct responsibility for this type of work.

In 1961 the Johns Hopkins Center for Medical Research and Training was established in Calcutta, West Bengal, under the direction of Dr. F. Bang, School of Hygiene and Public Health, Baltimore. Although the center is medically oriented, as the name implies, the organizers have realized that a meaningful programme of disease studies is possible only in a broad ecological context, one in which the behavior of the vectors and of the possible hosts of the disease organisms also is studied in detail. To gather such data, the programme formed an ecological unit headed by Dr. C.

Southwick. Some of the projects completed or in progress include work on the biology of flying foxes, rhesus monkeys, and various rodents, as well as the present study of deer and tiger.

At first I intended to study primarily the chital deer, but it soon became apparent that the most fruitful approach, the one that would yield the most information not only for the programme but also from the standpoint of conservation and management, would be to collect a broad spectrum of facts on a number of different species in one locality. After considerable searching I decided on a relatively undisturbed forest area in central India, the Kanha National Park in the state of Madhya Pradesh, as the site for the study. Fourteen months were devoted to research on the large mammals in this sanctuary, the remaining six months of the project being used to obtain comparative information in other areas. A broad study has one severe disadvantage—the danger of superficiality, of failure to collect the quantitative data needed for proper evaluation of the observed facts. On the other hand, a broad approach provides a better understanding of the interrelationship between species, which in the study of one area may be highly important. At Kanha Park, for example, observations on the chital automatically included the barasingha, with which they were often associated, and the tiger, which preyed on both. I hope that I have managed to present a reasonable compromise between the two approaches.

This report is concerned largely with the ecology and behaviour of the major hoofed animals in Kanha Park—the chital, barasingha, sambar, blackbuck, and gaur—and with the life history of the tiger, the most important predator in the area. The main purpose of placing all this information under one cover is not only to present new material about the habits of these animals but also to stress similarities and differences in aspects of behaviour, such as the time of mating and bearing of young, and to attempt to answer such questions on predator-prey relations as, what is the effect of tiger predation on the hoofed animals in Kanha Park? The report, furthermore, provides a summary of the available information about these species in the wild in India, indicating how little has been and is still known about them and how much research needs to be done in the near future if the large mammalian fauna is to survive in appreciable numbers. In India, perhaps more than in most countries, the basic problems of animal and human ecology are intimately related, and a solid body of facts is desperately needed if conservation and management practices satisfactory to man, his livestock, and the wildlife are to be initiated in time to save the last from complete extermination. If this report acts as a stimulus for other studies it will have served its purpose.

Conclusion

India's wildlife has reached a critical stage in its survival, and the country is fortunate in possessing a sanctuary like Kanha Park, where a remnant of the peninsular fauna still exists in fair number. The park is large enough and ecologically varied enough to support a considerable wildlife population on a permanent basis, especially since the forests surrounding it provide a buffer zone between the park and the heavily cultivated parts of the district. As a potential tourist attraction the tiger has few equals among animals. And the park as a whole can provide future generations with a view of how their country once looked before the forests were overexploited for timber and overgrazed by livestock and before much of the wildlife fell to the poacher's gun. The park can also become a study area unaffected by man's influence where the interrelationships between species and many other ecological problems can be investigated. A national park represents a specialized form of land use in which, ideally, the native flora and fauna are permitted to exist undisturbed by man. This in particular should apply to the predators, which have aroused the antipathy of man for centuries and have as a result been needlessly persecuted on the slightest pretext. Certain management practices in a park are sometimes necessary, and these should of course be based on a thorough study of the situation and be directed at the principal and not the superficial cause of a problem. The evidence presented in this report, for example, indicates that poaching and not tiger predation has been the general cause of the decline of the wildlife in the park. The most effective means of managing the tiger is obviously to manage the prey, which in turn means: (1) curtailing the activity of poachers, and (2) limiting and gradually eliminating all livestock from within the boundaries of the park. Only after these two tasks have been accomplished, and all forms of wildlife have been substantially increased, will the park be able to fulfill its unique potential as a living museum and natural laboratory. Above all, Kanha Park is part of India's cultural heritage, a heritage in many ways more important than the Taj Mahal and the temples of Khajuraho, because, unlike these structures formed by the hands of man, once destroyed it can never be replaced.

P.D.

Stracey

The Future of the Tiger

P.D. Stracey belonged to the Indian Forest Service and was a great spokesman for the study of wildlife. He fought unceasingly for the enforcement of conservation measures.

When P. D. Stracey wrote this article, the tiger's future hung in the balance as the period of 1950-1960 had taken a severe toll on tigers and their habitat. Would they survive the hunter's guns and the timber-merchant's axe?
(Photo courtesy Fateh Singh Rathore.)

Two hundred years ago the tiger population of India must have been very great. It must also have been high in relation to the human population which was kept at a low level by starvation, epidemics, child mortality and a generally low expectation of life. At the same time the jungles were vast and game plentiful. But *Pax Britannica* changed the picture by stopping local wars, enforcing the penal code for crimes against life and introducing peaceful conditions in which settled agriculture gradually developed. The human population began to increase and inevitably there arose a clash between tiger and man.

In his rapid and indiscriminate clearing of the jungle for cultivation, man came up against the game species as well as their predators and although his weapons were primitive, he still had the power to maim and injure, even if he could not always kill. The result was a gradual increase in the number of man-eaters. As game became scarce with the clearance of its habitat, cattle killing by tigers became more frequent. The habit developed naturally and it was not only injured tigers which found easy prey in the increasing number of cattle.

A hundred years ago the situation seems to have been really bad and many parts of the country were feeling the pressure: villages were being deserted and the jungle was re-invading cultivated land. One alleged reason for the creation of man-eaters in the past was the abundance of human corpses during the time of epidemics and famines. Hindus burn their dead but there were occasions apparently when the number of corpses completely outstripped the resources of the people in regard to cremation. Bodies were then left with at most a live coal placed in the mouth as a symbol of cremation. To what extent this practice encouraged man-eating tigers it is, of course, impossible to say.

The early British sportsmen were poor killers by comparison with the well-armed modern hunter. With their matchlocks and muzzle loaders, and even with the breech-loading smooth-bores of a later generation, they must have left many a wounded animal. It was the introduction of more efficient firearms, particularly the rifled

Extract from *Tigers* by P.D. Stracey (New York, 1968).

barrel and smokeless powder, which brought about a significant change. Although hardly anyone except Europeans was allowed to carry arms, the large increase in their numbers, particularly of the army after the 1857 'sepoy mutiny', meant a much greater volume of fire power being brought to bear upon the tiger population. By that time the pursuit of big game and the hunting of the tiger in particular had assumed the nature of a cult among empire builders. The slaughter of the tiger as well as of the lion was on. The turn of the tide against the tiger started from then.

The human population has since increased steadily and the tiger population has decreased. Perry claims that in the last century more than a hundred thousand tigers were killed in India, yet he wonders why the mortality of victims of man-eaters did not show any appreciable decline over the same period. He quotes the following figures: in the 1860's mortality was 1300 to 2000 victims annually and in the 1930's 1000 to 1600. I believe that the explanation for the decline in post-war years is probably due to the greater efficiency of modern hunting methods, brought about by the use of the electric torch as an adjunct to the rifle. In the old days tiger shooting was an uncertain business and if tigers were fired at during the hours of darkness, the odds were that they were usually wounded rather than killed, which incidentally meant more potential man-eaters. But tiger shooting became much easier once it was possible to fit a hand dry-cell electric torch to a rifle or a shot gun. The UP, where Corbett used to operate, is the only state in India in which it is forbidden to shoot tigers after sunset and this counters to some extent the destructive power of electric torch light. Elsewhere this unsporting but to some extent unavoidable method still prevails.

It must be borne in mind that man-eating by tigers is not prevalent throughout India. It is mainly confined to certain localities where it is generally of a long standing nature. While more tigers were being shot in the country as a whole, it does not follow that more man-eaters were being shot. The shooting of a normal tiger was an easy affair compared with the killing of a man-eater and all the advantages of darkness are in favour of the man-eater so long as the hunter does not have an efficient killing technique—and that came with the electric torch.

Even so there appears to have been an alarming increase during recent years of the incidence of man-eating, not only in areas where it has long been prevalent but also in hitherto uncontaminated regions. The scourge has assumed vexing proportions during the last few years in the Sunderbans, which for centuries has been a centre for this macabre man-animal relationship. In this vast stretch of tidal backwaters and waterways many people seem convinced that deaths from tigers are on the increase although the authorities tend to deny this. The victims are traditionally engaged in wood-cutting and honey gathering, both occupations that are conducted under the supervision of the forest department but by the very nature of their tasks the people cannot be completely protected from surprise attack.

At present there is no means of knowing whether the increase of man-eating tigers is real or apparent. The latter could well be the case, due possibly to the greater number of people being exposed as the result of a planned development now taking place in India, or to the depletion of the natural food of the tiger. Both these reasons imply that the tiger population may be subsisting on half rations. Normally a tiger requires to kill once every three or four days but this period could be extended to a week. One thing seems certain: there has been a great increase in recent years of the number of guns and activities of meat hunters, thus forcing the tigers to turn to man-eating. The increase in the number of inexperienced hunters may well have brought about a concomitant increase in the number of wounded animals.

The same grounds are offered as explanation for the position in Orissa which in the past few years has come into the news with reports of large numbers of people being killed by man-eaters. Recently there was an appeal from a missionary in the Bastar area, home of the warlike Maria Gonds who might be expected to be able to look after themselves. In this case it is the tribes themselves who have been responsible for creating a situation which encourages the attacks of tigers for they have decimated the game by unrestricted hunting. These central Indian tribes, once masters of vast forests where they lived mainly by hunting, are now restricted to a ritual *battue* once a year in which they kill everything that they can find. Their hunting instincts are so deep and their society so untrammelled by taboos that they have virtually cleared their jungles of game. It is small wonder that the tigers have turned on them.

Corbett's country—the Naini Tal district, the gateway of Kumaon and part of the belt of the Himalaya from the Ganges to the borders of Nepal—is periodically in the news and the scourge has certainly not ended there. In addition to these chronic sore spots, alarming news of tigers killing humans is occasionally received from various parts of the country. Only the most serious get into the newspapers and it is impossible to review the whole picture. The type of information on which Perry apparently based his figures is not readily available and the lack of a scientific approach to the subject of man-eating, with the failure to sift information regarding the explanations offered for the increase of 'bad' tigers, is both disappointing and frustrating. As a piece of applied research into an interesting aspect of animal ecology, the study of the man-tiger-game relationship would be well worthwhile. The facts should be ascertained before deciding on the application of long-term remedial measures in the interests of both the tiger and its human victim.

There are good grounds for believing that the boldness of the cattle-raider leads to man-killing and then man-eating. Many a killer has attacked its first human when being obstructed in the process of obtaining its meal from a herd of cattle. From killing to eating is but a small step and this may account for some of the cases of healthy tigers which have taken to man-eating. Nevertheless records indicate that it is injuries which are at the bottom of man-eating as such. In the USSR man-eating by tigers is unknown whereas it is widely prevalent in Malaya.

Of all the natural injuries that may lead to disabilities causing the tiger to take to man-eating, damage from porcupine quills appears to be the most common. In the majority of cases the paws and lower limbs are injured in such a way as to affect the tiger's ability to pull down and kill natural prey or cattle. Occasionally the quills penetrate the face and jaws. The quills are barbed and once they enter the flesh are practically impossible to remove unless they are cut out. A tiger will bite the quills off as far as it can reach with its teeth and will continue to rasp with its tongue until a raw wound is caused. Suppuration of the wounds adds to the pain and discomfort, increasing the degree of incapacity. Other natural causes of incapacity in hunting for food are old age.

Sometimes this deterioration can reach such a stage as to make one wonder how the animal can survive at all.

Another theory regarding healthy man-eaters is that they are the progeny of man-eating tigresses but doubt has been cast on this by no less an authority than Corbett who maintained that 'cubs of man-eaters do not become man-eaters simply because they have eaten human flesh when young'. Corbett's view is contrary to that expressed by other writers and I have no means of knowing why he held it. Did it stem from his generally big-hearted and slightly romantic view of the tiger? It is generally accepted that man-eaters do not subsist entirely on a diet of human flesh and that they also eat game animals and cattle. Corbett may have had this fact in mind. It is interesting that Kenneth Anderson, who has been described as the 'Jim Corbett of the south', claims that man-eating tigers are permanent addicts, unlike man-eating leopards which are said to lay off killing humans for long periods.

Corbett's conclusion that a liking for human flesh is not necessarily transmitted to the offspring of a man-eating tigress seems to be at variance with what would be a normal biological phenomenon. It is true that there have been one or two rare cases in India of carnivores, such as the lion and the tiger, subsisting on non-animal food but it cannot be denied that the natural food preference of these species is for flesh.

Whatever the natural causes responsible for man-eating they are likely to be outweighed by the artificial cause of injuries inflicted by man. Wounds from gun and rifle may enrage the animal to the point of taking revenge. The wounded tiger's reputation for ambushing its assailant provides support for this suggestion and although a wound may not be sufficiently crippling to prevent the tiger from killing its natural prey, once launched on man-eating it may well continue with this career. In fact it is these lightly wounded tigers which on recovery have no obvious reason for continuing as man-eaters that provide the puzzling features. Generally however the evidence is clear and leads one to fulminate against the persons responsible for the initial crime against the tiger.

The tiger that has become a man-eater or a cattle-killer has no future. The hand of every man is against it and sooner or later it falls victim to a bullet. To this extent, wherever the interests of the tiger and man clash there is a grave threat to the future of the tiger. This applies to all the peripheral forest areas so far as cattle-raiding is concerned for there are large numbers of cattle living outside the reserved forests that also graze in the protected areas. The right of pursuit into a government forest is granted in the UP only to an aggrieved cattle owner who may sit up for the marauder. To some people this appears to be almost a quixotic gesture in the light of the prohibition on the shooting of tigers later than forty-five minutes after sunset. Many sportsmen in the UP complain that after they have made elaborate and expensive preparations and are sitting up expecting the tiger at any moment, the authorities pull them down from their prepared hides in trees as they enforce the 'no shooting after dark' rule; at the same time a person from a neighbouring village, on the plea that his cow, which was probably illegally grazing in the forest, was killed by a tiger, is permitted to take his revenge without paying for the right to shoot in the reserved forest according to the rules.

It was reported some time ago that tigers in Mysore and Madras were being poisoned with pesticides supplied to cultivators and that their skins were finding their way to the local taxidermists. I recently came on a magnificent tiger skin for sale in a curio shop in Delhi. I enquired the price out of curiosity and was startled to find that a trophy which would have cost £20 twenty-five years ago now sold for ten times the sum. The proprietor of the shop calmly told me that he had sold four skins already at this price. One wonders how the tiger can stand up to such commercial pressure. Twenty years ago Jim Corbett expressed the opinion that the tiger would be wiped out in ten years but he was laughed to scorn by complacent persons in authority. His prognostications are now being borne out. Large areas of the best tiger habitat have been cleared at the foot of the Naini Tal Himalaya, within fifty miles of Corbett's home, in the interests of mechanised farming. With the disappearance of grass and trees, the game has also departed, as well as the tigers that preyed upon it. The same story applies elsewhere. Forests which were once the private shooting grounds of the Maharaja of Mysore have been closed to shooting because of the alarming decrease in the tiger population since the transfer of these areas to the Government forest department.

In India the sole hope for the tiger lies in the retention of large blocks of forests of sufficient extent and backed by hilly ranges, as is the case in the greater part of the sub-Himalaya and central India, where it can range freely and have sufficient game to prey upon. The latter is the crux of the problem, for a forest without game suitable for the tiger's diet is useless. This inevitably brings up the whole question of the general protection of wild life and of game animals in particular. Unfortunately the present position is not very satisfactory and if the tiger is to survive—not in a few isolated sanctuaries but in forests which were once its home—much more will have to be done regarding the protection of wild life. Destructive practices such as shooting from vehicles, both by day and night, the sale of game meat and the illegal shooting in government forests, must be stopped.

Fortunately the Indian tiger is not exposed to any great extent to persecution resulting from superstitious fancy in regard to the alleged value of its various parts for medicinal purposes. Among the Malays and Chinese this cult is said to be highly developed: the flesh is a remedy for debility, pills made from the eye-balls are said to cure convulsions and blindness, the skin either burned or roasted and mixed with water is a general cure for illness, the sexual parts are alleged to have aphrodisiac properties and the bones (chiefly of the head) are much prized by the Chinese as containing a soul substance or vital fluid, akin to that of man. The Indian faith in the value of the tiger's fat as a cure for rheumatism and the use of the clavicle, whiskers and claws as ornaments and lucky charms is shared by the Malays and Chinese. In India it is a common occurrence for a sportsman to lose some of the whiskers and claws of the tiger he has just shot to the crowd which always gathers on such occasions. To what extent these beliefs influence the survival rate of the tiger is a matter for conjecture. An ominous portent is the persistent drain on the world's rhinoceros population for its horn, mistakenly valued as a highly effective aphrodisiac. On this analogy alone there seems no future for the tiger in south-east Asia.

As a minor solatium we have the general respect, tinged with awe, in which the tiger is held in India. Some of the forest dwelling tribes of central India will not refer directly to the tiger by name but will use an indirect honorific title, such as the 'Great One'. The Datla tribe of the north-east Himalaya consider that they are the kinsmen of the tiger. The superstitions associated with the belief that men can turn themselves into tigers and vice versa are less common in India than in Malaya and countries beyond. This mystique is more prevalent among the less sophisticated classes and to that extent its protective value is less. Unfortunately it is not the common man alone who holds the key to the future of the tiger.

The tiger today is India's most valuable attraction to certain classes of foreign tourist and ranks with the Taj Mahal as a foreign exchange earner. The growth of safari organisations has been a feature of the post-independence period and tiger shoots arranged by them come under the category of luxury trade. Even the indigenous sportsman finds it expensive to arrange a shooting camp.

Providing this commercial activity can be properly controlled it could do a lot for the future of the tiger. Something for which there is a demand is normally considered as worth conserving but unfortunately the demand is increasing at such a pace that there are grave fears of the supply becoming exhausted. Certain steps such as the ban on the shooting of tigresses and a tightening of the rules governing the export of skins would help. By rationing the stock of tigers available for shooting for the tourist trade and above all, by protecting wild life on which the tiger depends for its natural food, it is possible that we might be able to ensure that the tiger will be with us in any appreciable numbers in the future.

Statistics are notoriously tricky things to play with but I cannot help quoting some figures: according to Burton, a total of 1579 tigers were shot in British India in 1877 but no figures are available for the additional numbers which were shot in the native States. Fifty years earlier, between 1820–8, an average of 138 tigers were shot annually in Bombay Presidency alone. A little more than a hundred years later, according to Chaturvedi an average of 280 tigers were shot annually from 1934–54 in all of the seven major tiger bearing States of India. In whatever way we interpret these figures, one cannot help asking the question: *'Quo vadis Panthera tigris?'*

B.

Seshadri

LT. COL. S. A. H. GRANVILLE

PROFESSIONAL HUNTER

BIG GAME SHIKAR ORGANISER

Recognised by the Govt. of India.

PACHMARHI

MADHYA PRADESH, INDIA

Inclusive price quotations for shikar tours in the world renowned tiger jungles of MADHYA PRADESH.

All parties under personal supervision of experienced hunters. Come as you are we provide everything—good camps, good food, good hunting.

Representative in United States of America, Ted Shatto, "Cloudwalk" Kenwood, California.

HIS LAST KILL

The Twilight of the Animals

B. Seshadri has been a prolific writer on the wildlife of India and, as early as the 1950s, put pen to paper on the crisis of India's wildlife.

In post Independence India, such advertisements, enticing the hunter, were common. Today Pachmarhi is not only an ecologically sensitive zone but the area around is one of India's most recent Project Tiger reserves.

Man has lost his capacity to foresee and to forestall. He will end by destroying the earth.

Albert Schweitzer

'The Natural Wilderness is a fragile thing; the material of poetry, art and music.' Thus said the late Dr. Olaus J. Murie, the distinguished American naturalist. As I now come to the end of my sad story of the ebbing fortunes of the wild life of India, my thoughts go back, now to a night spent in the wilderness in the north of this wonderful country, now to a day spent in the south, slices of time spent in the 'fragility' of the wild world even such as Dr. Murie spoke of.

I remember that first evening in the Chandraprabha Forest as I sat in an easy-chair outside the lodge, of which I was the sole occupant. The setting sun made a scene of splendour, as its rays struggled with the flying mist-cloud fronting the waterfall just beyond me. The water's roar seemed merely to accentuate the stillness around. The great copper-gold sun was poised deceptively still on the far edge of the forest, while in reality it was plunging fast beyond the western horizon. The long rays caught the treetops for a few moments, and all at once the great orb seemed to disappear with a rush and the forest around me was draped in a black hush. The trees stood motionless in the still air as if welded to the landscape and their dark outlines were silhouetted against the heavens, now beginning to be star-studded.

There was the morning after, when I was up and off, accompanied by the considerate forest ranger, Sukhraj Singh, long before dawn. It was fragrant and cool as we drove through forests beyond the sanctuary in perfectly delightful country, hills of the extreme eastern end of the Vindhyas, umber and pinkish in the background in the early morning light. The dawn was not abrupt as the dusk had been, and as the blurred outlines of the forest assumed shapes, bird song twittered from the trees. The sun arose and fought off the ground mist, revealing herds of white and brown cattle or big, black buffalo, already on the move for the eternal business of

Extract from *The Twilight of India's Wildlife by* B. Seshadri (London, 1969).

grazing. Sheet-swathed cowherds followed them listlessly and looked at us without interest. Suddenly, like a sprite, a pretty little chinkara buck stepped up to the roadside, and as quickly vanished into the parklike interior of the forest.

Later that day, as we were returning to the lodge after a long and tiring trek into the sanctuary's interior, I remember the little village in our way, perfectly harmonious with the wilderness around it, from which little cascades of grey-white smoke drifted into the sky. The smell of these fire-plumes mingled with the evening smells of the forest, as the toothless old man we asked for news of lion looked uncomprehendingly at us. Bird calls and the pad-crunch of our feet were the only noises in the stillness. We walked on, stopping only to look at a sloth bear's pawprints as it had shuffled from a cattle path into thick bush.

There was the memorable night in the great forests of the Godavari river, when with the forest officer of the range, I spent fourteen hours cruising in our jeep with scarcely a stop. He had told me that development projects had destroyed most of the wild life, but I hoped to see the wild things once the night had spread its protective and kindly shroud over the glorious wine-colour of the evening teak forests. The tall trees blushed like copper in the setting sun as we set out from the forest lodge. Soon would be the hour when the peacocks would step out of their roosts, the males to pay their dazzling court to the downright hens—the enchanted hour of the Indian jungle. It was a crisp evening, typical of the cold weather.

We were armed with the fell combination of jeep and spotlight, but our purpose was not to kill. I wanted to see how the animals that were left in these once-pristine forests lived in the changed circumstances. The first hour and the next passed without the forest showing anything but the peacocks, but I was not unduly despondent. Teak forests have very little undergrowth, and we had clear vision as we drove in and out of them. The first major encounter was as unexpected as it was magnificent. Across an irrigation canal, now dry, we caught in our roving lights a group of three chital stags, an uncommon party, two already so disturbed as to be hurrying down the far side of the embankment. But the third and the most splendid of the three, with his great antlers in velvet, stood still for a few seconds in the light-beam now trained solely on him, nostrils quivering, and made an unforgettable sight.

Every now and then we stopped to savour the stillness and to draw into ourselves the warm, gentle breeze which blew through the pillared trees all around us. Sometimes a bird sang like a tinkling bell as it flew home, rather late, to roost. Now we heard the sound of running water, tossing and swirling, in a jungle stream, although most *nullahs* were semi-dry at this time of year. As we passed a project area, now here, now there, we heard the babel of cutting, sawing, or hammering in the palpitating air. We hastily fled from the offending noises, away into the dark stillness, weaving in and out of the teak trees, picking out dead tree stumps and ravines in the headlights and avoiding them when we could, or crashing through when we could not.

We began to pick up numerous pairs of eyes in the light beam, but identification was difficult. Since I was going to be the one to make the novel attempt to take the photographs of their owners by flashlight, as my companion held the animal with his lights, by walking deviously and circuitously in the surrounding darkness to get as close to the quarry as possible, I did not like to base my effort on a rapid identification and walk on to a resting sloth bear or an irate leopard. The fallen leaves were dry and crackled noisily as I stepped on them in the utter blackness. Many times, as I got close to a nilgai or a sambar, the animal started to move off but still in the light, and I followed it for as long as I could simply for the pleasure of it.

There was a sloth bear, a round black bundle of fur, who melted away as the beam strayed to him. There were sambar and nilgai in ones and twos, almost always near the fringes of forest villages and inside fenced-in teak nurseries. I wondered what it was in the latter that attracted them. The numerous thatch-roofed platforms on bamboo poles in the cornfields were mute evidence of the incursions of deer, antelope, and pig, in search of the sweet, growing corn. Fleeing nilgai were comic with their little tails stuck straight up in the air. A pair of porcupines, husband and wife we presumed, moved as if they were on wheels, a continuous progression forward, feet never showing, only a flurry of quills. We drove parallel with them for a while, before they gave us the slip by a quick right turn into thorny bush, strictly penetrable only by porcupines. We saw more of them, but only singly or in pairs. It was the same uninterrupted movement, terribly purposeful in its forward slide-march, as if the animals had a date with destiny.

We put on an extra layer of clothing as the wind blew colder. Of jungle noises there were none, and no wonder. The ruthless slaughter of the preceding years had made all animals both wary and shy. We drove up a hill through a long, winding, and beautiful forest path, and it grew even colder. By the pathside stood a magnificent nilgai bull, feeding. Momentarily dazzled by the light, he stood still for perhaps five seconds. What an easy target these animals make, I thought, for the jeep-and-spotlight hunter! Recovering himself, he turned and ran into the forest.

The magic wand of dawn was already touching the tattered leaves of the great trees as we started on the long and weary drive back. The beauty was as transient as the wild animals we had seen. On this trip we had spent fourteen continuous hours in these jungles, and as we stepped out of the jeep another day had established itself.

Then there was our family week in the Hazaribagh National Park, of the kind we often talked about in our pedestrian and contentious city life. The two boys, very young then, had already begun to be imbued with our longing for nature's prodigalities and to share them with us. Our longing to get away from the worship of time and the banal details of appointments and teas had finally worked itself into a pattern—thrice a year in the wilderness, taking my annual leave in three parts to coincide with the school holidays of my wife, who was teaching, and of the boys who were in a public school. We were asked if it was safe to camp with small children amongst wild animals. Our secret lay in the fact that the boys thought of these animals as their particular *friends*. Animals, as a rule, prefer to bite the faint-hearted. They know if you are calm, if you are friendly, or if you are scared. A leopard may be unsociable, but he may be reckoned upon to leave you alone. A bear may be inquisitive, but has no reason to attack you unless you surprise him.

The forests were not village-free. People lived in their midst in tiny communities of mud-built and tumbledown huts, with pungent, musty, rotting smells. We spoke to village folk with betel-stained smiles, and watched the unrehearsed grace of their movements and the unchaperoned conversation of men and women, boys and girls. Our boys were continually in a high state of joyful excitement, and spoke of the numerous accidental meetings they hoped to have with animals of the forest. They came with us on foot into the heavily foliaged jungle, where the fecundity of the undergrowth was prodigious, and we stuck to the tracks smoothed by generations of animal feet. There were big tracts where no grass-grown ruins or green-grown moats, not uncommon in India's forests and suggesting man's intrusion in the long past, marred the landscape.

We listened with new ears to the whisper of the trees as they rippled in the cool north wind, and were enfranchised by bird song. If we were out early in the morning, we would get our feet very wet with the night's dew, but it was cool and soothing. We could see the sun drawing up the moisture in spirals of vapour. This was the time of day too when, as they dried, unknown herbs gave off their rich and cloying smells, and the children delighted in plucking and crushing leaves to savour the subtly different and spicy smells. Every sparkling stream in the woods carried an invitation to plunge naked into it. Often it was so marvellously still that their splurges of fun were the only sounds that sweetened the air. The pleasantly warm winter sun turned our skins from their forlorn seedy city look to a healthy brown. In the afternoons, between visits to the Park interior, as we lay on the grass and the sun threw its golden girdles round the canopies of trees, it was warmly sensuous enough to make us feel slumbrous, and yet not go off to sleep. We saw the boys with half-closed eyes, trapped in the city to live human lives, here chasing in and out of the wavering shadows, and heard their yelps of delight as they discovered a brilliantly coloured beetle or butterfly or the gossamer-spun home of a spider, or fed a cheeky little squirrel or wild bird which returned their friendliness by accepting a crumb from their outstretched hands. We lingered, listened, and watched the overflow from the reservoir next to the lodge, over the stone dam, which became an iridescent and glittering waterfall, and the water leaping and gurgling at its foot. The civilised world seemed far away, but the days fled, and we measured them not by their length but by their breadth. It was not all joy; sometimes a strange melancholy would flow over us, but even this had a mellow, unobtrusive beauty of its own. When the time came to leave, it was significant that even the children had nothing to say.

A remarkable fact in the world's history of the last two thousand years is that mankind has disputed all along the line the claims of wild animals to survive in their own right. If their survival was of no use to him—or so he thought—they had to go. The process of extermination of many species of animals has proceeded steadily during the Christian era, but was greatly accelerated after 1800. Today, over a thousand species and subspecies, at a conservative estimate, are treated as gravely threatened. With the apathy to wild life conservation and man's insatiable greed, the fact must be faced that many of these endangered animals will be extinguished in the next two or three decades at the rate of well over a species per year.

Till man appeared on the scene, an uneven increase of any one species was kept down by many natural causes: scarcity of food, predatory animals, disease, natural calamities. That is, a balance was maintained between the reproductive capacity of the species and the natural agencies of destruction—the so-called balance of nature. When man emerged from his savage state, he upset the balance. Animals whose flesh he coveted were killed off, while others he favoured multiplied. Thus, while some animals went over the edge once and for all, others spread and became pests.

It was only at the beginning of this century that thinking men began to appreciate that the wild things too had a right to live, within their habitats, side by side with man. Out of this thinking grew attempts to afford some measure of protection to wild life by the formulation of restrictive laws against indiscriminate shooting. In time, wild life areas here and there were closed in full or in part to shooting, and trapping of animals and trade in pelts and feathers were brought under some kind of control where such was possible. But the magnitude of the problem was so vast, and the general indifference of governments and the public so great, that these measures were woefully inadequate and touched only the fringe of the problem. The spiritual and cultural values of wild life conservation remained largely un-appreciated, and the scientific interest in the fauna did not extend beyond the naturalists.

This, then, is the position today in all parts of the world, to a greater or to a lesser degree. To appreciate the great wealth of animal life that has already been destroyed, we may take a look at one or two historic destructions. Africa was perhaps the world's greatest reservoir of wild life, but, after the advent of the Boers in South Africa, suffered cruelly. The stupendous antelope and zebra herds were destroyed without trace in an amazingly short number of years. Figures of these killings are hardly credible, and hundreds of thousands of these beasts were slaughtered during the Boer treks inland, comparable in scale only with the bison slaying in North America in the second half of the last century. With increased European occupation in the further north of Africa, professional hunters for ivory and other animal products took up the chase and decimated the equally vast animal congregations of those regions. All this was followed in time by legalised slaughter by white hunters hired to clear the bush on behalf of governments for African settlements or tse-tse fly control, and illegal slaughter by the Africans themselves as political, social, and environmental conditions began to change with a bewildering rapidity.

The curtain rose for wildlife slaughter in Asia a long time after the main herds in Africa and North America had been destroyed. In the colonial era, when most of southern Asia was governed either by European nations or by local kings and chieftains, wild animals, although extensively hunted both by Europeans and the local princes and their retainers, were comparatively unaffected in the absence of organised mass-killing, which was the characteristic feature of antelope, zebra, and bison hunts. It was fortunate that this was so, because wild life in Asia did not exist, except in a very few tracts, on the vast African scale. Asia's animals could not have survived man's slaughter on the African style. Their habitats, too, aided their survival, as more often than not the habitats were thick and heavy jungle as against the open plains of Africa and North America.

Since the last war, as the great colonial regimes came to a close, a period of unrest and strife began in many areas, which scattered large-scale destruction of every sort in Burma, Malaya, the new countries of Indo-China, and Indonesia, and is still doing so. India has been notably stable, but while war and lawlessness led to uncontrolled killing of wild animal life in other parts of southern Aisa, the immense development projects of India led to habitat-destruction without parallel in history. Today, only a very small fraction of the wildlife of twenty-five years ago is left.

Has India's wildlife a future? One cannot truthfully say it has, and the reasons have been discussed. One might ask, do these wild animals have to live on? Man in India wants more and more space, the population is increasing at an unprecedented rate, and has he not the right to clear and occupy the forests as he pleases, killing off the wild- life in the process? He certainly has no such right, no claim in the least to apportion to himself all the living-space of so many creatures allotted to them from immemorial time in the natural order of things. What is his right, the right of might and the gun? If progressive thought believes that might without justice is not right, how can such a theory be applied in justification of the slaughter of the animals? Wildlife asks for so little of man. It is this which has hit me with the force of a sledge-hammer each time I have set foot in a jungle and seen its wild residents. They ask for nothing except to be left alone in the pathetic strips of wild tract that are all that remain of their once populous homes. The animals have their simple rights too on this earth—to exist. In India, much too often there is pious talk of wild animals being in the cultural traditions of the land, as if this in itself will assure their eventual survival. On the other hand, it merely draws attention away from the problem of saving them.

All I have said about the animals applies equally well to the country's rich avian and reptilian life. Bird life is superbly rich. Including migrants, over 1,500 species find homes in the sub-continent. But they need trees and bushes, water and marshes, and protection from hunters to survive. Today, the most affected are those limited to specific breeding and feeding grounds through deprivation of their territory.

The beautiful pinkheaded duck *(Rhodonessa caryophyllacea)* has been feared extinct for some years. The last authentic record was in Darbhanga district in Bihar in June 1935, a long time ago. The whitewinged wood duck *(Cairina scutulata)* of Assam is so rare as to be nearly extinct. Others like the great Indian bustard *(Choriotis nigriceps)* and the monal pheasant *(Lophophorus impejanus)* are the ornithologists' worry, as they totter on the brink of extinction.

... What is an Indian jungle without its quota of peacocks *(Pavo cristatus)*? Who can forget, once he has seen it, the display of the cock bird before his small harem of hens, in the bewitching hour before dusk? And what a display it is! The erection of the gorgeous ocellated tail, the strutting, the posturing, the paroxysms of quivering! And when it is all over, the harsh *'may-awe'* and the gasping *'ka-aan'*!

What is a marsh landscape without a pair of sarus cranes *(Grus antigone)*, the largest birds of India? F.W. Champion called them 'the Darby and Joan of the jungle'. These huge, grey birds, with their long, bright red legs and heads which look as if they were covered with close-fitting caps of ruby velvet ornamented with tassels, are devoted companions—so devoted are they thought to be that tribal hunters who kill one for food kill the other too.

Many must have heard but not seen the collared scops owl *(Otus bakkamoena)*, pretty little 'horned' owlet, heard its soft, questioning *wùt*? and its lovely ascending note of bubbling pleasure, from out of the groves it is partial to. Some at least must have seen the crested serpent eagle *(Spilornis cheela)* as it has soared in wide circles high up in the sky in wooded country; seen too, perhaps, the openbilled stork *(Anastomus oscitans)* with the gap between his arching mandibles, and the smaller egret *(Egretta intermedia)* in his breeding plumage, in their favourite marshes and mudflats, busily searching for frogs, crabs, and snails.

But one and all must have seen the whitebacked vulture *(Gyps bengalensis)*, unloved bird, carrion feeder, useful scavenger, and drawing attention to itself by its quarrels with its mates, hissing and screeching, over an animal carcass in the countryside; seen too, if they had the stomach to wait and watch, the speed with which the flock demolish such remains.

Both kinds of crocodiles of India, the mugger *(Crocodilus palustris)* and the gharial *(Gavialis gangeticus)* have become extremely rare.

Both are now officially protected—which does not prevent week-end sportsmen from Calcutta from hunting them in the Sunderbans swamps, where alone the mugger perhaps survives in any number. Both the snub-nosed mugger and the long-snouted gharial were such interesting and integral parts of the Indian jungle scene, and though the mugger is by no means a likeable thing, their passing would sadly deplete the stage.

Another disapperaring reptile is the monitor lizard. The last one I saw was crossing the road as I was driving through the Mahanadi Sanctuary in north Bengal in 1964. There is a famous story attached to this lizard. Its best-known characteristic is its very powerful hold when it clings to anything. Tradition has it that when Shivaji, the Great Mahratta, laid siege to the Moghul-held fortress of Khelna, its walls were so steep that all the attempts of his soldiers to scale them were foiled. Then one of two brothers tied a rope to a monitor and threw it to run up the wall. As it found a vantage-point and settled itself, the other brother scaled the wall with the rope's aid, and opened the gates to let in the Mahrattas. Shivaji was so pleased with the achievement that he awarded the title of 'Ghorpade' to the clan from which the brothers came, from the Marathi name for the monitor, which is *ghorpad.* But true it is that it is immensely difficult to dislodge a monitor once it has decided to cling and stay put.

Devoted individuals, and the two premier natural history societies, the Bombay Natural History Society and the Wild Life Preservation Society of India, have worked assiduously for the cause of wild life conservation, and to persuade the authorities to evolve a policy by which the objects of such conservation can be achieved through sustained implementation of its component stages. But for such efforts, the situation today would be far worse. But in a problem of this nature it is increasingly difficult for single persons or non-official groups to act effectively.

No one can now dispute that the wild life of a country is not one of its most interesting and valuable assets. Sanctuaries where they have been created in India are for the ostensible purpose of conserving the natural fauna and flora in specific and characteristic areas. I say 'ostensible' because there is so little 'following-up' done to ensure they are adequately staffed and managed. There are no experienced naturalists or former hunters of big game on their staffs to advise Forest Departments on wild life management. Often the men whose supposed task is to look after the wild life in their restricted areas have very little useful knowledge of their charges.

Conservation of wild life should no longer be thought, of, as I am sure it is in many high circles, as a frill, an amenity that ranks low in any realistic scale of values. There are economic arguments for it, in addition to the scientific, the aesthetic, and the moral.

It was once the case that wilderness and wild life did not need human aid to survive. Both would indeed have conserved themselves had they been left alone. This, however, has not been the case. Both have been rendered unstable through man's interference, and therefore now need his aid to continue to exist. The science of ecology has thus assumed great importance in recent years. It is the branch of biology which deals with the habits of organisms, their modes of life, and their relations to their surroundings. Wild life no longer exists in merely physical or climatic environments, but in increasingly complex conditions which involve extended relationships with man.

But the utmost care is necessary in all stages of ecological research as applying to the wild life of India, lest conclusions are hastily drawn and universally applied. For example, I read recently a statement by a scientist working on prey-predator balances that these need to be improved in the sanctuaries. I did not understand it at all. In none of the Indian sanctuaries do predators cause any anxiety either because of their numbers or because of their taking too many prey animals. They are all comparatively slow-breeding, and a spectacular increase in their numbers can be quite ruled out. Neither are the prey animals excessive, and under the present conditions they are unlikely to multiply hugely in the foreseeable future. Denudation of forest grasslands is caused by domestic livestock, not by the wild herbivores. I should have thought that no interference whatever was necessary in the prey-predator relationship, as the sanctuaries are populated by too few of either group, not by too many.

In the end, wild life in India will be conserved only if it is kept on a national footing without reference to politics or political units. Time is not on the side of the animals. Conservation of wild life should continue to aim primarily at the maintenance of its habitats. All forest, scrub, marsh, and swamp are in charge of government departments, and the saving of adequate areas of these to provide living-space for the animals is the responsibility of the State.

Kailash

Sankhala

The Skin Trade

Kailash Sankhala was with the Indian Forest Service and was the first Director, Project Tiger, in 1973. He was at the time Chief Wildlife Warden of Rajasthan and played a vital role in securing the future of Rajasthan's protected areas. For many, he was India's first 'Tiger Man'.

Kailash Sankhala with his favourite tiger – Jim – from Delhi Zoo. After serving as Director of the zoo, Sankhala played a critical role in reviving the rapidly depleting tiger population of India. The first warning of the tiger's crisis was sounded at a meeting of the IUCN at the Delhi Zoo in 1969.

Over one hundred years ago, in 1872, Captain J. Forsyth, Settlement Officer and Deputy Commissioner of Nimar in what was then the Central Province, was one of the first to express concern at the losses in tiger population. He mentions particularly the Narbada valley of Madhya Pradesh, and in 1882 Captain J.H. Baldwin of the Bengal Staff Corps supported him. Baldwin spoke of the good old days when one could bag a dozen tigers in a fortnight, whereas in his time only two or three could be obtained in the same period. What a wonderful way of monitoring populations!

In 1900 Russell recorded his objection to the reward being offered for every tiger killed in Mysore (Karnataka) as he feared it might lead to the destruction of the tigers there. It did.

In 1930 A.I.R. Glasford drew attention to the commercialisation of tiger trophies; at that time the price of a skin was Rs 200 and a rug with mounted head cost Rs 300. The trophies were collected by local dealers and resold to cooperative societies in big cities like Bombay and Calcutta where Europeans returning home bought them as souvenirs.

Also in the early '30s R.G. Burton in *The Book of the Tiger* (1933) gave a warning that in Hyderabad the habitat was deteriorating and the number of tigers rapidly decreasing; but he came to the entirely false conclusion that after the withdrawal of British rule in India anarchy would prevail, agriculture and population would be reduced, and that tigers would once more be able to flourish. Quite to the contrary, as we know, peace prevailed, agriculture and the human population increased, and tigers dwindled.

His brother, R.W. Burton, was more perceptive. In 1952 he wrote in a history of Indian shikar that the tiger population was wasting away; it was, he said, a national asset and he pleaded strongly for its preservation. Jim Corbett also felt that the tiger was on the way out. His contemporary M.D. Chaturvedi, a retired Inspector General of Forests, who had witnessed the death of over 250 tigers and had himself shot more than 50, mentioned that the tiger was still holding its own but needed protection; however, he still

Extract from *Tiger! The Story of the Indian Tiger* (London, 1978).

continued to bag his tiger each year till he retired in 1954. When I met Chaturvedi on my arrival in Delhi in 1965 I reminded him of the advice he had given to us in the Forest Service: that we should ask our fathers-in-law to give us a pair of guns instead of ear-rings for our wives. Chaturvedi was crestfallen.

Such pious statements about the need to protect tigers coming from those who were still associated with hunting were naturally not taken seriously. In 1956 I circulated a letter to the members of the Wildlife Board of Rajasthan appealing to them to stop the shooting of tigers at least in the hot months of May and June. Unfortunately most of the members of the Board were those who were used to easy shooting, and my suggestion was overruled. Again in 1958 when I was drafting shooting rules for Rajasthan I pleaded for a close season for tigers from November to June. My boss did in fact declare July–October a close season, more for the convenience of the hunters than the tigers, as one would hardly go into the malarious rain forests at that time of the year anyway. This was in line with the regulations in other states. Tigresses are usually either pregnant or with cubs in spring and summer, and this was the open season for shooting, with the result that many pregnant mothers or mothers with cubs at heel were killed. Sometimes the cubs were collected as a bonus by the hunters, but many died of starvation or were killed by other predators. The fortunate ones were those who came into our hands, like Jim, Rosy and Ratna. An excited hunter would pull his trigger on any tiger whatever the size, and even some forest officers who ought to have known better did not spare cubs. I wish I could name them here.

In June 1954 when I was camping at Dholpur I received a message that a tiger had been killed in the Banvihar forests. I rushed to the scene in my old loading truck, and to my surprise found a police party in a jeep with the Superintendent of Police at the wheel. In the police truck that was following was a tigress with a cub about six months old, both dead. I asked the Superintendent to unload the bodies of my wards, and was told that the action had been taken in self-defence in the course of anti-dacoit operations. The explanation could hardly have applied to the cub, whether or not it was true in the case of the mother.

Even as late as 1968 there were no restrictions on shooting tigers in Orissa and West Bengal, and even after the introduction of a fee for a hunting licence it was nominal. Nowhere, except on paper, were any restrictions imposed on the shooting of tigresses; the pretext was that a hunter cannot identity the sex of a tiger in the jungle.

Every year more tigers were killed than were replaced by the process of reproduction. Tiger economics based on wrong assumptions led to depreciation of the capital as well as the interest. Yet in 1969–70, when a ban on tiger hunting was in the air even more licences than usual were issued.

The tiger had withstood the onslaught for decades, and he might have been able to stand it for another decade were it not for the predation by man. He began to destroy the home of the tiger and at the same time to kill the animals on which it preyed. The loss was greatest immediately after India became independent, when a few greedy and short-sighted citizens organized large-scale hunting campaigns for personal gain. Nets were spared, pits were dug, traps were laid, forests were burnt. No animal was spared—mostly to cater for city restaurants where venison suddenly became popular. Soon block after block of forest became a storehouse for timber and a wildlife desert. One has not to go far to see our actions at the time; they are reflected in the nearest hill.

The cattle population of India is far more than the human population and is one-fifth of the total cattle population of the world. Although less than 11% graze in tiger habitats, the grazing pressure is still intense in the deciduous forests, which produce excellent fodder. Cattle are competing with the wild ungulates, and in recent years there is a new threat to the wildlife due to the large influx of migratory cattle. Coming from distant non-forested lands, they are exerting unprecedented pressure on tigerland, especially in Rajasthan, Madhya Pradesh, Bihar and Maharashtra. The pastures and forage available for the tiger's prey have started to disappear. The meandering herds of cattle are eating the last straw of food, drinking the last drop from the waterholes, and spreading uncontrollable diseases like foot-and-mouth and rinderpest.

The pastoralists build camps, *bhattan* or *gwaras*, inside the forests and constantly disturb the habitat. The man guarding his cattle sings to break the monotony, keeping the wild animals in a state of tension and forcing them to go to more vulnerable areas where they are killed. Pastoralists enjoyed legal protection before the ban on tiger killing; in 'defence of their property' they killed tigers by any means, even poisoning and employing professional hunters to eradicate the predator.

The uncontrolled extension of agriculture is another cause of the destruction of wildlife. Areas like 'Tiger Haven' in Dudhwa, once the best area of tigerland in the Terai region, have been released for agriculture. Pockets of open areas inside the forests have been allocated to forest labourers for growing food; wild animals are attracted by the crops and are killed as a matter of right with the crop protection guns.

Farming communities newly settled near forests acquired the rights to remove firewood, charcoal, thatching grass, bark, bamboos, timber and fruits for 'domestic use', as well as having the right to kill wild animals for crop protection. When the population was limited and the demands were local the forests could sustain this pressure, but the introduction of fast mechanised modes of transport meant that supplies could be sent to distant places for commercial use, thus further accelerating the destruction of the forests.

When the population was limited, the *jhoom* method of shifting cultivation in the evergreen hills provided the wildlife with a better habitat by opening up the forests by felling and burning. Now the population in the hills is rising as everywhere else and pressure on the land is increasing, necessitating more intensive application of the *jhoom* method. When carried beyond a certain point, i.e. with a shorter rotation period, shifting agriculture upsets the ecological balance. Thus in the eastern hills we have the spectacle of a dwindling habitat and wildlife in the face of an explosion in human population. A visit to the area in March is revealing: the burnt hillsides are a potential danger for soil erosion.

Because he was not in his division when it was on fire, a forest officer was summarily dismissed in the Boat Club of Nainital and ordered to take the first ship back to England. This story is told to the trainees of the Indian Forest College year in and year out. The forest fire is the forester's nightmare. I saw my father fighting fires in the Aravali hills and I myself spent days and nights doing the same in the forests of Udaipur. It was a losing battle, as most of these fires were started deliberately. It should not be forgotten that *controlled* fires bring back nutrients to the soil much faster than the normal processes of decay; but quite obviously undesirable are the fires started by tribal people to drive wild animals into their nets; or ritualistic fires to propitiate the gods or to ask for favours such as the birth of a son or the cure of an ailment. Patches of forest are also burnt to beseech the gods for a good harvest, and the more effective the burning the better the gods are pleased. Some fires are started—at the wrong time, at the height of summer—by pastoralists to get a new flush of grass for their cattle. Others again are started to take revenge or to victimise the fire protection staff, and forests are even burnt when some VIP visits the block.

A forest burnt without thought or planning will remain a desert for at least a month, and wild animals will either leave the area or die of starvation. A repeatedly burnt forest deteriorates very fast. No watch-towers or walkie-talkie sets can prevent these deliberate fires; only better public relations can do it, and this is a slow process.

With a rapidly-growing demand for forest products, men and their machines leave hardly any area of tigerland undisturbed. For at least six weeks a tigress needs a secluded lair in which to bring up her cubs; where now can she find one? Unfortunately the season of forestry operations, when almost every corner is visited by man, coincides with the tigresses' breeding period. Often the cubs are abandoned, to get killed or picked up by poachers. This has acted as a further limiting factor on the enhancement of the tiger population.

The foresters' folly of felling trees that had no chance of regeneration because of heavy grazing or soil erosion paved the way to total destruction. These homes of tigers and their prey have been lost for ever, as the ghastly sights of the forests of Gwalior, Alwar, Bundi, Udaipur and Jaipur make only too clear.

Natural forests are also being replaced by 'man-made' forests for the production of paper, plywood, coffee, tea, rubber, cinchona (for quinine) and eucalyptus. Regions that had remained for so long more or less undisturbed were exploited, the victims of affluence and the attitude of foresters who wanted to 'squeeze the last rupee from the forests'. This was a complete contrast to the outlook even a decade ago when the old guards were conservators in the real sense.

The construction of irrigation and power dams also introduced a large influx of labourers into the forests. They thinned out the trees to meet their fuel demands and heavy machines operated round the clock, disturbing the habitat. Men working on the dams found shikar the only diversion and destroyed the wildlife recklessly.

Tiger hunting was always a tradition among tribal societies like the Nagas and those living in Manipur and Arunachal. There were tiger clubs called *keirups*, and any tiger coming to the knowledge of members was doomed. It was surrounded on all sides and as the circle closed it was killed by spears and axes. Originally it was a sport, but with the passage of time it became a profession to sell tiger skins. The population of tigers in the tribal areas began to decline very fast, but even as late as March 1972 tiger killing had not stopped in the Khasi hills.

During the festive season in Delhi in December 1968 I conducted a survey in the central fashion market and posh hotels. It was in its way one of the most interesting assignments I ever had, watching women dressed in their best for ten days between 7 and 9 p.m. What a contrast to studying deer and ducks! As my sample each day I took the first hundred women, and out of the total of one thousand there were fifty ladies wearing spotted or striped fur coats. Most of them were foreigners. I interviewed a few Indian ladies on the matter. 'It was given to me by my mother,' said one. 'My husband gave it to me as a wedding present; he is a forest officer,' explained another. They also informed me that they were only wearing them because they had them and had no desire to acquire a new one. The fault, they declared, was not theirs: the animals were killed long before the ladies got their coats ...

Delhi becomes very cold in December–January: there is a snow fall in the Himalayas, temperatures below zero are recorded. Indian women put on woollen capes, but, being largely vegetarian, they do not like the thought of skins being ripped to decorate themselves.

Spotted and striped skins, therefore, were almost entirely exported to the West and to the East.

Once I was deputed to conduct a Canadian minister and his wife to the wildlife sanctuaries of Rajasthan. At Jaisamand they watched a pair of leopards for nearly an hour. When I went to the airport to see them off although it was a cold January night I found the lady carrying her leopard coat over her arm. 'Believe me,' she said, 'I will not put this coat on again.'

The pace of the person-to-person campaign to stop the heavy drain on our leopards and tigers was too slow for me, and I decided to raise the tempo. But how? I talked it over with my friend Razia, a charming lady on one of the national newspapers, and we devised a plan. She was to pose as a lady shortly to be married who was to be given a choice fur coat as a present from her brother in England. A photographer would take a picture of her in the coat in order to get it approved by her brother before he bought it. And so we went from shop to shop, taking stock of the pelts and having a perfect excuse to photograph them.

One shopkeeper informed us he had a regular supply of 1000 snow leopard skins a year. Another specialised in clouded leopard skins and his annual supply was nearly 2000. Countless leopard skins were neatly piled up in his shop: he said he had nearly 3000 on view and double that number in his warehouse. An interesting piece of information came to light: most of the exports were to East Africa. I could not understand this carrying of coals to Newcastle, for Africa has far more leopards than we have in India. I was told that in Kenya leopard skins could be sold at a much higher price because of the numerous tourists who went there; also, the local traders could obtain a certificate of origin for these imports which came in handy for smuggling Kenyan leopard skins. The illegal killings of Indian leopards were being utilised to legalise the killing of leopards in Kenya. The vicious circle had no end, and the leopards of both countries were losing ground.

I counted 22 tiger heads and all seemed to be laughing at us; probably they were mocking at our mission. There were hundreds of tiger rugs, and I pulled out four and spread them out on the floor. The trader immediately offered me a 30 × 40 ft carpet for

$10,000. I asked if one was readily available. 'Yes,' said he, 'but you will have to place a firm order as I have to bring it from a palace.' I found a ready excuse to decline the offer.

The next shop had just as many skins. 'The fur of cubs is softer,' said the shopkeeper, adding that it required nearly 80 skins of leopard cubs to make a coat. After taking photographs of the lady wearing various coats and counting the stock we concluded our investigations.

The soft pelts of snow leopards, which the ladies love best and from which the shopkeepers earn a substantial profit, came in a steady flow of 600–800 skins per year in the fashion market. Snow leopards are so rare that even people living in the Himalayan regions hardly ever see them. They live at an altitude of about 12,000 feet where they prey on marmots, musk deer and snow hares. Occasionally they come down to the lower pastures but hardly ever have a chance to attack the sheep of the ever-vigilant Gujjars. But some of the graziers, renowned as tough walkers and climbers, who for the six summer months live above 8000 feet, are tempted by the lucrative offers of the valleys. Equipped with firearms and living in rugged mountainous areas where there is little chance of the civil law being enforced, these men become poachers and soon run amok, endangering the whole wildlife of the Himalayas. They chase the snow leopard relentlessly, showing no mercy to pregnant females or mothers with suckling cubs. Abandoning their sheep, they go all out to stalk snow leopards, leopards, lynx and martens for their pelts and musk deer for their musk pods. Down the valley they go to the emporiums, where they get their loans paid off quickly and even obtain the lure of extra money.

The story of the stripped skins is equally pathetic. In the Dehra Dun forests I heard of a tiger held in a snare for two painful days. When the Wildlife Officer came to dispatch the beast it broke its paw and ran off into the jungle to die an agonising death. Another tiger was stoned to death in the Umariya forests of Madhya Pradesh in 1912. Sometimes villagers trap tigers and invite influential persons to shoot them at point-blank range.

In my study area of Rajasthan I came across a special class of professional shikaris known as the Bavariyas who are expert burglars. After committing a crime a Bavariya could walk more than 8 km backwards, with his feet pointing in the opposite direction to his movement, to deceive police trackers. In March 1960 while I was camping at Ramgarh in Jaipur I received information that a tigress had been making regular kills so I went to investigate. While the forest guards were busy searching for the pug marks I sat quietly near the village well. Presently a man came towards the well with his clothes stained with blood. I thought he had committed a murder and was about to clean himself, so I loaded my gun and told him to stay where he was. He took me for a police officer but having committed no murder he made no attempt to run away. I told my driver to tie his hands with his turban. The man informed me that he had shot a tiger, not man. Meanwhile the forest guards had found another man running up the slope of a hill, but being no match for a Bavariya they had abandoned the chase. My captive Bavariya was fined Rs 500 (then $100), but the skin had already gone to market where he made good his loss.

In order to kill a tiger with a low-powered muzzle-loading gun the Bavariya has to hit a vital part from close range. Such country-made guns produce a large hole which reduces the value of the pelt, so they do not use this risky, noisy and uneconomic method of poaching. Instead they obtain free from the villagers a supply of Folidol, DDT or any other poisonous insecticide and smear it on kills made by tigers. After even one gulp the tiger is hardly able to walk away from the carcass, and sometimes a whole family of mother and cubs falls victim in this way. The poacher gets a skin free of holes, readily acceptable in the hungry foreign markets.

This large-scale poaching, especially by poisoning, has proved fatal to the big cats of India. I put most blame on the traders who purchase the pelts and are quite unconcerned how they were obtained. The price of a tiger skin in the later' 50s was hardly $50; ten years later it had risen to $599. This was too much of a temptation for habitual poachers to resist, particularly when the average annual income of a man working in the forests is less than what he could make by selling one raw uncured tiger skin.

The results of my investigation with my lady accomplice were published on the front page of the *Indian Express* in 1967. It was followed by numerous letters to the Editor and led to questions in

Parliament. A ban was immediately imposed on the export of all kinds of spotted skins, and the firms concerned raised a tremendous hue and cry, presenting their pre-ban commitments for not less than 20,000 skins. Many tigers and leopards not yet born were destined to honour these commitments. The case was presented to the Indian Board for Wildlife with a plea to the Grievances Committee of the Government. The Chairman of IBWL, a young and effective minister, Dr Karan Singh, reacted sharply: 'In that case we have grievances against the Grievances Committee.' The ban on the export of skins was imposed effectively in 1968.

Then of course the firms started to give wrong declarations, coining names of sources not to be found in any book. Skins started to come to me from the Customs Office for verification and I found most interesting cases of adulteration. Wild cat skins bearing the designs of leopard spots were printed with a special dye. My problem was whether I should call them the skins of a spotted cat, a banned item, or merely the skins of wild cats which were free of export control? To save the wild cats, whose pelts ran into a few thousands annually, I declared them to be adulterated skins which could not be identified for export.

Once the channel of commercial export had been stopped the skins started going out of the country as personal baggage, for which there were no restrictions. Also the cunning traders dispatched skins roughly stitched into the shape of pants and coats since the export of tailored pieces was not controlled. Traders and shikar companies formed a strong lobby, and the representatives of foreign trade argued against a total ban on the export of tiger skins on the grounds that these earned much-needed foreign exchange.

I waited for another opportunity and it was not long in coming. The Tenth General Assembly of the International Union for the Conservation of Nature and Natural Resources met in New Delhi in November 1969. In her inaugural speech the Prime Minister, Mrs Indira Gandhi, to everyone's surprise declared: 'We need foreign exchange, but not at the cost of the life and liberty of some of the most beautiful inhabitants of this continent.' This silenced the foreign trade advocates and shikar outfitters once and for all.

Up till then one always had to contend with the indifference of the public who continued to admire photographs of hunters with one foot on a dead tiger, their deadly telescopic rifle resting on the trophy. Such pictures constantly appeared in popular magazines, and the image had to be destroyed. That is why I had concentrated on a publicity campaign giving glimpses of the personal lives of the tigers in Delhi Zoo to the press. Having created the right psychological climate, the time was ripe to tell the people that the Indian tiger was on its way out. The people were shocked. My friend Sunil Roy (Director General of Tourism) and I pleaded before the Indian Board for Wildlife for nothing less than a complete ban on tiger shikar. Various people opposed us on the grounds of the rights of the 'honest sportsman', but they were never that.

My paper entitled 'The Vanishing Indian Tiger' was presented to the IUCN meeting on 29 November 1969. This proved to be a red letter day for the tiger, which was entered in the *Red Data Book* as an endangered species. The Report of the Expert Committee, of which I was Secretary, criticised the Forest Department for its neglect of the interests of wildlife. This enraged my colleagues in the Forest Service and I was declared a rebel. Though severely criticised at the time, the Report was to become a landmark in the history of nature conservation in India and a guide for all future measures, including the Wildlife Protection Act of 1972 and the inauguration of Project Tiger.

Meanwhile, in 1970 India placed a total ban on tiger shooting and soon other countries followed. Mrs Gandhi wrote personal letters to the heads of all the States, but unfortunately the short period between the IUCN meeting and the imposition of the ban proved to be the worst period yet for the tiger. Everybody wanted to bag his tiger before the law became effective. Short-sighted self-seekers distributed their last favours to friends, and more tigers were shot in those few months than in any year of the preceding decade.

Many protests and appeals were made to the Government, shikar companies pressed for last permits, fur traders pleaded for relaxation to enable them to honour their commitments. One shikar operator named A. Imam, popularly known as 'Two Two', wrote an open letter to the Prime Minister implying that she had been misguided. He quoted wrong figures, claimed the loss of foreign exchange, and alleged the capital loss of over 60 million rupees as a result of 50,000 cattle killed by tigers every year. In another letter, to Dr Karan Singh, the writer, P.C. Barua, Raja of Gauripur, claimed that the ban on tiger shooting cost India Rs 30 million annually. In a letter to *The Cheetal* I advised people to ignore these false claims. The claim of the shikar operators was that as free citizens of India they should enjoy freedom of trade. The ban on tiger hunting and the export of skins had, they said, deprived them of their legitimate trade and livelihood. The case was argued on behalf of the Government, or rather I would say on behalf of the Indian tiger, by a learned government lawyer.

In February 1971 Delhi High Court was the scene of this significant event. The hall was full to capacity with ex-maharajas, jagirdars and landlords who had taken up tiger shikar as a business, as well as travel agents who had joined them in their venture.

The judge read and reread passages from my paper on 'The Vanishing Indian Tiger' in which I had stressed that pregnant tigresses and tigresses with cubs at heel were being killed. It appealed to his heart as well as his head on the grounds of national interest and in the first hearing the tiger won the case. After that most of the shikar companies pulled down their shutters or changed their signboards.

Unfortunately the lucrative trade in skins did not stop, and curio shops and fur traders continued to encourage poachers to poison tigers. The next step was to ban the export of skins even as personal baggage, but still the traders continued to collect and hoard in the hope of some relaxation in the export regulations.

Clearly, more effective methods were needed. The timely visit of Guy Mountfort, a trustee of the WWF, on to April 1972 was just what was required. He met our Prime Minister and promised one million dollars to go towards tiger conservation. The next day Dr Karan Singh was appointed Chairman of a task force to conduct a thorough Inquiry and work out a proposal, while I was appointed Officer on Special Duty to prepare a plan of action; the minister presented the proposal to the Prime Minister in September 1972. This was the birth of Project Tiger.

Billy

Arjan Singh

The Lost Cause?

Billy Arjan Singh has been associated with wild tigers for fifty years. His focus has been Dudhwa National Park on the Indo-Nepalese border. His battles to save habitat and the tiger are legendary.

Billy Arjan Singh with the tigress Tara in Dudhwa National Park, Uttar Pradesh. He was the first person in the world to introduce a zoo-bred tigress into the wilderness.

One November day I was guiding a group of local officials through the forest to survey an area for the extension of the sanctuary. I took them to a wild and wanton stream which meandered through many miles of beautiful creeper-clad forest whose eternal twilight offered shelter to the tiger, the bear and the elephant. Then the silence was shattered by the raucous cries of graziers, herding their cattle through the undergrowth. The path which usually bore the pugmarks of tiger, bear and signs of the passage of forest deer was now churned up by a myriad hoofprints and showed nothing more exciting than the prints of the herders' misshapen toes.

As we surveyed the scene one of the forest officers murmured something about human interests being all-important, and immediately my mind went back to an important meeting of conservationists which had been held in New Delhi exactly a year before. The highwater mark of the meeting had come when India's Prime Minister, Mrs Indira Gandhi, had declared her support for the cause of wildlife conservation in India. By the time the Agricultural Minister, whose department is responsible for wildlife, had spoken, the mood of optimism had ebbed very considerably; in the end, he concluded, everything must be subservient to the human interest. Now the same words were being repeated in one of the few places where the animals might hope to be left alone. What chance was there of saving our wildlife, I wondered, if the politician with his eye on the votes, and the bureaucrat with his eye on the politician, were unanimously agreed on this order of priorities?

In the present situation it is not difficult to forecast the final result. India's population now exceeds 550 million. The first years of Independence saw the beginnings of our efforts to catch up with our food problems, and though this laudable objective still gleams fitfully ahead like the elusive Jack O'Lantern it has brought about the twilight of our wildlife. The 'Grow More Food' campaign was vigorously promoted, the legislators hoping that food production might thereby keep pace with our rampaging population. This was a new age, the age of the poor but adequately fed man. Somehow,

Extract from *Tiger Haven* by Arjan Singh (London, 1973).

however, the poor man has sneaked ahead of the pundit's predictions. It is a case of 'Man proposes, God disposes' or as some term it—Kismet.

The same unbalanced equation affects India's 300 million cattle. Most of these animals do not give an ounce of milk and religious sentiment prevents them from being slaughtered either for food or leather. Nor can they be put out of their agony when afflicted by disease or a broken leg. Vultures swoop down to peck out the eyes of the beast which has collapsed beside the road, while on the other side the mild wayfarer continues his journey to Nirvana. Thus men and cattle fill up the continent but the land available to accommodate them remains static. It does not need the stars to foretell that in the ensuing competition for living space it will be our wildlife which becomes expendable.

Yet these are conditions we have to live with and it should not be beyond man's inventive genius to devise a solution which would create enough room for everyone. For, though lower than the beast in many of his passions, he has the capacity to control his fate as well as that of others. Of course it has to be admitted that it is very difficult to promote the idea of wildlife preservation in an under-developed and democratic country. Even rich and politically sophisticated nations have destroyed their animals and birds by using pesticides on the fields, and their fish by discharging toxic chemicals from factories into the streams and rivers. In a poor and overpopulated country like India the case for protecting wildlife seems to conflict with every other priority. The cultivator hears his government talking endlessly of food production, of food prices and the need to avoid buying from abroad; he is freely issued with gun licences to protect his crops; and then after all this he has to listen to the same government lecture him, if only half-heartedly, on the importance of saving the deer which graze on his crops and handicap the very objectives he has been told to pursue. Is it any wonder that he remains unconvinced by his ruler's new-found concern for the animals?

Equally the politician who depends on the cultivator's vote remains very reluctant to speak of our national heritage, the million-year old evolution, the aesthetic pleasures of wildlife and its scientific and cultural values.

Despite the apparent contradictions, however, wildlife does have a place in an under-developed country. That it has been deprived of it in India is very much the responsibility of the politicians and the bureaucrats. Political manoeuvring has become so common that it is now an accepted part of our lives. Nearly a quarter of a century after Independence the various groups which endeavoured to maintain the balance of power in the early years have not polarised into mature parties; indeed today they resemble opportunistic mercenaries more than responsible rulers and their activities threaten the very grass roots of democracy. The politician is often only semi-educated with no qualifications except his party label and a desire to distribute the fruits of patronage which have come his way. Caste affiliations have probably earned him a place in the legislature, strong-arm tactics have kept him there, and circumstances have placed him above his mental superiors. His main concern is in forming *ad hoc* alliances for the purpose of toppling the party in power or, according to the situation, preventing his own party from being toppled. These alliances are very fragile affairs, for the partner of today may be the opponent of tomorrow. Right sides with Left and communist with capitalist as the merry-go-round of politicians endlessly revolves in the scramble for power. Naturally there are frequent changes of government which cause the administration to remain in a permanently demoralised state.

The bureaucrat for his part has to sail a tricky wind in the prevailing confusion. He will be a man of good education, for he has to pass out high in a competitive examination to secure a place in the civil service. Thirty-five years later he may become head of a department or be sent on some foreign assignment, and when he retires he will receive a respectable pension. Yet throughout his career he has to pander to the whims of the politician whose one desire has always been to impress the electorate before he too 'abode his destined hour and went his way'. Politicians are continually interfering with the day-to-day administration to please as many constituents as possible, and they can be exceedingly vindictive if officials do not take good care of their boss's public image. A civil servant dare not suspend a subordinate even for gross inefficiency or dishonesty in case he should discover that the man is related in some distant way to his political chief. Many a good official has had his chances of promotion ruined by failing to follow the correct line and many others have never looked back in their march to success through the simple precaution of saying 'Yes sir' at the right moment.

Such is the manner in which the state is administered and every aspect of our life suffers for it. Wildlife is particularly vulnerable since it is of no interest to the population as a whole and therefore none either to the politician or the bureaucrat at his command. This total disregard for nature can be seen in the way the forests have been torn down and replaced by cultivation. The main clash between the animals and man is now over. As we have seen the animals have emerged the losers, especially the larger mammals like the elephant, the tiger, the lion, the leopard and the rhinoceros, whose horn is so popular with the sexual athletes of the east despite family-planning drives.

The forest which remains is expected to yield revenue from its timber and other resources; if this was done skilfully and with moderation, wildlife could prosper even as an incidental part of the forest. Yet it is not: everything is exploited carelessly. Soaring revenue figures are produced by local officials to please their small-time party bosses and these statistics are then displayed in the legislature as proof of the advancing economy. If the economy is indeed benefiting, it will not do so for very long. I have already described the damage which has been done by replacing the old slow-maturing trees by new faster-growing varieties; what is even more remarkable about this policy is that it has so often failed according to its own standards. The plantation division of the forest department was specifically created for the purpose and enormous amounts of money were spent on equipment, labour, spare parts and all the other incidentals which such an enterprise involves. The results are at first impressive. Large areas of orderly and well-prepared fields are planted with young saplings and surrounded by fencing; this is apparently designed to protect the saplings against the wild pig, which might uproot a few of them while digging for roots, the porcupine, which might nibble their bark, and the deer who while grazing might browse on a few shoots. This reckoning excludes the ubiquitous cattle who have penetrated everywhere. For a few months the saplings flourish but then at the end of the year the graziers start burning off the coarse grasses in the surrounding area so that their cattle can feed on the tender shoots which replace them. With the grasses are burnt the fencing posts protecting the saplings, and as the fences collapse the cattle rush in to feed on the fresh pastures which have suddenly and miraculously been thrown open to them. The young trees are trampled underfoot or otherwise destroyed by the fires which spread into the plantations.

Not much is left after a few months of this treatment, but by this time the past has been forgotten. More tractors are bought, more land is put to the plough and the whole cycle of events repeats itself without any protest, for the public memory is notoriously short, and people seldom question the policies of their rulers. And as the monsoon torrents pour down the bare hillsides, eroding the soil as they go, our planners slide comfortably into retirement. They may never realise the damage they have done, for the economy of a country is not the product of a routine appointment, or even of a whole generation, and those who have sown the wind will unfortunately not be there at harvest time.

The presence of the cattle in the forest is an enigma so bizarre as to be Gilbertian if it were not so tragic. Cattle are mainly grazers and their wild counterparts, as far as food is concerned, are the swampdeer and nilgai, who hardly ever enter the forest, and the chital and hogdeer who mainly do so for shade and protection. Browsers like the sambar seldom leave it except occasionally at night. It may therefore be pertinently asked why cattle should be allowed the freedom of the forest especially as the dense cover of the trees prevents the growth of even the smallest amount of grass. The answer is both startling and pathetic. The civil servant maintains that he dare not restrict the grazing 'rights' of border villagers because a complaint will automatically be made to his political boss; the restriction order will then be lifted and the civil servant will suffer a loss of face. Thus the safe policy of *laissez-faire* prevails, according to which you see no evil, hear no evil and speak no evil. And in the meantime the graziers set fire to the reed beds in the forest to provide more fodder for their cattle; the stems of the reeds explode like rifle-shots as they burn, and one day the tall trees catch the flames and another place becomes a wildlife desert, where the wild chorus is replaced by the yells of the herders, who have now come to stay. Who is to blame for the cattle in the forest?

Whether it is the politician or the bureaucrat—I still blame the bureaucrat for being half a politician—it is a crisis of character which knows no other master than expediency.

The same principle operates when it comes to protecting the animals from hunting. The various laws banning tiger-shooting, the export of skins and so on, have been useful but collectively they may add up to a classic case of 'too little and too late'. In my own state shooting is still uncontrolled outside the forest; anyone can fire at wildlife in the fields, and though it may be technically illegal to shoot a tiger, in practice any number of excuses of the 'crop problem' and 'defence of property' variety can be invoked to absolve the individual of his crime. A Bill to correct this situation has been waiting for approval since 1966 but due to changes of government, lack of interest and political pressure from the agricultural lobby which has little sympathy for preserving anything which might damage the farmer's livelihood, however marginally, it still has not reached the statute book. The Bill would make it compulsory to report every kill outside the forest, and the carcass would then become the property of the state. Of course like many other laws it would probably not be strictly enforced, but at least it would give conservationists a much-needed weapon to deal with offenders. Whether it will ever come to law is another matter.

Similarly the skin trade continues to flourish despite the official ban. The headquarters of the trade are in the New Market in Calcutta, and shortly after the ban had been imposed I went there to see what effect it had had. At one time the turnover had been exceptionally heavy, both in raw hides collected by agents working round the country and in cured and mounted skins ready to be shipped abroad. These lucrative days were now over, I was told. One shopkeeper informed me regretfully that he had been able to handle only 200 skins a month since the ban compared to a thousand or so before. Nevertheless the trade continues and even the local customs are not averse to abetting a limited traffic. During a short tour of the dealers in the market I was shown one collection of thirty leopard skins and variously offered a monthly supply of fifty uncured tiger pelts at around three thousand rupees apiece, and two hundred leopard skins at a little over a thousand rupees each. There was also a plentiful supply of monitor lizards, crocodiles and pythons, and a whole range of finished products openly displayed including tigers, clouded leopards and pandas. This trade takes place under the shadow of the monumental edifice which houses the Forest Department of Bengal. Just across the road is the animal market, known for many years to both residents and visitors to Calcutta as the place where you can purchase almost any form of Indian wildlife. It is a dark, dirty building with animals and birds of every description packed into over-crowded cages. The smell is sickening and after a morning spent visiting this wildlife ghetto and the skin market nearby, one begins to understand why so many of our beautiful forests are becoming silent and deserted.

Of course the obvious way of dealing with these commercial operators would be to enforce the existing laws more efficiently. Perhaps some method could be found of accurately branding all skins and then declaring that any presented for sale after a particular date would be illegal; severe penalties could then be imposed on those caught flouting the law. After all, if the desecrators of the Taj Mahal can be put behind bars, why should the skin merchants, who trade in the fur of rare animals, go free? We have our engineers, but no alchemists.

Simple though it may appear, I think such action is too much to hope for. The law is too weak, vested interests are too strong, and there is always someone around to point out that human considerations must come first; in this scheme of things conservationists do well if they are merely relegated to a class of amiable eccentrics. The only chance of saving our wildlife is to adopt a completely new approach to the problem; new, at least, as far as India is concerned. We must realise that in the survival of the animals lies an outstanding financial investment which can be exploited by developing the tourist industry. Kenya's second largest asset is her wildlife while India, with potential resources not much inferior to the African veldt, earns practically nothing from them. With no commercial justification for their continued existence, the animals are killed, and as they disappear, so too does the rich financial dividend they would have paid in the future.

Once we have become aware of this undiscovered gold-mine we must establish a national service for wildlife which will co-ordinate the planning of parks and sanctuaries throughout the country. At a local level responsibility for the animals must be taken away from the forest departments and given to a separate body; in this way wildlife will receive the attention it deserves and not be dismissed, as it is now, as a tiresome pest. I think we will also have to accept that there is no longer any point in trying to protect every animal in the land; the idea that the cattle could be excluded from all the remaining forests along with the timber merchants and other contractors is nothing more than a fantasy. Instead we should concentrate on building up a few areas reserved entirely for wildlife. There should be more land made available for sanctuaries and it should be divided up into larger and more viable units. The total area of all reserves in India today amounts to 4200 square miles; in Tanzania the Serengeti park alone is 5700 square miles. Compare this to the Maldhan sanctuary in northern India which is precisely four square miles. Such places give absolutely no protection to the animals and are created merely to pay lip service to the idea of wildlife preservation. In my view a sanctuary must be at least 100 square miles; anything smaller should be abandoned, for as long as we persist with places like Maldhan we cannot be said to be taking the survival of our animals seriously.

Most important of all, sanctuaries will have to be properly protected. That means ending all forestry operations inside them and excluding everyone, from the graziers to the honey-collectors. The importance of removing the cattle cannot be exaggerated; until this is done no amount of planning will save the animals. As I have already mentioned deer are always driven out by livestock and often catch their diseases. The gaur of Madumalai and Bandipur were completely destroyed a short while ago by an infection transmitted by domestic animals. Africa has a safety valve in the tsetse fly which carries a sleeping sickness fatal to cattle but harmless to wildlife. India has nothing comparable and the only solution is total segregation.

When the borders of our sanctuaries are sealed the animals will at last be secure. In some places, of course, a whole species may have disappeared and then they will have to be replaced either with animals bred in captivity or from another well-stocked area. As we have seen it is not easy to return captive predators like the tiger and the leopard to the wild because they have lost their ability to kill and their fear of humans; nevertheless it will have to be attempted otherwise many of our sanctuaries will be protecting nothing more imposing than the mongoose.

All these proposals may sound and turn out to be no more than quixotic daydreams in the context of what is happening in India today. Yet I believe that they represent the only hope of saving our wildlife. The cheetah has already been lost, and many other animals, as we have seen, are in grave danger. The erotic sculptures of Khajuraho and Konarak are carefully preserved as part of our cultural heritage, yet the tiger, which is our outstanding heritage, graces the showcases and walls of tycoons thousands of miles away. We are exchanging our birthright for foreign gold and when the inheritance is gone no hand of man can bring back the vanished herds galloping across the plains or revive the resonant roll of the tiger's roar which echoes through the forest. Much has been destroyed already; this is our last chance to save what remains.

Threefold the stride of Time, from first to last!
Loitering slow, the Future creepeth,
Arrow-swift, the Present sweepeth,
And motionless forever stands the Past.

Schiller

Charles

McDougal

Tigers and Man

Charles McDougal started life as an anthropologist and then turned to tigers. He has spent the last forty years in the tiger country of Nepal and India. His work on the tigers of Chitawan National Park, in particular, is unique.

McDougal prepares a camera trap.

This picture, taken by a camera trap in Chitawan National Park, Nepal, is of one of the largest tigers ever photographed. 'Chuck' (Charles) McDougal follows the traditions of F. W. Champion with his camera. (Photo courtesy Charles McDougal.)

The future of the tiger depends entirely on man. Attitudes toward the tiger have begun to improve among the educated segment of mankind. Until quite recently the ultimate big game trophy, now the tiger is considered worthy of being saved for his own sake. This is heartening. But basic attitudes have not changed in the minds of millions of Asian villagers, many of whom have traditionally regarded the tiger as their enemy. Education is the only answer, convincing the farmer that without the tiger he will be worse, not better off; this will be a slow process. But even if mankind as a whole decides that the tiger should be preserved, ultimately his fate depends on whether or not human population growth is checked, and checked soon. The expanding number of humans, crying out for more and more land to produce food, is gobbling up the few remaining wild parts of Asia at an unbelievable rate. If there is no place left for the tiger to live and nothing to hunt for his food, the best conservation programmes and the goodwill of mankind will avail him little.

In bygone years there was an almost inexhaustible supply of tigers. 'At one time in parts of India at the beginning of the last century, they were so numerous it seemed to be a question as to whether man or the tiger would survive,' comments Brander. 'Over large areas in Bengal the villagers had to surround their habitations with high stockades for their protection', notes Hewett. He also mentions that: 'The town of Gorakhpur in the east of the United Provinces had for a long time to be protected against the ravages of tigers by lines of fires.' Today Gorakhpur is a major rail junction, a city surrounded by the barren sun-scorched plains, a long, long way from the nearest tiger jungle. Williamson, author of *Oriental Field Sports* published in 1807, tells of the incredible numbers that existed during the late eighteenth century, mentioning that a traveller being conveyed by palankeen saw three tigers lying by the side of the road along which he was proceeding.

In those days the tiger was thought to be an obstacle to progress; killing him was considered a service to mankind. After shooting a pair of man-eaters, Shakespear remarks: 'It was much that I had

Extract from *The Face of the Tiger* by Charles McDougal (London, 1977).

been the avenger, constituted by Him, who ordains all things, to slay these tigers, and to save further loss of life'. To only a slightly lesser degree the same attitude applied to all tigers. Forsyth emphasises 'The obstacle presented by the number of these animals to the advance of population and tillage.' Baker urges that although: 'There are persons whose minds are so ill-balanced as to regret the present paucity of tigers ... even the most morbid mind must allow that the country and people are better for the absence of the tigers which did patrol duty upon the roads close to Calcutta itself, and that too not at night only.'

The tiger's image in the minds of the early hunters was not a sympathetic one. Campbell calls him 'A cowardly, treacherous, and bloodthirsty animal', while to Inglis he was, 'The embodiment of devilish cruelty, of hate and savagery incarnate'. 'The very beauty of the tiger, the *beaute du diable,* in truth, and the vivid combination of black, yellow and white on his glossy skin, is terrible to look upon, let alone the malignant cunning shot from his eye, and the cannibal hunger expressed in his curling lips and flashing white teeth,' is the impression given by Baker. In those far off days there were few who had a good word to spare for the tiger. One of these was Sanderson, who urged that 'The tiger is no unmitigated evil in the land,' lamenting 'It is a pity to see the tiger proscribed and hunted to death by every unsportsmanlike method that can be devised, in response to unpopular outcries—chiefly in England—without foundation in fact, about his destructiveness'. Admitting that tigers took an appreciable toll of domestic livestock, he attempts to set the balance straight: 'It may be thought that even this loss is sufficiently serious to warrant the advocating of a war of extermination against tigers, but the tiger might, in turn, justly present his little account for services rendered in keeping down wild animals which destroy crops ... It is the pig and the deer—not the tiger and panther—that attack the sources of subsistence; and these are only to be kept in check by the animals appointed to prey upon them. Were the tiger and panther gone they would soon gain the upper hand.' Nevertheless, Sanderson concludes with the remark: 'Of course all tigers are fair game to the sportsman; they can never be unduly reduced by shooting.'

Not only was killing off the tigers a humanitarian task, it was also a very exciting pastime, one worthy of a gentleman. Tiger hunting already had a long history among the ruling elite of India dating back at least to the beginning of Moghal times, when the Emperor Baber and his companions went after tigers on horseback, armed with arrows, spears and swords. It was taken up with enthusiasm by the British army officers and, to a lesser extent, civilians serving in India. Rice describes tiger-shooting as 'The most exciting and glorious sport this world affords'.

The policy of exterminating tigers, which led, for example to the payment of rewards for the killing of 349 tigers in the Central Provinces during a period of only six months in the first half of 1864, amounting to a total of Rs. 16,480, no mean sum in those days, was in time discontinued. This was due mainly to concern on the part of hunters that the supply of tigers for sport was getting noticeably smaller. Tigers had long been preserved for this purpose in the princely states, and the British emulated their example. No matter which book from whatever period one examines, the author invariably states that tigers were much more common before his time. Thus in 1886 Baker remarks how much less numerous tigers were in Bengal than in Williamson's time; Hewett explains that there were far less in the *terai* region in 1886 than there had been twenty years earlier; and Forsyth, writing of central India in 1878 comments 'Tigers are certainly not now so numerous by a great deal in many parts with which I am personally acquainted as they were even six or eight years ago'.

The establishment of 'reserved forests', the system of hunting 'blocks', and the enforcement of a closed season, gave the tiger a large measure of protection in those jungles so set aside and managed. Tigers thrived there despite the regular losses which their population sustained through being hunted. The same was true in the Indian states, whose rulers took an especially narrow view of poaching. Heavy hunting may have kept their numbers down to a lower level than ordinarily would have been the case, but in those days tiger habitat was more continuous and covered vast areas. Since there was no deterioration of the environment in these protected areas, the tiger population remained an essentially healthy one despite recurrent losses; it was resilient and capable of making a rapid comeback if the steady hunting pressure was relaxed. Brander comments: 'Up till about the beginning of the present century, sportsmen only visited the Central Provinces in moderate numbers, but about this time shooting became a popular pastime amongst army officers, and tigers were much reduced. The war practically put an end to shooting, except by district offices, and during its duration the tigers rapidly increased.' He notes that at the time local hunters, who mainly shot for the pot, killed few tigers—although they certainly did so earlier during the period when rewards were paid for the destruction of these animals. 'It is the European sportsman that thins out the tiger'.

Indulged in as it was by a relatively closed fraternity, the elite of the British ruling class in India and the Indian princes, 'tiger shooting' in time came to possess very definite ethics, or rules of the game. One of the most stringent of these was the unwritten obligation that the hunter follow up and dispatch any animal not killed outright. 'Let it be said that, when a tiger is wounded and has to be finished off, every white man goes in and takes the risk without hesitation, many a good fellow paying the extreme penalty; may they find good sport in the happy hunting grounds', declares Best. In the end it became very important how you killed your tigers; un-sportsmanlike methods were universally condemned. Burton's motto was: ''There is no 'safety first' in tiger-hunting'.

There were greater restrictions on shooting, and a greater emphasis on sportsmanship. At the same time, the forests were being better and better managed. Despite the losses inflicted by many a tiger slayer, incredible though it may seem, tigers were not only holding their own in reserved forests, but in some places their population actually managed to grow. Hewett remarks that: 'In the Report on Forest Administration in the United Provinces for 1935–36 it is stated that tigers were tending to increase in numbers and that it is almost inevitable that as the numbers of tigers increase there will be a migration of surplus tigers into the surrounding forests.'

The ideals of chivalry did not survive the Second World War. Hunting in the post-War era was more characterised by the motto 'the end justifies the means', although there were exceptions. At the same time, hunting went commercial, as trophy seekers from overseas came to the sub-continent for what many of them considered the greatest trophy of all. The hunters from abroad were a different breed from the British army officers who had preceded them, and who had run their own show. Having no knowledge or experience of local conditions, the new hunters put themselves completely in the hands of their outfitters, some of whom obeyed the rules, while others had few scruples. It was a lucrative business, and it is not surprising that much of the resistance against giving the tiger full protection came from these commercial interests.

Poaching of tigers was never much of a problem before the War. The demand for skins was limited. Most of the tigers killed by village shikaris (hunters) were ones that had made a nuisance of themselves by preying on domestic livestock. The penalties for poaching in the Indian states, and in the Kingdom of Nepal under the Ranas, were so severe that it was almost unknown. The reserved forests under British rule were well controlled. In India after the War, however, the old rules went by the board; even if still on the books they were laxly enforced. An easing of regulations made firearms more generally available. As Seshadri describes the situation: 'Villagers who had lived, in the main, within the game laws, both from fear of punishment and lack of lethal weapons, assumed that the change of authority meant freedom from control and came to consider poaching as a democratic right in the new, free society'. Added to the village shikari was a new recruit, the 'gentleman-poacher', who roamed the forests by night in a jeep blazing away at anything caught in his lights. The situation in Nepal was not dissimilar. For some years after the overthrow of the Ranas in 1950, the protection which wildlife had enjoyed during their rule—for the benefit of their own hunting parties—was viewed as another form of Rana oppression. Poaching became widespread. Illegal hunting was also stepped up in East Pakistan (now Bangladesh) following the war. Bhutan, having a predominantly Buddhist population which deplores the taking of life, did not suffer so badly as its neighbours. Just as poaching became more rampant, the demand for tiger (and leopard) skins suddenly went up, their value increasing as the tiger became scarcer. At the same time a new and easy method was put into the poachers' hands. Large quantities of insecticides, rodenticides, and other poisonous chemicals were made available to the villagers with a view to increase agricultural production. These toxins also were most effective for poisoning the big cats at their kills. The widespread use of poison caused a rapid reduction in tiger numbers in some regions.

Poaching and hunting were important factors contributing to the tiger's decline especially in the post-War era. But, overshadowing them by far, the destruction of the tiger's habitat stands out as the major reason why the cat today is in such serious jeopardy. The *pax britannica* brought stability. The population grew and agriculture spread. More and more forest was cut back and what remained was increasingly exploited. Although this process has accelerated so much in recent decades that its effects are obvious to all, signs that the process had begun were noted 150 years ago. Burton quotes a Captain Mundy, who toured India in 1827–28 and who hunted tigers, commenting that, 'In these modern times ... the spread of cultivation and the zeal of English sportsmen have almost exterminated the breed of these animals'. At the time Mundy's remarks were only of local application. By the turn of the century the effects of agricultural expansion were more widespread. Hewett, after describing a hunt during the early 1880s during which a dozen tigers had been slain in 15 days, mentioned that he had occasion to visit the same spot 25 years later. 'The ground had been brought completely under cultivation, and no one could have imagined that there had ever been any cover there suitable for a tiger.' The same author explains how swamps which had provided natural sanctuaries for tigers, inaccessible to hunters even with elephants, had disappeared due to the changing of the countryside for cultivation. During the pre-War years in Nepal, the Chitawan Valley and certain parts of the *terai* region were deliberately kept free from cultivation, both to ensure sport for the Rana families and their guests, and for other reasons. This was the first lowland area to be opened up for resettlement after the War, as population growth in the highlands outstripped food production. Except for the Sunderbans delta of the Ganges, tiger habitat has virtually disappeared in Bangladesh as the result of development projects and the inexorable spread of shifting cultivation.

Let me recapitulate. Despite constant hunting pressure, which increased towards the turn of the century as tiger shooting became more popular, until the beginning of the Second World War the tiger continued to hold its own. Although appreciable habitat had been lost, huge areas still remained. The use of the reserved forests had become controlled and regulated, and reports indicated that in some of these areas tigers had actually increased. In the Indian states and in Nepal, tigers were still numerous despite the toll from shooting. Some overall decline had, of course, occurred as the result of loss of habitat as the human population increased and, to a lesser extent, as the result of poaching and hunting. Gee estimates there were perhaps 40,000 tigers in India at the turn of the century. Sankhala reckons there still were about 30,000 at the beginning of the Second World War.

The increased exploitation of the forests for the war effort and the poaching of wildlife by the military set the stage for events to follow. But it was accelerated human population growth, which made itself felt especially in the post-War era, increasing as much in 25 years as it had in the previous century, that caused irrevocable damage—widespread destruction and deterioration of the tiger's habitat. While previously, with large and remote tracts of jungle intact, the tiger population could recover from even heavy hunting losses, now, with the habitat reduced to smaller and more fragmented tracts, this was no longer possible, especially with the hunting outfitters ferreting out as many tigers as possible for their rich clientele from abroad. Nor could the tigers recover from stepped up poaching, an even greater danger now that it had become big business, with the price of skins soaring. Writing in 1964, Gee estimates: 'I don't suppose there are more than about 4,000 tigers left in the whole of India.' In 1975, just over a decade later, Sankhala concludes: 'It would ... be safe to put the total number of tigers in India, Nepal, Bhutan and Bangladesh at around 2,000.'

The tiger's present patterns of behaviour have been strongly influenced by his association with man over the years. A super-predator, the tiger himself has become the hunted, the harassed. Before the advent of firearms the tiger had little to fear from man. It was a much more conspicuous animal, much less strictly nocturnal, and in many cases occupied places where no self-respecting tiger would be found today. This was true even until the middle of the last century, when hunters were few and firearms still of the muzzle-loading variety. Rice gives a good account of hunting in Rajput country during the early 1850s. He and his companions met with tigers in isolated bits of cover in otherwise fairly open country, often quite close to villages and even small towns. They did not bother to tie out baits or make any special arrangements in advance. Hearing that some tigers were to be found near a particular village, they proceeded there, collected a gang of men, and beat the likely covers. The result was 158 tigers killed and wounded during five seasons of 'sport', most of the cats being found in what we today would think the most unlikely of places.

Brander, who did his hunting a half century and more later, comments: 'Tigers have vanished from the comparatively open nalas in which our ancestors found it so easy to kill them, and even in my time they have disappeared, or at the most are only occasional visitors in many of the outlying jungles.' More and more, the tiger did everything possible to minimise contact with man, as the latter became more ubiquitous and at the same time more lethal. The same author observes: 'Their chief endeavour in life seems to be to avoid being seen or having attention drawn to them.' Always far more secretive and retiring in its habits than, say, the lion, these characteristics became intensified as the potential for contact with humans increased. The tiger retreated to more remote and secluded jungles, became more nocturnal, especially near human settlements, and became more circumspect about returning a second time to feed on kills that it had made—especially when these were tethered baits which had been placed in its path. These efforts to avoid man are what led many of the early hunters to stigmatise the tiger as 'cowardly'. There was nothing cowardly about the tiger, it was just getting smarter. As early as 1878, Sanderson observes: 'The most unsophisticated tigers, after being hunted unsuccessfully once or twice, become so alive to danger from any source that it is most difficult to circumvent them.'

The tiger has no instinctive fear of man. He has learned that avoidance of humans is the best strategy for survival. This is a cautious cat, generally not taking risks of any kind. At the same time it can be extremely bold, caution and boldness being twin facets of its character, like two sides of a coin. The tiger is a confident, calm, collected animal that rarely loses its cool, even in sudden, unexpected encounters with humans; it is a much less dangerous beast to meet by surprise at close quarters than, say, a bear. The tiger usually gives way, but rarely loses any of its dignity in the process. Sometimes it stands its ground, expecting man to move away, like the time when I met the tigress Chuchchi on a knife-edged ridge, face to face; she made no move, and eventually I retreated. Not long ago, while walking on Bandarjola Island with Andrew Laurie, who was completing a three year study of the rhino in Chitawan, we suddenly came upon a tigress and her large, two-thirds grown cub, as they rested near a kill which they had made that morning. With a 'woof' the cub shot off to our left into the grass beyond the kill, while the tigress made tracks through the trees to the right. But then, as we stood there in the open forest, the large cub, having circled around, walked up the rise and on to the bank where we were. About forty yards from us he stopped and stood there looking at us for three or four minutes, making no attempt at concealment. He was not even alarmed when we took a step or two closer to get a better look. Finally he proceeded on his way, heading in the direction his mother had taken, but after a short distance he lay down by a bush and watched us for another minute or two before clearing off for good. Certainly in neither of these two close encounters, happening unexpectedly, did the tigers display any fear, although in the second one, surprised by the abruptness of our meeting, the first reaction of the two cats was to put some distance between us. In Chitawan tigers are, of course, strictly protected, and have been for some time. We may presume that their behaviour is less influenced by human threat than was true generally, and is still true today in most places.

In localities relatively free from human disturbance, tigers hunt readily by day as well as by night if the other conditions are right, although the cats hunt mostly by night because of the advantages for concealment offered by the cloak of darkness. This indicates that where tigers are strictly nocturnal, they have become so to minimise contact with humans. Seidensticker, who radio-tracked the large cats in Chitawan during the spring of 1974 reports: 'Though reported in the old literature as primarily nocturnal or crepuscular in their activity, I found both the tiger and the leopard active and moving about throughout the diel cycle. Both cats moved less during the mid-day period than in the morning or evening, but during all periods, 75% of the receptions indicated activity.' In Malaya, Locke reported the tigers inhabiting the remote, interior parts of Trengganu State to be less nocturnal and not as elusive as those in the relatively populated coastal region.

Hunted tigers became very knowledgeable about the methods employed to kill them. The predators were often shot when they returned to finish off a kill. Smart tigers became hyper-cautious when returning to feed, even smarter ones abandoned the carcass after a single meal. 'Every tiger in India has been hunted,' a well-known tiger slayer explained to me back in 1960. The survivors were a pretty clever bunch of cats. I cannot resist one example of this from the bad old days when I too used to hunt them. Not long before dawn a big male tiger killed a large buffalo and dragged it into the thick forest. Later the same morning, hearing the news from the villagers, a friend and I went to investigate on an elephant, taking with us a local tracker. We found the kill close to the hills. Only a small portion had been eaten. There was only one possible tree in which to construct a small, concealed platform for me to sit and await the tiger's return in the evening, a bare and spindly tree at that. The tracker walked up to the tree and slowly climbed the trunk to the first branches some 15 feet or so from the ground, which he tested with his weight by standing in them, declaring that the tree would only do as a last resort. Then we took the elephant up to the tree, and the man climbed out of the branches directly on to the beast's back, whereupon we headed back to the village, having decided against waiting over the kill.

In the morning we arose in the small hours and set off on our elephant for the site of the kill. Making the final approach very cautiously, just at first light, we hoped to find the tiger still in the vicinity. We were more than a little surprised to discover that the cat had not even visited the carcass during the night—it was untouched. Even though we knew it would probably be a waste of time—this was probably one of those tigers that never returned to a kill—I reconsidered the idea of the platform in the tree. The tracker, again with us, said he'd better have another look, so we took the elephant up to the tree and the man climbed directly from its back into the branches. He again tested all the possibilities and worked out his mental blueprint of how to build the small, one-man hide. By this time we had taken the elephant off some distance. The tracker climbed down the trunk of the tree and came after us on foot. Back at the village we tucked into a hearty breakfast, while the tracker gathered some assistants and materials, and started back to the scene of the kill. When the gang got there, at about ten in the morning, there was the tiger, ravenously devouring the carcass. Incredible as it may seem, from the hill-slope behind, the tiger must have had the spot under continuous observation since we had first visited it the previous morning. He saw the tracker climb from the ground into the tree and watched him moving about in the branches, but he did not note the tracker leaving the tree, for the man did not climb down, but stepped on to the back of the elephant. All the time that he thought the tree held a human being, he did not approach the kill, hungry though he must have been. The next morning the tracker climbed from the back of the elephant into the tree; after the elephant left the tiger saw the man climb down the trunk of the tree and go away. Thinking the coast was clear at last, the tiger moved in and made up for lost time. We were completely nonplussed at first, but sat down and reconstructed the events which I have related. I regret to relate that this tiger was subsequently shot—by a fluke, I might add—for he knew all about lights and men up trees. In a flash he leapt off the kill as soon as an electric torch was switched on, but then made the mistake of exposing himself as he moved between two trees. While skinning this animal, an old male with worn down canines, we found two old gunshot wounds, and dug a twelve bore slug out of one side of his body and six 'large game' pellets out of the other. He had learned the hard way.

The tigers whose behaviour was unpredictable were those that survived their association with man the longest. Baldwin in 1877 comments: 'It is often when least expected and likely enough in the most unlooked-for-quarter that you come across a tiger'. Sanderson, writing about the same time, similarly remarks: 'Tigers frequently astonish those most conversant with their ordinary habits by some erratic conduct, and it is unsafe to condemn as untrue almost anything that may be related to their doings (as long as it is nothing of which they are physically incapable) merely because it is unusual or unprecedented.'

A discussion of the relationship between man and the tiger would not be complete without at least touching on the subject of man-eating tigers, which may be defined as ones that deliberately kill humans for food. Happily such animals are rare, but they cropped up with some frequency in the past in a few regions and remain something of a problem in the Sunderbans delta of the Ganges. The point to make is that man-eaters are abnormal tigers; normal tigers avoid man and attack only if provoked or under some special circumstance, such as when a tigress thinks her cubs are threatened. Never did they constitute more than a fraction of the total population—even in the notorious Sunderbans region, only about three per cent of the tigers are confirmed man-eaters. Because stories about them make more exciting reading, they have been much in the public eye. This is unfortunate, for man-eaters have given the species as a whole a bad press. While unusual circumstances may account for instances of man-eating in some regions, most of the famous man-eaters, such as those of Kumaon made known by the books of Jim Corbett, not only were partially disabled, but operated in areas of sub-optimal habitat where natural prey was scarce.

Today we find the tiger with his back to the wall, with little remaining habitat left, and even that increasingly threatened by the inexorable expansion of human population. Truly, from the last ditch, the tiger is fighting for his life.

The Indian tiger was not officially recognised as being in jeopardy until 1969, when at the Congress of the International Union for Conservation of Nature held at Delhi, a resolution was passed to place it in the *Red Book of Endangered Species.* The concerned countries stopped tiger hunting shortly afterwards, while at the same time introducing new legislation to prohibit the export of skins. Under the auspices of the Indian Board of Wildlife, a 'tiger census' was carried out in India in 1972, resulting in a tally of 1,827 tigers for that country. At the time Nepal was thought to have about 150, and Bhutan roughly 180. Mountfort put the Bangladesh population at approximately 100.

In 1972 the World Wildlife Fund launched 'Operation Tiger', an international effort to save this cat, concentrating on the Indian race. It was also instrumental in causing many western countries to ban the import of tiger (and other) skins.

A joint project between WWF and the four countries having populations of the Indian race, Operation Tiger has concentrated on giving full environmental protection to the best existing areas of tiger habitat left in the sub-continent, enlarging existing sanctuaries and improving their management.

India has created nine 'Project Tiger' reserves in different parts of the country: Manas (Assam), Sunderbans (West Bengal), Palamau (Bihar), Simlipal (Orissa), Corbett (Uttar Pradesh), Ranthambhore (Rajasthan), Kanha (Madhya Pradesh), Melghat (Maharashtra) and Bandipur (Karnataka). A reserve in Bhutan, Manas, adjoins the Indian one of the same name. Bangladesh has a reserve in the Sunderbans not far from that in India. Nepal has set up three tiger reserves: Royal Chitawan National Park, Karnali Wildlife Reserve, and Sukla Phanta Wildlife Reserve. This makes a total of 14 tiger reserves in the sub-continent.

In order to survive the tiger needs more room and less disturbance; better protection for the whole ecosystem in which he plays a critical role. As [Kailash] Sankhala, the Director of 'Project Tiger' in India, comments: 'The tiger is exceptionally sensitive to any change in the environment. He will not stay to eat the last dead deer, but will leave an area well before the changes in his environment are clearly visible. He is the index of environmental quality'.

We cannot hope that the tiger will ever regain anything like its former numbers. Most of the habitat has been lost, forever, and a lot more will go, as the human population climbs even higher. All that we can expect is to maintain a few viable breeding populations of wild tigers in some places. Not all of the tiger reserves which have been established hold out equal chances of accomplishing even this. The IUCN Survival Service commission states that for an animal like the tiger a contiguous population of at least three hundred is necessary to maintain a gene pool of sufficient variety. All known populations are smaller than this, and there is no regular genetic exchange between them. In only two regions, Manas (India and Bhutan) and the Sunderbans (India and Bangladesh) have more than 2,000 sq km been set aside for management as tiger reserves. Only three other Indian reserves even come close to this—Melghat, Palamau and Kanha. The remainder of the reserves in India and those in Nepal are all less than 1,000 sq km.

Ultimately, unless the mushrooming growth of the human race can be controlled, wildlife will not survive. The subsistence farmer, representing the great bulk of the population of the sub-continent, is not concerned with what will benefit his grandchildren—he is concerned with feeding his family today. If the tiger disappears because it is a luxury that starving millions cannot afford, by that time it will be all over for man also—he will have lost his freedom, as more and more regimentation is needed to control the growing hordes. Thus the tiger is a symbol. There is nothing freer than a wild tiger on the loose. There are few things more tragic than a tiger behind bars, or for that matter even one enjoying the contrived freedom of an out-door zoo. But by the end of the century that is where all the world's remaining tigers may well be.

M.E.
Sunquist

Radio-tracking the Tiger

Melvin Sunquist has decades of experience with tigers, leopards and other carnivores. He is is a senior wildlife ecologist and works as a professor at the University of Florida.

Mel Sunquist with his tranquiliser gun. He was one of the first to radio-collar a wild tiger in order to find out more about its home range, behaviour and feeding habits. The late 1970s were a critical point in tiger-conservation history. Nepal's Chitawan National Park was the location for several scientific studies on the tiger.

Introduction

An understanding of how animals use space and time relative to conspecifics and to other features of their environment requires knowledge of their movement patterns. Because the movements of animals are frequently difficult to observe under natural conditions, most studies have relied on mark-recapture or study of tracks and signs. These studies, while providing data on population dynamics and predation, generally lack the precision necessary to understand the social-spatial organisation of essentially solitary and secretive animals. Information on social organization and how it relates to the animal's ecology are necessary to provide the predictive capacity on which future management decisions can be made.

Since the early 1960s, two major technological advances have been made which allow scientists to overcome the limitations of conventional methods of ecological research. First, the development of fast-acting immobilizing drugs and projectile syringes allowed the capture of free-ranging animals. Secondly, the development of efficient and portable telemetry equipment provided researchers with the means to mark and locate individual animals on a regular basis. By simultaneously monitoring several individuals within a population, information on social and spatial interaction patterns can be obtained. Movements and activities of individuals can also be related to other features (e.g. food, habitat) of their environment. Thus, the essential data needed to examine and define social structure in relation to an animal's ecology can be obtained.

A combination of these two techniques have been successfully applied to the study of social organization and ecology of grizzly bears (*Ursus arctos*) mountain lions (*Felis concolur*), and leopard (*Panthera pardus*). However, comparative information on the tiger (*Panthera tigris*) is lacking.

Study Area

Field studies began in Nepal in December 1974, in Royal Chitawan National Park with the permission and co-operation of the Ministry

Originally published as a symposium paper on 'Tiger Conservation in India', 22–24 February 1979, New Delhi.

of Forests, H.M.G. The Chitawan region has long been known for its rich vegetation and abundance of wildlife, especially the tiger and the one-horned rhinoceros (*Rhinoceros unicornis*).

METHODS

Tigers were initially attracted to an area by placing live domestic buffalo calves at sites along frequently travelled routes. The baits weighed 50–180 kgs. Bait sites were also chosen with regard to the proximity of dense cover and trees, which provide the best stands (platform) for darting. Baits were tied out late in the afternoon and checked the following morning. When a bait was missing, it was assumed that the tiger had taken it into nearby cover and was still there. A capture attempt was then organised. Several sections of drive cloth (*bhith*), each 37m long and 1.4m high, were positioned in such a manner as to create a funnel and two people with Cap-Chur guns were positioned in trees at the narrow end of the funnel. Trained elephants were then noisily driven from the wide to the narrow end of the funnel, thereby hopefully forcing the tiger to pass within darting range (approximately 20m) of the Cap-Chur guns. Immobilizing darts were aimed at the muscles of the hind quarters. Darted animals were found by following their tracks. The average time between darting and location of the animal was 25 minutes. The average distance travelled after darting was about 150m. All individuals were immobilized with the Parke-Davis drug CI-744 with initial dosages averaging 4.25 mg/kg of body weight. Animals were immobile for about 5–7 hrs. While immobile, animals were weighed, measured, ear tattooed, radio-collars were attached, general condition noted, and a photographic record made for future identification.

The response to darting and handling did not suggest that the animals were disturbed by the process. Tagged tigers returned the same day to feed on bait kills and occasionally tigers made new bait kills the same day.

Radio-collars which were recovered did not show signs of repeated scratching and the necks of recaptured tigers showed no signs of chafing or loss of hair, all suggesting that the tigers were not disturbed by the collars. All tagged tigers singly killed large prey and females successfully reared young.

Seven tigers were radio-tracked for period of 3 to 24 months. Tagged animals were located from elephant, vehicle, aircraft, and on foot using portable receiving equipment. An animal's location was determined primarily by triangulation or less commonly by circling the animal once a day, but this was usually impossible because some animals ranged over large areas and our range of mobility was often restricted.

The overall approach represents the most efficient method for obtaining behavioural and ecological data on a quantitative and unbiased level.

Many kinds of data were collected during the project, including activity patterns, habitat, use, extent of movements (home ranges), patterns of land use (territorial), social interaction patterns, population characteristics, and predatory habits. Radio-tracking data from Chitawan indicate that

(a) tigers maintain relatively small and exclusive (territories) home ranges,
(b) a male's territory includes the smaller ranges of several females,
(c) tigers socialize infrequently,
(d) tigers prefer riverine forests and grassland habitats,
(e) females make a kill about every 8 to 8.5 days, and
(f) Chitawan supports an adult resident population of about 15, with a 4 : 1 sex ratio favouring females.

Obviously, information on home range, range sizes, habitat use, food habits, and social organization are essential for the establishment and management of future and existing reserves. Information of this type can be applied to such management issues as habitat manipulation, reserve size, translocation, and packing.

Seven [illegible] were tracked for a period of [illegible] months. [illegible] animals were [illegible] from elephant, vehicle, [illegible], and on [illegible] equipment. An [illegible] location [illegible] circling [illegible] and [illegible] range of [illegible] was often [illegible].

[illegible] containing [illegible]

Many [illegible] activity patterns [illegible] patterns of land use [illegible] characteristics [illegible] predator [illegible] tracking data from Chitwan [illegible]

(a) [illegible]

(b) [illegible] observed [illegible] several [illegible]

(c) [illegible]

(d) [illegible]

(e) [illegible]

(f) Chitwan [illegible] about [illegible]

[illegible] habitat use [illegible] and management of [illegible] information [illegible] management issues as habitat manipulation, [illegible] translocation and tracking.

S.P.

Shahi

Battling for Wildlife in Bihar

S.P. Shahi worked in the Indian Forest Service of the state of Bihar. He was a great champion of the tiger and of wildlife generally. He loved watching animals and photographing them, and his comments on governance are pertinent even today.

S. P. Shahi's famous picture of a wolf watching a goat before the kill. Shahi was one of the first foresters in India to record and document what was then the splendid wildlife of Bihar. (Photo by S.P. Shahi.)

The idea that a country should preserve, unspoiled and unexploited, its natural grandeur, gave to the world its first National Park, situated in Yellow Stone in the USA, over a hundred years ago (1872). In the course of the century that followed, the National Park movement spread to other nations and more and more people have begun to discover that such parks are ideal institutions for creating an awareness of their environment among people and to educate them about the behaviour and habits of wild life. Its philosophy spelt out that park areas were not just vestiges of the past but symbols of the future—a future of growing understanding and compassion for all forms of life, plant and animal. In the course of this century, more and more areas were designated as National Parks permanently by legislation, to enable the region to be preserved, without any exploitation or denudation, for a fuller appreciation of its scenic and scientific values.

The park so dedicated by law becomes a heritage of the people—neither its boundaries nor its features can be altered easily by the government, irrespective of its political beliefs. All parks in the USA come under the National Parks Act of the USA, 1916 and those in Canada are backed by the authority of the Rocky Mountain Park Act. In Kenya, National Parks have been established under the royal National Parks Ordinance, which authorises the Kenyan Government, with the consent of its legislature, to gazette an area as a Royal National Park. A similar ordinance in Tanzania, which is famous for the Serengeti Park and the Ngorongoro crater, confers full legal status on its parks. In India, the five National Parks are Corbett in Uttar Pradesh, Shivpuri, Kanha and Bandogar in Madhya Pradesh, and Taroba in Maharashtra. They have all been established by legislation enacted by the respective State Governments. More are in the offing.

We in Bihar have not lagged behind. 112 square kilometres of our forest area, barely sixteen kilometres from the town of Hazaribagh, were set aside as a National Park about the same time as Kanha was established in 1955. However, no legal status has so far been conferred upon it. The Park, though twenty years old now, is still

Extract from *Backs to the Wall: Saga of Wildlife in Bihar, India* (Madras, 1977).

not covered by an Act. I submitted the draft of a National Park Bill as Chief Conservator of Forests in 1967 but it has yet to be examined, much less legislated upon. The Governments that came to power successively in Bihar after the 1967 general election fell so rapidly that they could not even settle down, leave alone find the time to legislate on National Parks. As a result, any demand for the release of park lands controlled by the Government was dealt with by the various ministers in charge of forests. This has led to a number of problems, as the following example illustrates. A certain person claimed fifty acres of land in the midst of Hazaribagh Park. This claim was examined by a law court and found fictitious. However, the minister concerned, who came from Hazaribagh, ordered the release of this land even though he knew of the court ruling and in spite of my protest that such a step would affect the campactness of the Park and undo thirteen years of wildlife conservation work. But before his order could be carried out, the ten-month old ministry to which he belonged was voted out of office. Earlier, three ministries, formed by various permutations and combinations of political parties, followed in quick succession but none of them could provide the State with a stable Government. One lasted for a bare three days, another for a month and a half, and the third for a slightly longer period of three months. They were too engrossed in finding political allies to survive, and had little time to think of state business let alone wildlife. Finally, President's rule was promulgated by the Central Government as a stop-gap remedy. I took this opportunity to represent to the State Government that the release order should be reconsidered. After reviewing the case, the Government agreed with me and rescinded the order in December 1968. President's rule lasted for seven months and a new ministry was formed after a mid-term election. The same gentleman who had ordered the release of the land in 1968 was again appointed Forest Minister. He lost no time in raking up the issue and, in the spite of objections raised by the Additional Member, Board of Revenue and the Chief Secretary to the Government—besides myself—re-ordered the release of the land, mercifully only thirty-five acres this time, to the same person. In his minute dated 8 April 1969, the Minister wrote:

> I take strong exception that Govt. orders communicated to the Chief Conservator of Forests (C.C.F.) on 24–6–68 were not acted upon till the middle of November. This only shows the scant respect with which the Forest Officers have treated Government orders.
>
> I would like the displeasure of the Government to be pointedly brought to the notice of the C.C.F. and the C.F. (Conservator of Forest) under intimation to me.
>
> I would like that Government orders contained in letter No. 2283 dated 24–6–68 should be implemented at once without any further fuss after rescinding the order contained in Govt. letter No. 4523 dated 3–12–1968.

But before this minute could be acted upon, the four-month old ministry was thrown out of office on 21 June 1969. At the same time, public agitation against the release of this chunk of land had reached considerable proportions and the press had also taken up the issue. As a result, the new ministry that followed, although unstable right from the start, had to take a decision urgently on this issue. The new Chief Minister, Bhola Paswan Shastri, was advised by his Cabinet colleagues not to release the land, to which he agreed. However, the mercurial character of the political parties that shared Shastri's Government toppled his ministry after a mere twelve days and Shastri resigned before he could record the advice of his Cabinet colleagues.

Inevitably, President's rule was imposed once again. This time the Assembly was, however, kept in animated suspension. The Adviser to the President ordered that the *status quo* be maintained until a popular ministry was formed again. According to him, it was not for the caretaker government to take a policy decision on so vital a matter. After a spell of seven months of President's rule, the Assembly was revived and a new ministry—the seventh in three years—came into existence. The new Forest Minister—the ninth in three years—who belonged to a different political party from the one who had twice ordered its release earlier, passed orders not to release the land 'in the larger national interest'. This is how the issue rests today, precariously, in the absence of an Act.

I have dealt with this case not to highlight the conduct of a minister but to underline the fact that although no law exists to ensure the legality of Hazaribagh National Park, the fact that we had improved the conditions of its fauna and provided facilities to the public to see and admire them was enough to prompt the general public, and members of the legislature and the press, to agitate on this matter. The new Wild Life (Protection) Act of 1972 prescribes elaborate procedures for enquiring into the claims over land before an area can be declared a National Park. The forest authorities are keeping their fingers crossed that the claimants will not raise their heads again when legal procedures for constituting the area into a National Park are initiated.

At our present stage of wild life conservation, there is a need for bringing more and more people to the parks so that they can experience the excitement and pleasure of being in the midst of Nature and, hopefully, offer us support at crucial moments. If we had waited for suitable legislation to designate the Hazaribagh area a National Park, we would neither have received the financial assistance of the Government nor the support of the public. The 'sanctity' associated with this name is a tribute to the National Park concept.

That the National Park idea is catching on in this country is also evident from the demand for having a similar Park in the Champaran (West) district of North Bihar. An excellent compact block of forests of over 30,000 acres known as Madanpur is an ecological entity by itself. With miscellaneous forests interspersed with cane brakes, swamps and open grass lands, there is no other forest of this type in the State so ideal for a rich faunal life. It is the second largest stronghold of the tiger in the State—twelve tigers reside permanently in this area. A prominent member of the Congress legislature party and also of the State Wild Life Board wrote to the Prime Minister, Mrs. Indira Gandhi, in June 1972 regarding this issue as the Government, for some unknown reason, began actively considering the release of over 100 acres of land in the Madanpur forests to an individual. He wrote:

> As a member of the State Wild Life Board, I have of late been having a feeling that the policy of the State Government runs at times counter to what you have been desiring. Your interest in the conservation of nature and wild life is well-known. I am told, you have been on this point writing to the various Chief Ministers of the States also.

Forest which is the habitat of wild life in this State is being honey-combed by release of forest lands under different popular Governments. You are aware of the status of the tiger in this country. In a recent census conducted by the Bihar Forest Department, I am told that there are 80 tigers in the whole State but except for my district of Champaran which has got 14 tigers in a small area of 300 square miles (775 square kilometres) of forest, the only other viable population is in the district of Palamau. Madanpur forest in my district of Champaran is still rich in wild life with concentration of over a dozen tigers. I am distressed to write to you that there are very dis-quieting reports about releasing forest lands to different persons in this forest. Even as much as plots of over 100 acres are perhaps under active consideration of Government for release to individuals. Madanpur forest will completely be ruined if this is not stopped. This is a sanctuary and we are keen to convert it into a 'National Park' because of the concentration of tiger population in this area but all our ambitions will be set at naught if lands are released from this area and from other adjoining forests of Champaran district.

I also like to bring to your notice, another instance of what Government is probably contemplating to do. The only place where chinkara (ravine deer) is available is in the district of Rohtas on the plateau. This has been declared as a sanctuary by the Forest Department to protect this species but attempts are being made by interested influential persons to get a part of this Sanctuary denotified because these persons are fond of shooting in the forest.

I feel that there should be a central legislation for the protection of wild life and from the reports in the papers, I find that some of the States have passed resolutions authorising the Central Government for such an enactment. It will be very greatly appreciated if you kindly write to the Chief Minister of Bihar to pass a resolution in the current session of the Assembly, as some other States have already done.

The Prime Minister forwarded this letter to Shri Kedar Pande, then Chief Minister of Bihar, and said in her covering letter dated 5 July 1972:

I enclose copy of a letter which I have received regarding the preservation of wild life in Bihar. You already know of my interest and concern. The Bihar Assembly has not yet passed a Resolution in favour of Central legislation on this subject about which I wrote to you on 12 April 1972. I hope you will get this expedited.

> I am disturbed by what the letter says regarding the release of forest land. Please look into this personally and stop it.

It is rather significant that this letter was written from Simla at a time when the Prime Minister was having the historic talks with Mr. Zulfikar Ali Bhutto, Prime Minister of Pakistan, and goes to show her keen interest and concern with the country's wild life.

The general issue of the release of lands from forests has not been settled satisfactorily so far although it is debated at most of the Forestry meetings. When Mr. C. Subramaniam was Minister of Planning, he brought to the notice of the Chief Ministers of all States, through his letter of the 29 August 1971, the need for preserving the forests of the country. He wrote, among other things, that 'further deforestation for agriculture can only be viewed with alarm.'

The Estimates Committee (1968–1969) of the Fourth Lok Sabha in its 76th Report (March 1969) had this to say on the subject:

> The Committee regret to note that an area of about 11 lakh hectares under forests has been lost since 1951 for cultivation and other development projects, etc., in the country. No attempts have simultaneously been made to bring an equivalent area under forest as stipulated in the First Plan and recommended from time to time by the Central Board of Forestry. It appears that the data furnished to the Committee is also incomplete. The Committee feel very much concerned over these *continuous inroads into the forest area which is already below the required proportion laid down in the National Forest Policy.* In their opinion, if the trend is allowed to continue unchecked the situation may assume alarming proportions, particularly in States having a small forest area. The Committee, therefore, strongly recommend that Government should immediately pay serious attention to this problem and take effective measures to ensure that simultaneously steps are taken to afforest suitable areas equal to those which have to be deforested on account of the implementation of plan projects, etc. The Committee suggest that, besides exploring other avenues, this matter may be considered by the National Development Council which is an appropriate forum for taking decisions on such important matters.

Despite such strongly worded reports, the situation continued to deteriorate and the Ministry of Agriculture had to bring to the notice of the States once again, in August 1974, the need not to alienate forest lands. In its 65th report the Estimates Committee (1973–75) of the Fifth Lok Sabha says:

> The Committee feel greatly concerned that no concrete steps have been taken so far and the very first step suggested in the First Five-Year Plan document that an immediate reconnaissance survey of waste-land be made so as to know how much of waste-land is available in every State and what proportion of this would be suitable for raising plantations has now been included in the Fifth Five-Year Plan under 'Social Forestry Programmes' after a gap of about 18 years. The Committee note that the programme of afforestation of waste-lands in some of the States has suffered as survey of waste-land has yet to take place ...
>
> The Committee are concerned to note that instead of increasing the forest area in the country so as to bring it to the proportion laid down in the National Forest Policy Resolution, *there have been continuous inroads into the forest area and there has been shrinkage of 3 million hectares of forest area since 1952.* (It increased from 1 million hectares in 1969 to 3 million hectares in 1974). The Committee in their report (1969) had expressed concern over this matter and had felt that if this trend was allowed to continue unchanged the situation might assume alarming proportions particularly in States having a small forest area. They, therefore, recommended that the matter might be placed before the National Development Council for their consideration and it was exactly after 4 years, i.e., on 8/9–12–1973 that it was actually placed before the Council. The Committee regret to observe that Government have not paid due attention to the Committee's recommendation and *during the period of last 3 years ending 1972–73 an area of 1.71 million hectares has been allowed to be deforested in different States.* The Committee is of the opinion that had Government paid serious attention to this problem and taken measures to implement their earlier recommendation that simultaneous steps should be taken to afforest suitable areas equal to those which had to be deforested on account of implementation of plan project, etc., the position would have been much better than it is today ... The Committee note that judging from the national and international standards, the position with respect to forest area in our country is extremely unsatisfactory. Having regard to the fact that forests are useful in many ways, viz., they increase the incidence of rainfall, regulate water supply, reduce the intensity of flood, restrict soil

erosion, are a vital ecological necessity and have important biological, aesthetic, wild life and touristic values, supply raw materials for forest based industries, provide employment to local people, etc., the Committee recommend that the following steps should be taken urgently:

(*i*) Waste-land utilisation survey included in the Fifth Five-Year Plan should now be undertaken and completed early by laying down a time-bound programme in this regard.

(*ii*) The proportion of the area which should be under forest in each State/Union Territory should be clearly indicated. The work should be completed by a specified time.

(*iii*) *No further shrinkage of forest area should be allowed to take place.* In this regard the Committee reiterate their earlier recommendation and also recommend that the proposal approved by the National Development Council that 'any time any forest land is taken out of its use for any purpose whatsoever, must be compensated with another kind of land anywhere else or else in *cash* not merging in the revenue account but remaining in a block fund to buy land under private ownership through acquisition' should be implemented. In this regard, the Committee would also like that in addition to acquisition of land the question of acquiring private forests may also be considered.

All these recommendations have remained merely on paper, and I am not sure if any action will be taken on them in the near future. The recommendations are basically unrealistic also. Lands that are shown as 'waste' on records are actually occupied by villagers and very little waste land is actually in existence.

The strangest part of the situation is that the same Ministry of Agriculture, which in August 1974 recommended the views of the Estimates Committee to the States, set up a Committee of its own three months later to examine the feasibility of leasing out blank areas of forests to farmers under some kind of an agreement. The terms and reference of this Committee are:

1. To assess the extent of blank forest area in various States;
2. To assess how much of these blank areas would be suitable for raising agricultural crops;
3. To recommend the best agency for raising agricultural crops on those forest vacant lands which are suitable for agriculture;
4. To assess the likely impact of these agricultural activities on the neighbouring forest areas; and

5. To prepare a draft agreement under which lease of forest land would be given.

The State Forest Advisory Board in Bihar has also ignored all the advice of the Centre, and the Board's first task, entrusted to it by the State Government, is to evolve methods for releasing further lands from the forests. The fact that nearly a lakh and a half acres of forest land has already been released, which in turn has led to further encroachments, does not seem to bother anyone.

I had known the area covered by the Palamau National Park (which is also not covered by any legislation) as its Divisional Forest Officer and was aware of its potentiality for wild life. One of my first acts as Chief Conservator of Forests in 1960 was to secure the Government's approval to convert this into a National Park and take speedy measures to conserve its indiginous fauna.

The term 'national park' suggests an area which the nation has by law decided to preserve because of its magnificient geological features, especial biological and historical characteristics and where nature displays its finest spectacles; 'Reserves' which appeal to the higher emotions in mankind, and provide opportunity to its people to appreciate environmental values. The Yellow Stone Lake with its shore line of over 160 kilometres, large areas of tundra and naked rocks above the tree line, and roaring geyser attracts over two million visitors each year.

The million head of wildebeest, zebra, Thomson's gazelle and other antelope that congregate on the central plains of Serengeti National Park (Tanzania) only to migrate with the advent of the dry season in a gigantic procession, provides an unique sight unparalleled anywhere in the world. 'To name just a few of the most abundant species there are now over 500,000 wildebeest, 180,000 Thomson's gazelle, 150,000 zebra, 65,000 impala, 50,000 buffaloes, and 25,000 topi' (Schaller). No less magnificient is the view of thousands of wild animals on the crater floor from the rim of the Ngorongoro crater. The very vastness of these unique, world famous parks—Yellow Stone is some 10,000 sq. kilometres, Serengeti 14,500 sq. kilometres, and Tsavo 20,000 sq. kilometres—gives one the feeling of being in a wilderness, as enchanting as what the first explorers had experienced when they came across them before the advent of civilisation.

Not all the parks in the world are, however, so vast. The two famous parks of Uganda which are noted for their lakes and geographical spectacles; the Murchison Falls (renamed Kabalega) and Queen Elizabeth (renamed Rwenzori)—are only 3,900 sq. kilometres and 2,000 sq. kilometres respectively in area. The Kidepo Valley Park in Uganda is a bare 1,300 sq. kilometres. Except for a park in Sweden (Sarek and its adjacent areas) which is some 5,000 sq. kilometres, the highly populated small countries of Europe do not have large wilderness areas: the Camargue Park in France is a bare 130 sq. kilometres in extent.

The National Park Movement in India is yet young, nor do we have Parks of the size and grandeur of Yellow Stone in America or Serengeti or Ngorongoro in Tanzania. The oldest National Park in India, Corbett, was set up in 1935 and covers only 560 square kilometres. Kanha in Madhya Pradesh—perhaps the best National Park we have—is a bare 250 square kilometres in extent. Nor, for that matter, do our National Parks boast of such spectacular natural wonders as the 'Old Faithful' and Mount Kilimanjaro. However, we have made a beginning and we can only hope that the movement will grow in this country in the years to come.

The two National Parks in Bihar—Hazaribagh and Palamau—have been poorly equipped by Nature. Besides, in neither of them can one see tiger as easily as one can in Kanha. But it would have been folly to lament over what nature had not given us and not done our best to develop what we do have. The progress in the last twenty years has been encouraging beyond expectations, and if any single measure can claim credit for bringing about an awareness about conservation among the urban educated it is the establishment of these two parks. For they are like two temples where anyone interested can learn what life in the wild is like and where they can develop an understanding of and compassion for the voiceless denizens of the forests. The sight of a sambar stag in Hazaribagh, or a herd of gaur in Palamau, moving placidly, unmindful of visitors, is exciting in itself.

It would also have been unwise to have waited till we had people trained in park management, desirable as that would have been, before starting these two parks. We would have been beaten by the ruthless march of time. Our park management practices are simple. Apart from permanent small water retention dams built especially for animals inside the parks, we dig and maintain, in the hot months of April to June, a large number of temporary water-holes in the forest to replace the parched streams. This is possible because they carry sub-soil water only a few inches below their dry sandy surfaces. Artificial salt licks and hundreds of synthetic mineralised salt-slabs provide additional nutrients. All animals need the same groups of nutrients (protein, carbohydrates, fats, minerals and vitamins) in similar proportions, and animals in the wild obtain them from forest vegetation. The ruminant herbivores like sambar, cheetal, gaur and nilgai—with which we are primarily concerned—employ the microflora of their rumen to alter the low value grass and other vegetable protein to high value microbial protein. The vegetation feeds the microflora which in turn feeds the animals. In the summer months, when the trees are leafless and the grass and shrubs on the forest floors dry up, the browsers and grazers have to do with a meagre diet; the artificial licks, mineralised synthetic salt-slabs and assured water supply that we provide are a great aid to them in these lean months. Otherwise, during the period from June to October, the animals get ample sustenance from natural growth when the first monsoon showers cause the forest floors and canopies to blossom forth in luscious greenery.

The rehabilitation of sambar in Hazaribagh and of cheetal and gaur in Palamau are examples of how animals respond to these facilities and to a protected habitat. Though preservation of the habitat and prevention of killing are the *sine qua non* of success, our achievements would have been more impressive had we succeeded in closing the park areas to grazing. In this effort, unfortunately, we have not succeeded and cattle continue to graze merrily inside both Hazaribagh and Palamau. In its report of August 1970, the Expert Committee of the Indian Board for Wild Life states: 'Grazing is a major problem in all the National Parks and Sanctuaries of India. In Kaziranga, Manas, Jaldapara, Kanha, Bandogarh, the problem is fairly easy to tackle. In Corbett, Madumalai and Taroba grazing has had disastrous consequences. Grazing in Bandipur, Periyar, the sanctuaries of Andhra Pradesh, Sariska, Bharatpur, Gir,

Hazaribagh, Palamau, Dachigam and Daksum is also a serious hazard to wild life.' To me, the future of Betla—the hub of Palamau Park—seems to hang by a tenuous thread. The damage to vegetation and competition for food caused by the presence of domestic cattle is being aggravated by wild elephants, and the locality is showing signs of biological instability, threatening the survival of cheetal, sambar and gaur. The danger to the Betla area is very real and steps must be taken promptly to combat it.

While Americans are legitimately proud of the success of the National Park idea that has travelled the world over from the country of its origin, the present day analysts of their park policy are in a great quandary: how can more and more people who own parks continue to enjoy them without damaging their natural qualities? While only some twenty thousand people visit Hazaribagh and Palamau annually, even this small number causes disturbances. This is specially so in the summer months when the thirsty animals congregate at the water-holes in the morning and evening which is when the majority of the visitors also gather and thereby disturb the animals. We do not have a 'Park Service' to help a visitor understand the Park's ecology and how best to use and enjoy Parks without impairing them or disturbing their inhabitants.

The tourist-park relationship needs to be understood properly. Some tourists want to have a relaxing holiday, others seek the excitement of exploring an untamed environment, and there are some—though only a microscopic few—who see in a park the opportunity to learn and understand the 'law of nature'. The principle of zonation to cater to these three needs, is being increasingly recognised in other parts of the world. The Hazaribagh National Park, with its limited area and little room for expansion, does not offer scope to put this zonal concept into practice, but Palamau National Park, in the very nature of its configuration, seems to be tailor-made for it. This Park, if expanded to include the whole of Baresand and other adjacent sanctuaries (now within Project Tiger), can be suitably divided into three zones. The Betla area at the Park's entrance with its modern amenities and easy accessibility, can cater, as in fact it does even now, to the needs of those visitors who, although they desire a holiday in a forest environment, do not want to do with-out modern facilities. This group of visitors forms by far the largest proportion of the twenty thousand tourists who come to Palamau annually. The area a little further south, covering all the forests around Mundu, Lat and Kumandih, can be the intermediate zone to cater to those who desire to probe into the wilderness and go for treks to enjoy wilderness life style. This will also reduce the strain on the tiny Betla area. The deeper forests of Baresand, still further south, could be the zone restricted exclusively for study and investigations by scientists and serious visitors.

That 'Project Tiger' at this stage of our park development covers not only the existing park area of 245 square kilometres, but also an additional area of 585 square kilometres described above, is a happy augury for the park's future. This compact area of over 800 square kilometres can be one of the finest National Parks in the country. All that is required is a will to put an end to commercial feelings, even after the expiry of the 'Project Tiger' period.

In any case, what we in the Forest Service can do to educate the people with respect to wild life is very limited. What is needed is a much greater and concerted effort on the part of the powers that be in this country. For a start, to quote the words of the Prime Minister, 'Forestry practices designed to squeeze the last rupee out of our jungles, must be radically oriented at least within our National Parks ...' She goes on to pose the fundamental question: 'Is it beyond our political will and administrative ingenuity to set aside about one or two per cent of our forests in their pristine glory for the purpose?' Part of the problem is that there was no uniform wild life code in the country till recently and each State has so far had the discretion to follow whatever policy it liked in this matter. Shri Fakhruddin Ali Ahmad, then Minister of Agriculture, said in a letter dated 29 March 1972 to Shri Kedar Pande, Chief Minister, Bihar:

> No nation has such a rich and varied fauna as India and yet of late the rapid decimation of India's wild life has few parallels. Areas once teeming with wild life are quite devoid of them and the few sanctuaries and parks where wild life now seeks refuge have a tenuous status. Some animals and birds are already extinct and certain others are on the verge of being so ... It is, therefore, imperative that the country should have a

uniform Wild Life Conservation and Management Bill which would make provision for the control of not only hunting but also of trade and traffic in wild life produce, and for the conservation and management of the wild life habitat.

In an informal meeting of conservationists held by the Prime Minister in September, 1970, it was resolved that the Union Government should bring forth such a uniform enactment, relating to wild life conservation. Since Wild Life (Protection of Wild Animals and Birds) is a State subject, before such legislation can be initiated in Parliament, the Legislative Assemblies of two States must adopt a resolution under Article 252 (1) of the Constitution delegating the power of passing such a law to Parliament. In those States where there are Legislative Councils also, the resolution will have to be passed by both Houses.

The Prime Minister herself followed this up by a personal request in her letter of 12 April 1972 addressed to Shri Pande and other Chief Ministers:

I have written to you in the past about wild life conservation and management. Although there is now greater consciousness about this problem than a few years ago, we have not been able to significantly arrest the continuing decline of our fauna, including many endangered species. Poaching is on the increase, and we continue to receive reports of a lucrative trade in the furs and pelts of even those animals, like the tiger, whose shooting is in law prohibited throughout the country. Regrettably some State emporia are also involved in this business.

My colleague, the Agriculture Minister, has already written to you about the difficulties of controlling trade and taxidermy in the absence of a uniform Central law applicable to the entire country. Experts are unanimous that only an integrated and country-wide policy of wild life conservation and management can arrest the present precipitous decline. I have also received several urgent appeals from the World Wild Life Fund.

It is for these reasons that we now seek your co-operation to enact Central legislation on wild life conservation and management. A new Bill incorporating the most recent thinking on wild life management has been prepared. The Bill also provides specific remedies in the Indian context which will make it possible for the Central and State Governments to deal effectively with the more insidious threats to our fauna.

> This is not a political issue. It concerns the survival of our famous natural heritage. It is hard to think of an India devoid of its magnificent animals, of the hard-pressed tiger, for instance, going the way of the now extinct Indian Cheetah. Past experience reveals the limitations of the regional approach, with State laws frequently at variance with one another and all the attendant difficulties of implementation. The Centre and the States must now act in concert on the basis of common legislation which should be strictly enforced.
>
> I, therefore, request you to get a resolution passed in your Legislature in accordance with Clause 1 of Article 252 of the Constitution as early as possible.

The President gave his assent to the Bill passed by Parliament on 9 September 1972 and it was applied to Bihar from February 1973. But the enactment of this piece of legislation did not improve matters straightaway. For example, it took the Government of Bihar sixteen months to approve the rules under the Act, and it has, on the whole, been indifferent to the necessity of enforcing the Act. As a result, the stringent penalties provided in the Act for illicit shooting in Sanctuaries and National Parks have yet to make any impact. To take an example, some five months after the application of this Act to Bihar, a motor car was apprehended in broad daylight at the Betla check post of the Palamau National Park with a dead cheetal in its boot and a gun inside the vehicle. The car and the gun were seized and the six occupants were prosecuted in the court for the alleged offence. While the accused persons were released on bail, the car and the gun were impounded. An appeal for their release was rejected by the district judge with the observation that 'the law was quite clear on the point that the vehicle could be seized, more particularly when it was found loaded with the killed animal and was caught in that condition at the check post. According to the provisions of the Wild Life (Protection) Act such vehicles are also liable to be forfeited to the State.'

With the judicial system as it is in this country, it takes two to three years, and even more, before cases are heard. This case was just coming up for hearing when, to our great astonishment, the Government decided to withdraw it on the grounds of 'State and Public Policy' without consulting me. I protested strongly against this. Those of us who have worked hard to save the wild life of Bihar feel frustrated by such incidents. We do not know what 'public policy' could be involved in this criminal case. This was the first case to be initiated under the new Act and we had pursued it zealously. In what way the criminal prosecution of the poachers conflicted with the Prime Minister's advice and directive that wild life conservation was not a 'political issue' and that poachers were to be dealt with effectively, is hard to understand. Unfortunately, politics and personalities seem at times to contaminate all policies and programmes in Bihar. This matter somehow reached New Delhi and at the intervention of the Cabinet Secretary to Prime Minister, the Bihar Government rescinded its order and the case is once more before the trial court. It is no wonder that the withdrawal of this case encouraged others to violate the sanctity of the Palamau National Park. Only a month later, on Christmas eve 1974, a two-year old gaur calf was shot at night and while the poachers were busy dismembering it the following morning, they were apprehended by the game warden. A member of a nearby Christian Mission is allegedly involved. The forest staff have been prompt in instituting the case in the court but are keeping their fingers crossed lest the ghost of 'public policy' raises its head again and the case is withdrawn by the Government.

Earlier, in January 1970, a prosperous farmer settled on the outskirts of Champaran forest adjoining Nepal is alleged to have shot a tiger assisted by the local Sub-Inspector of Police. To cover up the offence, the Sub-Inspector, it is said, manoeuvered to get a complaint filed in the police station by a villager to the effect that his grandfather had been eaten up by a tiger in the forest. Without informing the Divisional Forest Officer, the Sub-Inspector wrote directly to the Sub-divisional Magistrate, Betla (in those days only the District Magistrate could declare a tiger a 'man-eater') requesting that the tiger be declared a man-eater. But even before the magistrate could take any action, the tiger was shot dead in the Sanctuary. Ironically, at about the same time, Dr. Karan Singh, Chairman of the Indian Board of Wild Life, wrote to Shri Nityanand Kanungo, the Governor of Bihar, about the position of the tiger in India:

> The steady decline in the tiger population of our country has been causing great concern. The Prime Minister has expressed her anxiety over the situation and has suggested a complete moratorium on the killing of tigers for 5 years. A meeting of the International Union of Conservation of Nature and Natural Resources held recently in Delhi also took note of this grave threat to the tiger population and recommended a moratorium on the killing of this animal till the correct trend of the tiger population is ascertained through ecological studies.
>
> This problem was also subsequently discussed in the Executive Committee of the Indian Board for Wild Life, and it was decided to recommend that there should be a complete moratorium on the shooting of this beautiful animal with effect from 1st July 1970 for five years, so that the declining trend is arrested. Of course, an exception can be made in the event of a tiger being declared a man-eater.
>
> Wild life has come down to us as a priceless heritage and it is our duty to see that it is passed on to posterity enriched. I would, therefore, in my capacity as Chairman of the Indian Board for Wild Life, strongly urge that you may issue suitable instructions for the implementation of the recommendation of the Indian Board for Wild Life I have quoted above.
>
> I shall be glad to know, in due course, of the action taken by your Government in this regard.

On receipt of this report of a tiger having been killed in Champaran, I wrote to the Secretary in the Forest Department citing Dr. Karan Singh's letter and requesting him to institute an enquiry into this incident. I never heard anything in reply, in spite of my verbal reminders. No enquiry of any kind was made and the case, already over five years old, has yet to come up in the court even for a preliminary hearing.

In July 1973 in a forest Sanctuary of Rohtas district, a tiger trap was set by a poacher dealing in tiger and leopard skins, at the spot where a tigress, with two cubs by her side, had killed a buffalo calf the previous evening. While the tigress escaped with one cub, the second one was unfortunately trapped and was cruelly shot dead the following morning while it was still struggling to free itself from the trap. The Range Officer of Forests recovered the skull of the cub from the spot. He was also able to recover the uncured skin by laying a trap for the poacher. A member of the forest staff pretended to be a customer and offered him a handsome sum of money for the skin. The poacher accepted the offer and fell into the trap. The skin, some six feet in length, showed that the cub was probably about two years old. A case was filed in July 1973, the first offence concerning a tiger after the application of the Wild Life (Protection) Act to Bihar. It is now February 1975 and the case is yet to come up for a hearing.

There was yet another incident in the same area. A Government officer of the rank of Executive Engineer is alleged to have had the forest check post forcibly opened at night and shot a sambar using a government vehicle. As the incident concerned a Government servant, the matter was reported to the department concerned as well as to the Forest Secretary, and at the time of going to press no action seems to have been taken. Perhaps it is too early for the law court to take notice, the incident took place in April 1974. The latest that I have heard is that the accused officer has been granted a long adjournment of eight months by the court, at his request.

Much will also depend on how we go about the business of setting up a suitable administrative machinery for wild life management in the country. The notion that wild life should be looked after by an altogether separate service and that the present forestry personnel are ill-equipped for it, has been debated for quite some time. To support this argument, it is often stated the East African countries have different personnel for their game reserves and their forests. But few people realise that, in those countries, the wild life live in open grassy savannahs, unlike India where the bulk of wild life lives in forests. Wild life and forests have to co-exist in this country.

Even if a separate wild life service is created, I doubt if it will attract men with the necessary aptitude and dedication. As it is, the Indian Forest Service is less glamorous than the other two existing All-India Services. A Wild Life Service will be still less so. The Indian Forest Service was revived so that available talent could be dispersed and in the hope that meritorious youngsters would join this service. But this hope, unfortunately, has been belied. In the seven two-year courses between 1968–70 to 1974–76, out of the 116 persons who were selected for training at the Indian Forest

College, Dehra Dun, for the IFS, as many as forty left during the course of the training for other services. Not only that, they left largely for the Indian Administrative and the Indian Police Services a few of them went to the State Bank, and the Central Engineering, Revenue, Indian Ordinance and Railway Services. The situation in the country at present is such that it is not only the salary but the pomp and power that goes with a service that also influences meritorious young men wanting to join it. As long as such a situation exits, the Wild Life Service will continue to be unpopular, and will mostly attract the left overs.

Considering all the pros and cons of the matter, certain guidelines have very recently been issued to the State Governments by the Government of India to establish immediately a separate Wild Life Wing under the overall charge of the Chief Conservator of Forests. An Officer of the rank of Additional Chief Conservator of Forests will head this wing. An officer of the rank of Additional Inspector-General of Forests at the Centre is to co-ordinate and direct the activities of the Wild Life Wings in the various States. It is envisaged that members of the Forest Service trained or experienced in wild life management will join the new wing without loss of rank.

The Prime Minister approved this proposal for organising a Wild Life Wing in the various States in her note dated 18 September 1974:

> Training the next generation of wild life managers is crucial. I am not sure whether we have the necessary expertise within the country. We should not hesitate to look abroad for the skills we may need. Possibly UNESCO or UNDP could help in providing a small group of foreign experts to be deployed both at the Forest Research Institute, Dehra Dun, and at the Centre to help in training and to keep a watchful eye on our evolving wild life programme.
>
> In order to maintain performance standards, all persons directly or indirectly concerned with wild life management should be regularly assessed in their annual reports for their performance in wild life conservation work.
>
> The Unit at the Centre will have an important role to play, especially in the early stages. It should be staffed at a high level by specially selected officers, so that it has the means to persuade and assist the States.

Subject to these observations, the proposal regarding the Wild Life Wing is approved.

Success in the conservation of wild life will, in the ultimate analysis, depend on the interest taken by the State Governments and their Forest Departments. Forestry and wild life being State subjects, the Centre can only use persuasive methods. While there is no hostility as such against wild life, there is colossal indifference to it both at the political and administrative levels. Lack of political courage is another serious handicap to contend with. The future will hinge on how soon this indifference vanishes and is replaced by courage and keenness, and how soon those in power realise that ecology and conservation are no longer a matter of aesthetics, but one of survival—a biological necessity.

M. Krishnan

Looking Back on Project Tiger

M. Krishnan was a man of varied interests, as knowledgeable about Tamil literature as about India's wildlife, and a fine prose writer as well as illustrator. He wrote the famous 'Country Notebook' column in *The Statesman*, often highlighting the world of unspectacular, backyard animals.

M. Krishnan as a member of the Steering Committee of Project Tiger. He spent much of his time in the late 1970s and early 1980s reviewing Project Tiger and its management system.

(Photo overleaf courtesy Valmik Thapar.)

Project Tiger was inaugurated in April 1973 at the Corbett National Park, one of the nine Tiger Reserves. Three years have passed since then, and although the project got off to a necessarily slow start, much work has been done towards its implementation and it has received wide publicity. Still, most people think of it entirely as a concerted attempt to save the tiger in India, the land in which this most magnificent of the greater cats is best known and still has (inspite of sustained slaughter over centuries) its largest and widest-spread population. That it certainly is, but it is also very much more than that. In fact, is the most ambitious and realistic conservation scheme attempted so far, and I think it is the solution to certain conservation problems inherent in the democratic set up of India.

It is useful to recapitulate the circumstances that led to Project Tiger, to appreciate its magnitude and scope. That the tiger was declining rapidly in India was no new realisation—grave fears over its future were expressed fifty years ago. The need to save other animals typical of India's wildlife, some more seriously threatened and exclusively Indian (unlike the tiger), was also realised long ago. However, the attempt to save endangered animals was made piecemeal, on the basis of legislative and field protection accorded to particular species; this did achieve success in a few instances, notably in two feats of conservation of recent times, the saving of the Great Indian Rhinoceros in Assam and Bengal and the Asiatic Lion in Gujarat: it is significant that in both cases it was dedicated protection in the field and the preservation of the natural environment that led to success. But in spite of such instances, India's wildlife, both faunal and floristic, continued to decline generally, and several threatened animals were not conserved efficiently.

Two things happened to give a fillip to the country's conservation effort. In 1969, the International Union for the Conservation of Nature [IUCN] met in New Delhi, and the interest of western countries in our wildlife problems was roused. In 1970 the Expert Committee appointed by the Indian Board for Wild Life [IBWL] published its report: *inter alia*, this report stressed the importance

Extract from *The Times of India Annual 1977*.

of preserving the country's flora as an integral part of its wildlife and for the first time defined the term "wildlife" to include the flora, analysed the very small percentage (about 4 per cent) of forest land occupied by existing and even proposed sanctuaries, and pointed out the necessity for total environmental conservation and freedom from human disturbance in preserving wildlife.

Mounting concern for the alarmingly depleted tiger resulted in the Operation Tiger of the IUCN, which considered the problem and chose India as the country where the tiger had its best chance, and the World Wildlife Fund made a most generous offer of money for this purpose. The IBWL and Indian naturalists were also exercised, independently, by the problem: clearly the mere prohibition of tiger-hunting and the ban on the export of tiger skins would not suffice, and more constructive steps had to be taken.

It is at this juncture that the nature of conservation problems inherent in our democratic organisation and in any scheme soundly based on total environmental conservation, should be mentioned. Under the constitution, each state had sovereign power over its forests and, in fact, the entire wildlife wealth of India is in the hands of the states. Therefore, no national scheme for conservation can be enforced by the Centre, without the active cooperation of the states—and as mentioned already, the tiger today is thinly distributed all over the country.

Further, although unquestionably the roundest and most certain way to assure the continued survival of any wild animal is to protect not merely the particular species but its entire environment, such a scheme requires adequate territory—one cannot reasonably expect nature to maintain its own balance in too cramped a space.

It was necessary to secure large tracts of forests in different parts of India to constitute the Tiger Reserves and to eliminate human claims on these forests, and such vast tracts, free from human intrusion, were not readily available.

Project Tiger seeks to solve these problems by the Centre providing a substantial part of the funds (this includes the contribution of WWF, the Central provision being roughly four times that of the WWF's) needed to run each Tiger Reserve and asking the concerned state to follow the plan of Project Tiger—the state would also contribute to the expense of the project in some ways. The project is to be implemented in five years, and thereafter, too, the states will continue to conserve their Tiger Reserve according to the plan. The total contribution of the Centre and the WWF over the five-year period will be about Rs. 4 crores.

The response of the participating states has been generous in the large areas of reserved forests they have added to existing sanctuaries so as to make available the territory needed for a Tiger Reserve. In each reserve there is a substantial core area, which is free of human claims and activities, and a buffer zone around which will also provide for visitors and accommodation for the project staff. Villages are to be moved out of the core and no cattle grazing or other forms of human intrusion will be allowed in it. The nine Tiger Reserves selected for the project are widely separated and quite dissimilar in their terrain and flora, and even in their faunal features, though, naturally, all have been chosen because they are known to hold tigers, associate predators, and prey animals in plenty, and also adequate water, fodder and cover. Though more may be added to them in the future, for the present, these are the nine chosen reserves: the Corbett National Park of Uttar Pradesh; Ranthambhore in Rajasthan; the Kanha National Park of Madhya Pradesh; Palamau in Bihar; Simlipal in Orissa; Melghat in Maharashtra; Manas in Assam; the Sunderbans of West Bengal and Bandipur in Karnataka.

... The entire area of each reserve will be strictly protected, and a quite adequate organisation of this, fully equipped, has already been set up in each reserve. There is also provision for research studies in them.

The net result is that under Project Tiger there are now nine different large reserves, each with its distinctive individuality, and each typical of a part of India, where total environmental protection (something not so far attempted in India right from the time when wildlife conservation first began, in the days of Asoka) will obtain. It is not only the tiger that will be benefited by the provision of an entirely natural ecological setting. The wild vegetation on which varied and heavy human demands have been made till now, the other mammals, the birds and the lesser life will all be benefited.

The main contribution of the human effort will be effective and vigilant protection from poaching and disturbance. Indeed, if this is done, the rest can be left to the sure and infinitely complex ability of nature to look after itself.

A brief account of the dominant character and main animals of each reserve would be in order—but first things first—the tiger first. People all over the country, and even outside, must now be familiar with the figures cited to show the great decline of tigers in India, that there were 40,000 tigers a century ago but that today they have dwindled to under 2,000. The last figure, based on counts (mainly of pug-marks) is probably near enough to be acceptable, but on what basis was the figure 40,000 reached? I do not know. Reading the old shikar literature of India one does get the impression that tigers were quite common in the forests then, and that the forests were far vaster in extent, but then this old literature extends over a century. Even so, not the 40,000!

Beyond all question the main reason for the decline has been the systematic hunting down of tigers by all possible means over a long period. It had been argued by some that the decline of the natural prey species has probably not been a contributory factor, since the prey animals are still there in small numbers where tigers have become locally extinct. This argument is not valid. Always the predator dies out well in advance of the prey, and an abundance of prey is essential for its survival in the face of sustained human hostility.

However, tigers prey on a quite surprising variety of animals, big and small: when hard pressed, they will even hunt frogs; on the other hand, they take young elephants and rhino calves when they can, and can kill an adult gaur—though I have seen gaur in a herd effectively warding off a tiger by a concerted defensive action. All kinds of deer, nilgai (not much fancied, however), pig and even hares and peafowl are hunted. An interesting animal found in all the reserves is the porcupine, whose plump flesh all predators love. When desperately cornered, the porcupine charges in reverse gear and drives the strong, needle-sharp quills on its lower back into the face and chest of the incautious killer coming on it from behind. Leopards and tigers sometimes get badly spitted this way, and the barbed quills penetrate deeper and deeper into their flesh, crippling or even killing them, so that long after it has been killed and eaten, the porcupine extracts a postmortem revenge!

There is no proven record of a melanistic (black) tiger, but the white tiger is a distinct and exclusively Indian race. Or rather, it was. It now survives, apparently, only in captivity, in zoos all over the world. It is not a true albino (if it were, it should have pink eyes) but is albinotic, and is usually of very large size.

The leopard, second only to tiger in size and strength, and equally arresting in its looks, is found in all the reserves—excepting the Sunderbans, probably. Some say that being more versatile it can survive where the tiger cannot, but I think it is no less endangered and dwindling rapidly. Project Tiger should benefit it.

Dhole (the so-called 'wild dog') are the other main predators of these reserves. Jackals and hyenas, both much depleted today, often find their meat, not from god, but from tiger-kills (naturally, when the tiger is not there) and should also be helped by the project.

Chital (excepting in Manas) and wild pig are found in all the reserves. They are the two most adaptable and fecund of our wild animals, and have helped to sustain the tiger (and other predators) over the years. Dhole have served to keep a check on them and prevent them from overrunning the forests, with the decline of tigers and leopards.

Now for the reserves themselves: naturally, only the briefest mention is possible here.

Corbett Park, on the banks of the Ramganga, with the foothills of the Himalayas for a backdrop, has long been noted for its distinctive beauty and its tigers. Lofty stands of sal, sissoo along the river, and vast, rolling maidans are features of its vegetation. This is one of the few areas where the chital and its less attractive cousin, the hog deer, are both to be found: there is a small herd of elephants visiting the park in summer, and in the Ramganga there are mugger and also the rare gharial (fish-eating crocodile, now much depleted) and very large tortoises.

Ranthambhore is a dry deciduous hilltop forest, featuring *dhok* (*Anogeissus pendula*) and *ber* as its main trees. It is the smallest of the reserves, but so tight in its wildlife integrity that it is also one of the most promising. It teems with sambar and fine nilgai—langur, the sloth bear, chital and chinkara are the other main animals. The bird life is rich, and there are small lakes holding a few crocodiles.

Kanha was originally set up to try and save the hardground barasingha which used to roam it in thousands and which had dwindled to under a hundred. This deer now survives in a population of a little over a hundred only here. Sal forests and mixed deciduous forests interspersed with open meadows, and the Banjar valley, give Kanha its peculiar charm. The reserve has always been noted for its tigers and great herds of chital—sambar too, are there in the forests, as also gaur.

Palamau is almost encircled by the rivers Koel and Auranga, but the heat in its deciduous forests during summer dries up the pools, and still the animals stay on, finding such comfort as they can from the few scanty water-holes that remain. A small shifting population of elephants, chital and sambar, and a varied lesser life, and a small population of small-sized gaur, are the main animals of Palamau, besides the tiger and the leopard. The wolf, rare today even in the northern plains, has been seen here.

The Simlipal hills are noted for the vast stretch of sal covering them. Elephants, sambar, chital, peafowl (also found in most other reserves, but outstandingly beautiful here) and a rich and varied bird life are its features.

Melghat is the most recent of the reserves, a reserve featuring low hills and valleys in the Satpuras covered with teak and bamboo forests. Fine gaur, sambar, chital and the other animals of teak forests comprise its fauna.

Manas is a riverain forest along the Manas and its associate rivers, just below the Bhutan hills—there is a close link between the reserve and the Bhutan sanctuary across the water. Manas is noted for its scenic splendour, and the quite distinctive character of its lesser life—among the birds on the river are mergansers, and the Malay tupaia (tree-shrew) occurs here. Magnificent elephants, flights of great pied hornbills across the river, and wild buffaloes, swamp deer and sambar and hog deer are the main features of the reserves.

The Sunderbans, mangrove forests inundated each day by tidal waters, are undoubtedly the most peculiarly distinctive of the reserves. One would think it a poor place for mammalian wildlife but the mammals, including the tiger are there all right, having adapted themselves to a semi-aquatic life.

Bandipur, celebrated for its gaur, chital and elephants, is a mixed deciduous forest—it is the only southern reserve at the moment. It is one of the most promising of the reserves, with a vast tract of interior forest now comprising its core.

Will Project Tiger succeed? One may answer, but how can it fail, being so solidly based on nature's ability to recoup and maintain its own balance, provided depletive factors (all stemming from human activities) are removed, as the project plans to, and adequate territory is provided, as it has been? But, no, of course, it can fail. Any plan, however soundly conceived, can fail in its execution, not only out of lack of care, or ineptitude on the part of the people in charge of it, but also out of overmuch eagerness to get results. This is a project which needs much patience, and faith in nature, and unceasing vigilance, especially in protection, a long-term scheme that will take at least another decade to succeed, or even to fail. It is now very much in the hands of the participating states, and only time can show how well they have discharged their responsibility.

One may argue that as with the best-laid plans of mice and men, something wholly unexpected and freakish may happen. Well, all reasonable contingencies have been thought of. It is possible that with the most carefully guarded protection available to them in the reserves the animals may stray out of it and get killed—though the recent Wildlife Protection Act should take care of that. It is possible that some wholly unforeseen and unforeseeable catastrophe may undo everything in a reserve. But, as the inimitable Jeeves would have said, the contingency is remote.

John Seidensticker

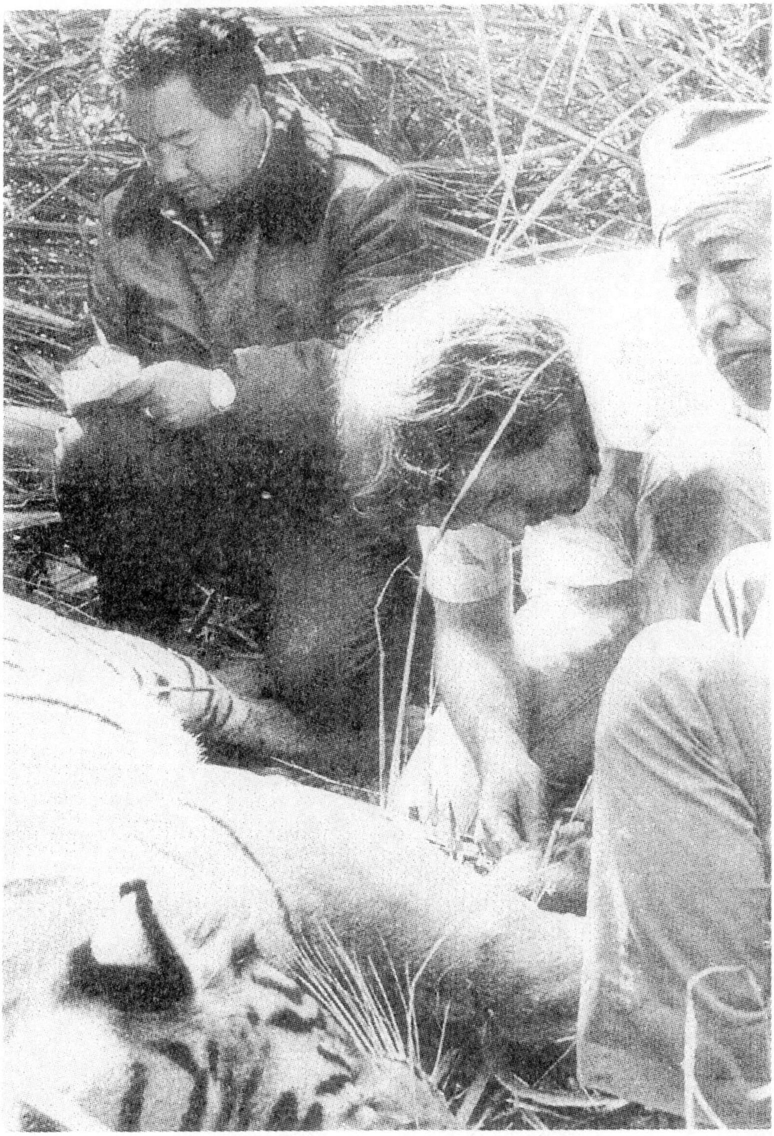

Bearing Witness

John Seidensticker worked in Nepal, and in the Sunderbans of India and Bangladesh. He studied tiger predation in Nepal's Chitawan National Park and was witness to the extinction of the Javan tiger. He is currently Curator of Mammals at the National Zoological Park of the Smithsonian Institute in Washington.

John Seidensticker (centre) after tranquilising one of the first tigers in the world that was radio-collared. This was in 1974 in Chitawan National Park in Nepal.

BEARING WITNESS

If you go to Bali Barat or Meru-Betiri national parks on the Indonesian islands of Bali and Java and talk with the people who live near them and who use the forest, you almost certainly will hear stories of recent encounters with tigers. When I worked there in the late 1970s, people had many stories to tell of encountering a tiger drinking near a temple, or of a tiger that regularly came and rested along a forest stream at a place called Pondok Macan (Tiger Place), and there were many other tiger stories. Animals as metaphysically important as tigers live on in our minds after they are gone. No one wants to be the bearer of the bad news; I too hoped. Why else would I travel half way around the world to be there asking these people about tigers? The lingering image of tigers and the hope they remain a part of the landscape make it difficult to date extinction events and to discover the proximal causes of the extinction.

Some of our oldest tiger fossils have been found in Java and tigers and man have mixed on these Sunda Shelf islands for about that long. Java is one of the most densely-populated areas on earth and yet the tiger was only recently lost and another great beast, the Javan rhino *(Rhinoceros sondaicus)*, still lives in Ujung Kulon, a rain forest jewel. A.R. Wallace described Java in 1861 as:

> Taking it as a whole, and surveying it from every point of view, Java is probably the very finest and most interesting tropical island in the world ... scattered through the country, especially in the eastern part of it, are found buried in lofty forests, temples, tombs and statues of great beauty and grandeur; and the remains of extensive cities, where the tigers, the rhinoceros, and the wild bull now roam undisturbed.

When I worked in Java in the mid-1970s, I was intrigued and impressed that tigers were still extant, a condition that seemed contrary to the dogma of extinction-prone species on which I had

Extracted from *Tigers of the World: The Biology, Biopolitics, Management and Conservation of an Endangered Species,* ed. Ronald L. Tilson and Ulysses S. Seal (New Jersey, 1987). The author-date bracketed references relate to Seidensticker's bibliography which readers may wish to pursue by referring to the book.

been weaned. A good system of nature reserves located in tiger habitat on Java and Bali was established in the mid-1930s and early 1940s but in the end this did not suffice for the Javan tiger.

In addressing the primary task of this symposium, 'A Global Tiger Survival Plan', it will be useful to keep in mind what we know about the extinction of two of the three Sunda Island tiger subspecies.

DATING THE EXTINCTIONS

Java

My Indonesian colleagues and I found tracks of at least three tigers living in the Meru-Betiri National Park (then reserve) in 1976. We found no evidence to suggest that 'effective' reproduction was occurring. Tigers were not confining their movements to the reserve, nor were they using all the reserve area. We found no evidence that suggested any tiger had been killed recently by man, but most people living in the area were misinformed about the plight of the Javan tiger and its survival needs. A track count indicated there may have been three tigers still alive in 1979. After 1979, there has been no confirmable evidence of tigers.

I have attempted to trace the tiger's decline in Java. Two hundred years ago the tiger ranged over most of the island, and as late as the 1850s, tigers were considered a nuisance in some populated areas. By 1940, tigers were found only in the most remote mountain and forested areas. By 1970, the only known tigers were in the Gunung Betiri complex on the eastérn, south coast. This is an isolated region of the Southern Mountains that has been protected in the past from extensive habitat alterations by precipitous and dissected topography. While the last tigers managed to survive there, it was not a habitat where tigers ever occurred at a very high density.

Bali

If we use crude density estimates for tigers in good habit of one adult per 40 sq. km as the basis for an estimate, there were never more than about 125 adult Bali tigers at best at any one time on this 5500 sq. km island.

As I outline below, the Bali tiger population could have been regularly supplemented with tigers from Java swimming the Bali Straits.

We cannot be as precise in reconstructing what happened on Bali as we have been on Java. Most of the known specimens of the Bali tiger entered the world's museums in the 1920s and 1930s and all but one came from western Bali. There are reports that tigers existed in Bali until the 1950s, but we have no specimens from that period. None of Clifford Geertz' informants told him about the presence of tigers when he worked in towns along the southwest coast in the late 1950s, and Lee Talbot did not find evidence of extant tigers when he surveyed Bali in 1960. The Bali Barat Game Reserve (20,000 ha) was established in 1941, and in the 1960s and 1970s, much of the adjacent forest land was planted in forest plantations. I suspect that most, if not all, Bali tigers were eliminated from the Island by the end of World War II. It is possible that the stragglers reported in the 1950s were immigrants swimming the 2.5 km wide Bali Straits from the Baluran Reserve on Java. Tigers in the Sundarbans swim much larger tidal rivers. The Bali tiger was extinct about half a century after it was first described to science by Schwarz (1912).

ENVIRONMENTAL STRESSES AND TIGER EXTINCTION

Java

Wet-rice or *sawah* agriculture is the basis of the high human populations on Java, and in some areas, Java supports 2,000 people per sq. km. *Sawah* cultivation developed in Java in the rich alluvial basins surrounded by volcanoes and un-irrigable limestone hills. The alluvial coastal plains that comprise about half of the island were malaria-infested and posed technical irrigation problems; they were largely ignored for cultivation until the mid-1800s. From the mid-1800s through the beginning of the World War I, the Culture System efficiently and systematically brought nearly all remaining cultivatable lands in Java under production.

The period between the Wars saw little increase in cultivatable lands. Just before World War II, it was estimated that 23 per cent of the island remained under forest cover. During World War II, there was widespread deforestation without replanting. From 1950 through 1970, many of the remaining forest tracts were converted to plantations of teak *(Tectona grandis)*, especially in east Java. These teak forests are generally depauperate of wildlife. By 1975, 85 million people lived in Java with less than eight per cent of the land under forest cover.

Tigers and other wildlife declined as forested areas, alluvial plains, and river basins were converted for use in agriculture. As habitat contracted rapidly, set-guns and poison were used to remove unwanted tigers, and it was also reported that many tigers fell victim to eating poisoned wild boar.

During the 1920s and 1930s, a system of reserves was established in Java. By the mid-1960s tigers survived only in Ujung Kulon, Leuweng Sancang, and Baluran. Tigers did not survive in these reserves after mid-1960s when major civil unrest rocked the island and the reserves were sometimes used as sanctuaries by armed groups. Also during this period, disease reduced the rusa *(Cervus timorensis)* population in reserves and in many forest areas on Java.

By 1970, tigers survived only in a rugged area on the Southeast coast known as Meru-Betiri. This was established as a 50,000 ha. game reserve only in 1972. Large-scale plantation agriculture came to this and much of the surrounding area after World War II. Most of the areas below 1,000 m surrounding the Meru-Betiri reserve were planted in teak, coffee and rubber trees. Tiger density and home range size are strongly and positively correlated with biomass of large cervid prey. Essential tiger habitat in the Meru-Betiri Reserve where we would expect good numbers of cervids, including the lower alluvial river flood plains, had been converted to plantations. By 1976, an estimated 7,000 people lived there. A few banteng *(Bos javanicus)* used the forest or plantation edge, but there were no rusa surviving in the reserve. The tiger did not survive under these conditions.

When the system of small reserves was established on Java in the 1930s, they were nestled in expanses of forest that still covered about 25 per cent of the island. These reserves became increasingly fragmented and isolated through the next decades as forest was removed and plantations expanded. The areas where the last

Javan tigers did hang on were in the largest, most diverse, and remote blocks of contiguous habitat on the island. Gunung Betiri and associated river systems, Ujung Kulon-Halimun, and the Southern Mountains. With fragmentation, the largest contiguous forest blocks are 500 sq. km or less, and tigers did not survive in blocks of tropical high rain forest of this size. We would not expect these areas to support over 5–10 adult tigers, at best, at any one time (Sunquist 1981). Today there is no room on Java for tigers.

Bali

The Balinese culture and political system developed around intensive wet-rice agriculture on palm-fringed terraces up to 700 m., especially on the southern slopes of the volcanoes. Major land-use changes were late in coming to Bali. When plantation and small-labour agriculture for export did become established in the late 1880s, development focused on the northern slopes of the volcanoes and the narrow alluvial strip around the island. The relatively barren and unproductive southern peninsula and eastern end of the island were largely ignored. The Dutch did not establish colonial control until about 1910. The major gorges and spurs and the instability wrought by frequent earthquakes made establishing a road net for the island difficult, and it has only recently been completed. The collection sites for the last tigers were largely at the end of the road system as it existed in western Bali in the 1930s. Dutch tourist literature describes tiger hunting in western Bali in the 1930s and apparently that is where the Dutch hunters, A. and B. Ledeboer, killed most of their tigers.

The Bali Barat National park, located on the western tip of Bali, includes the area where the last Bali tigers were collected in the late 1930s. This is an important conservation area. The area of the Park that includes the former Bali Barat Reserve has been fragmented and there is little natural forest remaining. On Bali, as in Java, there is no room today for tigers.

Coup De Grace

The *coup de grace* to tigers in these small areas was stochastic processes or the human condition, depending on your point of view: (1) widespread poisoning during the period while habitat was being rapidly reduced, (2) uncontrolled fragmentation of the forest during the social disruption of World War II and events following, (3) loss of critical ungulate prey populations to disease, and (4) civil unrest of the 1960s resulting in tigers killed by armed groups seeking sanctuary in these reserves. There is not much a wildlife manager can do about this class of problem. However, we can learn the lessons from the extinction of these Sunda Island tigers: (1) it is dangerous to rely on small, isolated reserves as a means to assure the long-term survival of wild tigers; (2) large tracts of contiguous habitat are essential to assure the long-term survival of wild tigers. What will become of other wild tiger populations if these lessons do not become principles in long-term tiger conservation efforts?

Guy Mountfort

WANTED

ALIVE

for its beauty, grace, and contribution to the living world.
Fifty years ago there were 100,000 tigers.
Now there are barely 5,000.
The tiger is doomed unless we act now.

Support Operation Tiger

the World Wildlife Fund's International Campaign to save
the tiger and its forest home.

REWARD

satisfaction at having helped to save
a species threatened with extinction.

Back from the Brink

Guy Mountfort was a naturalist whose interest in wildlife began in childhood. He was a founder of the World Wildlife Fund and played a critical role in the launch of Project Tiger. He worked tirelessly to save tigers, specially within South Asia.

This advertisement reveals the campaign of the early 1970s which went a long way to save wild tigers. Mountfort spearheaded this campaign and travelled across South Asia in his efforts to keep the tiger alive.

I was convinced that there was still a fair chance of saving at least the Indian race [of tiger], which the world knew best as the 'Royal Bengal Tiger', providing that three conditions were fulfilled. First, the scientific resources of the IUCN would have to be brought to bear on the techniques involved in such a difficult operation. Second, the willing cooperation of the governments concerned would have to be obtained. Third, the considerable cost of such a multi-national effort would have to be underwritten by the World Wildlife Fund.

I had taken negotiations concerning the first and third conditions as far as I could. The task now centred on the second and I therefore set out to see whether I could interest the heads of state in my proposals. I knew from previous negotiations that I had undertaken on behalf of the World Wildlife Fund, that if I could obtain the backing of the head of state, all doors would be open to me when it came to working out the details with government departments; whereas if I opened negotiations at lower levels I was often frustrated by bureaucracy.

My first visit was to Mrs Indira Gandhi, the Indian Prime Minister. With me were Charles de Haes, now Director General of the WWF, and Zafar Futehally, Vice-President of WWF India. I knew that Mrs Gandhi had inherited a deep interest in wildlife from her father Pandit Jawaharlal Nehru. She said she had seen me on television the previous night and was therefore aware of my interest in the tiger, which she regarded as a national symbol of India.

Seizing this opening, I outlined my proposals. If the Indian government were to support us and would also create a number of special reserves in areas where tigers were still relatively numerous, the IUCN would help in drafting plans for their scientific management and the necessary research. Also the WWF would raise the equivalent of a million dollars (£400,000 at that time) so that the reserves could be equipped to the highest standards. Although it was impossible to save all the tigers elsewhere in India, if these reserves were established and effective legislation against poaching and the black-market export of skins were enforced, the tiger could still be

Extract from *Saving the Tiger* by Guy Mountfort (London, 1981).

saved from extinction. De Haes, with his wisdom in negotiations of this kind, was quick to remark that such a programme could only succeed if directed and co-ordinated by the highest authority.

To my delight, the Prime Minister agreed without hesitation. 'I shall form a special committee—a Tiger Task Force,' she said, 'and it will report to me personally.'

A little stunned by the speed of her decision. I asked tentatively if I might repeat this at my press conference that evening. 'Certainly,' she replied.

India Takes the Initiative

The Tiger Task Force was appointed the next day. The chairman was Dr Karan Singh, one of India's most dynamic politicians and at that time Minister of Tourism and Civil Aviation. My old friend Kailash Sankhala was put in charge of implementing the programme, which later came to be called 'Project Tiger'. Zafar Futehally served as the link with the IUCN WWF. Field surveys were made and a list of reserves proposed. A six-year plan, involving the expenditure of no less than £2,300,000 ($5,900,000) was approved by the government. A further budget that extended the programme until 1984 was approved later, nearly doubling the original figure. Bearing in mind India's tremendous economic and social problems, this set a magnificent example to the rest of Asia.

Before moving on to Bangladesh I attended a big press conference convened by Dr Karan Singh. In the course of a splendid speech, he said, 'During the hundred years of the British Raj, Englishmen slaughtered our tigers. Now an Englishman is leading a crusade to save them.' I thought this rather a wry comment even though justified by history. However, it was said with a smile.

In Dacca, capital of the new state of Bangladesh (formerly East Pakistan), I quickly obtained a meeting first with the new President, Justice Abu Syed Choudhury, and then with Prime Minister Sheikh Mujibur Rahman, the leader of the revolution which had succeeded, with India's aid, in gaining independence from Pakistan. Everyone was still in a state of euphoria over the victory, as well as being shocked at the devastation that it had brought. I feared that I could expect little interest in the tiger.

Nevertheless, the President welcomed my plans, saying Bangladesh must take every opportunity to gain any international assistance which could restore the country to a normal condition. Moreover, the creation of wildlife reserves would help to attract tourism and foreign currency. He promised his support, adding rather sadly that the country's natural beauty was one of its few assets to have survived the war. This was a promising beginning, but I knew that real power lay with Mujibur Rahman and that without his backing I might still fail.

I met him that evening, having pushed my way through a milling throng of officials, journalists and petitioners to the ministerial offices. Press photographers were playing with a young leopard which someone had presented to the Prime Minister. The atmosphere was chaotic and very different from Mrs Gandhi's quietly efficient surroundings.

We were being served the inevitable tea when the Prime Minister burst in, greeting us with complete informality. His secretary had warned us that he was always in a hurry. In fact, while we talked, he never stopped pacing up and down, radiating vitality and nervous energy.

I outlined my proposals again, this time against constant interruptions and questions. He obviously liked them. His face lit up and from then on he did most of the talking.

'Conservation is part of my plan,' he declared. 'The destruction of forests has been terrible! But do you know what I did? Two days after becoming Prime Minister I issued a decree forbidding the felling of any more trees and the killing of any more wild animals. The tiger? Why, it's now our national emblem and on our new bank notes! Of course we shall protect it. We shall have a great national park in the Sunderbans!'

His enthusiasm was wonderful. I began to understand how such a man could have broken through the apathy of the patient Bengali peasants and led them in a war to create a new nation. He also meant what he said. Within a few years we had not a national park, but three tiger reserves in the Bangladesh Sunderbans. Like India, Bangladesh also issued special postage stamps depicting the tiger. Poor Mujibur Rahman. Little could I know that he was soon to fall to a hail of assassin's bullets. A few years later, after I had been negotiating with President Daoud of Afghanistan on behalf of the World Wildlife Fund, he too was assassinated and I began to wonder if I carried around a jinx with me.

It was nine o'clock before we left Mujibur Rahman's office. Although I was exhausted after a week of constant meetings and press conferences in India, I now had to meet the Bangladeshi press to ensure that the campaign received good coverage. I then had to summarise the meeting for the local radio station, which I did against a background of shrill chatter and honking taxi horns which probably made it unintelligible.

Early next morning I was on my way to Nepal. As the snow-capped Himalayas appeared through the aircraft window, I felt again the familiar thrill which landing at Kathmandu always gives me. John Blower, the project manager of the local United Nations wildlife conservation programme and adviser to the Nepalese government, was there to meet me; so also was George Schaller, whom I had last seen at the other end of the Himalayas, when he was studying snow leopards in Chitral. We exchanged news as we sat over coffee in the sunshine.

The situation in Nepal had changed since my last visit. Previously I had been able to discuss conservation developments directly with HM King Mahendra. Now, alas, he had died. He had been succeeded by his son, HM King Birendra, whom I had not yet met.

I dined that night with the British Ambassador, Sir Terence O'Brien, and Sir Edmund Hillary, who was just back from the Himalayas. Although the Ambassador tried to arrange an audience for me with the new king, none was forthcoming. The king was still in official mourning and very busy with Cabinet appointments, and could not see me for at least a week. By that time I had to be back in Switzerland to present my proposals for the tiger project at a joint meeting of the IUCN and WWF. I agreed to wait as long as possible, but meanwhile briefed John Blower, who would be involved in the implementation of the proposals if they were accepted. During the next few days I visited the Royal Chitawan National Park, to find out how its tigers were progressing, and discussed with John Blower the possibility of creating two new reserves at Sukla Phanta and Karnali, both of which I knew were excellent tiger areas. There was time also for John to take me in a light aircraft to examine the Mount Langtang area, which he wanted to turn into a national park because of its extraordinary beauty. We managed to land somewhat precariously in a stony valley at an altitude of 12,400 feet near some scampering yaks, just short of the Langtang glacier. I agreed enthusiastically with John's proposal, for the peaks and lakes in the surrounding area were truly superb.

Fortunately, it was not long before HRH Prince Bernhard, at that time President of the World Wildlife Fund, visited the new King of Nepal and succeeded in obtaining agreement to all our proposals. In addition the King's brother, HRH Prince Gyanendra, took charge of the whole conservation programme, which has made great progress ever since. Today Nepal has three splendid tiger reserves at Chitawan, Karnali and Sukla Phanta, and both Langtang and the Khumbu areas surrounding Mount Everest have become spectacular national parks.

I had previously visited the small kingdom of Sikkim and satisfied myself that very few tigers were resident here. Bhutan certainly had tigers, particularly in the Manas forests, but was very difficult to enter, so I decided that both these countries would have to be tackled later. In any case, I now had to return to Switzerland for a joint meeting of IUCN and the WWF. At the meeting it was agreed that the tiger project should now be given top priority. The WWF immediately organised a world-wide fund-raising campaign, to be called 'Operation Tiger', and to be carried out by all its national organisations. The IUCN meanwhile appointed some of its most highly qualified people to liaise with their Indian, Nepalese and Bangladeshi counterparts in planning the creation and management of the tiger reserves. Some were to be entirely new; others already in existence were to be enlarged and improved.

The creation of an effective wildlife reserve is not simply a matter of erecting a fence around a protected area. The reserve has to be skilfully planned and managed, and its wildlife constantly monitored. First the site as to be accurately surveyed to ascertain its geophysical features, vegetation and water resources. The populations of its major animal species have to be determined in order to calculate the biomass in relation to the available food sources and the maximum carrying capacity of the reserve. In the case of the tiger this means knowing the numbers and sex ratios of its prey species. If necessary the amount of land available for grazing and browsing may have to be increased if the tigers are to have sufficient food to prevent them from wandering outside the reserve. If the deer and pigs are too numerous they may have to be culled to prevent them from destroying their habitat.

Guards must be able to patrol the reserve effectively. This involves the construction of roads and guard huts. Watch towers and water for fire-fighting have to be available and wells may have to be dug. Guards have to be recruited, trained and properly equipped with uniforms, vehicles, firearms, binoculars and two-way radio sets for controlling poaching. The cooperation of the local police, forestry officials and neighbouring civic authorities has to be obtained. Sometimes, to satisfy local requirements, a properly controlled hunting area has to be established outside the reserve, where surplus game can be shot on a sustained yield basis. Finally a long-term management plan must be prepared to cover not only the reserve but the protective buffer zone around it. Here the willing cooperation of the villagers is essential.

New reserves can rarely be established without imposing some restrictions on local activity. When planning a reserve one has to give a high priority to problems involving human interests. In Malaysia and New Guinea, for example, it was found that small numbers of aboriginal people inhabited the rain forests where new wildlife reserves were to be created. As in neither country were they seriously depleting the wildlife, but were living in peaceable equilibrium with it, no attempt was made to remove them. These reserves indeed now protect both the aborigines and wildlife as part of the same ecosystem.

But particularly in Asia, villages may have to be translocated, a matter which requires very careful handling if friction is to be avoided. Both India and Nepal have shown particular skill in this difficult task and by generous treatment have re-settled numerous villages in new sites. Arrangements have to be made to exclude domestic cattle, which occur in thousands in almost all new reserve sites. Those which enter after a reserve has been created are put in a pound and have to be reclaimed on payment of a nominal fine. In some reserves villagers are allowed entry for a few days each year to harvest essential fodder, firewood, thatching, fruit or wild honey, under a controlled programme. The annual burning of grass, which is usually a dangerously uncontrolled affair, has also to be strictly managed.

The creation of a wildlife reserve involves a considerable number of jobs for villagers in road-making, building, transporting, the hiring of elephants, bullocks and boatmen and in miscellaneous labour. Moreover, unlike many enterprises run by remote city-dwellers or foreigners, the money earned continues to circulate locally, thus enriching the community.

After the reserve has started to operate, plans usually have to be made to cater for tourism. People cannot enjoy wildlife unless they can see it. But here again great care must be exercised. Uncontrolled tourism can destroy a reserve by sheer success and weight of numbers. In the United States, for example, only 350,000 people visited the already fully established national parks in 1916; by 1978 the number had risen to 45 million and restrictions had to be introduced to prevent serious disturbance and the destruction of vegetation by tourists. Tourism, however, generates local employment and is an important source of revenue that offsets the cost of managing and guarding a reserve.

When a new wildlife reserve is created full account must be taken of the social and economic needs of the human community if the reserve is to have an assured future. It must never be seen as detrimental to man. Conservation is invariably a compromise between the need to protect wildlife and the aspirations of the local human population. In Asia particularly, where the density of the population is so high and the economic problems so great, much skill and patience are needed in balancing these priorities.

'Operation Tiger' is Launched

In September 1972 HRH Prince Bernhard launched Operation Tiger at an international press conference. The media gave us remarkably generous support. The tiger was a glamorous and newsworthy subject, and its plight aroused immediate popular interest. Prominent feature articles and pictures, television films and interviews rapidly multiplied.

Some remarkable efforts were made by our supporters to raise money. The most outstanding was the contribution of David Shepherd, the famous wildlife artist. He had already raised very large sums for the WWF through the sale of his animal paintings and had recently presented a helicopter to President Kaunda of Zambia, for the control of elephant-poachers. He now painted a magnificent picture of a tiger, which he donated to the WWF. His idea was that a limited edition of signed, full-size reproductions should be sold at £150 each for the benefit of the appeal. Despite the high price the demand for his work was so great that the entire edition of 850 copies was sold in six weeks. As some of them are now changing hands at three times this price they were obviously a good investment! After paying for the cost of reproduction, which was done at cost price by the generous printers, David handed over the proceeds, no less than £112,000, to the WWF. In recognition of his services to conservation, HRH Prince Bernhard later decorated him with his personal Order of the Golden Ark.

David Ogilvy, described as the world's leading advertising man and a member of the Executive Council of the WWF, put the full resources of his international company at our disposal and produced some compelling advertisements appealing for donations. These appeared in many countries, the cost being borne either by the newspapers and magazines or by other donors.

Young people of many nations took an active interest in the campaign, buying 'Save the Tiger' T-shirts and collecting money. In Great Britain, Switzerland and the Netherlands the WWF. Youth Service raised the remarkable sum of £300,000. Some of the youngsters in the United States even took to hissing women who wore tiger-skin coats, so that very soon it became socially unacceptable to do so. In London a tiger-skin coat was burnt in public by one protest group. Several large multi-national companies which used the tiger as an advertising symbol made substantial donations to the fund and the officers and crew of H.M.S. *Tiger* also contributed. The Armed Services agreed to replace tiger-skin aprons worn by their ceremonial drummers with synthetic furs. The International Fur Trades Federation introduced a voluntary ban on the importation of tiger skins. Fashion houses co-operated by producing excellent imitations of many animal furs, which have since become very popular. Virtually every airline signed a WWF agreement to stop advertising the hunting of tigers and other endangered species as a means of promoting air travel.

At about this time the IUCN achieved a major break-through for conservation. An international treaty it had prepared, the Convention on the International Trade in Endangered Species of Fauna and Flora, was adopted at a multi-national meeting convened by the United States Government. This made it illegal for any country to export or import, either alive or as skins, any animal species listed in the IUCN Red Books as endangered. The treaty has since been ratified by fifty-nine nations, including those where tigers occur. As a result the once very large international trade in tiger skins has almost been wiped out.

In eighteen months the campaign raised nearly £800,000 ($1,700,000), the largest contributors being Switzerland, the United States, Great Britain and the Netherlands, in that order. Contributions had come from as far afield as South Africa and Australia and it was the most successful campaign yet organised by the WWF.

With this money the WWF has already supplied about forty vehicles and two launches for the Sunderbans reserves, complete radio networks for all the reserves as well as tractors, fencing, camping and fire-fighting equipment, night viewing apparatus, telemetry and capture equipment, elephants and camels, generators and water-pumps, projectors and laboratory equipment and uniforms, binoculars and arms for guards.

The money raised by 'Operation Tiger' has been well spent. In 1976 a midterm appraisal of progress with the new reserves was carried out by Professor Paul Leyhausen and Dr Colin Holloway of the IUCN and Mr M.K. Ranjitsinh, the United Nations Environment Programme representative for Asia and the Far East. Their report stated that quite outstanding successes in furthering the tiger's chances of survival had already been achieved.

Only four years later, in 1980, there are reports that the numbers of tigers in all the established reserves have increased substantially. In one or two instances the population has even doubled, thanks to more successful breeding, the high standards of protection against poaching and, probably, to an influx of tigers from the unprotected regions outside the reserves. There has also been a remarkable increase in the populations of deer and antelope, as a result of the improved management of the grazing areas. Moreover, the reserves, which represent a total of many thousands of square miles of forest, are providing sanctuary for every kind of wildlife, from tigers and leopards and their prey species to wild elephants and rare birds, reptiles, butterflies and plants.

One important result of 'Operation Tiger' was that it quickly attracted the attention of other countries where tigers occur. Within a short time Malaysia, Thailand and Indonesia had expressed themselves willing to create new tiger reserves. Contact had also been established with HM King Jigme Singh-ye Wangchuk of Bhutan, who had created a big reserve in the Bhutan Manas forest adjoining the Indian Manas reserve. The two were put under joint management and now form one of the largest population centres for tigers. Fortunately sufficient funds were by then becoming available, although the extra demands on the tiger specialists at the IUCN became a problem.

In 1979 Sir Peter Scott, Chairman of the WWF, visited China, where he achieved another long awaited breakthrough for conservation. The Chinese government not only became members of the IUCN, but also agreed to sign the Convention on the International Trade in Endangered Species. A wide-ranging programme of wildlife conservation was planned, including the creation of many new reserves. One surprise was to learn that about 150 tigers, reported to be of the Siberian race, existed in four reserves in the northern part of Heilungkiang Province. Since the Russians had recently announced that the number in their Sikhote Alin reserves had now risen to 150, this doubled the known population of the race. According to zoologists at the Academia Sinica in Peking, the Chinese tiger still existed in small numbers and is now protected. It is also believed locally that both the Indo-Chinese and Indian races of the tiger may still survive in the more remote western and southern parts of China. A very rewarding outcome of Sir Peter's visit was an invitation to send an expert from IUCN to make a two-year study of the now rare Chinese giant panda, of which perhaps only 400 exist in the wild. By a happy coincidence the panda is the symbol of the World Wildlife Fund.

THE TIGER IS SAVED

Thanks partly to 'Operation Tiger', but chiefly to the wholehearted efforts of the various countries concerned, a large number of well-managed reserves are today providing the tiger with a real chance of survival. Their locations are as follows:

India

The Manas Reserve, in Assam.
The Palamau National Park, in Bihar.
The Simlipal Reserve, in Orissa.
The Corbett National Park, in Uttar Pradesh.
The Ranthambhore Reserve, in Rajasthan.
The Sariska Reserve, in Rajasthan.
The Kanha National Park, in Madhya Pradesh.
The Melghat Reserve, in Maharashtra.
The Bandipur Reserve, in Karnataka.
The Sunderbans Reserve, in West Bengal.
The Jaldapara Reserve, in West Bengal.
The Periyar Reserve, in Kerala.

Bangladesh

Three reserves in the Sunderbans.

Nepal

The Royal Chitawan National Park.
The Royal Karnali Reserve.
The Royal Sukla Phanta Reserve.

Bhutan

The Bhutan Manas Reserve.

Malaya

The Tamng Neggara National Park.
The Krau Game Reserve, in Pahang.
A new reserve in Trengganu.

Thailand

The Khao Yai National Park.
The Khao Soi Daow Reserve.
The Huai Kha Khaeng Reserve.
The Tung yai Reserve.
The Salak Pra Reserve.
The Phu Hkien Game Sanctuary.
The Phu Khiew Game Sanctuary.
Other reserves in formation.

Indonesia

The Meru Betiri Reserve, in Java.
The Gunung Leuser National Park, in Sumatra.
The Sumatra Selatan Reserve, in Sumatra.
Several new reserves in formation.

USSR

The Sikhote Alin Reserves, in Manchuria.
The Suputinsk Reserve, in Manchuria.
The Lazovsky Reserve, in Manchuria.

China

The Chang-bai Shan Reserve.
The Mengyan Reserve.
The Fangjinshan Reserve.
Other reserves in formation.

Korea

Several new reserves in formation.

The situation in Burma remains obscure, although it is known that both the Indian and Indo-Chinese races still survive there in spite of their lack of legal protection. Information is also still lacking from Vietnam, Cambodia and Laos, in all of which some tigers probably still exist. News has, however, been recently received that at least 50 tigers of undetermined race (probably the Siberian) are now known to have survived in northern Korea.

In 1979 revised estimates of total populations of the eight races of the tiger were still partly guesswork, but were as follows:

Siberian Tiger *P.t. altaica*	350–400
Chinese Tiger *P.t. amoyensis*	small numbers?
Indo-Chinese Tiger *P.t. corbetti*	about 2,000
Indian Tiger *P.t. tigris*	about 3,300
Caspian Tiger *P.t. virgata*	extinct?
Sumatran Tiger *P.t. sumatrae*	600–800
Javan Tiger *P.t. sondaica*	1–2
Balinese Tiger *P.t. balica*	extinct
Total	about 6,400

The numbers of the doomed Javan race have continued to fall. A survey made in 1979 could find no proof that the survivors were still breeding. Moreover, it seems that the small food sources available in the Meru Betiri reserve were subject to increasing competition from leopards and wild dogs.

Ten years previously there seemed little hope of saving the tiger species from total extinction. Today it can be said that the Indian, Indo-Chinese, Siberian and Sumatran races now have an excellent chance of long-term survival if the present measures for their protection are maintained. There is every hope that they will be, although poaching in Sumatra is not yet fully controlled.

Nevertheless, it would be unrealistic to deny that new problems are looming ahead. Many of the tiger reserves, particularly those in India, are only 200 to 400 square miles large and are therefore too small to sustain increasing populations for long. While some of them may successfully be enlarged, it will not be possible to extend the boundaries of others in more highly developed and crowded areas; perhaps their tiger population will be stabilised by natural means, but overcrowding brings heavy penalties. If this arises, tigers will have to be translocated, either to new reserves created in suitable areas of low human population density, or perhaps to the very few reserves large enough to accommodate additional numbers. Another obvious problem is to maintain an adequate gene-flow in small reserves. The IUCN scientists have already calculated that in order to maintain a viable breeding stock for an indefinite period, a minimum contiguous population of 300 tigers is required. Others believe that 200 would be sufficient. In the Indian subcontinent only the Sunderbans reserves in India and Bangladesh, the joint reserves in the Bhutan and Assam Manas forests and the joint Tung Yai and Huai Khaeng reserves have this capability. It may therefore become necessary to exchange a certain number of surplus tigresses between small reserves. Obviously tigers of the surviving races must not be intermixed.

Yet another problem is the over-spill of tigers from over-crowded reserves into the surrounding country. When this happens, domestic cattle are liable to be taken in the unprotected buffer-zone around reserves and people may be attacked. To calm the fears of villagers near tiger reserves, it has already been necessary to make arrangements for compensation to be paid quickly if any cattle are taken. Problems such as these rarely arise in countries where wildlife reserves are measured in thousands of square miles, but in densely populated Asia they are vitally important and will have to be watched very carefully by the reserve managers.

The question will probably be asked, 'Was it worth while and necessary to spend so much effort and money on preventing the extinction of the tiger, when so many other problems are facing humanity?' It is the kind of question which faces all conservationists.

The answer must be 'Yes'. If no effort were made to protect the natural world, humanity would be suffering far more than it does at present. Already, to our loss, we have caused the extinction of countless animals and plants. More than one thousand animal species of various kinds and twenty-five thousand species of plants are now listed as endangered. Each loss impoverishes our environment and weakens man's prospect of long-term survival by further unbalancing the ecosystem. We dominate this planet by our skill and technology, but still cannot escape the fact that all life is interdependent. The tiger has been referred to by an eminent scientist as a 'most sensitive indicator of the health of the natural area and the country at large'. This may perhaps sound far-fetched, but it is not. Like all other animals, the tiger has a part to play in its natural community. Remove it and the community is at once unbalanced—deer and pigs, for example, can multiply to excessive numbers, which in turn are able to increase their damage to man's crops. Saving the tiger and its forest habitat was not, however, merely a matter of preventing extra damage to crops in Asia. It was a remarkable demonstration, by a large number of relatively poor Third World countries, of their awareness of the importance of protecting their natural heritage. Can we in the affluent West question their decision to spend money and effort on such a cause? Was it wrong to hasten to help them achieve such a goal? I think we had a duty to do so, because, as the Prime Minister of India said at the 1979 Symposium, the tiger campaign 'was not just for the survival of our heritage of wildlife, but also for the survival of man'. And this, I believe, is the real answer to the question.

As for the cost involved, one has only to compare it with what the nations of the world are willingly spending on new weapons of destruction. In 1978 military expenditure amounted to £212,000 million ($530,000 million). Saving the tiger and its habitat will have cost, taking everything into account, less than the price of a single short-lived modern bomber aircraft. Or to put it another way, the equivalent of about the cost of seven miles of a six-lane highway. One may ask which of these represents the best long-term investment for humanity. The tiger is part of everyone's heritage and I, for one, am proud to have played a part in the crusade to save it.

Nicholas

Courtney

If All the Beasts Were Gone, Man Would Die

Nicholas Courtney is a freelance writer and broadcaster. His book grew out of his fascination with the tiger as a cult symbol in several cultures of the world. He has studied, in particular, this aspect of the tiger:of the 'cult' of the tiger across the globe.

Man painted like a tiger. Even today, across the western coast of Karnataka, people dance in worship of tigers. Nicholas Courtney's book, The Tiger: Symbol of Freedom, *is about the tiger's cult and its impact on man. (Photo courtesy Ullas Karanth.)*

At one time in parts of India at the beginning of the last century, they [tigers] were so numerous it seemed to be a question as to whether man or the tiger would survive.' Dunbar Brander was reflecting on the early 1800s when the tiger population was at its zenith. There is no possible way of knowing the exact numbers of tigers at the turn of the twentieth century but the figure generally quoted is 40,000 for India and a further 100,000 throughout the rest of Asia. By 1969 barely 5,000 tigers survived in the wild in small isolated groups.

It was then realised that if such an astounding rate of loss continued unchecked there would soon be no tigers left, other than in zoos or safari parks. Two species were already extinct, four more were listed in the IUCN *Red Data Book*, the International Union for the Conservation of Nature and Natural Resources' record of endangered species. The remaining two sub-species, the Indian and the Indo-Chinese tigers, were sinking fast.

The reasons for this rapid decline were obvious; reasons accurately pin-pointed by Captain Mundy as early as 1833 when writing of a particular tiger hunt in 1827: 'Thus in the space of about two hours, and within sight of the camp, we found and slew three tigers, a piece of good fortune rarely to be met with in these modern times, when the spread of cultivation, and the zeal of the English sportsmen have almost exterminated the breed of these animals.' In addition to the growth of the human population which led to the inexorable spread of farming throughout the tiger's range and the excessive contrived slaughter, there was also a lucrative market for tiger skins.

Mundy's thoughtful attitude was unusual, for few sportsmen throughout the whole history of tiger hunting really believed that their prolific quarry could ever be shot to extinction. They occasionally expressed mild concern that they had fewer tigers to shoot than their predecessors but seldo m attempted to discover the cause for this. One verbose writer sportsman in 1875 writing from Central India did comment that 'tigers are certainly now not so numerous by a great deal in many parts with which I am personally acquainted as they were even six or eight years ago'.

Extract from *The Tiger: Symbol of Freedom* by Nicholas Courtney (London, 1980).

By the turn of the century the more intelligent hunters began to exercise some measure of control in order to protect their sport. Forest reserves were divided up into hunting blocks and a closed season introduced. The Indian princes set aside vast tracts of land solely for the tiger, in order to preserve their sport. The Ranas, the former ruling family of Nepal, also kept huge tracts of Chitawan on the border with India exclusively for tiger hunting. Poaching was virtually unknown, so severe were the penalties under the new game laws. The tigers thrived as a direct result of these changes, their numbers keeping pace with those culled in the protected areas. Some areas were hunted more than others, like the central provinces of India with their many army encampments but during World War I with only a few district officers hunting, the tiger population actually increased.

Between the two world wars the relentless slaughter continued but in some of the controlled forest areas these resilient animals actually managed to increase their numbers. A report on forest administration in the United Province in 1935–6 even states that 'it is almost inevitable that as the numbers of tigers increase there will be a migration of surplus tigers into the surrounding forests.'

When shooting was relaxed during World War II the tiger population expanded again. Hunting was resumed with ruthless vigour after the war. Many professional shikar companies sprang up to cater for the growing demand of the very rich to 'bag the ultimate of trophies'. Their clients shot with superior weapons, regardless of expense or the effect on the species and the environment. However, not all these professional shikars were unscrupulous. Being experts in their field, with an intimate knowledge of the tiger, a few turned conservationists once the final ban on hunting forced them out of business.

The sudden post-war demand for skins gave the poachers a new market. Everything was in their favour after Independence in India. 'Villagers who had lived, in the main, within the game laws, both from fear of punishment and lack of lethal weapons, assumed that the change of authority meant freedom from control and came to consider poaching as a democratic right in a new, free society.' The game laws, although still extant, were never enforced. The 'reserved' forests, formerly well managed during the British Raj, were now considered free for all. In Nepal the Ranas' tiger forests, formerly shot every few years, were heavily poached after their overthrow in 1950 as the 'people's right'. As the restrictions on owning firearms were relaxed a new type of hunter emerged. These 'cowboys' with searchlights mounted on jeeps roared through the forests blazing at anything that moved. Toxins and rodenticides, freely given by the governments to aid new agricultural schemes, were all too often used to poison tigers. Only in Bhutan, with its predominantly Buddhist population that abhorred needless killing, was the tiger relatively safe in this post-war orgy.

The systematic massacre of tigers at this time was by no means confined to the Indian subcontinent. Like the British in India the French hunted the tiger for sport throughout Indo-China although not with the same ruthless dedication. The latter-day political structures of Russia and China did not entirely fit with the 'elitist sport of hunting' although the many professional hunters doubtless accounted for just as many tigers as the shikar companies and their clients. In China there was the added incentive of the high price that was given for the carcass because of its supposed medical and mythical properties.

In Sumatra the tiger still suffers from the attentions of the oil-rich natives and expatriate staff who pursue their quarry for his skin, a prized souvenir.

The number of tigers killed for sport, self-protection or of their skin is horrendous but is in fact small compared with the effect of 'the spread of civilisation' on the tiger's decline. The population of Asia increased more in the twenty-five years after World War II than in the whole century before and is now alliterating at an even faster rate. Obviously the physical boundaries of the continent cannot expand to accommodate this population explosion so it is the land within the borders that is used to feed them. Captain Mundy's comment on the spread of cultivation in 1827 was then the exception but in time it was to become the rule throughout all Asia. Hewitt describes one spot in northern India in the 1880s where a dozen tigers had been shot in a fortnight; he returned twenty-five years later to find 'the ground had been brought completely under cultivation, and no-one could have imagined that there had ever been any cover there suitable for a tiger.'

In central Asia, the Caspian tiger inhabited the dense reed and *turgai* thickets in the river valleys. When the vegetation was destroyed by steppe fires or brought under cultivation for rice, tea and cotton crops and the marshes had been drained, the tiger was forced out and eventually became extinct. Parts of the Sundarbans, the aquatic home of the Royal Bengal tiger, have also been cultivated for rice, thus squeezing the tiger into smaller and smaller ranges. In China the tiger was officially declared 'an impediment to agriculture and pastoral progress' and as such is almost exterminated.

Although the drainage of swamps and the use of former unproductive land for farming whittled away the tiger's range, it was the destruction of the forests and jungles that most affected the tiger. The enormous demand for timber during the last war began the indiscriminate felling of the mature hardwood forests of Asia. Unfortunately this trend, a valuable foreign currency earner, has continued and escalated to the present-day level. The cleared forests are either taken for agriculture or planted with unsuitable softwoods. With these new plantations there is no undergrowth, and like the cultivated areas, they cannot 'hold' a tiger. With no cover there can be no tigers. In Nepal the malaria-carrying mosquito effectively kept man from cultivating the former Rana-controlled forests of the Chitawan Valley. A United States aid project checked the spread of these mosquitoes, so encouraging the colonisation of parts of that 1,000 square mile bastion of tiger country, an all too common example of man moving in at the expense of the tiger.

In the coastal mountain ranges of China the unending search for firewood has effectively destroyed the forests. Full-scale commercial ventures that felled the forests of Sumatra and Java have critically reduced the tiger's habitat, forcing these vulnerable sub-species into smaller and less suitable area. In Malaya the tiger fares rather better than elsewhere because in that country there has been less damage to his habitat. Little is known of the forestry operations in war-torn Vietnam, Laos and Democratic Kampuchea, but the news is unlikely to be encouraging as the tiger has probably been much disturbed by man. In parts of Vietnam millions of hectares of forest were defoliated by the United States Air Force using napalm and arsenic-based chemicals. The resurgence of secondary growth created ideal conditions for the tiger and his prey species but much of the area was heavily mined and 'booby-trapped' and is littered with unexploded shells and bombs. Although these obstacles now effectively keep the areas free of humans and leave the tiger in peace, he, too, can be blown up by accident.

The fate of the tiger is not only affected by hunting and the loss of habitat to forestry and cultivation. The ever-expanding Asian population requires more and more space in which to live. Over the last few decades even the remotest areas have been opened up for settlement. These developments disturb the formerly wild areas, hounding the few remaining tigers and their prey species to extinction. The tiger has to contend with major hydro-electric power stations, oil refineries and oil fields, all with their operators, motor-trucks and helipads.

In the conflict between man and the tiger it is invariably man that wins. The conflict is entirely of man's making, for the tiger has no quarrel with humans. In India there are now an estimated 300 million cattle. A very large percentage of these give neither milk, food nor leather and are prevented from being slaughtered, even for humane reasons, on religious grounds. These cattle either stray or are driven into the feeding grounds of the tiger's prey species, competing for their food and spreading disease. The prey species are effectively driven off leaving the tiger no choice but to take these cattle to survive. In many cases a villager will cultivate right up to the boundary of the tiger's range. There have been reports of a tigress giving birth to her cubs actually in a sugar cane field. Very occasionally a cane cutter has been mauled or sometimes killed by a mother protecting her cubs. Farmers have been killed or attacked in their paddy fields for the same reasons, and still the tiger is labelled a man-eater.

It is a short-sighted farmer who complains that his weak and near worthless cattle are being 'lifted' by a tiger. The farmer struggles to grow enough food for his family, guarding it night and day against wild pig, deer and destructive monkeys. If the tiger takes domestic cattle he is, in fact, doing the farmer a service for his very presence will keep those herbivores off the farmer's crops. The value of cattle taken rarely exceeds his value as a 'game keeper'. In his capacity of controller, the tiger's worth has always been appreciated by some like this *jagheerdar* (headman of an Indian village) described by a nineteenth-century forester:

> While sitting at breakfast we were alarmed by hearing cries of distress proceeding from the Jagheerdar's hut, and on running out to ascertain the cause, we found old Kumah in a furious state of excitement, his left hand firmly fixed in the woolly pate of the hopeful scion of the house, and belabouring him soundly with a stout bamboo. We inquired what crime young Mohadeen had been guilty of to bring upon himself such a storm of parental indignation, and learned to our astonishment that it was owing to his having killed a tiger. To most this feat would have been considered brave in a boy of fifteen but not so the old man who recognised the value of the tiger to the village.

This perceptive headman recognised one of the important functions of the tiger. As one of the great carnivores the tiger stands at the pinnacle of the wild life pyramid, a primary predator who controls stocks of prey species, that in turn affect the environment. If man in his ignorance lops off the pinnacle, then a fearful chain reaction starts that alters the structure of the pyramid, making it unstable.

An illustration of this occurred in the Red Indian reserve of Kiabab in the United States of America. Congress passed a preservation order on a particularly rare species of deer only to be found in the Kiabab, but did not put a preservation order on the mountain lion as it was considered dangerous vermin. Eventually the lion was hunted to extinction for sport and for the high price its pelt fetched. The controlling factor removed, the deer multiplied unchecked. They began to strip the bark of the aspen, the predominant tree, as they were short of scrub and grass on which to browse. The young saplings were also eaten leaving nothing to replace the dead and decaying trees. The cool of a forest condenses the vapour of the air which in turn falls as rain, and so, with fewer trees, it rained less, and the water table fell. With no rain the undergrowth shrivelled up and the Red Indians in the reserve suffered from crop failure and lack of pasture for their stock and horses. They in turn began to die out. Those that survived moved from the barren land believing that a curse from heaven had driven them away.

The devastating effects of interfering with the environment can be seen in the desert near Kahtan, in the Takla Makan region in the far west of China, which was once 'tiger country'. A Swedish archaeologist discovered that the city there had been constructed almost entirely of wood, undoubtedly felled from the surrounding forest. With the loss of the forest and the proximity of man the tiger moved away. What remained of the forest and the cultivations around the city soon dwindled and, with no rainfall, erosion set in and reduced the environs to desert.

A similar example in the last fifty years is the town of Gorakhpur in the United Province of India. In the 1930s the town 'for a long time had to be protected against the ravages of tigers by lines of fires'. Today there is not a tiger to be seen near this straggling city set in a barren sun-baked wilderness.

Those who advocate that the tiger is better off in a zoo or safari park living a trouble-free existence clearly do not appreciate the ecosystems of nature or the habits of the tiger. Some of these people believe the tiger is better protected in captivity, where they breed with relative ease, in quite large numbers and more frequently than in the wild. Others believe that nature is cruel. Nature is not cruel. Animals are not ruled by fear as Rudyard Kipling suggests in his *Second Jungle Book*, but by hunger or thirst. Where permitted by man, tigers live carefree lives—except where experience has taught caution.

For the most part these latter day Polito Menagerie owners are quick to defend the presence of tigers in their zoos and safari parks as their bid to save an endangered species from extinction, but it is likely their real motive is financial. There are of course many notable exceptions among these establishments where scientific study is stressed and regular cross breeding occurs with the establishment of sperm banks. London, Basle, Frankfurt, Phoenix, San Diego and Delhi zoos are among the pioneers of this work.

Although adequately fed and watered, a caged tiger can never be happy, even if he has been bred in captivity. Six paces at the most in each direction on a concrete floor and behind iron bars is no substitute for the many miles a tiger normally travels in a night when hunting in the wild. Swimming, another favourite pastime of the tiger, is nearly always denied him. Without these and the other necessities, it is no wonder that tigers become lethargic and deteriorate. The normally acute eyesight, hearing and sense of smell fade from lack of use. These defects become increasingly pronounced with in-breeding. The result from the average zoo is a tiger which is a mere caricature of his former majestic self.

The now fashionable safari parks are marginally better than the average zoo but still open parkland is no substitute for a home range of forest or jungle with cover, game and water. As with the zoos, there are exceptions, like the Marwell Zoological Park near Winchester, Hampshire. Here the accent is on gathering practical knowledge that can be applied to conservation in the field and on educating the public rather than concentrating on the gate receipts—although these too are important to finance the projects.

Private collectors like John Aspinall, make a significant contribution to the greater understanding of many of the endangered species. John Aspinall's breeding programme of Indian and Siberian tigers has been particularly helpful. His 'zoo parks' at Howletts and Port Lympne, both in Kent, are open to the public most of the year.

For a tigress to teach the basic skills of stalking and hunting to her cubs can take up to two years of intensive tuition. A tiger cub bred in a zoo or safari park cannot possibly be taught these essential skills by his captive-bred parent and so would be helpless if returned to his natural habitat. However, 'Billy' Arjan Singh, a great naturalist and conservationist, has achieved what was thought to be impossible by returning a captive-bred tigress to the wild. In a scheme sponsored by Frankfurt Zoo a tigress cub, Tara, from Twycross Zoo was sent to Tiger Haven, Arjan Singh's farm in the Dudhwa National Park on the Indian-Nepalese border. There she roamed completely free and every day accompanied Arjan Singh on his rounds in the forest. Gradually she began making sorties to the forest on her own, becoming increasingly independent. Eventually she left 'home' completely when her mating call was answered by a tiger. She has been seen again, once, remarkably, being taught to hunt by the tiger. The success of the operation was in doubt for some time when she disappeared, but Tara has recently been photographed, proving that a captive-bred tiger can be returned successfully to the wild. It is encouraging to think that this reintroduction could work on a larger scale, but only when the nations concerned are ready to receive and protect them for ever. For some sub-species it is already too late.

The extensive search and subsequent photographic evidence of Tara was sponsored by a new organisation, the International Trust for Nature Conservation. This trust is made up of a team of dedicated conservationists who channel all their funds, expertise and energies into a few selected projects, like the tiger and leopard schemes at Tiger Haven. One of the principal advantages of the I.T.N.C. is that their sponsors can actually see where their money is being spent and are kept fully informed of particular projects.

Unquestionably the tiger's only place is in his natural habitat, free from the interference of man. It is still a close run race between the tiger's survival and his destruction. In some countries the race has already been lost, in others the tiger is disappearing fast while elsewhere there are encouraging signs that the tiger population is on the increase.

The last recorded small Bali tigress was shot in 1937. Reports that a few survived in the west of the island were unfounded. Since a Caspian tiger was shot in Iran in 1957 there have been a few hopeful signs of pug marks, like those in the Elburtz mountains, and sightings in eastern Turkey, but these have not been repeated so there is little hope that any of this species survives.

There are tragically few Javan tigers left in Java. In the latest survey, 1978, evidence rather than sightings of only three, possibly five, tigers was found. With only one captive-bred tigress in Budapest Zoo it is all too likely that this species will soon become extinct, a far cry from the 1830s 'when the Javan tiger was found all over the island'.

Numerically the Sumatran tiger is stronger than the Javan. A conservative estimate puts their numbers at 800, scattered over the island in small groups. Although there are still viable breeding stocks, hunters and the loss of environment are steadily whittling away the numbers.

A report from *Novostrov*, the Russian press agency, in 1979 confirms that, despite belated conservation measures, there are no Caspian tigers left in their last known habitat in the U.S.S.R., a spot called Tiger Gulch in Tagikistan. The same press release announced that 'naturalists believe that there is no longer any danger of the Amur or Ussuri [Siberian] tiger dying out in the Soviet far east. Thanks to strict protection their number has doubled to about 200 in the last 20 years.' Conflicting reports have come out of the People's Republic of China on the numbers of Siberian tigers still extant there and in Korea. Some believe that there are as many as 100 or 200 in the northernmost Heilungkiang Province but a 1973 report suggests, regrettably, that only 'several tens of tigers remain in China and Korea.'

Atlhough the numbers of Siberian tigers in China are minimal, the Chinese tiger slipped from being 'very rare' to 'on the verge of extinction'. A few tigers exist in isolated pockets about the Yangtse river valley where they compete with the Chinese for land. The latest news is that the decline has been checked but this has not been authenticated.

The little that is known about the numbers of the Indo-Chinese tiger indicates that he is faring better than the other sub-species. The population is not large being in the 'very low thousands' and is still on the decline. It may be some time before any information on numbers comes out of those war-torn countries of south-east Asia where it would appear that the preservation of the tiger is not a high priority. Despite having the best tiger forests, the number of Indo-Chinese tigers in Malaysia is falling from an estimated 3,000 in 1954 to between 600 and 700 in 1978, and is still declining. The tiger's lot is little different in Thailand where the population of 500 is also on the decline. The census carried out in 1960 showed 1,125 tigers to the east of the Irrawaddy, the great Burmese river that divides the two species of tiger, the Indo-Chinese and the Indian. Since that date the Burmese borders have been closed to foreigners but the news of the tiger population is disturbing as the species is believed to be 'much depleted although widely if thinly scattered and to have completely disappeared from many of its old haunts such as the Maymyo Game Sanctuary.'

Across the Irrawaddy the same 1960 census revealed 496 Indian tigers, but they too were sharing the same fate as the Indo-Chinese tigers. Towards the end of the 1830s the fact that the race type of the species, the Indian tiger, was rapidly heading towards extinction was finally appreciated. For decades naturalists, like the celebrated E.P. Gee and the ex-hunter Jim Corbett, had been canvassing the plight of the tiger and the reason for his decline, but such was the power of the shikar lobby and the short-sightedness of the government that their warnings went unheeded. However, the position was eventually understood in 1969 when the total number was thought to have fallen to only 2,500 in India. Bangaladesh was thought to support a further 150, Nepal about the same, Bhutan 200 and Burma not many more. The total, a possible 3,500, was a far cry from the estimated 40,000 at the turn of the century and the figure of 30,000 at the beginning of World War II. These figures were presented to the IUCN Congress in New Delhi which resulted in a resolution to add the Indian tiger to the IUCN *Red Data Book* which lists endangered species.

Once the tiger's plight had been registered an all-out ban on hunting was passed by the governments of all countries in the Indian tiger's range. The export of skins was also prohibited. The battle for this legislation was hard fought but proved even harder to put into operation. The hunting ban was openly flaunted, often by those with the authority to enforce it, the excuse being that every tiger killed was a proven man-eater. The penalties for killing tigers were small when compared with the inflated prices of tiger skins the export ban produced. Even today skins can be bought openly in the New Market in Calcutta. Clearly legislation by itself was not enough to check the dwindling stock of tigers. In order to act effectively, the exact tiger population and its various locations had to be established. In 1972 a census, carried out by nearly 5,000 men in two massive swoops, showed an estimated 1,827 tigers in the whole of India. Armed with this information, Guy Mountfort, a founder member of the World Wildlife Fund, prepared a paper for the Fund outlining his proposals for saving the tiger. After some initial opposition, mainly financial, and the uncertainty of its reception in the countries concerned, the scheme 'Operation

Tiger' was adopted. Finance for the project came quickly by way of a world-wide appeal that raised, not the target figure of 1 million dollars but 1.7 million dollars. The money came from donations and the sale of books, pictures and almost anything with a tiger logo. David Shepherd's brilliant picture 'Tiger Fire' raised £120,000 in signed lithographs. The success of the scheme showed the world cared about the tiger.

The suspected opposition to 'Project Tiger', the Indian version of 'Operation Tiger', did not materialise. The way having been carefully paved by Guy Mountfort, Mrs Indira Gandhi took up the scheme with enthusiasm and appointed a cabinet minister, Dr Karan Singh, as chairman and Kailash Sankhala, director of the Delhi Zoological Park, as overseer of the six year plan. Two million pounds, a massive sum considering India's economic and social problems at that time, was voted to the scheme. It set a fine example to the rest of Asia.

The aim of 'Project Tiger' is to protect specific areas by eliminating the interference of man and letting nature take its course. This interference covers everything from forestry operations, the grazing of domestic stock and poaching to the removal of whole villages.

Since 'Project Tiger' was launched on 1 April 1973 eleven reserves have been established, each in a separate state and containing different types of tiger habitat. The eleven are situated in Bandipur, (Karnataka), Corbett (Uttar Pradesh), Kanha (Madhya Pradesh), Manas (Assam), Melghat (Maharashtra), Palamau (Bihar), Periyar (Kerala), Ranthambhor and Sariska (Rajasthan), Simlipal (Orissa) and Sundarbans (West Bengal). There are also 125 smaller sanctuaries throughout India, perhaps the best known being 'Billy' Arjan Singh's 'Tiger Haven' on the border with Nepal.

Mountfort went to Bangladesh, which was then only just recovering from a devastating war, and persuaded the government to set aside part of the Sundarbans as a tiger reserve and this trend is encouraging. Despite this magnificent start, continued success is by no means assured. Tigers are resilient animals and given the right facilities, notably protection, they will increase up to, but not beyond, their optimum number for each reserve. But even in some of these reserves the tiger is still disturbed. Villagers still graze their cattle in the tigers' forests, the felling of hardwood continues, possibly to offset the loss of revenue from the 12,000 square kilometres given over to the tiger.

In Nepal the conservation of the tiger is centred on the Royal Chitawan National Park, the 1,000 square mile valley between the Shivaliks and the Himalayas, with another two reserves, Karnali and Sukla Phanta, to the far west of the country. Coinciding with the ban on hunting, the Nepalese Government adopted the World Wildlife Fund's proposals in 'Operation Tiger' and designated 210 square miles of the Royal Chitawan National Park as a sanctuary for the preservation of tigers. Adjacent to this reserve is an hotel, Tiger Tops, where wildlife enthusiasts can stay and watch the fauna of the reserve in its natural state. The thorough studies and intimate knowledge of this Reserve's tigers since 1972, have made the Tiger Tops director of wildlife activities, Dr Charles McDougal, one of the leading authorities on tigers today.

The retort of high powered rifles still echoes round the *terai* forests of the Royal Chitawan National Park. Armed men still ride on elephants at the head of a funnel of beaters as they draw a known tiger range. There are still cries of 'Hey, Hey, *bagh, bagh*, tiger, tiger!' as the flash of orange and black and white streaks through the trees. As the tiger approaches the guns a single shot is fired. The tiger, hit in the flank, continues crashing through the undergrowth. The beaters follow to claim their prize. But these are no Rana hunters, or even poachers, but Nepalese and American scientists sponsored by the Smithsonian Institute in Washington and the American arm of the World Wildlife Fund. The tiger is not dead, merely heavily sedated by a tranquiliser dart.

It was no accident that the Smithsonian chose the Chitawan Valley to study the tiger for the Nepalese government take their conservation seriously—the army patrol the reserve day and night and take a fatalistic view of poaching. The scientists spent five years in a management-oriented, scientific study of the tiger in the wild. Their method of monitoring their tigers was simple. Twenty-six tigers, mostly sub-adults, were selected, tranquilized and fitted with a light radio transmitter built into a collar fitted round their necks. From then on their movements were followed, either by receivers on the ground or from light aircraft. These movements were plotted, giving the scientists an accurate picture of the tiger's life in the day time, their kills, feeding patterns, associations with other tigers and matings and, most significantly, their search for new home ranges once the family group had split up. The study proved to be a success and their findings of great practical use. The original reserve has now been increased to 360 square miles with the aid of a fund set up by the Frankfurt Zoological Society which will allow the increasing tiger population to expand into new home ranges. Eleven tigers are still collared and their movements monitored, not only by radio tracking but also by traditional methods. For obvious reasons the radio tracking is useless at night and as the tiger is a nocturnal animal there is still much to be learned about his night time habits. The results of these exhaustive studies and the continuing work in the field have done much to further the understanding of the tiger and his habitat.

These conservation measures were not confined to saving the Indian tiger. Other countries were actively involved in their own projects to save their particular sub-species. Tiger hunting and the export of skins was universally banned, with the exception of Burma where, according to a local newspaper article, 'hunting and dealing in tiger skins were so lucrative that buying centres have been opened in Akyab and Momeik.'

With the expertise and financial backing of 'Project Tiger' the Indonesian government set up the Meru-Beriri Game Reserve in 1972 to protect the pathetically few remaining Javan tigers. In Sumatra, where, despite legislation, tigers are shot and skins exported, the government has set aside nearly one million hectares at the Gunung Leuser Reserve for the tiger and the many other threatened species. So far the scheme is proving a success, but the tiger is so persecuted in other parts of the island that the overall position is still not healthy.

The Indo-Chinese tiger is being protected by the Malayan government in a reserve being set up in the state of Trengganu as part of a five year plan. In Thailand there are already four reserves, the National Park at Khao Noi and three sanctuaries in the upper basin of the Khwae Noi river system. The day may still come when the governments of the war-torn Vietnam, Laos and Democratic Kampuchea view the tiger in his proper light and consider him worth saving.

Although they were too late to save the Caspian tiger, the Russians have had some success with their conservation programme for the Siberian tiger. That sub-species has doubled and is still increasing in their Sikhote Alin Reserve of 310,000 hectares, the Suputinsk Reserve of 16,500 hectares and the Lavaski Reserve where a policy of *laissez faire* has produced encouraging results.

A start has been made on planning a tiger reserve in China. With the increasing political and cultural ties between China and the West the tiger's chance of survival may be increased.

In some areas these conservation programmes may have come too late, for not all these reserves hold an equal chance of success. The IUCN Survival Service Commission states that an animal like the tiger needs a contiguous population of at least 300 to a maintain a viable gene pool. All known populations of tigers are below this figure with little chance of natural genetic exchange with other groups.

The future of the tiger depends entirely upon man. A fine start has been made among those who believe in saving the tiger for future generations. The results of 'Project Tiger' are encouraging but will count for little unless man is willing so share his environment with his fellow creatures. Since the earliest civilisations, the tiger has been a symbol to mankind, representing power and strength, good and evil, courage and ferocity, sometimes even luck. It would be a tragedy if this most beautiful and free of animals was lost to the world forever. The tiger's survival lies in all our hands.

Peter Jackson

Problems and Solutions

Peter Jackson is Chairman of the Cat Specialist Group of IUCN (the world conservation union). For eighteen years he was Chief Correspondent of Reuters in India and was closely involved with the birth of Project Tiger.

Peter Jackson examinining a human dummy in the Sundarbans Tiger Reserve, West Bengal. The dummy is wired to a battery to deter man-eating tigers – they get an electric shock if they attack the dummy. This, it is hoped, will keep them from attacking humans!

Tigers lived for hundreds of thousands of years in an ocean of forests, heavily populated with prey, where people existed in small numbers in isolated groups. In a few decades in this century the situation has been transformed. Now it is the tigers that live isolated in small numbers. An ocean of people has replaced the ocean of trees and is pressing in on the remaining islands of tiger habitat. Tiger prey is equally under siege.

The human population explosion in the twentieth century resulted from improved medical treatment and technological advances in industry and agriculture. The world population of 5,234 million represents as much as 10 per cent of all who have ever lived on Earth in the last 10,000 years. Human feet have trodden the highest summits and reached the most remote and wild lands. Despite all controls, the human population will continue to grow for several decades yet. The increase will be mainly in the developing countries, where most of the remaining wild lands lie.

To support humankind, the natural resources of the Earth are being strained by the spread of mining, fishing, agriculture and forest exploitation. Rivers are dammed and diverted; wetlands are drained. Tropical moist forests originally covered 4,300,000 km^2 (1,660,000 sq. miles) from India through southeast Asia. More than half has already been cleared. By the end of the century, at least a further 200,000 km^2 (77,200 sq. miles) are likely to disappear. Apart from clearance for agriculture, well over half the wood is cut for firewood, the only source of energy available to tens of millions of Asians, and for building material. The remainder goes to developed countries, especially Japan. The consequences for all wildlife are obvious. And the tiger, which lives at the top of the food chain, will be among those that fare worst. Fragmentation of forests into islands surrounded by agriculture isolates tigers, which will not cross open land.

Scientists calculate that a contiguous population of at least 500 tigers is needed to maintain full species evolutionary potential. In other words, that is the minimum number needed in any one area to maintain the genetic ability to adapt to a changing environment. Only in the Sundarbans mangrove forests does this condition clearly

Extracted from *Tigers* by Peter Jackson (London, 1990).

exist. Most other reserves in the Indian subcontinent hold fewer than 100 tigers. Some reserves are still linked by belts of forest. Unfortunately, these forest corridors are threatened by the pressure for agricultural land.

Tigers exist in large tracts of continuous forest in Burma and parts of southeast Asia, but their numbers are not known. Again the forests there are being cleared and tigers isolated. To counter the ill-effects of inbreeding in small, isolated populations, the translocation of just one unrelated breeding animal in each generation is sufficient. If tigers are moved around a group of reserves, it makes them the equivalent of a much larger, and therefore genetically healthier, tiger population.

Reserves themselves are subject to the destructive pressures of cattle grazing and wood collection. There are too few guards. And those few are usually miserably under-equipped and under-paid, struggling to keep the human waves at bay. Local people often have good reason to resent the protected areas. Formerly, they could graze their livestock there, and collect wood and other products. That has been stopped. Outside the reserves, cattle and goats have often turned grazing lands to near desert. Demand for firewood for cooking and heating has devastated wooded areas. Within the reserves people can see lush grasses and forests of useful wood. Moreover, the reserves are sanctuaries for animals that emerge at night to ravage crops, and sometimes injure and kill people. It is no wonder that conflict arises between people and protected areas.

The Indian tiger reserve of Ranthambhore is a case in point. It consists of 500 km^2 (193 sq. miles) of rocky hills covered with light forest intersected by luxuriant valleys, near the eastern edge of the Rajasthan desert. Ruined fortresses and palaces bear testimony to centuries of human occupation. When it was declared a tiger reserve in 1973, some villages still existed inside it. To improve the integrity of the reserve, the people were moved out, given good agricultural land and helped to rebuild their village communities.

But the life-giving monsoon is a fickle visitor to this part of India. Many years it fails and there is little or no rain to promote the regeneration of crops and grazing land. Some 50,000 cattle and 50,000 goats belonging to 66 villages around the park need fodder.

Inevitably, the villagers want to send them into the reserve, where the grass grows tall. Battles have developed between guards and villagers, in which at least 15 forest guards, including the director, and some village people have been injured since 1980. Graziers have even built roadblocks to prevent guards reaching areas where they have been illegally grazing their cattle.

During a severe drought in 1986, thousands of cattle entered Ranthambhore. Armed police were despatched to drive out cattle and graziers. Last year a tiger killed a child. Such episodes only increase the bitter conflict between people and the reserve. Ranthambhore is probably one of the best protected reserves in India, possibly in Asia. Even so, a recent study found that 126 of the 157 compartments into which the reserve is divided were affected by illegal grazing, and 86 by wood poaching.

Wildlife authorities know that they need the understanding and support of local people, but they are often handicapped because they have no authority or funds to operate outside reserves. There is insufficient cooperation from other wings of government.

A private Ranthambhore Foundation is now trying to relieve pressure on the reserve by improving facilities for local people. The foundation provides mobile clinics for health care and family planning, and high-grade cattle to improve local breeds and milk production. These cattle can be stall-fed instead of being sent out to graze. Experts are helping to rehabilitate village grazing lands, which have been destroyed by over-use. Village children learn about the wildlife in their neighbourhood and visit the reserve. If the programme is successful, it will be extended to other reserves. Furthermore, it can be hoped that, once governments have seen what can be achieved, they will undertake similar schemes.

In Nepal, the government is already taking action. Local people are allowed into the Chitawan National Park for two weeks each year to collect the tall grass for thatch and fodder. Outside they cannot get sufficient supplies because of excessive grazing by their cattle and goats.

Wildlife tourism helps to promote conservation, but it has become a problem in popular viewing areas. People from all over the world now want to see tigers, which, protected by Project Tiger, have become bold and visible in a few reserves. Urban Indians, who formerly had little interest in their country's wildlife, visit the reserves in increasing numbers. At peak times, in the early morning and in the evenings, tourist traffic in prime areas of Ranthambhore has become intense. Too many vehicles disturb wildlife, including tigers, and damage forest tracks. Tourist numbers and entry times in Ranthambhore and other popular reserves are now being limited.

Poaching is another constant threat. The tiger has legal protection in all countries of its range, except Burma. International commerce in any part of a tiger has been banned since 1976 by the Convention on International Trade in Endangered Species of Wild Fauna and Flora (CITES). Anti-fur movements in western Europe and North America have reduced demand for skins. Nevertheless, clandestine trade continues to encourage poaching. The principal markets for tiger skins are Arabian countries, Taiwan and Japan. Western tourists still conceal skins in luggage, seldom checked by customs. From time to time, illegal hoards of tiger skins are uncovered by the authorities. Increased vigilance and firm action, with public support, are required to reduce poaching and illegal trade to a minimum.

China has few tigers left to provide bones for popular medicines, but appears to be getting supplies from other Asian countries. In Taiwan, the public slaughter of tigers for gourmet meat caused an international scandal in 1984. Tigers have never existed in Taiwan, and, after the scandal, the government clamped down on imports.

People in developed countries support tiger conservation but the problems are not theirs. Tiger attacks on livestock or local people breed resentment and opposition to conservation of dangerous animals. Villagers poison tigers which become a nuisance. The question: 'Are tigers more important than people?' is raised, not only at local levels, but at the national level after a spate of attacks, or if villages are moved from reserves. In one incident, when a man was killed by a tiger, his friends began shouting at the guards: 'You're not trying to catch that tiger. You don't care about us. If we kill a tiger we go to prison, but if a tiger kills one of us, nobody cares. We are just dogs.' However, when the tiger was captured, there was jubilation and the overt anger abated.

Sympathy for the problems of people living close to tigers arouses concern among a wider community. Indian newspapers challenge any over-emphasis on saving tigers to the detriment of people. Such adverse public reactions worry conservationists, because the future of the tiger, and all potentially dangerous wildlife, depends on public support. Wildlife authorities thus face the challenge of placating people, while saving tigers.

In Kheri District, near India's border with western Nepal, where there has been an epidemic of tiger attacks around the Dudhwa National Park, tiger specialists say the trouble has arisen because sugarcane is grown up to the very edge of the park. They want sugarcane cultivation near the park banned. But local farmers do not want to give up this highly profitable crop. Controls on grazing and firewood collection are also proposed. People are urged to work in groups, which are less likely to be attacked by tigers than lone individuals. Tiger Watch teams have been ordered to follow the movements of tigers in the area, and to deal with any incipient problems. Tigresses with cubs are provided with baits positioned so as to draw them back to the park. If necessary, a tiger may be trapped and removed to a zoo. Some have been shot.

The family of anyone killed receives compensation. Farmers are also compensated for loss of livestock, provided that it was not inside the reserve.

Some local people argue that tigers are welcome because they keep deer and pigs out of their crops. In an area of Sumatra, where wild pigs proliferated after elimination of the tigers which preyed on them, a farmer said he no longer informed the authorities if he found signs of tigers, because he feared that they would be hunted down for trophies.

Wildlife authorities in India are confident that an occasional outcry against tigers will not affect the tiger conservation programme. Even in politically turbulent West Bengal, where legislators have from time to time aroused passions over the human toll in the Sundarbans, governments of all persuasions, including Communist, have stood firmly in support of conserving the Sundarbans and its tigers. They have evicted people who have tried to settle in the reserve.

Hemendra Panwar, director of the Wildlife Institute of India, has played a leading role in both tiger conservation and improving the lot of local people. He declares: 'Our programme is not just for the tiger. It aims at conserving whole ecosystems consisting mainly of forests, which are of vital importance to human welfare. The tiger is an important component of these eco-systems. Despite the occasional incidents of man-killing—and there have been only a small number outside the Sundarbans and Kheri—the programme must go on because it is in the larger interests of humanity.'

Can the Tiger Survive?

> 'Of the many ways of measuring a land's wealth, one of the surest signs of ecological richness and diversity is an abundance of predator species. Because each species sits at the top of a different food chain, belonging to a different cycle of organic matter, we can be certain of the existence of a large animal community for every predator. This is, in turn, sustained by vegetation. The existence of carnivores carries the implications of a larger ecological community and of millions of years of evolutionary struggle.'
>
> Jonathan Kingdom, *East African Mammals*, Vol. IIIa (Academic Press 1977).

Tigers, like people, can only exist if they have sufficient food. In the case of the tiger, as of all carnivores, that food consists of other wild animals. A tiger requires about a hundred large prey every year. It follows that a genetically healthy tiger population of 500 tigers needs up to 50,000 large prey. To produce sufficient young to sustain such an off-take, a total population of 500,000 prey animals is required. They, in turn, are dependent on plants—palatable grasses, leaves and shoots. All require an adequate supply of water and sufficient living space. The health of the ecological community also involves many other species, which form part of the working 'machine' of nature. Birds spread seeds. Carrion eaters and insects break down dead matter and return the nutrients to the soil. These nutrients, essential to all life, are recycled through the living community. The whole provides a balanced world eco-system into which the human race fits.

Between 6,000 and 9,000 tigers roam the forests of 12 countries in Asia today. They represent only a tiny relic of the numbers which once spread from Turkey in the west to the Sea of Okhotsk in the Far East. The decline has been mainly in our present century, during which the human population has more than quadrupled to over 5,000 million. The increase has largely been in the developing countries, which includes the tiger's habitat through south and southeast Asia. Natural areas, never before disturbed, have had to be converted to living space and agriculture to produce food for the billions.

Large wild animals are in future, likely to be confined to reserves. Outside them their prospects are poor. But the scope for more and larger reserves is rapidly decreasing. Moreover, tigers and other large predators, which are always relatively few in number, may face genetic decline and ultimate extinction through inbreeding when confined to small areas, unless mankind comes to their aid. Ideally, forest corridors should link reserves so that as many animals as possible can interbreed. That is not always possible. To maintain the gene pool, it will be necessary to translocate some animals between reserves.

Scientific breeding of threatened species is being increasingly attempted to ensure maximum genetic variability in the captive population. The Siberian tiger, which is a prime example, now numbers over 600 in captivity—about twice the number in the wild. Captive-bred antelope and deer have been successfully reintroduced to the wild, but reintroducing large captive-bred carnivores to the wild is fraught with difficulties. They need parental training in capturing prey. They may continue to try to be familiar with people. This can be alarming, and might lead to accidents. Adverse public reaction can hamper conservation efforts.

The only answer is to maintain an adequate network of reserves. But, for this, an enormous investment in funds and people is required. The funds must be sufficient to provide guards to protect tigers and other wild animals; managers to ensure habitat protection and monitor the wildlife; and scientists to investigate the requirements of various species and make recommendations for management. Political will and international support are required for such a big programme.

In the past twenty years, the tiger has become a symbol of wildlife conservation, its successes, and its problems. Its continued life on Earth challenges us all.

Alan

Rabinowitz

Wildlife Abuse

- **Alan Rabinowitz** has worked with jaguars, tigers and leopards, and is highly regarded as a big-cat expert. His work on the status of tigers in Indo-China is remarkable. He works as a scientist for the Wildlife Conservation Society, New York.

A man rides the tiger in his effort to ward off evil. This picture is from the Grand Palace in Thailand. (Photo courtesy Valmik Thapar.)

Before leaving for New York, I had hoped to spend a few relaxing days in Bangkok. But during my first two days there, what started as a pleasant shopping excursion turned into something quite different.

The morning after I reached Bangkok, I went to visit the famous Chatuchak Weekend Market, an intricate maze of over five thousand vendors which spreads over twenty-eight acres. It's like a massive flea market and Thai-style country fair rolled into one. There were stalls selling everything from wild boar meat to human skulls. If shopping became tiresome, you could go watch a cockfight in progress.

I'd seen some of these Thai oddities before. There were scores of open-air shops in Bangkok selling stuffed cobras, or caiman and crocodile handbags and wallets by the hundreds. On all the major streets, stalls hawked up-country jewellery alongside cases upon cases of beautifully mounted butterflies, scorpions, and bats. Many of these species, which are so abundant on the street, are rare in the wild.

Anyone looking for something more exotic can visit the numerous leather shops selling boots and handbags made from the skins of snakes, turtles, sharks, lizards, crocodiles, and elephants. On one pair of cobra-skin boots, I saw the snake's heads were still attached, hissing at me from the toes. Or there were numerous stores with bear, tiger, and leopard teeth and claws, all beautifully mounted in gold and silver settings. Twice, I was offered the skins and heads of the animals that went with these accoutrements.

When I got to the wildlife section of the Weekend Market, I was stunned at the variety of animals that could be bought openly and cheaply. There were hundreds of cages filled with wild jungle fowl, beautiful little pittas, hill mynas, pheasants, hawks, eagles, falcons, macaws, and parrots. The harder-to-obtain or illegal species were sold in darker, more hidden areas of this part of the market. One cage housed both a baby gibbon and a baby langur, the animals clinging to the wire of their cage. Their mothers were most likely

Extract from *Chasing the Dragon's Tail: The Struggle to Save Thailand's Wild Cats* by Alan Rabinowitz (New York, 1991).

killed to get them. Another cage held a python, and still another contained two leopard cats.

But the most pitiful sight was the squirrels—one of the more popular 'pet' items at the market. Burmese striped tree squirrels, Indochinese ground squirrels, grey squirrels, and white-bellied flying squirrels were all tied by little strings around their necks to the top of a table, with no food or water nearby. The sun found its way through rents in the awning and beat down on the more unfortunate ones. Nails were clipped, sharp teeth were filed, tails were fluffed, all in order to make them cuter playthings.

I watched Thai children pass by with their parents, poking here and there, trying to play with the cute furry balls. When one young boy went to pet a white-bellied flying squirrel, its stiff body simply shifted space. A look of puzzlement flashed across the child's face, and the vendor quickly replaced the dead animal with a young golden-coloured ground squirrel. The boy smiled and giggled as the new little squirrel snuggled against his finger. The sale was made.

What struck me most was that there was no conscious maliciousness on the part of the vendors. These animals were commodities to be bought and sold like anything else. I looked at the body of the dead squirrel that had dropped to the floor. How many in a day? I wondered.

The next morning, while jogging in Lumpini Park in the middle of Bangkok, I was attracted to an area on the perimeter of the park where groups of people were milling about. As I approached, I saw cages of snakes, and then a curtained-off area where a live king cobra hanging from a hook was being slit open for its warm blood and gallbladder. At a table nearby, joggers, the majority of whom were Chinese, finished up their runs with a cocktail made of cognac, cobra or Russell's viper blood and gall. There were several of these stands open six days a week, except Monday, when the streets were cleaned.

At this point, I was thoroughly disgusted by all I had seen and I decided to spend the next few days in Bangkok talking with people, following leads, and looking through old newspaper files. I wanted to try to understand how extensive the illegal wildlife trade situation here was because it directly reflected on the government's true attitude toward protecting what wilderness was left in Thailand.

Thailand's only Wild Animal Preservation and Protection Act was enacted in 1960. This was the first major attempt by the Thai government to protect its increasingly depleted wildlife populations. This legislation created two categories: reserved wild animals, which are not permitted to be captured, hunted, or kept in possession, under any circumstances, and protected wild animals, species which can be captured and sometimes killed but only with a special permit. Nine species, considered to be Thailand's rarest and most endangered wildlife, were placed in the reserve category.

Javan rhinoceros	Schomburgk's deer	hog deer
serow	goral	Sumatran rhinoceros
kouprey	wild water buffalo	Eld's deer

Today, four of these species are considered extinct in the wild in Thailand. Two more species, Eld's deer and the hog deer, if any still exist, are close to extinction. The goral and the wild water buffalo exist only in small numbers in a few restricted pockets. The serow, or goat-antelope, is still holding out—only because it makes its home on steep limestone mountains and cliffs which are relatively inaccessible.

In January 1983, because of increasing international pressure, Thailand finally ratified the Convention for International Trade in Endangered Species (CITES), the most widely accepted conservation agreement in the world. Thailand signed the bill initially ten years earlier. But it was not until 1983 that the Thai government actually agreed to pass legislation to implement the convention, which would enforce protection for species classified by CITES signatory nations, now numbering nearly a hundred. But to this day, none of this new legislation has been enacted in Thailand and endangered species from other countries are still openly and legally bought and sold.

The results of a 1984 internationally funded survey called Operation Tooth and Claw found that 95 per cent of the jewellery stores in Thailand that cater to tourists still carried large-cat products. The average store carried fifteen large-cat claws and seven large-cat teeth. That same year, Bangkok was denounced by the Associated Press International as a major regional market for wildlife souvenirs.

In 1985, one of Thailand's biggest exporters of wildlife, Suchino Corporation, was openly distributing a shopping list which included thirty-three species of mammals and seventy-five species of birds for sale. The more expensive items included:

Baby Asiatic elephant	$19,500
Baby Malayan tapir	$ 5,500
Young clouded leopard	$ 5,000
Eld's deer	$ 2,000
Douc langur	$ 1,200
Great hornbill	$ 250

During this same year, TRAFFIC, an organization set up to monitor illegal animal trade activities, documented that a large number of the thousands of pangolin and python skins which had arrived in Japan had originated in Thailand. In addition, countless numbers of birds and mammals were discovered in the luggage of people travelling between Bangkok and Tokyo. Most of these animals died en route.

In 1987 (just months after an official from the Thai Forestry Department was quoted at the biannual meeting of all CITES signatory countries as saying. 'Thailand will cooperate to control trade in some of the over 5,000 endangered species of fauna and flora listed in the CITES ...'), the 'Eating Out' section of the *Bangkok and Beyond* newspaper favorably reviewed two new restaurants. Their delicacies included snake flesh, tiger penis in whiskey, snake blood cocktails, sea turtle, black monkey, and black dog.

As the wildlife trade became publicized internationally and it became more difficult to get certain species out of Bangkok, animal exporters started shipping from Vientiane, the capital city of Laos, a country that had not signed CITES. In the 1987 listing of wildlife, Suchino Corporation now had an addendum: '... our company has [an] Export License for live animals in Appendix I and II (CITES) from Laos. We can supply [these] to you legally by official texts. [For] the animals in Appendix I and II (CITES) and species out of stock, please give us more time.' Appendix I species are animals considered to be in danger of extinction, Appendix II contains species that could be threatened with extinction if trade is not controlled.

Suddenly, in August 1987, Laos arrested three of the largest Thai wildlife dealers on wildlife-smuggling charges and sentenced them from one to three years in prison. Two months later, a Thai government official flew to Laos and convinced the Supreme Court to set them free. 'After all,' the Thai official said, 'through the nature of their work, the men had earned a large amount of foreign exchange for Laos.'

In 1987–88, a survey of the bird and mammal trade of the Chatuchak Weekend Market listed 225 native bird species, 51 exotic bird species, and 24 native mammal species. Of the native birds, 78 percent were protected, and less than 3 per cent could be legally sold through the market. The offices of the Thai Forestry Department and the Wildlife Conservation Division are less than two miles away from this marketplace.

After a few days of research I knew I had only scratched the surface of this enormous problem, so I decided to talk with some of the officials whose job it was to protect Thailand's wildlife.

'You have only been here a short time, things have gotten better,' was a common response from Forestry Department officials.

'Our hands are tied,' one man told me. 'We patrol these areas, but wildlife officials don't even know what is protected and what is not'.

'There are too many ways around the law,' another said. 'People can legally possess two of any protected species as long as they don't capture or sell them.'

'The police are corrupt and don't care. They hinder all our efforts.'

All these statements were, to some degree, true. But I was bothered by a feeling that had been plaguing me at Dancing Woman Mountain. It seemed that much of the sentiment expressed in Thailand, the constant assurance that 'things have gotten better,' was all just a façade to keep up appearances both for the international community and for Thais themselves. The reality was that the wildlife was being exploited more than ever before. I was starting to believe that the poorest villager cared more about conservation than the highest banking officials.

Symbolically the forests and wildlife represent many things to the Thai people: life forces to be protected and nurtured, the spirit world, fear and power, beauty and strength. However, in day-to-day practices, animals and trees represent resources to be tapped and land to be utilized. Wildlife is to be used, strong animals are put to work, beautiful animals are worn, dangerous animals are eaten to gain power, and anything can be caged or chained for man's entertainment. Three hundred years ago there was a thriving trade in rhino parts between Thailand and its neighbours. Now that the rhino is extinct, other species have taken its place.

Even Buddhist practices in Thailand have been severely corrupted. I was especially offended by the Thai tradition of buying little containers or cages containing birds, fish, and turtles, then setting them free during special occasions such as festivals or birthdays. Through this beneficent act the buyer gains 'merit' for his next life. Yet it is obvious that the sale of such animals, captured for just this purpose, is a thriving business in death and torture which contradicts the most fundamental Buddhist beliefs. Most of these animals soon die or are quickly recaptured after their release. One vendor told me that she addicted her birds to opium so they'd return to her. Now, she bemoaned, opium was too expensive.

I stopped counting the gibbons and macaques I saw chained by the neck at Buddhist temples. Monks accepted such gifts freely from the people, sometimes believing they were doing the animal a service by caring for it. Often, however, the monks knew the value of such animals to their temples. Sometimes the abbot of a temple requested certain species of animals because they brought in tourists and increased the temple's donations. Many temples had little zoos. One temple compound in Uthai Thani kept a leopard cat, a civet, a Javan mongoose, and numerous forest birds in pitifully cramped little cages to attract the townspeople. The monks fed them what little remained from their own meals. The water dishes in most of the cages were bone dry.

Then there were the buckets of frogs in the marketplace. I watched as women skinned them alive, then severed the legs from their bodies to sell. With eyes bulging, the still living naked torso was thrown into a separate pail to be discarded.

'Why don't you kill the frogs before you dismember them?' I asked repeatedly.

'It is not right for Buddhists to kill,' I was told.

Geoffrey
Ward

Massacre

Geoffrey C. Ward is a prolific author whose bestselling work is *The Civil War: An Illustrated History*. In the 1950s he was based in India (with his parents) and saw much wildlife. He has written on the subject of India's wildlife for the past two decades.

The early 1990s in India were marked by enormous seizures of skins and bones, especially of the tiger. By 1993 the world woke up to its worst-ever tiger crisis. Geoffrey Ward records a critical moment in the tiger's history. (Photo courtesy Valmik Thapar.)

In late June 1992 I received a letter and a set of newspaper clippings from Fateh [Fateh Singh Rathore]. Several poachers had been arrested at Ranthambhore; they had confessed to the police that they had shot more than fifteen tigers there over the past two years. And they were not alone. Several other poaching gangs, they said, were at work in and around the park.

Rumours of tiger poaching had swirled around Ranthambhore since 1990, but the Chief Wildlife Warden of the state had dismissed them all as 'baseless,' the products of 'vested interests' (by which he seems mostly to have meant Fateh, without a job again and noisily unhappy at what was happening to the sanctuary he still considered his). Some 31,000 tourists, more than half of them foreigners, visited the park during the winter of 1990–9, an all-time record, and a good many complained that they had seen no signs of tigers, let alone the tigers themselves. Noon—the tigress that had mastered the technique of killing in the lakes, the animal I had watched feeding with her cubs in the grass two years earlier—seemed suddenly to be missing. So was the magnificent tiger called the Bokhala male. So were other individual animals well known to Fateh and Valmik [Thapar] and to the guides and jeep drivers who made locating tigers their business.

A story about the mysterious death of tiger sightings at Ranthambhore appeared in the *Indian Express* in February 1992. The field director claimed there was nothing to worry about: because of an unusually heavy monsoon the previous summer, the tigers were simply keeping to the hills. In March, the erstwhile Maharani of Jaipur, whose hunting reserve Ranthambhore once had been, also expressed her concern. She, too, was told nothing was wrong, and when the census was taken that summer, sure enough, the official total was forty-five tigers, one more than had been claimed the year before.

Fateh made more trouble for himself by publicly denouncing its accuracy: If there were that many tigers, why weren't they being seen? He was sure there weren't more than twenty tigers left in the park.

Extracted from *Tigerwallahs: Encounters with the Men who Tried to Save the Greatest of the Great Cats* (New York, 1993).

The rumours persisted. During our visit to Ranthambhore that winter, the corpse of Badhiya, a forest guard who had been one of the most knowledgeable and dedicated members of the forest staff, was found sprawled along the railroad tracks outside the park. There were whispers he'd been murdered because he knew too much about poaching.

Something was very wrong. Even the Forest Department began to worry, and when the census was undertaken the following May, Valmik Thapar was asked to help conduct it. The results were devastating: he could find concrete evidence of only seventeen tigers in the park, and tentative evidence suggesting there might be three more. Again, the Chief Wildlife Warden denied everything. The census was faulty, he insisted, botched by the same amateurs he himself had asked for help.

But then came the arrests. Gopal Moghiya, a member of a traditional hunting tribe who ordinarily worked as watchmen for local herdsmen, was seized by the Sawai Madhopur Police, along with the skin and bones of a freshly killed tiger he had shot.

Fateh was devastated:

> Geoff, it is a massacre [he wrote]. When the police chief showed me the skin, I could not control myself. Tears were rolling down my cheeks. He had to take me away. It's heartbreaking and sometimes I feel guilty that I taught them to have faith in human beings. ... All the tigers were shot at point-blank range, just innocently looking at the man with the gun. ... Everyday some bad news is coming. ... Somebody shot a tiger two years ago and somebody else shot one three months before that. It shows that nobody bothered about these animals.

I called Fateh. He was again in tears. 'I sometimes think it was my fault,' he shouted over the long-distance line. 'I taught my tigers not to fear people and see how they have been repaid.'

Gopal Moghiya's confession led to the arrests of several others, including his own brother, a Muslim butcher, and four Meena herdsmen who admitted killing four tigers to protect their livestock.

Again, the Forest Department's initial instinct was to cover things up. One or two animals might have been killed, it said, but poaching on such a large scale was impossible. (Gopal Moghiya did eventually recant his confession, yet he had airily bragged of his poaching skills to several disinterested journalists before doing so.)

But the facts could not be denied: eighteen tigers and leopards were already gone from Sariska, perhaps twenty tigers missing at Ranthambhore, and reports of more poaching were filtering in from everywhere. In Uttar Pradesh, for example, where the Forest Department stubbornly insisted that Dudhwa and its adjacent forest still held one hundred and four tigers, Billy [Arjan Singh] estimated there were now no more than twenty.

Valmik did a hasty calculation of the total number of tigers thought to have been poached, based on just five years' worth of official seizures of skins and skeletons. It came to one hundred and twenty animals. And it seems reasonable to assume that several times as many more went unreported.

At that rate, the Indian tiger is surely on its way out. (So, evidently, is the Nepalese: Twenty-five tigers disappeared from the Royal Chitawan Reserve between 1998 and 1990 alone, so large a percentage of the park's resident population that it may be impossible for it ever to recover.)

Tigers have always been poached. Villagers poison them to protect themselves or their livestock, and some skin smuggling has continued despite an international ban on the trade. But compared to the twin menaces of expanding population and dwindling habitat, poaching has been a relatively minor threat to the tiger's survival. Now that has changed. If allowed to continue at its current pace, poaching will swiftly undo whatever good Project Tiger has managed to do over the past two decades.

The immediate crisis was caused by the peculiar demands of Chinese medicine. For hundreds, perhaps thousands of years, tiger bones and other tiger by-products have played an important part in Chinese healing. The catalogue of physical ills which tiger bones and the elixirs brewed from them are supposed to cure includes rheumatism, convulsions, scabies, boils, dysentery, ulcers, typhoid, malaria, even prolapse of the anus. Tiger remedies are also said to alleviate fright, nervousness, and possession by devils. Ground tiger bone scattered on the roof is believed to bar demons and end nightmares for those who sleep beneath it. A 'miraculous medicine' made from tiger bone and sold in Vietnam and elsewhere promises '6 love makings a night to give birth to 4 son.'

The demand for these products is enormous, not only in China and Taiwan, but in South Korea and in Chinese communities throughout Southeast Asia and some Western communities as well. A single brewery in Taiwan imports 2,000 kg of tiger bones a year—perhaps 150 tigers' worth—from which it brews 100,000 bottles of tiger-bone wine.

The Chinese themselves have finally run out of tigers—wild populations that once ran into the thousands have been reduced to fewer than one hundred animals—and so they have begun importing tiger bones on a massive scale, ignoring the complaints of conservationists and willing to pay prices smugglers find irresistible. From the Indian reserves—where tribal hunters are paid a pittance to take the risks and do the actual killing—shadowy middlemen, perhaps with the connivance of some Forest Department and police officials, spirit the bones of poached tigers northward across the Nepal border, then on into Tibet and China.

More because of the inefficiency of this process, evidently, than out of concern for the wildlife of other countries, the Chinese have set up a tiger-breeding farm near Beijing. There, using Siberian tigers obtained from North American zoos, they are now raising carnivores whose only *raison d'être* is to be disassembled, ground up, and sold to clients at home and abroad. Its managers predict they'll have bred some two thousand tigers in the next seven years, and they have recently asked the Convention on International Trade in Endangered Species for a permit to peddle their tiger products overseas. 'If we don't get the permit,' one official told a visitor to the breeding farm, 'we'll just kill all the tigers.'

Sentiment aside, some urge that the Chinese breeding programme should be encouraged since its success might relieve the pressure on dwindling wild populations. Opponents argue that farms will never be able to provide enough tigers to satisfy Chinese demands, while legitimizing trade in tiger products would only make it easier for poachers and smugglers to continue their deadly work.

The Ranthambhore scandal could not have come at a worse time for Project Tiger. 1993 was to be its twentieth anniversary, and a celebration was already planned at which a brand new national census figure was to be announced: 4,300 animals, almost two and a half times the number there had been when the project began.

All the old problems still persisted. The hostility of local people had intensified: arsonists had recently set fires raging through the hearts of Kanha and Nagarahole, where K.M. Chinnappa, the ranger responsible for defending it for so long, had been forced to flee for his life. And there was already one disturbing new problem, a sad side effect of the national struggle with sectional and ethnic separatists that threatens to tear apart the Indian union. Armed militants of one kind or another had taken shelter in seven of the nineteen reserves, intimidating forest staff, slaughtering animals for fun or food or profit, making a mockery of the parks' supposed inviolability.

Now, massive poaching has been added to that already bleak mix. A three-day International Symposium on the Tiger was to be held in New Delhi in February 1993. Nearly two hundred and fifty delegates were coming from every region of India and many parts of the world, and the government's more strident critics predicted little more than a desperate exercise in defensiveness.

They were wrong. The new All-India Census figure of 4,300 was bravely announced, though almost no one believed it; 3,000 tigers seems a far more realistic figure, according to most of those with whom I spoke, and even that may now be far too high. And the delegates were made to sit through an appallingly self-congratulatory film: 'Forest cover is increasing,' the narrator intoned. 'The tiger reigns supreme'; and in the reserves, 'all is well.'

Everyone in the hall already knew that all was anything but well, and for the first time in my experience Indian government officials were willing to say so in front of one another and in public. The Forest Secretary, R. Rajamani, set the tone of candour: the anniversary conference, he said, should be an 'occasion for introspection, not celebration.'

For three full days, the tiger's champions talked and argued and agreed to disagree. Billy had come all the way from Dudhwa, looking out of place as he always does once he leaves his jungle. 'I don't know which will outlast the other, the tiger or me,' he said with a grin. I told him my money was on him.

Fateh was there, too, newly reinstated in the Forest Department by the courts—'I have my dignity back,' he said—but relegated for the moment to a desk job. He kept his trademark Stetson on inside the assembly hall, and, while delivering a paper on the problems of censusing tigers, mimicked in cunning pantomime a forest guard trying to trace a pug mark when he had never before held a pencil. Ullas Karanth, the researcher from Nagarahole, eagerly shook the hands of Billy and Fateh and other Tiger-Wallahs he had only read about, and lobbied hard for a more scientific approach to tiger management. Research should be free and unfettered, he said; India needed objective facts upon which to make its hard decisions.

Valmik Thapar seemed to be everywhere, delivering a battery of papers, demanding complete honesty about poaching and other potential embarrassments, and vowing to defend those forest officials willing to bring them to the public's attention.

Everyone seemed to agree that a much greater effort had to be made to involve local people in the creation and management of parks. The poaching crisis would never have occurred had local people felt they had any stake in the tiger's survival. And both central and state governments seemed serious about undertaking ambitious ecodevelopment projects—electricity, water, alternative forms of fuel—to provide benefits at last to the people who live in and around the parks. Some plans seemed so ambitious, in fact, that Ullas Karanth gently pointed out that the government already had access to 96 per cent of the country on which to experiment with economic uplift, and might do better to leave alone the mere 4 per cent left over for wildlife while one field director suggested that before government came to the aid of the herdsmen he'd been trying to keep out of his park, he hoped it would at least provide trousers for his forest guards.

There was also a good deal of what seemed to me to be very romantic talk about the importance of maintaining intact the ancient 'sustainable lifestyles' of the tribal peoples who live in and around the besieged reserves. I couldn't help but remember the *gujjars* whose herds I'd seen avidly eating up what was left of Rajaji National Park. Their lifestyle was ancient all right, but it was no longer remotely 'sustainable'; if Rajaji is to survive, some creative alternative will have to be found for them. If it is not found, the forest will vanish, and so will they. And though every park is unique, it is hard for me to see how the same won't ultimately be true for most if not all of the people now living within India's reserves.

In any case, I left the Delhi conference in better spirits than I had expected. The poaching crisis had brought together the tiger's most eloquent advocates. They were talking to one another now, working together instead of on their own, for the first time more united than divided.

Before flying home to the States, we wanted to revisit Ranthambhore and Dudhwa once again. It had been five years since I had sat on the roof of Valmik's farmhouse watching the village women heading home while he tentatively outlined his plans for the Ranthambhore Foundation. I had been sympathetic then, but privately unconvinced that the hardscrabble landscape around his home could ever be coaxed back to life, let alone that the gulf between wildlife enthusiasts and villagers might one day be breached.

I could not have been more wrong. Valmik's house is now the heart of a green oasis, alive with birds and small animals, shaded by some fifty species of trees, many of them native varieties grown from seeds gathered in the forest. A lush nursery grows 500,000 seedlings for villagers to plant during the monsoon. And a cluster of outbuildings behind the house constitutes a full-scale demonstration farm: a sleek, stall-fed murrah buffalo, already the father of hundreds of handsome progeny scattered through nearby villages; a herd of cross-bred cattle whose milk yield is ten times that of the ordinary Indian cow; heat for cooking provided by a bio-gas plant powered by the animals' dung. Just down the road, village women of all castes and faiths meet in their own handsome, mud-walled building, producing handicrafts which provide needed extra income to some sixty households.

Villagers from as far as fifteen miles away are asking for seeds with which to reforest their land. In at least two villages, the people themselves have formed Forest Protection societies with nurseries of their own. The people of Sherpur, Valmik's nearest neighbors, asked for and then helped dig a cattle ditch two kilometers long so that their approach to Ranthambhore at least can be made as green again as it was in the time of their ancestors.

Valmik is the executive director of the Ranthambhore Foundation and divides his time between his farm and his home in New Delhi, from which he does almost ceaseless lobbying on behalf of wildlife in general and Ranthambhore in particular.

The man in change of day-to-day activities around Ranthambhore is Dr. Goverdhan Singh Rathore. He is Fateh's son and has his father's chesty swagger and Rajput mustache, but he is a Tiger-Wallah of a different kind: he seeks to serve the tiger by ministering to the needs of those whom he hopes will one day be its protectors.

Five mornings a week he climbs aboard a medical van and sets out for one of fifteen villages. He and his medical team have now offered immunizations and basic health care—heavily dosed with messages about family planning and the importance of preserving the forest—to more than 25,000 people, and more villages have expressed their interest in participating in the program.

The Ranthambhore Foundation is just one of many non-governmental agencies now at work around India's parks, but partly because of the park's fame at home and abroad, it has become a symbol for a new kind of Indian conservation effort. The Indian branch of the World Wildlife Fund has launched a similar project of its own just down the road, and as part of a large-scale ecodevelopment plan intended to serve as a model for other parks, the Rajasthan Forest Department has begun planting fodder to be given away to graziers so that they needn't take their animals into the park.

It is the foundation's work with children that seemed to me to hold the brightest promise. When foundation workers began taking jeeploads of them into the park, the children liked the birds and animals well enough, but what first struck most of them was the novel sight of seeing so many intact trees in one place. Born and raised within a kilometer or two of Ranthambhore, in the heart of what had once been a thick forest, many had never seen more than two or three lopped trees at a time, had never realized before just what had been lost to cattle and goats and the woodcutter's ax.

On our last evening of Ranthambhore, Goverdhan took us to the mud-walled children's educational center the foundation has constructed beneath a huge tree on the outskirts of a nearby village. Lit by the white glare of a hissing kerosene lamp, fifteen boys sat in a circle while one of them rattled out a steady rhythm on the bottom of an upturned kettle and they all song a specially written song about the wonder of trees and the importance of caring for the wild animals that lived beneath them.

These boys had come from miles away to spend the weekend and some had ridden two different buses to get there. Represented among them were several of the communities that live around the park—Meenas, *gujjars, malis,* Muslims—all eating from the same pot, singing about the same forest.

As we watched and listened from just beyond the circle of light, other voices could suddenly be heard moving along the dark road behind us. Several more boys, hurrying home to their village, had been moved to join in praise of the forest which ultimately only they can save.

From Ranthambhore, we returned to Delhi, then made the long drive to Dudhwa to visit Billy. The court cases against him seemed at least momentarily forgotten, and late one afternoon, he did something he only rarely does these days: he accompanied us into the park.

Dudhwa seemed especially handsome as dusk approached and as we drove through the red-brown grass—tiger-stripped by the smoke from fires deliberately set to char the undergrowth and allow fresh green shoots to spread for the deer to eat—thousand of swallows and bee-eaters tumbled through the air in pursuit of their evening meal.

But the few animals we saw—chital, a herd of thirty swamp deer, a lone sambar calf somehow separated from its mother—seemed frantic with fear, plunging deeper into the forest as soon as they spotted us, evidence perhaps that they had recently been shot at from vehicles that resembled ours. And only once, along all the miles of dusty road we travelled, did we see a set of tiger pug marks.

Gloom seemed almost palpably to settle around Billy's shoulders as we turned off the metalled road that leads out of the park and onto the rutted track to Tiger Haven that runs for two kilometres along the Neora. The sun was hanging very low in the sky now, and as we came around a bend in the river, wisps of mist rose from the elephant grass and its damp sweet smell filled our nostrils.

A big male tiger lay motionless atop the riverbank, fifty feet across the river, his brassy coat burnished by the dying sun, his opaque eyes fixed upon us.

I stole a look at Billy as he watched the tiger. It seemed almost an invasion of his privacy: Head cocked to one side, smiling, he was rapt, adoring, his face lit up as if he had unexpectedly come upon a lover.

The tiger gazed back at him for a time, then rose slowly to his feet and—stretched out to an almost unbelievable length, belly nearly touching the ground—slipped into the underbrush and disappeared. Under Billy's vigilant eye, this tiger, at least, still occupies his range, still reminds us of what will be lost if the new hopes stirred at the Delhi conference are allowed to die away.

As the Land Rover started up again. Billy beamed at me and raised one thick thumb in silent delight.

John

Seidensticker

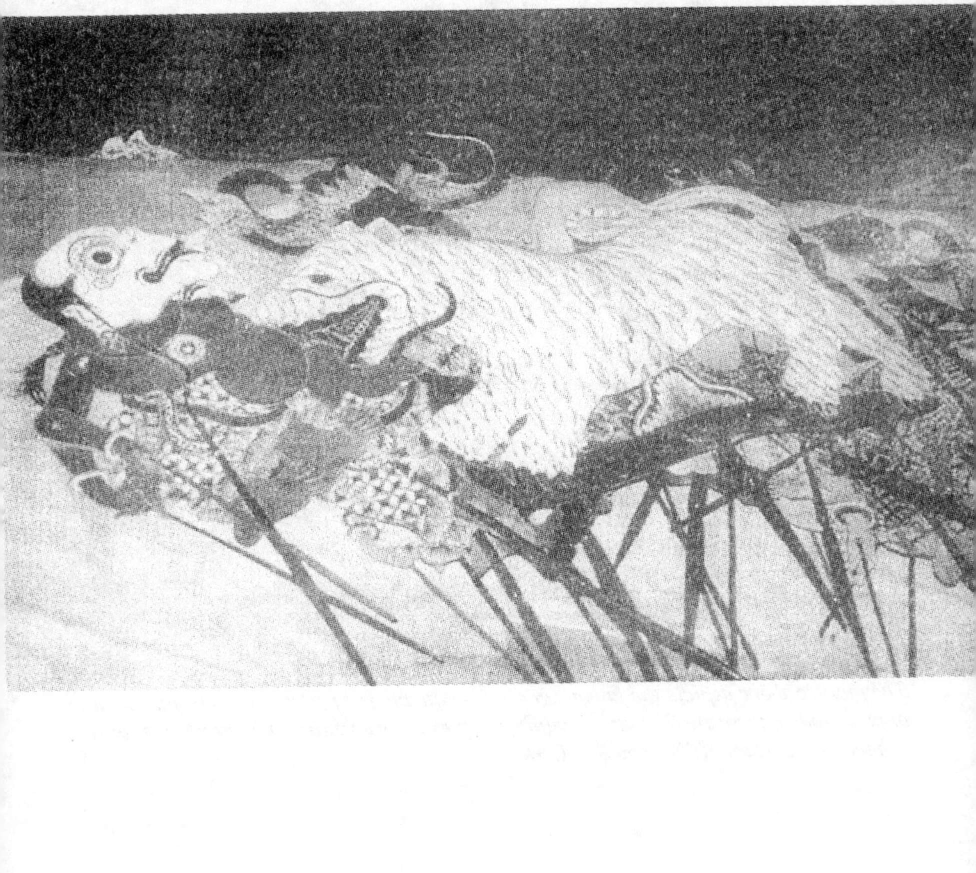

Why Save Tigers?

The picture above depicts the Javan tiger in shadow puppet performances in the island of Java. Today, these are the only remaining memories of an entire sub-species that once inhabited the island. (Photo by Sue Earle.)

The tiger lives in a world of sunlight and shadow
Always secretive—never devious
Always a killer—never a murderer
Solitary—never alone
For it is an irreplaceable link
In the process and the wholeness of life

TIGERS

I wrote those words in the fall of 1974 while I was studying tiger predation and predatory behaviour in Nepal's Royal Chitawan National Park. During several months of daily tiger encounters, real tigers living their lives, often within the sounds of busy village life, I found tigers so unlike the tiger depicted in the oft-quoted William Blake poem 'The Tyger' *(Tyger! Tyger! burning bright/ In the forests of the night/ What immoral hand or eye/ Dare frame thy fearful symmetry?).* Hearing a tiger roaring in the night or seeing a tiger track on a dusty forest road brings a sense of power and tension and grace to landscape that only the largest predators can invoke.

In our rapidly changing world, the endangered tiger's decline represents real and symbolic loss of quality of life. Landscapes where the endangered tiger and people live together, and the tiger and its living area are viewed and supported as a positive feature in the landscape, are landscapes to be treasured, as are the lessons to be learned from them. The continued survival of the tiger completely depends on this. To me, landscapes where tigers live today represent the highest levels of ecological integrity and ecological completeness, the very existence of which reaches into and affects the quality of our own lives.

There is something special about tigers that evokes strong feelings in nearly everyone. For anyone living in tiger-land, special care is always taken when moving about to avoid surprise encounters. For the armchair traveller, just thinking about tigers conjures up images of lush jungles in exotic far-off lands. Tigers are among the most recognisable of all animals, embodying great power, lithe and

Extract from *Tigers* by John Seidensticker (Vancouver, 1996).

awesome grace, mystery, stealth, and danger. Tigers serve as symbols of freedom and nature untouched. Tigers are the steeds of gods.

In Hinduism, the god Shiva is both destroyer and reproducer. As destroyer, he is pictured wearing a tiger skin and riding a tiger. His consort is Parvati the Beautiful, who in her dark side, appears as Durga the Terrible, riding a tiger. In some Asian cultures, tigers incarnate mystery and potentially dangerous beings. Shamans and magicians adopt the guise of tigers to promote powerful images. Tigers are believed to be the avengers of their Supreme Being or to punish sinners on behalf of Allah.

In ancient China tigers were considered regal and beneficial during some periods. At other times they were regarded as potent messengers between the human and spirit worlds. In still other periods, tiger images were used to deter evil spirits from the graves of the deceased. A tiger, sleeping or sitting at the feet of monks, demonstrates Buddhism's power to harmonise and tame nature's forces. A roaring tiger symbolises a fury and fighting spirit. Tigers and dragons together symbolise the two great forces of nature. In Taoism *yin,* or evil, is controlled by the tiger and the dragon controls *yang,* or good. The role of the tiger is reversed in Buddhist thought, in which the tiger represents *yang.*

Just watching a tiger walking down a forest road or patrolling the edge of a moat in a zoological park, you can see that everything about its movements speaks of an easy power and grace. In a blink, a tiger can recast into an awesome killing machine. Muscles tensed in a stalk, an explosive rush, abrupt turn, graceful leap, unanticipated stop, the tiger's great size amplifies our perception of its agility, We see the motions we expect in a house cat, only one per cent of a tiger's size.

Tigers are the largest of 37 species of living cats. Once widespread and abundant over their vast range in southern and eastern Asia, tigers lived in habitats including rain forests, mangroves, scrub and thorn forests, forests and tall grass areas on river flood plains, and even in the temperate forests of the Russian Far East. In addition to cover and water to drink and cool off in, this largest cat needs large mammalian prey to survive. The tiger is a specialised predator of large hoofed mammals (ungulates). Large deer, such as the sambar and red deer, and wild swine are mainstays in their diet throughout their range. They also prey on wild cattle, such as gaur and banteng, where they occur in the southern reaches of their range. Tigers also kill domestic cattle and buffalso where these are made available to them in their habitat. Occasionally, tigers kill people.

For much of this century, ridding a region of tigers was considered a sign of progress and a step on a path to positive economic development. No one gave much thought to what the world would be like without tigers. Describing the Sundarbans, the magnificent mangrove forests at the mouths of the Ganges where it interfaces with the Bay of Bengal in India and Bangladesh and one of the largest expanses of tiger habitat remaining today, E.E. Baker wrote in 1887: 'The sole distinctive characteristic of this tiger, so far as is known, is its utter fearlessness of man, and its inveterate propensity to kill and devour him on all and every opportunity.' Writing a management plan for the tiger and other wildlife in the Bangladesh coastal zone nearly a century later, my colleague M.A. Hai and I concluded: 'The survival in the wild of the powerful metaphysical symbol of Bangladesh, the royal Bengal tiger, hinges upon the capability and the will of man. In the Sundarbans, tigers, deer, forest, and men are linked inseparably and so must be their management. Any attempt to separate the tiger from its prey, the deer from the forest, or people from their needs will surely fail. The tiger must be managed with all wildlife as an integral part of forest management that ensures the sustainable production of forest products and maintains this coastal zone at the level of best achievable ecosystem function to provide for the needs of the people of Bangladesh.' And so it is throughout the tiger's range today.

It comes down to this: the largest of the cats, the predator powerful enough to kill all but the very largest of mammals, is endangered. Endangered means that if present trends continue as they are now, the tiger will become extinct in the wild. Most experts agree that, even with more than two decades of intensive international and national efforts to conserve tigers, they are worse off today than when their endangered plight was first recognised in the late 1960s.

Two events have brought the tiger to the brink. First, there has been a massive reduction in suitable tiger habitat throughout its range since the end of World War II, as more and more former wildlands have been turned to agricultural production to support our ever expanding human population. Further, what remains of tiger habitat has been divided again and again and the tiger population as a whole has been divided into smaller and smaller fractions, a process called fragmentation, until there are no longer any large expanses of tiger habitat left or any large populations of tigers left living in any one area.

Second, people have continued killing tigers. There are a few legitimate reasons for removing a problem tiger now and then, such as insuring the personal safety of people living in tiger areas or to reduce depredation on livestock. However, concerted efforts to stop a massive haemorrhage in tiger numbers from illegal killing for their elegant fur and as a source of tiger parts and products for traditional medicine makers, supplying increasingly demanding and affluent markets, have not been successful. So, even in many regions where there are areas of suitable tiger habitat, tiger numbers are greatly reduced, or the tiger is no longer present.

Is the tiger doomed in the wild? The tiger is certainly 'On the Brink', as *Time* magazine shouted in a 1995 cover story. Leading conservationist and USA Secretary of Interior Bruce Babbitt put the chilling fact this way: 'There may not be another chance to save the tiger.' If our collective attitude towards the tiger is one of antipathy and intolerance the tiger will disappear from the wild. This would be a terrible loss, symbolising a morbid disregard for natural places and wildlife conservation is general. The tiger's future rests in our hands and is completely dependent on our awareness of its plight and upon the level of support we provide for its survival.

Saving the Tiger

... I am deeply concerned by the great trouble in tiger-land. We are at a decisive moment in the life of this splendid predator. The tiger, a most cherished symbol of power and grace, has been pushed to the edge of its existence in the wild. Bearing witness to the passing, to the death of tigers in wild Asia, is a horrible experience. I know this experience first hand. I was there at the passing of the Javan tiger.

This is our last chance to save the wild tigers. While the tiger's unbroken range once spanned south and southeast Asia and into the Russian Far East, there has been a virtual collapse in the tiger's geographic range and in tiger numbers in the fifty years since the Second World War. Today, there remain only a few small tracts where we can hope to maintain the vestige of an Asian wildlife heritage, where the tiger can remain part of wild Asia in the face of ever more people and their need for land.

Consider this: Of the eight subspecies, only five remain. The tiger subspecies that once lived in the vicinity of the Caspian Sea is gone; extinct. The Bali Tiger: extinct. The Javan tiger: extinct. The central Chinese tiger has been reduced to just tens of individuals in the wild. The Siberian tiger is reduced to a few hundred individuals. Only 500 or so Sumatran tigers, the last of the island tigers, remain. These last three tiger subspecies are critically endangered. All could blink out and be lost forever in less than a decade, or even by the turn of the century, without our immediate and full attention and intensive conservation action. And what of the other two tiger subspecies? The Indo-Chinese tiger, the tiger of Thailand, Cambodia, Malaysia, Vietnam, Laos and Myanmar, has been reduced to 1500 or even fewer. Fewer than 4000 or so Bengal tigers remain in small remnant populations, scattered through the Indian subcontinent. We will lose these wondrous animals in the first decade or two of the next millenium if we do not take up the challenge of saving the tiger with a new and powerful urgency.

The challenge of saving the tiger is at the heart of conservation. The tiger is in trouble. People are responsible for the tiger's plight and only people can ensure the tiger's survival needs are met in the wild so it can survive. Saving the tiger depends on co-ordinated and thoughtful support from all people throughout the world.

Saving the tiger rests on a sophisticated scientific knowledge about the tiger's needs for quality space and adequate prey.

Saving the tiger rests on the well-being of its prey and the forests where they still live, its critical habitat, in blocks large enough to support viable tiger populations.

Saving the tiger rests on the stewardship, the skill, and the dedication of the professionals entrusted with seeking the ways and means for the tiger's survival.

Saving the tiger is stopping the killing—the massive haemorrhage in tiger numbers—from human-induced mortality to tiger populations.

Saving the tiger is breaking the economic demand for tiger parts and products that leads people to kill tigers.

Saving the tiger is making tigers and critical tiger habitats positive features in regional land-use and economic advancement programmes so that the people that live in tiger lands benefit from the tigers living there.

Saving the tiger depends upon the support of the citizens of the countries where wild tigers still live. Saving the tiger depends upon the support of people everywhere.

Ullas
Karanth

The Brutal Encounter: Man and Tiger

Ullas Karanth has spent the last two decades injecting tiger conservation with a strong dose of science. He has done new and innovative work on the population estimation of tigers and their prey across India. He is a wildlife biologist with the Wildlife Conservation Society, New York.

Ullas Karanth checking the canines of a tiger that has just been tranquilised and collared in Nagarahole National Park, Karnataka. Science is a vital ingredient for keeping tigers safe and Dr Karanth has fought for the use of science in wildlife management over the last fifteen years. (Photo by Praveen Bhargava.)

As long as human population densities remained low, and the technological capability to extirpate prey species or hunt tigers were primitive, tigers were safe over much of their range. Their ecological adaptability and high reproductive potential ensured their survival. No doubt, even centuries ago, landscape modifications had rendered many productive tracts such as the Gangetic and Deccan plains of India, the rice belts of Thailand, Vietnam and Java, unsuitable for tigers. Yet there remained extensive forests where unsuitable climate topography, soil and diseases kept out agriculture and high human population densities.

The picture began to change with the colonial penetration of Asia in the eighteenth and nineteenth centuries, when fire-arms teamed up with the traditional hunting skills, enabling colonials, kings and commoners to launch a war of attrition on tigers. At the same time, political stability and improved drugs against epidemic diseases increased human population densities, opening up hitherto inhospitable areas to intensive agriculture, often with new crops like sugarcane, coffee or tea. Probably the only positive factor favouring tigers in this era was the banning of shifting cultivation and protection of extensive wooded tracts as government-owned 'Reserved Forests' which could not be cleared and farmed by the expanding human population. Therefore, despite considerable unsustainable logging by forestry departments, by the middle of this century most remaining tiger habitats in India and Burma survived only in Reserved Forests. During the same period, in the absence of any protection to her forests against agricultural invasion, China lost most of its tiger habitats, while relatively lower population pressures alone saved tiger habitats in parts of Thailand, Indochina, Malaya and Sumatra.

By the middle of the twentieth century, the Bali tiger subspecies was driven to extinction. When India gained independence in 1947, tigers were in full retreat. There were official bounties for killing tigers, enticing villagers and tribals to shoot, poison or otherwise slaughter tigers at every opportunity. The 'Grow More Food' campaign encouraged the honey-combing of remaining blocks of tiger habitats with agricultural enclaves, setting the stage for endless

Extract from *In Danger: Habitats, Species and People*, ed. Paola Manfredi (Ramthambhore Foundation, 1997).

man–tiger confrontations. A liberal issue of gun licenses under this campaign added to the decimation of ungulates already caused by the more 'traditional' techniques. The advent of jeeps and dry cell torchlight in the post-war era provided new tools to aid the poachers of tigers' prey. Simultaneously, licensed 'sportsmen', both foreign and Indian, contributed their own unsavoury bit to the massacre. A well-known taxidermist estimates that during the 1940s he annually processed over 600 tiger skins for 'sportsmen'. A flavour of this era can be got from the fact that even less exalted bounty hunters, like my old friend nicknamed 'Naribodi' (tiger shooter) Chengappa, killed 27 tigers in the vicinity of a single village close to Nagarahole between 1947 and 1964.

In the early 1960s, as a schoolboy helplessly witnessing the terminal period of this war on wildlife, I was certain that tigers would be extirpated during the next decade. What made the situation seem so utterly hopeless was the fact that, other than a few 'étitist' conservation pioneers, like E.P. Gee, Salim Ali, Billy Arjan Singh, Zafar Futehally and M. Krishnan, nobody seemed to realise or care about what was happening to India's wildlife. In 1967, George Schaller from the Wildlife Conservation Society, New York, completed the first ever scientific study of tigers. Besides elucidating key facets of the tiger's ecology, Schaller forcefully drew attention to the tenuous status of the animal through his classic study *The Deer and the Tiger*.

THE FIRST TIGER RESCUE: 1970–1990

In response to the concerns of the international conservation community over the imminent extinction of tigers, several Asian governments duly passed laws protecting them in the early 1970s. However, effective on-ground protection materialised only in a few reserves in India and Nepal. In India, a fortuitous combination of three factors—the committed political leadership of Prime Minister Indira Gandhi, the campaign by a small but informed wildlife lobby and the presence of a disciplined protective force in state forest departments, led to the actual implementation of the new wildlife laws in several reserves. At least in these refugia tigers, their prey and habitats were protected. With the partial exception of Nepal and the USSR, tiger-range countries lacked the necessary ingredients for effective tiger protection. Consequently, over most parts of Asia, the tiger's decline continued. The Javan and Caspian tigers were blanked out in the 1970s, even as international campaigns to save the tiger were launched.

To learn the right lessons for the future from this conservation history, it is important to analyse the factors anchoring the Indian tiger rescue effort. The most effective component of this effort was the practical, protectionist orientation given to the whole enterprise by Indian foresters who had to implement the new wildlife laws. Pioneers like J.J. Dutta, Saroj Raj Choudhury, Kailash Sankhala, Sanjay Deb Roy, H.S. Panwar, Fateh Singh Rathore and others charged with the task of protecting tigers did the most obvious, commonsense things. Controlling the hunting of tigers and their prey by employing sufficient, well-equipped guards in tiger reserves was one step. Reducing biomass exploitative pressures on tiger habitats by curbing cattle grazing, forest fires, removal of timber, firewood and non-timber forest products (MFP) was another. At least in the designated Project Tiger Reserves, their directors even succeeded in stopping official logging by their forester colleagues. Another far-sighted measure was the attempt to reduce human population densities within tiger reserves, by relocating human populations away from prime tiger habitats. Although this protectionist thrust of early tiger conservation efforts was sometimes inimical to the short-term interests of local people, the fact that tigers and the entire wildlife communities around them benefitted immensely from this thrust is a certainty.

Dramatic recovery of habitats, followed by a strong rebound of prey and tiger populations, was witnessed in the first decade of protection (1974–84) in many tiger habitats both inside the Project Tiger network (Kanha, Ranthambhore, Corbett, Manas, Kaziranga) and outside it (Nagarahole, Anamalai, Dudhwa, Bandhavgarh). In protected areas exposed to tourism, like Kanha and Ranthambhore in India, or Chitawan in Nepal, visitors could even crowd around and watch tigers from atop jeeps or elephants. The flavour of those heady days is beautifully captured in the superb photographs and movies shot by Belinda Wright, Fateh Singh Rathore, Valmik Thapar and others. By the early 1980s this situation gave rise to a sense of complacency, with the Director of Project Tiger rhetorically asking 'what do you do after you have succeeded?' International conservation bodies, eager for a 'success story' rushed around claiming that they had 'saved' the big cat. Nobody realised that these few hot spots of high tiger density represented only a minuscule fraction of total tiger habitat. Over the rest of its range, the tiger's decline continued.

IGNORANCE: THE MOTHER OF COMPLACENCY

Although the hierarchical, authoritarian mind-set which characterised the Indian forestry departments was a major factor underlying the effective implementation of tiger protection in Indian reserves, the same insular mind-set also filtered out any possible infusion of wildlife science into tiger conservation measures from the very outset. For decades, Western ecologists had known that objective monitoring of animal populations is essential for evaluating the success or failure of any wildlife management programme. Realising early that it is impossible to count all individual animals over large areas, ecologists developed several standardised sampling techniques to objectively estimate animal population densities, or, at least, to measure population trends.

Ignoring such objective, sampling-based techniques right from the beginning, Indian park managers set about the impossible task of counting every single individual of an elusive, low-density species like the tiger on a countrywide basis. For this enterprise they even invented a simplistic, completely invalidated method called 'pugmark census'. Essentially the method assumes that track impressions of all tigers in India can be collected simultaneously, and from that collection each individual tiger can be distinguished and counted. There is, of course, anecdotal evidence that some individual tigers can be identified from peculiarities of track shape, by experienced field men, if all four tracks can be seen imprinted on fine dust on hard substrate. The problem, however, is with the assumption that every tiger can be identified this way, a premise which has never been validated even on zoo tigers. In fact, in limited validation tests carried out by me, this assumption failed.

Compounding this basic false premise are ground realities such as a 15 to 20 per cent annual turnover of individuals in a tiger population, variations in track shape caused by differences in soil, the speed of the animal, the collection of multiple prints of the same paw, and the absence of suitable tracking substrate in most areas. Consequently, the tiger 'numbers' which were touted to 'prove' the success of conservation efforts bore no logical relationship to real tiger numbers. Worse still, these seemingly exact numbers, which were derived so easily, made the more complicated task of applying good science to tiger conservation seem totally unnecessary.

How does one apply good science to tiger conservation? To estimate densities of prey animals in the forest, I got several three-kilometre-long straight trails (called transects) cut through the forests of Nagarahole. At dawn, I walked at full alert along these transects, scanning the forest for animals. Every time a gaur, sambar or other prey animal was seen, I recorded the species, number and distance from the animals to the transect line, using an instrument called a range finder. After about 460 kilometres had been covered on the transects (with six assistants, over two weeks), these data were used to estimate the area covered in sampling, and the population densities of herbivores. Karnataka's forest rangers who worked with me were able to calculate the densities of different ungulates quite accurately using this 'line transect sampling'.

By walking along forest roads which tigers patrolled regularly, my field assistants and I collected tiger scats (droppings), which, although they smelled like hell, were a mine of information on tigers. Since more tigers in an area meant there were more scats to find, a simple index of the number of tiger scats seen for every 100 kilometres walked could be derived. This simple index could not tell how many tigers were in the area, but by accurately reflecting increasing or decreasing trends, it provided all the information which a park manager really needs to monitor his tiger populations objectively.

To identify individual tigers without any confusion, the best way is to use camera-traps, which are fixed on forest paths and electronically triggered by the tigers themselves. Their dramatic self portraits show stripe patterns which are unique to individual tigers. Such identifications can then be used to estimate tiger populations in an area accurately, particularly if used in combination with 'capture/recapture' computer models which can analyse the frequency with which tigers repeatedly appear.

To know basic facts such as sizes of home ranges of tigers, hunting frequency, use of corridors, dispersal routes, long-term survival rates, and to observe their behaviour closely, radio-telemetry is an invaluable tool. Equipped with a receiver slung around my shoulder and a hand-held antenna, I covered the Nagarahole forests driving on elephant back or on foot every day, radio-tracking my four collared tigers. With this technique I was able to enter the secret world of tigers, an impossibility otherwise in the dense forests of Nagarahole.

Findings from Chitawan's tiger research project, and later from the work in Nagarahole, showed up inconsistencies in the results of Indian tiger censuses. However, a decade ago, tiger policymakers and managers chose to ignore all criticism. They were equally apathetic to exploring alternative techniques: simple trend indices of tiger sign, prey density estimation or direct estimation of tiger densities using camera traps.

The Second Tiger Crisis

By the early 1990s, several adverse socio-economic factors combined to seriously undermine tigers. The three pillars of the earlier limited success were collapsing. Political support for wildlife conservation weakened under successive prime ministers. The tough, no-nonsense field mangers at the bottom gave way to smooth-talking officers more at home in the new political cultures which emerged. The pro-wildlife lobby of the 1970s was subsumed by a larger and more vociferous environmentalist lobby which, despite paying lip sympathy to the cause of 'biodiveristy', fought to promote market-driven forest biomass exploitation by local people.

Internationally, major conservation groups and funding agencies, prodded to be politically correct by social activists who knew little and cared less about wildlife issues, began advocating 'sustainable use' of even the three per cent land earmarked to be the last refuge of tigers. An international symposium to mark the twentieth anniversary of Project Tiger in Delhi turned into a forum to debate 'people's needs', while the tiger's own minimum ecological needs receded from the minds of the participants. An official documentary crowed that 'all was well with the tiger'. To say the least, this complacency was misplaced. In fact, in addition to the traditional pressures on tigers, a new threat was raising it's ugly head: the burgeoning demand for tiger bones to supply the medicine men of the Far East.

The initial disquiet of a handful of tiger conservationists, based on scattered evidence like illogical census results and the poaching of known tigers in Ranthambhore, gave way to serious alarm by mid-1993, following the relentless efforts of Delhi-based tiger conservationist Ashok Kumar and his undercover agents at uncovering hard evidence of large-scale tiger poaching in India. Although the Director of Project Tiger initially maintained that the tiger was not a 'dying patient' and 'continued to be perfectly safe', mounting evidence from wider investigations showed otherwise. The true extent of this poaching or its impact are still unquantified in the absence of reliable estimates of tiger numbers and the numbers poached. However, it is clear that there is certainly no room for such complacency any longer. As the Indian Minister of Environment finally admitted, 'there is a serious problem'. The question is, are we doing anything about it?

Reversing the Tiger's Decline

There are those who argue that loss of genetic variability caused by habitat fragmentation may become a long-term threat to some tiger populations. Others believe that only 'people friendly' conservation policies can save the tiger in the long run. But as Lord Keynes said, in the long run we will all be dead anyway, and we must not ignore the immediate crisis on hand. By over-emphasising long-term threats to the survival of tigers and thereby diverting scarce resources towards those, we may in fact be dooming the species to extinction in the next couple of decades.

My research on tigers in Nagarahole, in conjunction with those of biologists Melvin Sunquist, George Schaller and Alan Rabinowitz shows that the low numbers of tigers over much of Asia is caused by the loss of their prey base on account of hunting. Superimposed on this decline, the poaching of tigers for 'traditional medicines' (the bone trade) may now be driving the final 'coup de grace' into the big cat.

As we now know, tiger home-range sizes, densities and survival rates are all strongly linked to the maintenance of high prey densities. There is evidence that at higher densities, big cat populations can even withstand some degree of hunting pressure, because of the presence of 'surplus' transients. With lowered prey densities this 'buffer' of transients is lost, home ranges become larger, numbers of breeders decline, recruitment drops, and the tiger population becomes increasingly vulnerable. Ultimately, although a few individuals may linger on for a decade or so, extinction is dramatic and final, as the exit of the Javan tiger showed us two decades ago.

It is obvious that the tiger cannot change its natural traits, large size and carnivorous diet, to accommodate our changing policies. Either we accommodate the tiger's biological needs into our world view, or the big cat will go extinct. Therefore, the strategy to prevent the tiger's extinction has to be built around this vulnerable species' ecological needs rather than around social attitudes which we perceive to be politically correct. This inevitably means making several tough, unpopular decisions.

Firstly, we have to recognise that tigers cannot coexist with high density human settlements living off market-driven economic activities like agriculture and forest biomass exploitation. Therefore, human and livestock population densities need to be reduced inside prime tiger habitats through sensible and fair relocation policies, to allow wild ungulate prey to recover from habitat pressures, poaching and competition with livestock. It is even worth sacrificing some non-priority forest areas to accommodate such relocation, if critical tiger habitats can be physically isolated from poaching and habitat pressures.

Secondly, recognising that market-driven biomass exploitation is the leading cause of habitat deterioration, all extractive linkages between tiger reserves and local or distant markets for forest biomass derivatives such as fuel, timber, fodder, dung and other 'minor' forest products should be snapped. Moreover, this forest–market linkage must be broken, regardless of whether the agencies extracting such products are governments, NGOs or local people.

Thirdly, we need to appreciate that, despite our best social engineering efforts, there will always be criminals in any society, who can only be stopped through the effective use of force. Therefore, our effort to promote eco-development around tiger habitats has to be balanced by adequate investments in manpower and material resources for policing tiger habitats. Threat from poachers operating inside tiger habitats and the threat from distant wildlife traffickers should both be ruthlessly countered.

Fourthly, we have to critically and continuously evaluate how our tiger conservation efforts are faring, by employing universally accepted methods of science. For this, our policymakers have to shed their intellectual apathy and weave the science of wildlife biology into the fabric of conservation strategies.

Finally, without a committed political leadership and public awareness, it is impossible to usher in any such major changes. The only force which can perhaps induce the necessary attitude changes among politicians, officials, media, social activists and the public is an articulate, passionate 'tiger lobby' which clearly understands the ecological fragility of the feared predator.

When I see a tiger pad silently through the forest brush, literally melting into it, a deep sense of admiration and awe seeps through me, which no captive tiger can arouse. I cannot but help feel that it is this elemental passion we all feel for its wildness, one way or the other, which can either save the tiger—or destroy it forever.

WHY SAVE THE TIGER?

There are several sensible arguments which can be marshalled to justify why we should save the tiger. For instance, the productivity and welfare of our predominantly rural, agricultural society is critically dependent on the regulation of run-off and soil erosion, on the recharge of ground water, and the mitigation of local climatic fluctuations. Forests, which clothe the watersheds of most of our important river systems, play a dominant role in performing these functions, besides harbouring the tiger. If wisely managed, some of the forested landscapes can also provide our rural and urban populations the fuel, timber, bamboo, rattan and non-timber products needed for their sustenance.

More importantly, as the earth's mineral resources get exhausted rapidly, the need for food, fibres, shelter, fuels and life-saving chemicals of an expanding population seeking better lifestyles will increasingly depend on biotechnology. However, so far, scientists have explored only a tiny fraction of the rich forest biota, which is literally a treasure house of potential life-supporting products. The tiger is a key species of these forests, which harbour millions of plant and animal life forms. Moreover, the tiger is at the end of a complex chain of ecological relationships; this also includes plants which directly produce energy from the sun, and the herbivorous animals upon which the tiger preys. These relationships are so complex that it is virtually impossible to isolate and preserve only those life forms which may become useful to humans. One of the most effective ways of being sure of saving complex life-form linkages and ecological processes is to ensure that top-predators, such as the tiger, are thriving in an intact assembly of predators, prey and plant communities. Surely, sacrificing the remaining three percent land on which tigers live now, to solve some problem or the other which society has not been able to solve despite full access to the remaining 97 percent over centuries, does not make sense.

There are other arguments one can advance: the last refugia of tigers are also wonderful natural laboratories to observe and from which to learn. The tiger forests are our last links to a natural world from which we came, a rich source of education. They are an irreplaceable library of nature for generations to come, and advocating their destruction in the name of progress or temporary local benefits is akin to burning down an ancient library.

However, for all their impeccable logic, the above arguments for saving the tiger are basically utilitarian and rather selfishly human-centred. In addition, I believe there are strong ethical compulsions for trying to save the tiger. Tigers (and other wildlife species) are products of millions of years of evolution. Global climate change, the movements of continents, the advance and retreat of glaciers, volcanic eruptions and other mighty natural forces led to the evolution and radiation of life on earth. During these upheavals, life forms evolved and died out, only to be replaced by new ones. However, humans have now so drastically modified the earth's landscape that the wonderful process of evolution has been virtually negated for all but the smallest creatures.

The amazing process of natural selection (jokingly but appropriately attributed to a 'blind watchmaker' by evolutionary biologist

Richard Dawkins) gave rise to a species like the tiger. Do humans who evolved during the last few 'seconds' of the history of life on earth have a fundamentally superior moral right to wipe other species off the face of the earth? Or do we have a moral duty to protect some of these creatures on at least a tiny fraction of the earth's landscape? If the latter, at least in its last refugia, the tiger's right to survive as species overrides the rights of individual men to extirpate them. I believe such preservationism is ethically justifiable under any moral or social code we can think of.

Alan

Rabinowitz

The Status of the Indochinese Tiger

Alan Rabinowitz has walked the tiger forests of Indochina. Here he sits with the local people during his tireless efforts to survey some of the toughest terrain in the tiger range.

INTRODUCTION

In 1993, the number of tigers that comprised the Indochinese subspecies was listed as between 1050 and 1750. These numbers were based on little more than speculation. At present, we know less about the tiger in Indochina than we do about tigers throughout any other part of their range. This is due to the animal's secretive, forest-dwelling habits, and the fact that the range of this subspecies mostly encompasses six countries: Myanmar, Thailand, Lao PDR, Cambodia, Malaysia and Vietnam. Since many of these countries have been involved in wars, social unrest and political upheavals over the last several decades, there have been few opportunities to obtain reliable information about tigers in the region.

The use of Geographic Information System (GIS) technology to map existing habitat where tigers are assumed to be present was proposed in the late eighties, but only recently has this idea been developed in a more comprehensive manner to identify tiger priority areas and suggest a broader landscape approach to tiger conservation. However, the assumption that tigers exist in all intact forest areas is based more on historical fact than current reality. Since factors such as prey availability, water resources and hunting play a role in tiger distribution and abundance, modelling tiger demographics based on habitat alone can only be a first step. Field research is needed to provide data concerning tiger numbers and the factors affecting their survival ... Here I consider the history of protection afforded to tigers and their habitats, and the reasons behind the decline of tigers in Indochina's countries ... there is little recent data on known tiger distribution, and even where tigers are present, they are not uniformly distributed throughout available forest habitat. Finally, I summarise the current status of tiger conservation within the region and recommend some immediate actions to improve tiger protection and management ... Since the 1940s, Indochina has lost 80 per cent of its forest cover, partly due to three decades of uninterrupted warfare. Since the end of

Extract from *Riding the Tiger: Tiger Conservation in Human Dominated Landscapes,* ed. John Seidensticker, Sarah Christie and Peter Jackson (Cambridge, 1999). Published by permission of the Zoological Society of London.

the Vietnam War in 1975, slash and burn agriculture, fires and fuelwood collection have caused continued forest loss. Today only 10–15 per cent of the country's original forest remains, much of it in relatively small and fragmented pockets.

Of 59 protected areas listed as of 1992 in Vietnam, only eight were declared before 1986, and only one area is greater than 1000 km^2. Recent surveys in both protected and unprotected areas have indicated relatively high levels of hunting, illegal logging and collection of forest products. These activities, along with population growth and agricultural expansion, continue to eat away at the remaining forest areas.

A recent checklist of mammals in Vietnam lists the tiger as present throughout much of the north, and most of the border provinces with China, Laos and Cambodia. Although the tiger has been legally protected since 1960, and a 1989 law prohibits the trade of tigers, tiger parts are still easily available in Vietnamese markets. A 1993 survey found a total of 37 tiger skins and 1166 tiger claws on display in five Vietnamese cities. Despite continuing hunting pressure and loss of forest habitat, the 1996 'Status of the tiger' report lists tiger numbers in Vietnam as 200–300 individuals, the same number given three years earlier. There is no indication how these numbers were derived.

There are few large forest areas left for tigers in Vietnam, and there are not many recent tiger data even from these areas. With a rapidly expanding economy, increasing population pressures, and much of the remaining forest in very small isolated pockets, Vietnam needs to concentrate its conservation efforts in areas where the forest is still intact and where tigers and their prey still exist in some numbers. If any tigers are to survive in the future, Vietnam needs more field data that can be used to establish a few special 'tiger protection sites'. In conjunction with this, the government must show initiative in eliminating the wildlife trade.

Discussion

Since 1993, with the establishment of The Delhi Declaration at the Global Tiger Forum in India, there have been numerous regional and international workshops and conference discussing the status of tigers. At a trans-boundary biodiversity conferences for the Indochina region, the Indochinese tiger was declared an important flagship species for promoting regional conservation efforts along border areas. In 1995, the US National Fish and Wildlife Foundation and the Exxon Corporation launched the Save the Tiger Fund, pledging $50,000,000 over a five-year period. All of these actions have helped keep tiger conservation a high-priority issue among government officials, but there have been too few actions 'on-the-ground'.

The establishment and maintenance of a well-managed protected area system is a crucial component of tiger conservation. Local communities, left completely to their own devices, will not save tigers. I concur with the opinion that while incentive-based community conservation schemes are a laudable future goal for conservation, the current tiger situation is too critical to rely solely on long-term mechanisms. However, the idea that tigers are protected simply by establishing protected areas is no longer a valid concept, if it ever was. Even in the largest remaining forest areas, poaching and the wildlife trade continue to be the most insidious threats to remaining tiger populations. The many small tiger populations in isolated forest blocks are at the greatest risk and may not be salvageable. As poaching in these areas continues over time, the probability of population extinction increases drastically. And while any one factor alone may not bring a species to extinction, the effects of other factors, e.g. habitat loss and prey reduction, become compounded as extinction mechanisms become synergistic.

To protect tigers, two realities must be faced. First, land must be designated, protected and managed for tigers and their prey in perpetuity. High-priority tiger areas cannot be compromised. This will increasingly conflict with the needs and desires of growing numbers of local people. Secondly, not all tigers alive today can be saved for the future. Areas in which small populations may not survive should not drain the limited human and financial resources available for conservation. 'Triage', defined as the allocation of treatment according to a system of priorities that maximises the survivors of a battle or disaster, is how we must now go about our efforts to save the tiger. Otherwise, the tiger may follow the example of the Sumatran rhino whose continued demise has been assisted by years of inaction, misdirected initiatives and political correctness.

The sections that follow summarise some of the most basic issues concerning the conservation of the Indochinese tiger and recommend a few actions that should be immediately implemented if tigers are to be better protected and managed in the region.

The Current Realities of Tiger Conservation in Indochina

Data collection

1 There is a startling lack of substantiated, quantitative data on tiger presence and distribution throughout most of the region. Most field survey teams are poorly trained and lack appropriate guidelines for standardised tiger surveys.

2 Interviews and/or questionnaire surveys that attempt to obtain information about tigers are often done in a haphazard, subjective manner that does not provide reliable or accurate information.

3 Field survey data are often not published or made easily available to others involved in tiger conservation. When such data are reported, it is frequently difficult to evaluate or repeat the methodology.

4 Much of the prime tiger habitat, consisting of lowland forests with good water resources and a diverse large prey base, has been converted to other land use practices. Many protected areas, particularly those created in the last two decades, are in rugged, often degraded habitat that is suboptimal for the survival of tigers and prey populations.

5 Many areas where tiger live consist of relatively small, isolated forest blocks that may not support viable tiger populations in perpetuity.

6 Many protected areas and other forests with tigers are being degraded by human settlements and activities that destroy or change the forest structure. Access by tigers to reliable water sources is often cut off by such activities.

7 Any landscape or community approach to tiger conservation

will not be effective without a core of well-managed protected areas in place.

8 As human populations grow and the demand for land increases, increasing pressures will be brought to bear on remaining forests and protected areas.

Management and protection

9 Most protected areas containing tigers are inadequately staffed and have little or no monitoring and management of wildlife.

10 The staff of most protected areas are poorly trained, and are not given sufficient financial or social incentives to create a feeling of respect for themselves and the importance of their jobs.

11 No effective tiger management policies have yet been designed and implemented in any of the Indochinese tiger range countries.

12 There is a lack of real commitment by many government officials towards any conservation actions that are difficult or controversial.

Hunting

13 Partly due to increased market demands and partly due to the increased political stability of the region, the hunting of tigers and their prey has increased in recent years. Much of the hunting is for animal parts, using non-selective and inhuman hunting methods including snares, jaw traps, poisoned carcasses and traps.

14 Primarily as a result of hunting pressures on both tigers and their prey species, tigers are no longer present in many forest areas where they once occurred.

15 Where tigers do occur, surveys generally point to lower than expected tiger and/or prey densities due to hunting pressures.

Trade

16 The trade in wildlife, particularly tiger parts and their prey, is more extensive today than a decade ago. Such trade occurs at local, regional and international levels.

17 Although the wildlife trade is acknowledged as a major issue in tiger conservation, Cambodia, Laos and Myanmar are still not party to the Convention on International Trade in Endangered

Species (CITES). (Subsequent to the Symposium, Cambodia and Myanmar have signed the Convention.)

18 If the trade in tiger and other wildlife parts cannot be effectively controlled, the protection and management of tiger populations will become an almost insurmountable task in most range countries.

RECOMMENDED IMMEDIATE ACTIONS TO CONSERVE THE TIGER IN INDOCHINA

Data collections

1 Establish simple and inexpensive methods to quickly and accurately assess tiger presence, distribution and relative abundance throughout the different tiger range countries of the region.

2 Publish a manual in each of the range country languages dealing with tiger survey and research techniques, track identification and simple, inexpensive management practices to help existing tiger and prey populations.

3 Create tiger survey units to conduct field surveys and to monitor tiger and prey populations in areas of remaining tiger habitat.

Management and protection

4 Following up on the results of action 3, identify and prioritise the most important tiger areas within each country.

5 Design tiger management action plans for each country in the region, with a timetable for implementation. Progress on implementation should be reviewed by a 'tiger committee' once a year.

6 Ban the use and sale of all equipment used in non-selective and inhumane forms of hunting, particularly snares and jaw traps.

Trade

7 Create a government mechanism within each range country that can deal quickly and effectively with wildlife trade issues. Any range country that has not signed CITES should do so immediately.

Regional

8 Initiate a regional training programme for mid-level and senior government staff. Emphasise coordinated protection and management of tiger populations along international borders.

9 Bring together delegates from all the Indochinese tiger range countries once every two years to exchange information, promote trans-boundary conservation, and establish multi-lateral mechanisms for addressing wildlife trade and other conservation issues.

John
Seidensticker, *et al.*

Approaches to Tiger Conservation

Two fourteen-month-old tiger cubs swat at each other as their mother watches in Ranthambhore National Park, Rajasthan. The tiger is a great symbol of not only the wilderness but also of vital water catchments. John Seidensticker articulates the issue with rare eloquence.

Were it not for reserves we surely wouldn't have many tigers left. But obviously protection alone is not enough.

—George Schaller

[Reserved land has been an essential tool in tiger conservation, but] ... The conservation of species and undamaged habitats is like a three-legged stool. Each leg is necessary but not sufficient. The legs of the conservation stool are sustainable use of renewable resources, species recovery, and habitat preservation. Conservation can progress by focusing on each of these, defining their limits, developing improvements, and preventing dysfunction.

—Humphrey & Stith

Long-term success is managing reserved land with viable tiger populations lies in linking these areas with surrounding landscapes through ecological and genetic mechanisms that promote and preserve natural landscape dynamics. The tiger is in its present precarious state in part because of the growing imbalance between the expanding numbers, needs and wants of people and the limits of the capacity of landscapes to support these wants and needs. Making the economic case for inclusion of tigers in land-use formulations means showing that the benefits gained from including the tiger are as good as, or better than, those to be had by converting the habitat for other purposes. A core hypothesis that emerged from the presentations and deliberations at Tiger 2000 [see 'Introduction' in this book] concerned the linkage between the needs of the tiger and the welfare of the people living near it. Human needs are a part of any ecological system and securing a long-term future for wild tigers requires consideration of the needs of tigers and people together ... authors emphasise the need to shift the domain of our conservation theory, doctrine and practice from what goes on inside reserve boundaries to the landscape, the region and the world beyond. Our efforts to secure a future for wild tigers will necessarily include economic, cultural and ecological resources, environmental education and active

Extracts from *Riding the Tiger: Tiger Conservation in Human Dominated Landscapes,* ed. John Seidensticker, Peter Jackson and Sarah Christie (Cambridge, 1999). Published by permission of the Zoological Society of London.

recruitment and retention of partners locally, regionally, nationally and internationally, working together to achieve a common purpose—saving the tiger.

Zoos are obvious partners in securing the future of wild tigers. Zoos and related institutions have secured a future for tigers living there. And in the last three decades zoos have provided many of the human intellectual resources and the animal populations that led to the formulations of small-population biology. Our expanding understanding of the risks confronting small-sized animal populations and the technologies to assist in overcoming those risks, such as more precise understanding of genetics and the development of assisted reproduction technologies, have been of central concern for conservation biologists.

The World Zoo Conservation Strategy. '... urges the entire global zoo network and all other conservation-orientated networks to integrate and intensify their efforts towards their mutual goals. This great mustering of all available resources will be crucial to giving our Earth's biosphere the best possible chance for survival of its biological wealth of genes, species and ecosystems.' Yet, there has been and remains a tension between those who look after tigers living in zoos and those who have invested their time in the stewardship of wild tigers. Some to conclude that the goals of both tiger conservation paradigms are the same; securing a future for wild tigers. It is argued that many of the organisational principles and lessons from efforts to make tiger-breeding programmes in zoos goal-driven can be employed by the larger tiger conservation community in learning to work together to save the tiger.

We come from both sides of this issue and believe that the tension is not trivial and at times is crippling for tiger conservation. It is useful to explore the historical and cultural contexts of wild and zoo tiger conservationists as a means of separating the people issues from the problem, focusing on interests and inventing options for future partnerships. In our experience, stewards of wild tigers see in tigers a fundamental essence of nature, living in ideal natural places. Much of the moral authority for saving the tiger stems from the fact that tigers and their 'Edenic' habitats represent an external source of non-human values against which human actions can be judged with little ambiguity. Tigers are living symbols of power and grace and wild Asia.

Tigers are always value-laden and it is we humans who affix value in the way we perceive them. We do so in many different ways. For those of us who have seen, or who someday want to see, or simply place great value on tigers living out their lives in an ideal nature, tigers living in zoos can be seen as the antithesis of wild tigers. In this view, zoo tigers are living unnatural lives and tigers are a commodity being exploited for financial gain. We contend that there is nothing unnatural in the awe on a child's face the first time s/he really sees a zoo tiger. Wildlife films and beautiful colour photographs of tigers can be informative but simply do not replace living, breathing, roaring tigers. We think of zoo tigers as ambassadors for wild tigers. This is how the vast majority of people will ever witness the wonder of a tiger. The numbers of zoo visitors are staggering. Zoos have embraced the environmental movement to support endangered species conservation, and zoo visitors are an essential tiger conservation constituency. Zoo visitors and the public at large must be a partner in saving the tiger, because it is the public who supports the legal framework that protects tigers and it is the public which foots much of the bill. Zoos have moved substantially beyond being entertainment centres and are becoming conservation parks with goals focusing on conservation and education; in fact, zoos are playing an enormous role in environmental education. Zoos see their role as a support, not a substitute, for wild tiger populations ...

Will zoo populations ever serve as a source of tigers for 'reintroduction' into the wild? Reintroduction of tigers is not a conservation technology that will be used in the immediate future, but enough has been learned recently from the reintroduction of other large carnivores that it remains a viable option if the ecological, valuational and organisational challenges are met. Certainly zoo tigers are an insurance policy against ever losing the tiger completely, but the goal for zoo-based tiger conservationists and the stewards of wild tigers alike is to provide the support needed to maintain sustainable tiger populations on their home ground. The challenge for all of us is to keep these special places where tigers now live from becoming places where tigers go to die.

The first call to save the tiger led to one of the most famous and extensive wildlife conservation campaigns ever undertaken. With the passage of CITES and better protection for tigers in range states through the 1970s and into the mid-1980s, there was some success in efforts to save the tiger. But beginning in the late 1980s, tiger parts, especially tiger bone, began turning up in staggering quantities, indicating that a major haemorrhage in tiger numbers was occurring. In 1993, 'The International Symposium on the Tiger' held in New Delhi, India, and 'the Amur Tiger: Problems Concerning Preservation of its Populations', a symposium held in Khabarovsk, Russia, both concluded that the tiger was in crisis because of poaching and trading of its parts to supply the demand from traditional East Asian medicine (TCM).

There has been a focused and sophisticated response to this increase in tiger poaching by a number of NGOs, working with governments to stem the trade in tiger parts and products. Can we see a beginning of an end in this trade? Significant headway has been made in curtailing the legal trade in tiger bone, but tigers are still being poached and tiger products are still being sold as ingredients in several traditional East Asian medicines. This stubborn residual trade remains to be eliminated. Tackling the demand problem means taking tiger bone out of TCM, and enlisting would-be consumers of tiger bone in tiger conservation efforts is the key concept. TCM is a health care system with ancient roots that hundreds of millions of people depend on; the question is not whether there will be or should be TCM, but how to ensure that TCM will not endanger the survival of the tiger and other endangered species. Important first steps for tiger conservationists are to reject an anti-TCM stance and understand the need for treatment of the pains for which products containing tiger bone have traditionally been used; to help promote the acceptance of substitutes for tiger bone in TCM; and to talk with TCM specialists about the conservation status of tigers and the role TCM trade has played in endangering the tiger's survival. An alternative suggestion has been to 'farm' tigers to supply parts and products. Aside from the animal welfare and other emotive objections to this, there is no way to tell a wild tiger bone from a 'framed' tiger bone; debate on the possible effects of such a legal market on the illegal one is both heated and inconclusive, but the bottom line is that without a purposive approach to remove the demand for tiger bone, the future for wild tigers is very bleak.

Operation Amba (the name for the tiger used by the Udegai people of the Russian Far East) has added a new dimension to the toolbox of tiger conservation. An international effort has unfolded to deter the lethal slide of the Amur tiger into extinction in the Russian Far East. A conventional approach to containing the poaching of Amur tigers was unsustainable for financial and managerial reasons; rather, they describe Operation Amba as a strategic defence of the tiger with PsyOps (psychological operations) as a key component. Operation Amba has made the critical difference to the survival of the tiger in Russia. With low densities of humans and roads, the context for a protective scheme for the Amur tiger in the Russian Far East is strikingly different from that in other reaches of the tiger's range, but there are important lessons to be learned from Operation Amba: involve local people, develop skilled personnel and equip and pay them on time, secure political backing, communicate with relevant agencies abroad and maintain good public relations.

The wildlife trader or middleman is the link between the market and a poacher with a dead tiger in hand. Operation Amba focused on identifying and neutralising tiger traders in the Russian Far East. We need to focus on removing the city-based wholesaler in tiger parts in controlling tiger poaching in India. There is essentially no demand for tiger parts and products within India; the demand comes from outside. They estimate that a tiger a day is poached in India and this will continue and as long as punishment of city-based traders is not imposed, which it rarely is. Tiger conservationists must take up and effectively address the concerns of the people who live with tigers on a daily basis.

Tiger conservationists have seemed preoccupied with determining the number of tigers and doing so has been problematic and contentious. When tiger habitat has been identified it has usually been referenced as the amount in reserves, although it is commonly accepted that many more tigers live outside reserves than in them. There has not been an equal emphasis on determining the amount of habitat remaining for tigers throughout their range in Asia, or what the essential components of that habitat might be. The importance of adequate prey density as a habitat component has to be emphasised. With an adequate prey base a moderately sized tiger population could compensate for even relatively high mortality regimes imposed by poaching. There is an entirely new way of thinking about tiger conservation options and this is the idea of tiger conservation units—TCUs, an important conceptual change in thinking about the future of wild tigers. Tiger conservation planning in this view shifts from a taxonomic to an ecological basis because a conservation strategy must account for the behavioural, demographic and ecological variation present among populations across their range. The underlying principle is that tigers are adapted in all these ways to the ecological conditions where they live. Conservationists have identified major habitat types within each bioregion, and a process to identify both remaining blocks of habitat where tigers may still be able to live and the essential linkages within these habitat blocks or TCUs. They prioritise these blocks through a process that orders risks and opportunities, and suggest that the highest probability of securing a future for wild tigers can be achieved by focusing conservation efforts on the top 50 of the 160-odd blocks of potential types. We now have maps of Asia that accurately reflect where the tiger may survive in the next century ...

The process of including the tiger in long-term land-use plans is further advanced in the Russian Far East than anywhere else in Asia. The inaccessibility of the Sikhote-Alin Mountains where most of the remaining Amur tigers live has been a primary factor in their protection, but these mountains are now becoming more accessible as road density increases to support the extraction of timber and other resources. Using ecological criteria for sustaining the Amur tiger population conservation scholars have defined and implemented a planning process, and proposed a habitat protection plan for the Amur tiger. Reserves would be linked by multiple-use zones, providing connectivity and habitat for 70 reproducing females overall. With the ecological criteria fully developed, the political criteria necessary for sustaining the Amur tiger in the future and the essential factors that enable people and tigers to share forest resources have been made clear: what exactly will constitute a habitat that will sustain the Amur tiger into the future? This process has not so far been replicated anywhere else in the tiger's range. It is a process that will maintain the largest TCU in the world.

When the first call to save the tiger was heard in the late 1960s, India, like other countries responded with a top-down, command and control programme in which the tiger was treated as a public good. New protective legislation was passed. Habitat for tigers was provided through specially designated reserves that have grown from the initial 8 to 23 at the time of writing. In these reserves every effort has been made to separate tigers from people, usually by restricting commercial harvest of forest products and by relocating inhabitants. The underlying assumption was that these reserves would serve '... to increases the tiger population to optimum levels through improvement of the biotope ... this situation will provide a breeding nucleus [of tigers] from which surplus animals can migrate to surrounding forests' (Task Force, Indian Board for Wild Life 1972). The limitations of a heavy-handed, top-down approach, especially with dissipating central power in India, have become apparent to Valmik Thapar. Because of human population growth in and around tiger reserves, people and their livestock have been spilling into reserves rather than tigers spilling out as was originally envisioned. Tigers are very sensitive to dispersal barriers and, because of the small size of active tiger reserves, tigers living in them are at considerable risk from the potential impacts (demographic, genetic, environmental and catastrophic) of stochastic processes. Valmik Thapar reports that after 25 years the much-vaunted tiger reserve system initiated in India at the inception of Project Tiger is in tatters. There are some notable exceptions, such as Nagarhole, but many reserves (e.g. Panna) are rapidly becoming more isolated and degraded through massive extraction of resources to support growing populations of people, and their livestock, living in and around them. While the tiger remains a public good and national treasure in India, the people who live near tigers on a daily basis are having an increasingly loud and negative voice in the tiger's future.

This contribution is a cry to arms for tigers in India. Although Valmik Thapar does not talk about this, he watched the increasing threats to tiger habitats driven by the needs of local people as he studied tigers in the Ranthambhore National Park during the 1980s. In his book *Tigers, The Secret Life* (1989) he railed against a government that seemed not to care or at least did not give the tiger any priority status. The final chapter of his book is a prescription on how to better the lives of those who live near tigers. He did not just write about it, he then did something about it. With his teacher, Fateh Singh Rathore, and others he set up the Ranthambhore Foundation which is dedicated to bringing both the public and private sectors together to better the lives of those who live near Ranthambhore. And he established 'Tiger Link', a tiger support network that strives to bring together the many people throughout India and the world that believe there should be a place for wild tigers. Herein lies hope for a future for wild tigers when such efforts are duplicated and adapted to local circumstances throughout the tiger's range.

Often in tiger conservation, planning and actions have focused on a single threat, such as poaching, to the exclusion of the larger problems tigers face in the shifting social and political Asian landscape. The lands where tigers live contain resources—timber, minerals, hydropower—needed to fuel rapidly expanding Asian and world economies and the extraction of resources requires an improved transportation network, including the widening and straightening of roads. Bittu Sahgal has prepared a map that highlights—wildlife 'hotspots' is his word—the locations of planned or ongoing major projects threatening tiger reserves and other tiger habitats. The power of his map is that in a single page you can grasp how all-invasive and overwhelming these threats are to the future of the tiger in India. Largely financed through multi-national and international structures, these direct pressures are being brought to bear on tiger lands in India in response to the needs and wants of people who have never heard a tiger's roar in the still of the night or seen a tiger track along a dusty forest road. There are not the local people but those of us who live in India's and the world's urban and suburban centres. Most of these people may be personally natural or even supportive of sustainable tiger populations but are unknowing participants in the tiger's continued demise. What is so frustrating for the stewards of wild tigers is that these root challenges to securing a future for wild tigers are largely beyond the control of local people and in many instances even beyond control at national or international levels. Securing a future for the tiger on its home ground requires broad understanding of how international forces are threatening the tiger's future. No legal mandate can completely exclude economic considerations from the conservation process. Making the case to preserve the tiger and tiger habitat specifically and biodiversity generally means showing that the benefits to be had from preservation are as good or better than those to be had by converting the habitat for other purposes. This is where partnerships and linkages with local people specifically and the private sector in general will make all the difference. The lessons from Tiger 2000 were that the place to begin is in securing local partnerships based on sustainable land-uses and recovery because the long-term interests of both tigers and local people are usually at risk from these extractive pressures ...

How to make it worthwhile for people to live in proximity to tigers and how to increase their tolerance of tigers? These are examples of large- and small-scale investment in tiger conservation to the benefit of the local people. The Global Environmental Facility (GEF) is supporting projects that attempt to improve protected-area management and ecodevelopment for communities living within and adjacent to protected areas. At their core these projects seek to take the pressure off reserves and to rebuild natural capital around them. Strategies include planning for micro-credit, alternative livelihoods, conservation agreements, special programmes for joint forest management, education, conservation-awareness building and monitoring; all designed to promote better living conditions and public support for conservation at the local level. The GEF is spending tens of millions of dollars in this effort around reserves in India, Indonesia, China and Laos.

Do the GEF-sponsored programmes adequately address the needs of tigers as well as those of people? This contentious issue was expressed and discussed at Tiger 2000 because the needs of the tiger are not explicitly recognised or addressed in the GEF programme. Our advancing understanding of the ecological criteria that must be met to sustain tiger populations as outlined throughout these chapters will move this discussion from a theoretical plane to pragmatic on-the-ground assessment, consultation and action in each case. Ullas Karanth has demonstrated how this understanding can be furthered with an ongoing, statistically valid system to monitor the density of ungulate prey and tigers, based on his work using trained volunteers in India's Nagarhole National Park.

Eric Dinerstein and his associates report on a small-scale project that promotes local guardianship, including that of tigers, on degraded lands adjacent to the Royal Chitawan National Park in Nepal. They recognised that the main threat to biodiversity in Chitawan is the poverty of the surrounding villages, which hold 290,000 people and have a population growth rate of over 2 per cent a year. Lacking suitable alternatives for the fulfilment of their daily subsistence needs, many local residents believed that their livelihoods were threatened by the creation of the park in 1973. As is the case with many tiger reserve areas with a weak economy and a lack of supplies from outside, people in Chitawan are dependent on the park for fodder and firewood. This project focuses on rebuilding natural capital by developing a sustainable supply of fodder and firewood, and increasing habitat for wildlife, in the park's degraded buffer zone. The local community was responsible for resource management and protection in the Park's buffer area. By providing economic incentives and developing self-sufficiency, villagers have created alternative sources of the forest resources previously available only in the Park. They have also regenerated 16.5 km^2 of prime habitat for the tiger and the Asian Greater One-horned Rhinoceros. This wildlife resource has attracted ecotourists, and local communities are making money for community improvement, such as schools and health clinics, by charging fees to local hotels that use the regeneration area for wildlife viewing. This also provides funds for gas digesters that encourage stall-feeding of cattle with improved milk yields; this facilitates dung collection and reduces the size of the free-ranging cattle population around the reserve. Poaching in this area of the Chitawan Valley has significantly decreased. These authors provide principles for adapting this programme to other areas in tigerland. Indeed, this Chitawan site welcomes local groups from other TCUs who want to learn more about approaches that link tiger conservation with local development. As neighbours watch the communities involved with this programme prosper, the project is expanding regeneration activities from the site level to the landscape scale. Dinerstein calculates that when the full potential of this programme is reached there will be enough regenerated habitat to double both tiger and rhino populations in the Chitawan region. Chitawan is recognised as a primary success story in tiger conservation; the lessons from this valley provide one roadmap for securing a future for wild tigers.

Steven
Russell Galster
& Karin
# Vaud Eliot

Roaring Back

Steve Galster and **Karin Vaud Eliot** have played key roles in their work for the protection of Siberian tigers and Operation Amba.

A sixteen-month-old male tiger snarls from his position on a rock in Ranthambhore National Park. (Photo courtesy Valmik Thapar.)
The Siberian tiger was at a point of virtual extinction. With the anti-poaching Operation Amba, the tigers of this region have got a fresh lease of life. The authors explain how this operation evolved and then succeeded.

INTRODUCTION

'Imminent extinction.' That is how Russian and international wildlife experts described the situation facing the Amur (or Siberian) tiger by 1993. As with other subspecies of tiger, the Amur tiger's critical situation was relayed to the international community through press reports and via the Convention on International Trade in Endangered Species of Flora and Fauna (CITES). In four consecutive meetings in 1993 and 1994, CITES gave high priority to the plight of the tiger. While some hope was held out for the future of the relatively numerous Indian tiger, little was expressed for the remaining 200–300 Amur tigers being pursued by commercial poachers in Russia's wild Far East.

Thanks to a handful of government and non-governmental organisation (NGO) representatives, who believed otherwise, by 1997 the situation had changed dramatically. Instead of losing 50–60 Amur tigers a year to commercial poachers, experts were happy to report a rising population of Amur tigers and a lower level of commercial tiger poaching in the Russian Far East. This feat was achieved during Russia's post-perestroika transition—a period marked by widespread organised criminal activity—in Primorski Krai, a territory in close proximity to the world's largest tiger-consuming markets. Lessons from this positive experience must be applied to future protective efforts in the Russian Far East if a healthy and sustainable population of Amur tigers is to be maintained well past the turn of the century. Remember the Indian tiger, which was also brought back from a slide towards extinction two decades ago. India's Project Tiger was initially successful in the 1970s, but then deteriorated during the late 1980s and early 1990s, demonstrating that no endangered wild animal is ever 'saved'. Vigilance is the key to continued survival.

The authors of this chapter represent the Global Survival Network (GSN), an environmental security NGO that works closely with wildlife biologists and enforcement personnel worldwide to develop effective species recovery programmes. GSN co-sponsors

Extract from *Riding the Tiger: Tiger Conservation in Human Dominated Landscapes,* eds John Seidensticker, Sarah Christie and Peter Jackson (Cambridge, 1999). Published with permission of the Zoological Society of London.

anti-poaching operations in the Russian Far East, where we approach tiger conservation from a strategic, 'environmental security' point of view. Therefore, we will examine the objective of the Russian programme, code-named 'Operation Amba', the impediments to this objective (i.e. the threat), the strategy designed to overcome the threat and the tactical plan that the rangers of Operation Amba continue to follow. This analysis will cover four distinct stages of anti-poaching operations, from 1994 to 1997.

Background to the Tiger's Slide

Wildlife protection is too often analysed in a vacuum. It is necessary to examine the threat to a species within its local political, economic and social context before devising effective ways to overcome it. Russia and its Amur tigers are no exception to this rule. The fragmentation of the Soviet Union caused a breakdown in law and order across Russia and the former Soviet republics. There was an outbreak of crime, which continues today and is likely to continue until the turn of the century despite attempts to control it.

Russian law enforcement efforts have focused on high-level organised crime groups, also known as 'Mafia'. Between 1992 and 1996, drug dealing, plutonium and weapons smuggling, money laundering and the war in Chechnya absorbed the resources and time of Russian authorities in charge of the government's war on crime. Environmental crimes—commercial poaching, illegal timber cutting, toxic dumping, etc.—were not genuinely treated as national security issues and therefore were left in the hands of local authorities. The only central (i.e. Moscow-based) authorities who continued focusing on environmental security issues were in the Ministry of Environmental Protection and Natural Resources, renamed as the State Committee for Environmental Protection, but referred to in this chapter as the Ministry of Environment. (The exception was Alexy Yablokov who served as President Yeltsin's Ecological Security Advisor. Yablokov found it difficult to push an environmental agenda in the Kremlin and eventually went back to this position as Director of the Russian Centre for Environmental Policy.)

During the post-perestroika transition, the Ministry of Environment experienced severe budget cuts, forcing it to leave its local branches across Russia (called 'Ecology Committees') to fend increasingly for themselves. This was particularly true the farther away the Ecology Committee was from the Kremlin. Primorski Krai, home to an estimated 85 per cent of Russia's Amur tiger population, is seven time zones away from Moscow. Among many unfortunate consequences of these budget cuts were layoffs and salary reductions for wildlife rangers in places like Primorski Krai. Those rangers who braved the budget cuts and remained working inside or outside nature reserves (zapovedniki) were left with few resources to fight against well-equipped commercial poachers. Local hunters—hungry for meat—ravaged the populations of deer and wild pig. Opportunistic hunters and self-made middlemen—hungry for money—targeted wildlife whose parts yield high profits on any scale: bears for gallbladders, musk deer for musk glands, wild ginseng for its roots, and tigers for their pelts, organs and bones.

By the winter of 1993, officials from Russia's Ministry of Environment and the Primorski Krai Ecology Committee estimated that 60 tigers were being poached each year, and that at this rate the tiger could reach such low numbers that extinction was possible by the year 2000. With decades of wildlife conservation experience behind them, the Ministry and local Committee representatives developed a plan to reduce poaching, but this plan required money. Since it was unlikely that any funds could be obtained from the Kremlin, foreign assistance was required.

International Cooperation to Address an International Threat

Thanks to international publicity, by 1993 the plight of all tiger subspecies was well known to the world. The US government and CITES had highlighted the need to protect tigers by threatening trade sanctions against states that continued to trade in tigers. The time was clearly ripe for Russia and the international community to join forces to save the endangered Amur tiger. By December 1993, several foreign NGOs and Russian authorities in charge of protecting the nation's endangered species of flora and fauna met and agreed on a joint two-fold objective:

1 Stabilise the tiger population by the year 2000. 'Stable' was defined as a measurably increasing population. (Several officials in the Ministry of Environment, including Dr Valentin Ilyashenko, Vsevold Stepanitsky and Vladimir Shetinin, thought the tiger could rebound before 2000 if an effective mobile anti-poaching programme were put into place by 1994. American scientists from the Hornocker Wildlife Institute thought the same, and made their case to the US government for anti-poaching assistance by 1993).
2 Secure sound habitat for a stable population of tigers well into the next century. Sound habitat was defined as consisting of good tree cover, food (healthy prey base), water and 'connectivity' (eco-corridors).

Interviews with Russian tiger experts revealed a uniform view of the nature of the threat to the tiger:

1 Commercial poaching for the underground market in skins, bones and organs outside of Russia.
2 Poaching of the tiger's prey base (wild pig and deer) for local human consumption.
3 Habitat loss, caused mainly by legal and illegal logging throughout the taiga forest.

Interviews with enforcement officers revealed specific details about this threat assessment:

1. Commercial poaching and trading:
   a. Tiger poaching was being conducted by two sets of hunters: organised poaching gangs and opportunistic poachers. In either case, the poacher would sell the tiger parts (in some cases full bodies) to middlemen operating out of several cities, mainly Vladivostok, Khabrovsk, Ussuriysk, Nakhodka and Plastun.
   b. The middlemen buying and selling tigers were usually Russian, Russian-Korean, or Chinese. Most tiger parts, it appeared, were being smuggled to The Peoples Republic of China, South Korea and Japan.

c. Tiger parts smuggled to China were usually taken across the border by road or train through only a few channels, namely Pogranichniye and Poltovka, and possibly by air between Khabarovsk and Harbin, China. Tiger parts smuggled to South Korea and Japan were transported by boat from the ports of Plastun, Vladivostok and Nakhodka, or by air from Khabarovsk and Vladivostok.
d. Commercial tiger poachers and smugglers were often connected to organised criminal groups that would lend firearms, vehicles, or a 'roof' (protection) to poachers. Sometimes the Mafia group would simply buy the tiger parts from the poacher. Some poachers were unconnected to Mafia groups and resorted to open advertisements of bones and skins for sale from tigers they had killed.
e. Tiger kills were highest in the winter, when poachers found it easiest to track the animal through the snow.

2. Reduction of the tiger's prey base:
   a. Both legal and illegal hunting were responsible for the decline of the deer and wild pig that serve as the tiger's main diet. The hunter was usually familiar with the taiga and the lack of wildlife law enforcement in and around it.
   b. The reduction of the tiger's prey base caused the tiger to roam further and wider for food. This meant that the tiger—and its killer—could be found almost anywhere.
3. Habitat loss:
   a. Logging meant an increased number of roads into formerly pristine and inaccessible tracts of forest. This in turn facilitated poaching of tigers and other wildlife. Defending the taiga forest became even more difficult. Poachers could now use logging roads to penetrate deep into the taiga within minutes. Some timber company employees became poachers. Once having killed a tiger, the poacher could make a quick exit by the same road, and stood little chance of being stopped by a law enforcement officer.
   b. Actual deforestation affected the tigers' roaming patterns. Where logging occurred, for example, wild pig would migrate in search of ground food produced by trees of the taiga

(especially Korean pine cones), and this movement lured some tigers deeper inside the forest in search of them, or farther outside the forest in search of domestic animals.

c. Overall, deforestation was fracturing key habitat for the tiger. The animal's access to tree cover for safety, to ungulates for food, and to water in and near the forest was being slowly eliminated.

The Plan to Stabilise the Amur Tiger: Operation Amba

It is important to revisit the goal established by the Russians and their foreign supporters, just as it is critical to frequently revisit the goal of any strategic plan if it is to lead to success. If the law enforcer in the battle does not do this, the battle will eventually be lost to the law breaker. In the case of the tiger, the law breakers (poacher and illegal trader) maintain a focused approach to their objective because that objective is short-term, i.e. to make money quickly and avoid getting caught. Their strategy to reach this goal is equally simple: kill a tiger wherever protection is absent and sell it to a buyer as quickly as possible.

The more difficult goal of the law enforcer has been to stabilise the tiger population by the year 2000. Deciding on the strategy and tactics to achieve this goal was even more difficult. This was where foreign support entered the equation.

Some Russian authorities recommended an ambitious and expensive counter-poaching plan, which we shall refer to as 'plan #1'. They sought to determine where the poachers were striking and to deploy newly hired and trained rangers in these 'problem areas' using newly purchased vehicles, boats, and snowmobiles. From a strategic stand-point, we claimed, this was equivalent to 'containing' an insurgency, which was only possible when the insurgents (in this case poaching gangs) operated in distinct locations. But the tiger and its stalkers were scattered throughout Primorski Krai, inside and outside nature reserves, and around towns and villages. This was a war without borders. Plan #1 would only work if the taiga forest was saturated with reliable, well-trained and well-equipped rangers. That would require much more money than was available, would create massive managerial problems (i.e., supervision of numerous rangers), and was almost certainly unsustainable from an economic point of view. The tiger's range was just too vast to monitor it all at once.

Russian plan #2 recommended a mobile anti-poaching operation. Under this plan, several small teams (four to five men apiece) would rove the taiga in order to (1) maintain a periodic presence in areas no longer protected by rangers; and (2) follow up on reports of poaching and trading gangs. This appeared to be closer to a workable plan, but it still had holes. Its main problem was that with only several ranger teams roving the huge taiga, the poacher could strike wherever the teams were absent. The poachers and traders would eventually win in this equation. Anti-poaching patrols would end up chasing the poacher after the poacher had already killed the tiger.

Restricted by limited resources, we chose to work with and amend plan #2. The government, in exchange for financial support of this plan, agreed to establish a new, specialised 'Tiger Department' within the Ministry of Environment's branch in Primorski Krai. We code-named the special task of this department 'Operation Amba' ('Amba' being the indigenous Udegai name for the tiger). Money for 15 rangers, a commander and a small administrative staff would be channelled by foreign sponsors into Department Tiger to implement Operation Amba. Amba's strategy was to eventually put the poachers and traders—who at the time were on a very profitable offensive—on the defensive, and to raise the stakes and costs of killing and trading tigers. But how could this be done with only 15 rangers in an area roughly the size of England and Wales combined? In one word: 'PsyOps'.

State One (1994): Getting Started—The Strategic Defensive

'PsyOps' is a strategic term short for 'psychological operations'. PsyOps have been a key component of counter-insurgency or insurgency operations throughout history. In this case, we sought to make Amba appear to be bigger than it was, and to possess the power of operating invisibly. We wanted the poachers to think that an Amba ranger could walk or drive up behind them at any moment, no matter where they were; or that an Amba informant was positioned somewhere along the trail to the tiger. We wanted the tiger trader to think that Amba informants were everywhere, and that the chance of getting caught and going to jail had suddenly increased dramatically. PsyOps work only when they mirror an expanded version of reality. We sought to create an expanded image of Amba operations by doing the following:

1. Using the element of surprise: Amba patrols were quietly deployed to three distinct areas of the taiga at once. Rangers would randomly check vehicles coming out of the forest as well as hunters walking inside the forest. This activity would be concentrated in three days. Then without a word, rangers would depart for a new area, may be to return the next week, sometimes the next months.
2. Developing an intelligence network: During these patrols, Amba rangers would inform local citizens and authorities about their mission, inviting them to provide information on poachers and traders. A surprising number of people stepped forward. Over time, a network of informants was formed.
3. Using the press: As the Russians say, 'bad news has wings' and Amba was bad news for poachers and traders. Besides spreading word of Amba by mouth, press coverage was used to maximise publicity of Amba's presence.

The first four months of Operation Amba—January to April, 1994—were learning ones. The winter of '93/94 turned out only slightly better for tigers than the previous two winters. Amba rangers found themselves turning up at the crime scene after the crime had been committed. Poached tigers and signs of poached tigers were found throughout the Krai. Commander Vladimir Shetinin reckoned that the number of dead tigers discovered by rangers represented between 10–20 per cent of the true amount killed. Between January and April, Amba discovered five tigers shot by poachers.

But several things that Amba achieved during this period paid off later. Local citizens were suddenly aware of Amba's new presence. Poaching would no longer be so easy. Furthermore, information was compiled from new Amba agents about the structure of the underground wildlife trade in the Russian Far East. This information allowed Amba to design several undercover investigations targeting major tiger traders. These initial investigations were 'passive'—in other words we did not yet feel prepared to act on an illegal incident on the spot. We watched and learned.

By the Spring of 1994, through joint undercover investigations, GSN and Amba personnel had discovered several major poaching and smuggling operations in Primorski and Khabarovski Krais. Three are worth mentioning in that they were typical of others discovered later. The first involved professional hunters killing tigers, storing them whole and selling them to Chinese citizens in the city of Khabarovsk. The Chinese traders were purchasing the tigers at $5000 cash per frozen carcass. Sometimes only bones were sold to the Chinese at a rate of about $300 per kg. The Chinese traders would transport the tiger carcasses or parts back to China by air and by vehicle (also reportedly by train). The tigers were sold to traditional Chinese medicine companies in Heilongjiang and Jilin Provinces in northeast China. When investigators visited these firms in China, they learned that the tiger's bones were mixed with bones from other animals and ground into wines, pills and plasters and sold locally and to companies in Singapore and South Korea.

The second illegal operation involved poachers employed by a governmental department in Khabarovski Krai. These corrupt officials sold dead tigers to members of a Russian-Korean community in the city of Khabarovsk. Running low on tigers in Khabarovski Krai, the poacher would link up with colleagues in Primorski Krai where he would shoot the tiger. The poacher would immediately skin the tiger and maintain the rest of the body in a frozen state (easily done in winter). The poacher would then contact the Russian-Koreans who would arrange to sell the dead tiger to South Korean or Chinese merchants in the city of Khabarovsk. During our investigation we met the poacher and the traders, and viewed one of their dead tigers in the back of a government truck. The Russian-Koreans could speak Russian and Korean, and a smattering of Chinese, and were therefore well situated to act as middlemen. They sold skins for $3000–$4000 on average and the price of bones fluctuated wildly.

The third illicit operation we discovered involved a Russian government employee working with an employee of a joint Russian-

Korean logging operation. The logging employee was a driver for the logging company. He had full access to the taiga by the roads his company created and the vehicle he drove. He would carry a rifle with him during his work and poach deer and wild pig, and tigers on the side. Once the tiger carcass was in hand, the poacher used two contacts to sell the dead tigers. One was a customs officer working in the port of Vladivostok who could facilitate a sale and secret export of the tiger to any country by ship. The other contact was an employee of the shipping port in Plastun, which is situated along the eastern seaboard (Sea of Japan). The second contact would sell tiger skins and bones to Russian sailors and Korean workers heading by ship to South Korea or Japan. The tiger parts were easily concealed on board the ships amidst commercial containers and tons of Russian logs.

Amba received no support whatsoever from other enforcement agencies to do follow-up work on these investigations. But during these investigations, Amba learned three important lessons:

1 The line between the poacher and the market was becoming increasingly direct. Some Russian traders had supplanted foreigners as middlemen.
2 Amba could not yet rely on the police and courts to back it up in the field. Amba needed its own roof, preferably from within the government.
3 Networking paid off. By talking with local citizens and authorities, Amba rangers were building up a network of support and information. Not only through the press, but also through these direct contacts, Amba was becoming known throughout major parts of Primorski Krai. Amba was growing bigger and would soon be able to operate invisibly.

Stage Two (1994/95): Going on the Strategic Offensive

By late August 1994, a survey among Amba agents and tiger experts (conducted by GSN personnel) revealed that the volume of tiger bone trading had decreased. It was not clear at the time how much of this was attributable to anti-poaching and how much was due to the time of year. Amba undercover agents claimed that Amba's presence was slowing down trading activity by raising the risk of getting caught, which raised the financial costs of trading tigers.

Amba's new vehicles and uniforms projected a professional image of rangers who operated more like police. While in fact many Amba rangers deserved this reputation, as a whole Department Tiger was still very much in the learning stages. Could it have been, we asked ourselves, that tiger traders exhausted their supply of bones and were waiting until the winter of 94/95 to stock up again? Since only time would tell, it seemed wisest to prepare for a new onslaught of poaching by snow-fall.

While Amba prepared for winter, GSN took aim at the second part of our objective; securing tiger habitat for the future. Though sophisticated radiotelemetry technology, Hornocker Wildlife Institute personnel and their Russian scientific colleagues were amassing critical data on tiger roaming patterns and habitat. The Hornocker team was compiling scientifically credible data that would empower environmental officials to halt logging and certain levels of hunting within prime tiger habitat.

But the Kremlin was fighting a war with Chechnya and, at the time, afforded very little attention to environmental degradation in the Far East. The Russian Duma (parliament) took up issues such as commercial poaching of endangered species very slowly, if at all. GSN searched for and found a channel to the Prime Minister, whose advisors offered to draft a national decree on saving the Amur tiger. By the following year this draft decree would become a reality.

On the anti-poaching front, Amba rangers set out to find allies within local enforcement agencies. Their investigations showed that poaching gangs and traders detected by Amba were too well connected to the Mafia for Amba to fight alone. Thus, rangers looked to develop better relations with local police and FSB (formerly KGB) officers. Good relationships developed between two Amba teams (based in Ussuriysk and Luchegorsk) and local enforcement authorities. New investigations were set up in these two areas. With police and FSB support, the investigations could be more 'active' (e.g. once the perpetrator was detected performing an illegal act, Amba and the police could move in for the arrest).

Amba suspected that tiger parts were being smuggled to China by road from Ussuriysk to a border checkpoint called Poltovka. Before Amba could solicit information from the Chinese community in

Ussuriysk about tiger smuggling, they received a call from a potential informant. Alias 'Mr. Chang' offered information about wildlife smugglers in exchange for an agreement by Amba to arrest a particular smuggler. Although Amba rangers and the FSB concluded that Chang wanted to use them to undermine a competitor, they verbally agreed with Chang's condition. Chang subsequently informed Amba about the movements of a truck illegally carrying sea cucumbers and tiger parts. The information at first turned up nothing. But after four days of road checks the truck was found. Besides three metric tonnes of sea cucumbers, a tiger skin was found. Customs officers working the border point of Poltovka, where the contraband was impounded, refused to cooperate with FSB and Amba, insisting on forwarding the evidence to the Department of Transportation. Although no one was prosecuted for the incident, the smugglers were surprised and disappointed to have lost perhaps $50,000 worth of contraband. Better interagency cooperation would have led to a successful prosecution.

In another investigation, in the Bikin Valley, GSN and Amba investigators turned up evidence of tiger poaching and trading. In July 1995, undercover investigators negotiated the purchase of a tiger skin, a tiger skeleton and bear gallbladders from a local citizen. The tiger parts came from a one-year-old tiger that had been shot the previous winter. Investigators filmed the tiger parts in his possession and the conversation in which he revealed how he had come to obtain them. The seller was asking $11,000 for the skin and bones together. The film was later shown to local police who searched the dealer's house and found the tiger parts, together with narcotics and dynamite, which he was using to blast bears out of their dens. The dealer went to jail. It was decided that each Amba team should have its own video camera, and later these were supplied.

When local enforcement agencies do not help out with wildlife investigations, the work can be dangerously lonely for Amba. In May 1995 an Amba investigation was compromised by apathetic or corrupt officials, nearly causing one ranger to lose his life. Four Amba rangers discovered a tiger-smuggling channel between the city of Arseniev and Vladivostok, Primorski Krai's capital and major sea port. They learned that hunters near the city of Arseniev (north of

Vladivostok) were paid to kill tigers by a Mafia group, which then smuggled the remains to Vladivostok. Further examination by Amba revealed that this channel was also used to trade drugs and arms. Amba rangers took the information they had gathered to police and prosecutors in Vladivostok District. The police told Amba that they already knew about this channel, and that they should 'leave it alone' because the police 'were on top of it'. Several days later, the lead Amba ranger who discovered this smuggling route was attacked by a group of young men outside his home and badly beaten. An investigation by OMON (Police Special Forces) confirmed that the beating incident was linked to the discovery of the smugglers.

State Three (1995/96): Amba Gains a Roof

On 7 August 1995, Russian Prime Minister Victor S. Chernomyrdin issued National Decree number 795 'On Saving the Amur Tiger and Other Endangered Fauna and Flora of the Russian Far East'. This high-level political support for tiger protection sent a serious message to Russian law enforcement agencies and courts. The Russian courts had previously shown very little interest in tiger poaching, agreeing to hear only two tiger poaching cases between 1992 and 1995, and no cases relating to trading tiger parts during the same period. In 1995–96 alone, seven people were indicted for these crimes. More importantly, tiger kills were still down.

Taking advantage of their increased legal support, Amba investigators turned up the heat on wildlife traders in Ussuriysk, which informants consistently pointed to as the hub of tiger smuggling activity. Over the course of the year, information was gathered on a disconnected ring of tiger dealers around Ussuriysk who were sitting on a total of 15 tiger skins and approximately six sets of bones. Based on a tip from an Amba informant (an ex-hunter), investigators used fresh American hundred-dollar bills to lure the traders into position for an arrest. It worked twice, and failed a third time. The two traders caught, however, were persuaded to give details on other tiger traders and poachers before they were indicted. Some of the bizarre details included a middleman from Azerbaijan who was trading in tiger parts and leopard skins between Ussuriysk, Central Asia and China.

While the Ussuriysk Amba team focused on underground traders, the Iman Amba team made significant progress deep inside the forest where it was focusing on poachers. In July, after an eight-day stake-out near Novopokrovka, Iman caught a poaching gang involved in all aspects of wildlife smuggling, ranging from bears to salmon. Iman rangers videotaped the entire bust and the tape was used in court. A heavy fine was issued by the judge and the case made headlines in local newspapers.

Recognising that interagency coordination on wildlife law enforcement was still weak, and that Amba's ability to win cases in court against poachers and traders needed to improve, Amba officials invited wildlife law enforcement trainers from the US Department of the Interior to address Amba rangers and customs authorities. The US trainers provided training and technical assistance in the areas of CITES implementation, species identification, anti-smuggling and anti-poaching. A CITES manual was provided in Russian as well. Shortly after this training took place, the CITES Secretariat provided a short course in CITES regulations to Russian environmental officials, including Amba's Deputy Commander.

Stage Four (1997): Turning the Corner

Interagency cooperation and coordination improved in 1997. On 11 April 1997, officers working for Russian customs, police and Amba cooperated on an arrest of a tiger dealer who had attempted to smuggle a tiger skin out of Russia through Vladivostok's International Airport.

In fact, Amba investigations have improved over-all in 1997. When Amba began operations, some of the tiger dealers' internal smuggling routes had been discovered, but the actual destinations for the skins and bones of poached tigers were rarely confirmed; cooperation from police and customs officials working the border points was lacking. In the first three months of 1997, however, investigators discovered a major tiger skin trading route from Khabarovsk to Japan by way of Vladivostok. They also discovered a tiger skin channel by sea from Vladivostok to South Korea. Furthermore, a tiger skin and set of bones were discovered on the ship 'Kapago' in the port of Nakhodka; Nakhodka customs and local police offered to help with the investigation. Investigators also discovered other endangered fauna being smuggled out of Primorski Krai. Amur leopard skins, snow leopard skins, deer musk glands and bear gallbladder are some of the highly priced derivatives of endangered fauna recently detected by Amba investigators. For several years now, Amba investigations have also routinely turned up wild ginseng being smuggled to China.

Smoother operations by Amba are also attributable to improved coordination of outside financial aid. GSN and the World Wildlife Fund (WWF) now coordinate all assistance to anti-poaching patrols. Lack of such coordination can slow anti-poaching efforts. One slow or inaccurate money transfer can ground one anti-poaching team for a month while they wait for money to buy gasoline. Unfortunately, coordination of aid was not so good during the first two years of operations. In the first quarter of 1997, however, Amba was on the road almost constantly, stopping and/or inspecting 1700 vehicles, 1900 hunters and potential poachers, and 76 hunting shacks.

Amba public relations has also steadily improved. In the first quarterly field report of 1997 Amba Commander Vladimir I Shetinin states that, 'Video equipment was used to make more detailed assessment of crimes. This film, and information obtained during patrol, is used in the mass media—journalists have used our materials in four articles, two radio broadcasts, and three television shows.'

Shetinin's latest report added a sober note about the situation surrounding the Amur tiger. After detailing the involvement of local officials in tiger trading, he concluded that the Tiger Decree of 1995 was still not being adhered to by all Russian agencies. 'This inaction will make it very difficult to ensure biological diversity in Primorski Krai. This is especially true given the tremendous economic pressure to overuse natural resources at a time when neither legislation nor governmental funds can ensure the necessary protection from environmental degradation, especially of protected nature areas (national parks).'

Such an honest assessment of the situation is what caused most foreign conservationists to dismiss the possibility of saving the Amur tiger. However, on 8 July 1997, the Office of the Prime Minister informed the Minister of Environment that the Russian Duma had approved governmental funding of the Tiger Decree of 1995. And the most recent Amba investigations (summer of 1997) confirm that illegal tiger exports are low enough to allow Amba to eventually reduce them further. As Amba and its supporters move forward, it is critical to review the lessons learned thus far, key components of which may be applicable to similar situations elsewhere.

John

Seidensticker, *et al.*

Vision and Process in Securing a Future for Wild Tigers

John Seidensticker worked in Nepal, and in the Indian and Bangladeshi Sundarbans. (See p. 236 for further details.)

By the end of the 1990s, at the 'Tiger 2000' conference organised in London, people from all over the tiger's range assembled to assess the state of the tiger before the turn of the millennium. (Photo courtesy Valmik Thapar.)

In a remote Javanese village, a farmer went out one morning to find a tiger sound asleep beneath his rice barn. Even sleeping, this tiger was a problem the farmer knew was beyond his ability to solve. So the farmer hastened to consult with his village head. The village head accompanied the farmer back to the barn, where the tiger still lay sleeping. Agreeing that this problem was beyond both their abilities, they hurried a few miles to tell the subdistrict officer about the tiger. All three returned to the barn to view the sleeping tiger, then went off to enlist the help of the district officer. Progress up the bureaucratic chain to seek a solution to the sleeping tiger went on all day until finally a by-then large group of men reached the regional commander of the army. The commander marched out to the village and laid out a plan to deal with the sleeping tiger, but before it could be implemented the tiger woke up and moved away. So now they had a different, but still real problem; there was a tiger near the village but no one knew where it was. Suddenly leaving the barn was a very risky proposition.

This story was told to anthropologist Clifford Geertz in the 1950s in the Southern Mountains region of Java, an area where some of Java's last tigers lived. It may be a local joke about bureaucracy, as Geertz believed the story too well formed to be literally true, but we believe it to reflect the central dilemma in saving tigers. Lurking unseen or asleep under a barn, a tiger is perceived to be a problem requiring a solution. ... The vision that emerged from Tigers 2000 is that the tiger can be a star; not a fading star as a barometer of human intrusion and destruction of habitat, but a guiding star in consensus-building for sustainable relationships between people and resources, from which the tiger also benefits.

It is well understood that the metaphorical 'holocaust' for species on the brink of extinction, such as tigers, is the clearing of forests. The renewed tiger crisis of the early 1990s was the fear that the tiger could be lost because a new economic reality was driving demand for tiger parts. There has been some success in reducing

Extract from *Riding the Tiger: Tiger Conservation in Human Dominated Landscapes*, ed. John Seidensticker, Sarah Christie and Peter Jackson (Cambridge, 1999). Published with permission of the Zoological Society of London.

this demand and a process has been initiated for eliminating it entirely in time. The shock of this crisis for everyone who values wild tigers was that the tiger could be lost not only in the holocaust of species extinction but also to E.O. Wilson's metaphorical rifle shot. Could it be that with literally a few shots and snares tigers would be erased from ecosystems where they otherwise would persist?

Strong protective legislation and the means to strictly enforce it go hand-in-hand with the process of reducing and eventually eliminating the demand for tiger parts. Increasing the capacity of countries to control the illicit trade in tiger parts through strengthening law enforcement infrastructure should be a priority investment for the future of tigers. Needs include specific laws with meaningful penalties, government agencies with clearly defined responsibilities, trained people-power and intelligence-gathering networks. These are lacking or remarkably ineffectual in nearly every tiger range specific measures to control the tiger tráde; we applaud these measures, but wait to judge their effectiveness. Discussions at Tigers 2000 emphasised that these critical short-term responses need to be linked to solutions that give living tigers and the places they live sufficient value for the people who also live near them. Good intelligence is the lifeline of effective enforcement and security, and an important insight from Tigers 2000 was the need to form partnerships with local people when establishing intelligence-gathering networks. But payment for information must be timely, as must payment be for lost livestock where compensation is practised; delays here erode credibility and the tiger loses. NGOs are usually more effective in the timely disbursal of funds than are governmental agencies.

The 1990s tiger crisis was a wake-up call and a time to re-examine the status of tiger habitats throughout tigerland. Even though it is generally known that many more tigers live outside reserved lands than in them, tiger habitat has usually been equated with reserved lands in conservationists' minds. This has trapped our thinking and remains a trap for many tiger conservationists. Surprisingly, no one had attempted to assess the extent and character of the entire suite of potential tiger habitats that still present opportunities to secure a future for wild tigers until Eric Dinerstein and his colleagues did so in 1997. Their report was subsequently revised by Eric Wikramanayake and associates and presented at Tigers 2000. The broad outline of this tiger conservation unit or TCU concept provides a firm foundation on which we can base more detailed work to advance the limits of our knowledge about where tigers can and do live. Contributors to Tigers 2000 suggested that geographical priorities for tiger conservation actions should be based on bio-regional distribution rather than on ill-defined sub-specific designations and ranges for tigers. This shift moves tiger conservation from a taxonomic to an ecological emphasis, while still recognising the importance of the ecological, behavioural and demographic difference in tiger populations throughout their vast range.

Tigers 2000 was a chance to synthesise what new research was saying about the tiger's resilience and its ecological needs, and a more complete picture emerged than we have ever had before. While habitat loss, fragmentation and degradation remain as primary threats to the tiger's future, it is not the loss of habitat that has placed the tiger in its recent state of crisis. There are substantial blocks of potential tiger habitat remaining. The immediate problem facing tigers is that Wilson's metaphorical rifle shot in the forest has been all too literal and has substantially reduced prey populations in many of the remaining forest tracts that could otherwise harbour tigers. No large mammal prey, no tigers, is the crux of this newly highlighted threat. The advice that emerged from Tigers 2000 was to take the stress off tiger numbers and focus our resources on maintaining and monitoring habitat quality—especially an abundance of large ungulate prey—and on identifying and maintaining the connective habitat linkages within tiger conservation units.

Many of us think of those few places where tiger still live as natural wonders—little Edens, if you will. Saving Eden at whatever cost and means has been thought to be the goal. The vision emerging from Tigers 2000 is that we should not limit our vision to just the Edens with tigers, but think instead about recovering landscapes. We should put aside the notion that tiger reserves are self-contained islands, disconnected in a sea of non-compatible land-uses. Our vision should be of landscapes with their ecological and genetic processes intact. Protected areas are principal building blocks in this vision, but they cannot stand alone. We have emphasised the linkages between the needs of the tiger and the welfare of the people living near it. The future of wild tigers lies in a recovery process for tigers that includes, as essential elements, establishment and maintenance of sustainable relationships between people and their resources in habitats surrounding reserves, and maintenance of the connectivity within TCUs that is essential for ensuring long-term tiger population sustainability. The future of the tiger lies in recovering natural capital. Continued environmental deterioration is the alternative; along this road, the tiger and much else will be lost.

The specifics of shifting the boundaries of the problem domain and crafting effective solutions for 'the large carnivore problem' are dependent on the ecological and sociological contexts prevailing where remaining tigers live. Ecological factors are one of five variables in defining the 'problem' and seeking the solution. Cultural history, valuation, management system and policy process are all equally as important. These factors will interact very differently in different regions of the tiger's range, as the contributors to Tigers 2000 have shown.

Tigers 2000 anchored a vision, and initiated the beginning of a process to define and manage the flow of problems that emerges as we seek to secure a future for wild tigers and shift the diffuse concept of 'tiger conservation' to a far more focused goal of 'securing a future for wild tigers'. Because of the shifting social and political Asian landscape this will never be a completed task; we see it as a search for road maps to the tiger's future. Tigers 2000 shifted the domain of the problem of saving tigers to the ground where wild tigers live. It shifted the focus from the alarm generated by declining tiger numbers to the opportunity presented by the substantial amount of tiger habitat remaining. It shifted thinking about saving the tiger from a 'bunker' mentality to one of reaching out to forge partnerships with neighbours. It shifted thinking about saving the tiger away from crisis management towards a recovery mode and towards understanding and encouraging landscape patterns and conditions where tigers can persist in all the bio-regions over their vast geographical range; it also sought the vision needed to work towards encouraging these patterns. What the contributors and we as editors have done, in short, is to translate the many languages of tiger conservation into one language—the language of conservation biology.

Tigers 2000 highlighted the many good initiatives already in place to save the tiger. Going forward with this process is a matter of building on these efforts. We need to proceed with a consensus-driven process that moves beyond the domain of special interests—yet captures the power of those efforts—and seeks to improve the policy environment for the tiger, integrate conservation and development, and mobilise financial resources. Supportive partnerships are a central part of the vision for the future of wild tigers. Following Tigers 2000, we attended the Tiger Link meeting in New Delhi in December 1997. At this meeting more than 60 NGOs and government officials sat together to discuss present threats to and needs of India's tigers. We believe we were watching the process that will secure a future for the tiger in India. Later that same month we attended The First International Symposium on Endangered Species used in Traditional East Asian Medicine: Substitutes for Tiger Bone and Musk, held in Hong Kong, and watched a remarkable effort by TCM practitioners and manufacturers to interact and work with conservationists in an effort to remove tiger bone and musk from TCM. There is a long way yet to go on this road but the threat TCM poses to wild tigers is being communicated and heard.

There are good building blocks for realistic tiger conservation in place. Money, political will, key legislation, cooperation and integration are needed to start cementing these building blocks together into a future for the tiger. In the Chinese Year of the Tiger, the Save the Tiger Fund—a partnership between the US National Fish and Wildlife Foundation and the Exxon Corporation—convened a follow-on conference to Tigers 2000 entitled The Year of the Tiger Conference: Securing a Future for Wild Tigers. John Seidensticker and Peter Jackson represented the Save the Tiger Fund Council on the organising committee for the conference, along with Ron Tilson, Howard Quigley, Maurice Hornocker, Joshua Ginsberg, David Phemister and Nancy Sherman. Sarah Christie set up a network for, and served on, the conference advisory committee. Many of the authors contributing to his volume also served on the advisory committee. The Save the Tiger Fund invested in The Year of the Tiger Conference because there is simply no substitute for bringing so many of the critical players together in one place. There is no substitute for direct human contact in the evolution of co-operative relationships and strategies. It was a unique opportunity to pull together, and to build on the existing work in which so many people have invested so much of their energy and their lives to save the tiger.

Participants from 13 of the 14 tiger range countries (no one for North Korea was able to attend) met in Dallas, Texas, on February 10–13, 1998, to find what works and what has not worked, what fits and does not fit in seeking to secure a future for wild tigers. At this conference we sought to break down the problem of saving the tiger to technically practical and politically feasible scales. We wanted to be sure that we had identified the present context for action in order to support programmes that address present conditions, not problems in contexts that are no longer germane. Also we needed to be sure that we do not ignore the challenges of new problems arising from this shifting context that is the norm throughout tigerland. In more specific terms, The Year of the Tiger Conference asked how we are doing and appraised our current practices in tiger conservation. We wanted to be able to assess our tiger conservation efforts, and to clarify our standards of performance. We wanted to identify and build on the positive trends and conditions that are emerging in tiger conservation activities, especially efforts that make tiger conservation less combative and more cooperative for the people who live beside and in the midst of tigers. We wanted to build on the cooperation and goodwill that developed from the Tigers 2000 symposium, and on the power of coming and working together to foster and encourage innovation, diffusion of ideas and adaptation in tiger conservation activities. Also we wanted to ensure that the tiger's conservation needs were made apparent to the people living in tiger range countries and around the world.

The important difference between The Year of the Tiger Conference and Tigers 2000 is that the latter focused on using science to support tiger conservation. In London, and in these chapters, we have sought the ecological criteria that must be met in conservation strategies in order to sustain viable tiger populations and significant habitats. The Year of the Tiger Conference moved on to examine the political criteria that must be met if conservation actions that will maintain viable wild tiger populations are to proceed with confidence and success. Cory Meacham, an astute observer of tiger conservation activities, has noted that we must be able to articulate what we are about in a single sentence that cannot be misinterpreted. Thus, we selected as our theme, 'Securing a future for wild tigers', a theme that resonates throughout this volume.

This was the largest international gathering on behalf of tigers ever held and an unprecedented multi-country collaboration to share ideas and to develop plans. This conference fostered cross-disciplinary and cross-regional communication, with participating government officials, representatives from NGOs, conservation biologists, forestry specialists, engineers, land managers and others. Lines of communication were opened that may help to secure tiger habitats that span international borders, including many of the largest TCUs. Small and large conservation groups found opportunities to form partnerships for more effective conservation action. Further consensus-building exercises, focused at the TCU and bio-regional levels through the tiger's range, will be an essential foundation for bringing people and institutions together in our ongoing efforts to secure a future for wild tigers.

The endangered tiger is an indicator of eco-systems in crisis. We must direct our attention to the tiger's long-term future and support sustainable ecosystems and landscapes. We must move from viewing tiger conservation as an isolated part of ecosystem conservation to viewing the maintenance of viable tiger populations as an essential component of an integrated system of sustainable ecosystem management. Protecting tigers means managing tiger habitats for long-term rather than short-term exploitation. This is good for people living in tigerland and for their economy in the long-term, and the tiger also benefits. It is not possible to separate the interests of tigers from those of humans on any temporal of spatial scale, yet many of our past conservation prescriptions have attempted to do just that. Instead, the tiger can be the star in our ongoing efforts to implement actions that enable people to live in balance with natural resources.

R.S.
Chundawat
& Neel
Gogate

Saving Wild Tigers in
Dry Forest Habitats

R.S. Chundawat did his Ph.D. on the snow leopard. Over the past four years he has worked on a tiger ecology project, which entails following the only three radio-collared tigers in India, at Panna Tiger Reserve in Madhya Pradesh.

Neel Gogate has been working with the Panna Tiger Ecology Project and completing his Masters in this field.

Raghu Chundawat is busy tracking his radio-collared tigers in Panna National Park, Madhya Pradesh. He has thus far collared three tigers and provided fascinating insights into the natural history of the tiger. (Photo courtesy Joanna Van Gruisen.)

Tiger, *Panthera tigris*, has attracted and benefited from the attention of the conservation community over the past couple of decades. In spite of the overwhelming attention received by the species, its population status remains precarious the world over and continues to decline. Three subspecies—the Bali tiger, the Caspian tiger and the Javan tiger—have already become extinct, and the South China tiger is on the brink of extinction. Populations of Siberian, Sumatran and Indo-Chinese tigers are holding on against great odds. Over 80 per cent of the Bengal tigers still alive are reported from the Indian subcontinent. It is this subspecies which promises some hope for the future survival of the species—and thus the chances of saving the tiger for posterity rest mainly within the Indian subcontinent. Perhaps half of the world's tiger population is in India, yet its future continues to be threatened by habitat loss and degradation, the depletion of prey base either due to poaching or to other forms of human disturbance, and by the poaching of the tiger itself.

A population of perhaps 2,400 to 3,700 tigers in India may look promising, but a closer look reveals that the situation is grim. Besides the above problems, there are two characteristics of the tiger population in India which could doom the future of the subspecies—the small and isolated nature of the tiger habitat and tigers populations. Over 80 per cent of the protected areas that have tigers in India are less than 400 km^2 and the average population size of tigers in these protected areas is less than 15. Such small and isolated populations are extremely vulnerable to extinction. Human-induced factors, mentioned earlier, have a deterministic effect on tiger populations by fragmenting tiger habitats and isolating the tigers into smaller populations. This brings them within the realm of demographic and environmental catastrophes and the future of such populations is extremely difficult to predict due to the stochastic nature of these catastrophes. If we consider India's tiger population of 2,400 to 3,700 as one large contiguous population for modelling, the projection will give a longer survival period than a population which is smaller. We know tiger populations in India are fragmented into many small isolated populations and the extinction processes, both deterministic and stochastic in nature, will be active simultaneously on each of these isolated populations. The projected time of survival for these isolated populations will be much shorter than for one large undivided population.

These projections will vary in different habitats. The tiger is not a habitat-specialist and occurs in diverse habitats ranging from the hot arid regions of western India to the mangroves and humid rainforests of tropical Asia and the Arctic climate of Siberia. The tiger, however, has achieved its maximum density in areas of high productivity with a moderate tropical climate such as the flood plains of Chitawan, and the moist tropical forests of India as in Nagarahole National Park. Like other large carnivores, its density is also governed by the availability of appropriately sized prey, which in turn is determined by the productivity of the system and degree of anthropogenic pressures. We knew that the tiger population had declined in the past and that it continues to decline but, till the present study, it was not known where this decline was taking place and in which habitat the tiger was most vulnerable.

A simple analysis of the presence and absence of tigers in protected habitat (sample size for over 350 PAs) either as national park or wildlife sanctuary in peninsular India (excluding the north-east states) shows where tigers were present at the start of this century and are absent now. Such an analysis indicates that tigers have disappeared from 70% of their original protected habitat in semi-arid forests and from 35% of such habitat in dry tropical forests. These two habitat types together form the largest (more than 46%) tiger habitat in India. This shows that an extremely large proportion of the tiger population in India is highly vulnerable to local extinction. Low rainfall, a long hot dry season, extreme climatic conditions and a high conflict situation are some of the characteristics that make these habitats sub-optimal. In such sub-optimal habitats the loss of a single breeding tiger by poaching can have disastrous consequences and management has to be ever-alert to this threat in order to keep the tiger population stable. Moreover, protected areas are small (mean = 290 km^2) and the average tiger population in each PA is less then ten tigers. The tiger here will be extremely vulnerable even to normally operating demographic and environmental stochasticity. The problems are amplified in semi-arid and dry forests where the tiger is likely to require larger areas to maintain viable populations. The tiger still survives in most of the protected habitats in more productive areas. The analysis indicates that the tiger is extinct only in extremely small protected areas (mean = 180 km^2), and even if they are in productive moist habitats.

Nevertheless, however small and isolated tiger populations in these habitats may be, each and every population is crucial to ensure the long-term survival of this subspecies. To manage the highly vulnerable tiger populations, detailed information on the ecology of tigers in such sub-optimal habitats is vital for planning suitable conservation measures. In the past, several ecological studies on tigers have been conducted in the Indian subcontinent but most of these have been carried out in optimal tiger habitats in moderate tropical climates with high productivity and prey abundance. No study has so far been conducted in a habitat like Panna, which is typical of the tiger habitat of India and where the tigers are most vulnerable. Therefore the study in Panna Tiger Reserve is looking at the essential ecological requirements needed to maintain a demographically viable population and at identifying factors responsible for the decline of tiger populations in sub-optimal environments.

The Panna Tiger Reserve encompasses an area of 543 km^2 and is situated in central India. The dominant vegetation in the Reserve is 'Tropical Dry Forest'. The summer is long and hot, maximum day temperatures during the peak going over 46°C and in winter down to below 4°C for several days. The Reserve receives an average of 1100 mm rain but most of it falls between July and September. However, due to the nature of the terrain and the long dry season, water is a limiting factor. Dry and short grass habitat with open woodland is the most extensive habitat type in the Reserve and this supports nilgai and chinkara. The low-lying tall grass habitat with associated closed woodland supports higher densities of sambar and chital. These more mesic habitats are distributed along the major seasonal drainage system. The distribution of these habitats creates a heterogeneous landscape where ecological conditions vary seasonally. Shade and water availability vary spatio-temporally, influencing the distribution of wild ungulates. The Tiger Reserve is characterised by widespread human disturbance. There are 15 villages within the Reserve with human and cattle populations of about 5200 and 8500 respectively. In addition there are about 79 villages on the periphery of the Reserve, at distances varying from 1 to 10 kms, which also put immense pressure on the Reserve primarily through grazing.

Being predators, tigers prefer to remain under cover and difficult to spot. It is therefore extremely difficult to locate tigers at one's will, which is essential to get unbiased information on its ecology. Radio-telemetry is one way to gather information in an unbiased manner and in much greater detail. After tagging the tiger with a radio transmitter it is possible to locate the tiger any time and anywhere and follow its movements without being too close and without disturbing it.

Tiger movements and home-range size are influenced by prey biomass and other key resources such as cover and water. The wild prey biomass in the dry forest habitat of Panna is low, when compared with other productive tiger habitats of the Indian subcontinent. Moreover, human-induced disturbances are high and other key resources, such as water and cover, are also sparsely distributed and their availability changes with the seasons. This makes the availability of these resources unpredictable. All these factors create a difficult ecological condition for tigers and their responses vary as these ecological conditions change. These variances could be in their density and home-range sizes.

Monitoring these radio-tagged tigers reveals that the home ranges of tigers are much larger than in other more productive habitats of the subcontinent. The male tiger ranged over 277 km^2 in the dry forest habitat in Panna, whereas in more productive systems the male on average ranged around 80–100 km^2. The female ranges in Panna are also larger (40–60 km^2) when compared to those in Chitawan and Nagarahole, where their ranges could be as small as 14 km^2. The larger ranges indicate that in dry forest habitats, such as Panna, tiger densities are sparse. This finding has significant conservation implications. When we look at the average PA size (316 km^2) in dry forest habitats, we find that it can only support five to seven breeding territories. This is an extremely small breeding population, unlikely to keep the population viable. It is also estimated that approximately

20–30% of the habitat in dry forest habitats is unsuitable as a breeding habitat for tigers and when this is taken into account then the present scenario in terms of viability of the existing population in dry forests is even more precarious. This is an important issue in saving the tiger in our largest tiger habitat and one that needs to be addressed by wildlife managers.

In two adjoining female territories that have been monitored over the years, it has been observed that tigresses' responses differ with the variable ecological conditions that exist in these territories. One of the female's territories has a more even distribution of resources, high prey density and no disturbance, resulting in the tigress being able to raise all her cubs (three litters and eight cubs) successfully. Whereas in the neighbouring territory, with uneven resource distribution, including disturbed habitat, the tigress had only 35% success in raising cubs to adulthood.

During the study the food habits of tigers are determined from the remains in the scats of the prey eaten. It is estimated that tigers in Panna kill approximately 60 to 70 cattle each year, which translates to 11% of all the prey killed. However, the kill data of collared tigers show that the contribution by cattle can be as high as 39%, and for some individuals it is even higher. There are extensive parts within the protected areas which are used by both tigers and cattle. In these areas cattle comprise one of the major prey species for tigers and therefore play a critical role in their ecology. Wild prey availability is at its lowest here and tigers are largely dependent on cattle. The collared male's territory includes a large proportion of such habitat and its monitoring reveals that 70% of its kills are of cattle. Similarly, another collared female, who had established her territory at the periphery of the park in similar habitat, also takes a large number of livestock (60%). This is a serious issue for management, especially in the case of the breeding female. Moreover, over 50% of the tiger population lives outside the protected habitat, sharing it with a large number of livestock. Livestock predation is widespread and a common problem in tiger habitat, wherever cattle are grazed. Persistent killing of livestock by tigers and their dependence on livestock as observed in Panna bring them in direct conflict with local people.

The regular monitoring of tigers helps us determine how tiger density is likely to be affected by the composition and availability of wild ungulates. The two large ungulate prey, nilgai and sambar, form the bulk of the ungulate biomass in the area. The nilgai's preference for open habitat precludes it from substituting as the principal prey for tigers in dry forest habitats. Nilgai is not killed by tigers in proportion to its availability, although they are preyed upon when in habitat frequented by tigers. This implies that a high nilgai or wild ungulate biomass in open and disturbed habitats need not necessarily translate into high prey availability for tigers.

In the subcontinent, medium-sized animals, especially chital, form the major prey and contribute substantially to the prey biomass available to tigers in all the habitats where tigers are found in higher densities. Looking at the contribution made by different sizes of prey in the availability of prey biomass, if we compare Panna with high tiger-density areas, it is obvious that medium-sized prey is almost absent in Panna. Contribution by medium-sized prey is over 40% in high tiger densities areas, whereas in Panna it is less then 10%. Large prey such as sambar and nilgai together contribute over 80% to the prey biomass availability but in low prey density areas they cannot provide the numbers required for the tiger. Medium-size prey can attain higher densities and make it possible for a tiger to get food at regular intervals. The collared tigress, raising three one-year-old cubs, was able to kill a medium- to large-sized prey on average once in every six days in an area with high sambar density and low chital (medium-sized prey) density. Scat analysis, however, showed that the tigers in Panna fed more on smaller prey (34%) than did tigers in any other area. The tigers in Panna are able to compensate this low availability of medium-sized prey to some extent by preying more on smaller mammals such as langurs and four-horn antelopes. But for large predators like tigers it is demanding on their energy: the role of medium-size prey in the ecology of the tiger could therefore be an important factor in affecting the tiger's responses (such as tiger densities and reproductive success) significantly more than other prey species. A wider availability of medium-sized prey with increased abundance will have a positive effect on tiger ecology. This is especially since one of the major prey, the nilgai, which occupies open habitats is not preferred by the tiger and therefore limits the prey availability.

The problems faced by the tiger population in Panna concern their small population size, low abundance of suitable prey and widespread human disturbance. These factors can affect the reproductive success of the population. The preliminary analysis based on the existing survival/mortality rates estimates that a minimum of seven to nine female breeding territories are required for a demographically viable population. But the field situation is different: the 543 km^2 reserve possibly protects one breeding unit (includes three female territories) entirely and the other partly, with two female ranges within the park. The survival rate in these protected territories is highly variable. Only 60–70 km^2 of undisturbed habitat with high prey abundance, which partly supports two breeding territories, is the only area where high breeding success is observed. Ecologically, for the survival of tiger populations in an area, the number of tigers is not a very important issue but to know what proportion of the tiger population is breeding in good habitat is critical for the management of the species.

This problem for tigers is further accentuated in dry forest habitat due to very high human and cattle dependence on forest resources, creating sub-optimal conditions for tigers. At the end of the growing season, when most of the pastures are grazed, pressures intensify on the intact plant biomass of the reserve. In these habitats livestock populations are largely dependent on forest resources for most of the year. The cumulative effect of higher human pressure, small and fragmented habitats, high cattle dependence and low prey availability, makes tiger populations in these habitats more susceptible to the extinction process. The slightest perturbation will have a pronounced effect on such tiger populations. This is evident from past trends, which show that tigers have disappeared from about 70% of the semi-arid and from 35% of the dry forest habitats. This loss of tiger populations is very high in comparison to the loss in larger and more productive and moist habitats, where tigers still survive extensively. To manage tiger populations in these sub-optimal habitats more inviolate breeding habitats need to be created, the availability of suitable prey needs to be increased and further scientific studies aimed at specific management needs are required. Inviolate breeding habitats that ensure the tigers' reproductive success, the raising of cubs to adulthood and the successful dispersal of progeny must be central issues for the conservation of the species. A further critically important recourse for achieving tiger conservation is that conservation planning for the species must look at the larger landscapes rather than focus on single isolated units. These considerations will be crucial if we have to save India's wild tigers.

Valmik
Thapar

The Big Cat Massacre

Valmik Thapar has spent twenty-five years working to save wild tigers. He has written eight books on tigers and presented the BBC film series 'Land of the Tiger'. He has been chairman of the Cat Specialist Group of IUCN for South Asia and a member of several committees relating to India's Ministry of Environment and Forests. He is the founder of the Ranthambhore Foundation which both works to save the tiger across India as well as networks on tiger-conservation issues across the planet.

Valmik Thapar watches a tigress glide by him in Ranthambhore National Park, Rajasthan. Ranthambhore is today the best place in the world to watch wild tigers. (Photo courtesy Sanjna Kapoor.)

I thought I would end this century feasting on the extraordinary recovery of the wild tigers of Ranthambhore Tiger Reserve in the state of Rajasthan and in a way I did. I spent nearly thirty minutes reversing my Jeep some 4 kms in the face of a tigress that at 3 p.m. decided to move from one end of the valley to another and it was a day to remember as I quietly clicked my camera and loved every minute of it. It was also confirmed around then that after forty years a male wild dog had been sighted in Ranthambhore—what a recovery!

But I was rudely awakened on 19 December 1999 to the grim horrors of what is happening to the wilderness when, purely by accident, the sales tax inspectors in Ghaziabad, a small town in north India, intercepted a truck and found instead of illegal garments 50 leopard skins, 3 tiger skins and a handful of other skins. The story came in and out of the papers, as most things do these days, and some of us in and out of government remained in shock for a couple of days. After all it was probably the second largest seizure of big cat skins since Independence and brought home the fact that our precious wilderness was vanishing. Something must have needled me and finally, gathering courage to face the slaughter, I went with some of the seniormost officers of the Ministry of Environment and Forests to the city of Ghaziabad.

It was 7 a.m. and the smog and mist of the filth of both Delhi and all its satellite towns was only just lifting. We drove for over an hour and then into the sprawling mess of Ghaziabad's bylanes until we arrived at the District Forest Officer's (DFO) residence. I was with the Inspector-General of Forests and as we stepped out of the car and walked a few yards round a corner—there in front of us were laid out and hanging the skins of so many dead leopards that the first sight of them took our breath away and stunned all of us into silence. In a numb state we moved forward, looking slowly at what must be the tip of an iceberg in the ongoing massacre of India's wildlife. How many thousands of mornings I have waited even for the faintest sign of a leopard in India's forests. I have craved a glimpse of them. In over 25 years I have only seen 28 living leopards and here I was surrounded by 50 dead ones.

Some were enormous in size, the skins shining in the early

morning sun. There were hardly any marks on them—probably poisoned or electrocuted—a couple appeared to have been caught in foot traps and then smashed on the head, as suggested by congealed blood. They all looked freshly killed—over the last six months. They had been cured somewhere and waxed, and even had the signature of the 'artist' at the back. They were perfectly folded like table cloths—it was a blood curdling sight. I could imagine the horrors that these animals must have been put through—their agony, their death howls. Standing silently in the midst of the skins my head, my heart, my every pore seemed sent to oblivion. I realised that the recovery of Ranthambhore was probably only an illusion.

I touched, looked and turned over some of the skins—my colleagues from the ministry were shocked. In a way, we were as close to tears as anyone could be. I moved to an enormous tiger skin—its foot looked punctured by a foot trap, its flank had spear or knife marks, suggesting the tiger had roared in fury and pain and the poaching gang had come by and speared it down. My vision of the end of the century had been ripped apart, torn in pieces; it was covered in blood. There was no doubt that hundreds of leopards and tigers were being decimated by the co-ordinated working of poaching gangs right across India. Were skins being ordered like garments? Why were there exactly 50 leopard skins booked from Delhi to Siliguri, a small town close to the border of Nepal? Are there other such '50' consignments? How many gangs are out there engaged in this horrific slaughter?

One century has just ended, another has just started, but as a conservation community we have totally failed. The government, the ministry, the states, the NGOs, and people like myself—we have entered the twenty-first century with no intelligence, no information, we are totally impotent because there is hardly any effective mechanism of wildlife governance and enforcement. All our laws are violated with impunity. We are mute spectators to the massive slaughter in every forest of India. If big business has ripped apart India's wilderness for mining, illegal traders have picked out our precious wildlife for commerce and none of us have worked out a way to counter either. Our natural treasury is being devastated.

The twentieth century could not have ended on an uglier or more hideous note.

Now, in this disastrous dawn of a new century, the wildlife of India is dying. It is national shame, an unmitigated disaster that our country has not been able to take on the challenge to save its superb natural heritage. There is really no room for lip service any more, no room for complacency. There is only one goal ahead. Those who care must engage in the battle to save some of India's natural treasures and secure their future—so far we have failed.

In the core of my head I carry into the new millennium only a vision of skin and bone, of congealed blood, of a mass of skins, of the horrors of what man does. This is my 'new millennium', my utter, utter shame at our total impotence to save the wilderness of a great nation, my devastation at the global indifference to protecting our wilderness across the planet.

I didn't realise that the beginning of the twenty-first century would get even worse. On 12 January 2000, a day I will never forget, acting on a tip that must have resulted from the 19 December seizure, a police party with wildlife inspectors raided three premises in Khaga, Fatehpur, in the North Indian state of Uttar Pradesh, and seized 70 leopard skins, 4 tigers skins, 221 blackbuck skins, 18,000 leopard claws, and 132 tiger claws. It appears that both these seizures are linked. The three premises were illegal factories that were tanning and curing skins. By 15 January, from around these premises more than 185 kgs of tiger and leopard bones were recovered, revealing the horrifying state of affairs. Wildlife governance was in a complete state of collapse and clearly 'operation wipe-out' was on. As if this was not enough, by May two more seizures in Haldwani resulted in a recovery of 80 more leopard skins and endless other skins.

The twenty-first century had dawned with a nightmare. The biggest haul of large cat skins had taken place over a few weeks at the end of one century and the beginning of another. Never before had there been a haul of this magnitude and scale in the history of India. Skins, bones and derivatives of 1400 leopards and 50 tigers—all in one state! Imagine what has been processed in these factories over the last decade.

We are already losing at least 10,000 sq. kms of dense forest each year to timber mafias and so-called developers. We believe that at least 12 billion dollars worth of forest is exploited from India's natural treasury each year, and I am convinced that hundreds of tigers and leopards are trapped, poisoned and poached so that their skin, claws and derivatives feed the international market. The skin market across the world is booming with demand and the planet is losing its best natural treasure. This is not just India's failure. We have failed globally. Much of the responsibility must fall on our international organisations, both inter-governmental and non-governmental.

The last two seizures are the tip of an iceberg. India's wilderness heads for disaster. To prevent it requires global will and urgent reform in the enforcement mechanisms that prevent illegal trade across the world. Can we hope for a global political will that brings effective international co-operation and not lip service? Can we hope that innovative mechanisms for enforcement do not get lost in endless rhetoric and diplomacy? Can we even begin to hope that human beings everywhere will act before it is too late to reverse the horrors that envelope us all, across the planet? Can we greet the new century with effective global field action?

I have followed the trail of the tiger for twenty-five years and it has led me over the richest part of India, forest India. In this forest land there is a vast amount of timber, marble, gems, manganese, iron ore, bauxite and so many minerals that everyone's mouth waters. Minor forest produce abounds and everyone wants a bit of the land. Big dams, infrastructural projects and land mafias want their piece too. It is India's natural treasury and this natural wealth is under so much pressure that its very survival is threatened.

This is 20% of India, and the most neglected sector of governance, probably by the explicit preference of our ignorant political leadership. In this country we don't create mechanisms for protection but we excel at creating mechanisms for exploitation. We must work out ways to stop it and put public pressure on our political leadership to restructure existing mechanisms and focus on real issues. For instance, take the federal arm involved with saving tigers in the Ministry of Environment and Forests: 95% of its time, effort and money are spent on clearing public and private sector projects and dealing with city pollution. The 20% of India which is forest India has been allocated a tiny insignificant 'wing' to deal with its issues. Can you imagine—the richest part of India has only a 'wildlife wing'? The richest part of India never has a decent allocation of money from the Planning Commission. The richest part of India has no ministry to protect it.

No one cares. Everyone lives by rhetoric. The problems of the forest get only lip service and countless recommendations gather dust in different offices—what a tragedy of governance! What a mockery of administration.

How do you save tigers in the twenty-first century? We must start from scratch and restructure all our mechanisms for wildlife and forest administration. To start with we need

(a) A new federal ministry for the protection of forests and wildlife
(b) A review of the Indian Forest Service for encouraging specialization in the protection of biological resources
(c) We need to have a national armed force for the forest officer, on call like a Forest Police Force, to minimise the enormous damage to our natural treasury
(d) We need rapid financial mechanisms to disburse money from the federal structure to the field for better management
(e) We need to declare this sector ESSENTIAL so that the huge vacancies that plague forest staff are filled and the gates to looting are closed
(f) The time has come in the twenty-first century to disband Project Tiger that over the decades has become only a disburser of money and has no power to govern. Instead, under this new ministry a 'Tiger Protection Authority of India' must be created that is empowered under the law to appoint, recruit, transfer and assess all officers in Tiger Reserves from the rank of Ranger upwards. This 'authority' must also be able to disburse money directly to the field and have the final say in the management of all our twenty-seven Project Tiger Reserves

Only when these mechanisms are actually and effectively put in place can we even *begin* to start tackling the details of the most vital and most seriously neglected area of our planet—the forests. Land-use policy, community conservation schemes, joint forest management, and so much more requires innovative brain-storming. The first priority is to set into motion the six measures outlined above. The rest will follow. Only then will we be on the path of saving wild tigers in the new millennium.

P.K.
Sen

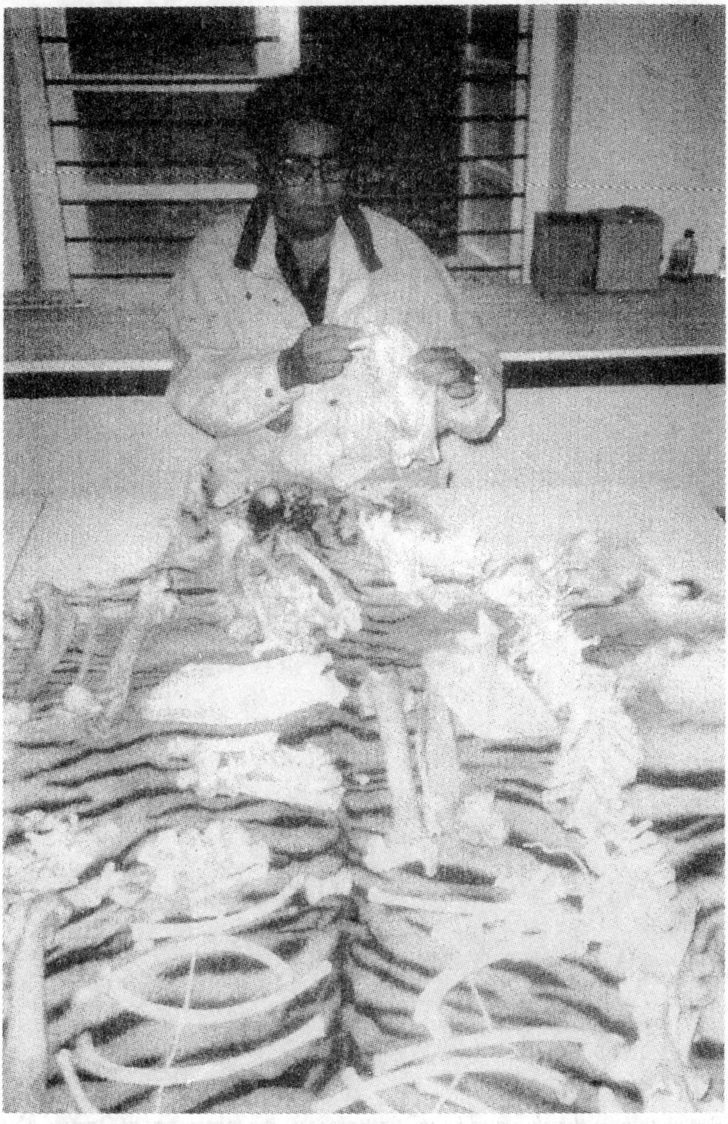

The Future of the Tiger in the Twenty-First Century

P.K.Sen has spent more than thirty years in the Forest Service of India, in the state of Bihar. Over the past four years he has been Director, Project Tiger, in which position he has watched and worked to prevent the decline of the tiger.

P. K. Sen examines the skin and bone of a tigress in the laboratory of Periyar National Park, Kerala. The managers of tiger forests face enormous problems because of the illegal trade in tiger derivatives. (Photo courtesy Valmik Thapar.)

(1) Today few care about the value of living tigers and they are killed for the cash they bring in, be it skin or bones.
(2) Tigers die every day, either on account of man destroying their habitats or because of poaching. In the first six months of the new millennium, more than 100 tigers are dead because of poachers, man–animal conflicts, and other reasons. Many deaths go unrecorded and I believe that the number of tigers has now crashed to below 3000 and is falling rapidly.
(3) The overexploitation of natural resources has reached a peak and no one wants the tiger to survive, be it politician, bureaucrat, industrialist, human activist or villager. Even foresters are casual in their approach.
(4) Thoughtless development activities have resulted in enormous natural calamities, be it drought, flood or landslide. The myth of the green revolution is being exploded as agriculture in much of our country produces less than had been envisaged. In fact, because of this there is a vast increase in the pressures on our forests, both human and cattle.
(5) Few realise that tiger habitats not only harbour tigers but also recharge most of our river systems.
(6) Globalisation ruthlessly plunders our natural resources and we enter a doomsday scenario for the tiger.

SAVING WILD TIGERS

The future is bleak but if we want to save wild tigers and prevent the tiger catastrophe, we need the following immediate steps:
(i) Split the Ministry of Environment and Forests, Government of India, to give it more focus and power and create a special Ministry for Forest India which is, 20% of our land mass.
(ii) To control poaching of wildlife, create a new force and also involve existing forces so laws are enforced and culprits caught and punished
(iii) Give full protection to those protecting our natural resources; cease political interference
(iv) Give a share of development benefits to forest-fringe dwellers and do not allow so-called human activists sitting in cities to

act as their sympathisers. Give the people the right to choose and make their own decisions

(v) Make 1% of the country's land mass completely inviolate and dedicate it to wildlife. A country which cannot meet its needs with 99% of land has no right to be governed by its existing system. Identify that 1% land within a stipulated period of six months and declare it an exclusive area for wildlife

(vi) Seal the eastern, north-eastern and sea borders with Nepal and Bangladesh to prevent large-scale smuggling of wildlife derivatives and tiger skin and bone.

FURTHER READING

This is a select list: a full bibliography requires a separate book in itself. Additional material will be found in the copyright statement.

Ahmad, Yusuf S. *With the Wild Animals of Bengal* (Y.S. Ahmad, Dhaka, 1981)

Alfred, J.R.B. *et al. The Red Data Book of Indian Animals, Part 1: Vertebrata* (ZSI, Calcutta, 1994)

Ali, Salim. 'The Mohgal emperors of India as naturalists and sportsmen' (*Journal of the Bombay Natural History Society* 31 (4): 833–61, Bombay)

Alvi, M.A. and A. Rahman. *Jahangir—The Naturalist* (Delhi, 1968)

Baikov, N.A. *The Manchurian Tiger* (Hutchinson, London, 1925)

Baker, S. *Wild Beasts and their Ways* (London, 1890)

Barnes, Simon. *Tiger* (Boxtree, London, 1994)

Baze, W. *Tiger, Tiger* (London, 1957)

Bedi, Rajesh and Ramesh Bedi. *Indian Wildlife* (Brijbasi, New Delhi, 1984)

—*Wild India* (Brijbasi, New Delhi, 1990)

Biscoe, W. 'A tiger killing a panther' (*Journal of the Bombay Natural History Society* 9(4): 490, Bombay, 1895)

Brandar, A. Dunbar. *Wild Animals of Central India* (Arnold, London, 1923)

Breeden, Stanley and Belinda Wright. *Through The Tiger's Eyes: Chronicle of India's Vanishing Wildlife* (Ten Speed Press, USA, 1997)

Campbell, T. 'A tiger eating a bear' (*Journal of the Bombay Natural History Society* 9(1): 101, Bombay, 1894)

Chakrabarti, Kalyan. *Man-eating Tigers* (Darbari Prokashan, Calcutta, 1992)

Champion, F. *In Sunlight and Shadow* (Chatto & Windus, London, 1925)

—*With a Camera in Tiger Land* (Chatto & Windus, London, 1927)

Choudhury, S.R., Khairi. *The Beloved Tigress* (Natraj 1999)

Corbett, G.B. and J.E. Hill. *The Mammals of the Indomalayan Region* (Natural History Museum/OUP, London/Oxford, 1992)

Corbett, G. 'A tiger attacking elephants' (*Journal of the Bombay Natural History Society* (7)1: 192, Bombay, 1892)

Corbett, J. *Man Eaters of Kumaon* (Oxford University Press, Oxford, 1944)

Courtney, N. *The Tiger—Symbol of Freedom* (Quartet Books, London, 1980)

Cronin, E.W. *The Arun: A Natural History of the World's Deepest Valley* (Houghton Mifflin, Boston, 1979)

Cubitt, Gerald and Guy Mountfort. *Wild India* (Collins, London, 1985)

Daniel, J.C. *A Century of Natural History* (BNHS/OUP, Bombay, 1986)

—*A Week with Elephants* (BNHS, Bombay, 1996)

—*The Leopard in India—A National History* (Natraj, Dehra Dun, 1996)

Davidar, E.R.C. *Cheetal Walk* (OUP Delhi, 1997)

Denzau, Gertrude and Helmut. *Konigstiger* (Tecklenborg Verlag, Steinfurt, 1996)

Desai, J.H. and A.K. Malhotra. *The White Tiger* (Publications Division, Ministry of Information & Broadcasting, New Delhi, 1992)

Dharmakumarsinhji, R.S. *Reminiscences of Indian Wildlife* (OUP, Delhi, 1998)

Divyabhanusinh. *The End of a Trail—The Cheetah in India* (Banyan Books, New Delhi, 1996)

Eisenberg, John F., George McKay and John Seidensticker. *Asian Elephants—Studies in Sri Lanka*, (Smithsonian, Washington, 1990)

Fend, Werner. *Die Tiger Von Abutschmar* (Verlag Fritz Molden, Vienna, 1972)

Flemming, Robert L.Jr. *The Ecology, Flora and Fauna of Midland Nepal* (Tribhuvan University, Kathmandu, 1977)

Gee, E.P. *The Wildlife of India* (Collins, London, 1964)

Ghorpade, M.Y. *Sunlight and Shadows* (Gollancz, London, 1983)

Green, M.J.B. *IUCN Directory of South Asian Protected Areas* (IUCN, Cambridge, 1990)

—*Nature Reserves of the Himalaya and the Mountains of Central Asia* (OUP, New Delhi, 1993)

Gurung, K.K. *Heart of the Jungle—the Wildlife of Chitawan, Nepal* (Andre Deutsch, London, 1983)

—*Mammals of the Indian Sub-continent and Where to Watch Them* (Indian Experience, Oxford, 1996)

Hanley, P. *Tiger Trails in Assam* (Robert Hale, London, 1961)

Hardy, Sarah B. *The Langurs of Abu* (Harvard University Press, Cambridge, USA, 1977)

Hillard, Darla. *Vanishing Tracks—Four Years Among the Snow Leopards of Nepal* (Elm Tree Books, London, 1989)

Hooker, J.D. *Himalayan Journals*, 2 vols (John Murray, London, 1855)

Hornocker, M., *Track of the Tiger* (Sierra Club Books, 1997)

Israel, S. and Toby Sinclair. *Indian Wildlife* (Apa Publications, Singapore, 1987)

Ives, Richard, *Of Tigers and Men* (Doubleday, New York, 1995)

Jackson, Peter. *Endangered Species—Tigers* (The Apple Press, London, 1990)

Khan, M.A.R. *Mammals of Bangladesh* (Nazima Reza, Dhaka, 1985)

—*The Handbook of India's Wildlife* (TTK, Madras, 1983)

Krishnan, M. *India's Wildlife 1959–70* (BNHS, Bombay, 1975)

Lahiri Choudhury, D.K. *The Great Indian Elephant Book* (OUP, New Delhi, 2000)

Littledale, H. 'Bears being eaten by tigers' (*Journal of the Bombay Natural History Society* 4(4): 316, Bombay, 1889)

Locke, A. *The Tigers of Trengganu* (London, 1954)

Manfredi, Paola. *In Danger* (Ranthambhore Foundation, New Delhi, 1997)
Mathiessen, Peter. *The Snow Leopard* (Chatto & Windus, London, 1979)
—*Tigers in the Snow* (Harvill, London, 2000)
McDougal, C. *Face of the Tiger* (Andre Deutsch and Rivington Books, London, 1977)
McNeely, A. Jeffrey and P.S. Wachtel. *The Soul of the Tiger* (Doubleday, New York, 1988)
Menon, Vivek. *On the Brink: Travels in the Wilds of India* (Penguin India, New Delhi, 1999)
Meacham, Cory. *How the Tiger Lost Its Stripes* (Harcourt Brace, New York, 1997)
Mishra, Hemanta and Dorothy Mierow. *Wild Animals of Nepal* (Kathmandu, 1976)
—and Jefferies, M. *Royal Chitawan National Park; Wildlife Heritage of Nepal* (The Mountaineers, Seattle, 1991)
Montgomery, Sy. *Spell of the Tiger* (Houghton Mifflin, Boston, 1995)
Morris, R. 'A tigress with five cubs' (*Journal of the Bombay Natural History Society* 31 (3): 810–11, Bombay, 1927)
Moulton, Carroll and Ernie J. Hulsey. *Kanha Tiger Reserve: Portrait of an Indian National Park* (Vakils, Feffer & Simon Ltd., Mumbai, 1999)
Mountfort, G. *Tigers* (David and Charles, Newton Abbot, 1973)
—*Back from the Brink* (Hutchinson, London, 1978)
—*Saving the Tiger* (Michael Joseph, London, 1981)
Mukherjee, Ajit. *Extinct and Vanishing Birds and Mammals of India* (Indian Museum, Calcutta, 1966)
Musselwhite, A. *Behind the Lens in Tiger Land* (London, 1933)
Niyogi, Tushar K. *Tiger Cult of the Sundarbans* (Anthropological Survey of India, Calcutta, 1996)
Naidu, M. Kamal, *Trail of the Tiger* (Natraj, Dehra Dun, 1998)
Oliver, William. *The Pigmy Hog* (Jersey Wildlife Preservation Trust, Jersey, 1980)
Owen Edmunds, Tom. *Bhutan* (Elm Tree Books, London, 1989)
Panwar, H.S. *Kanha National Park—A Handbook* (CEE, Ahmedabad, 1991)
Perry, R. *The World of the Tiger* (Cassell & Co. Ltd., London, 1964)
Philips, W.W. *A Manual of the Mammals of Sri Lanka*, Parts 1–3 (Colombo, 1980–84)
Prater, S. *The Book of Indian Animals* (BNHS, Bombay, 1988)
Ranjitsinh, M.K. *The Indian Blackbuck* (Natraj, Dehra Dun, 1990)
—*Beyond the Tiger, Portraits of South Asian Wildlife* (Brijbasi, New Delhi, 1997)

Richardson, W. 'Tiger cubs' (*Journal of the Bombay Natural History Society* 5(2): 191, Bombay, 1890)
Roonwul, M.L. and S.M. Mohnot, *The Primates of South Asia* (Harvard University Press, Cambridge, USA, 1977)
Saharia, V.B. *Wildlife in India*, (Natraj, Dehra Dun, 1982)
Sanderson, G.P. *Thirteen Years Among the Wild Beasts of India* (W.H. Allen & Co., London, 1896)
Sankhala, K. *Tiger* (Collins, London, 1978)
Schaller, G.B. *Mountain Monarchs—Wild Sheep and Goats of the Himalaya* (Chicago University Press, Chicago, 1977)
—*The Deer and the Tiger* (Chicago University Press, Chicago, 1967)
—*Stones of Silence; Journeys in the Himalaya* (Andre Deutsch, London, 1980)
Scott, Johanthan. *The Leopard's Tale* (Elm Tree Books, London, 1985)
Seidensticker, John, Sarah Christie and Peter Jackson. *Riding the Tiger: Tiger Conservation in Human-dominated Landscapes* (Cambridge University Press, 1999)
Seidensticker, John, *Tiger* (Voyager Press, 1996)
Shah, Anup and Manoj. *A Tiger's Tale* (Fountain Press, Kingston-upon-Thames, 1996)
Shahi, S.P. *Backs to the Wall; Saga of Wildlife in Bihar* (Affiliated East-West Press, Delhi, 1977)
Sharma, B.D. *High Altitude Wildlife in India* (Oxford & India Book House, New Delhi, 1994)
Sheshadri, B. *The Twilight of India's Wildlife* (John Baker, London, 1969)
Singh, Billy Arjan. *Tiger Haven* (Macmillan, London, 1973)
—*Tara, A Tigress* (Quartet Books, London, 1981)
—*Tiger! Tiger!* (Jonathan Cape, London, 1984)
—*The Legend of the Man Eater* (Ravi Dayal, New Delhi, 1993)
—*Tiger Book* (Lotus Roli, Delhi, 1997)
Singh, K. *The Tiger of Rajasthan* (London, 1959)
—*Hints on Tiger Shooting* (The Hindustan Times Ltd., Delhi, 1965)
Skaria, Ajay. *Hybrid Histories: Forests, Frontiers and Wildness in Western India* (OUP, New Delhi, 1999)
Srivastava Arun, *Primates of North-East India* (Megadiversity Press, 2000)
Stebbing, E.P. *Jungle By-ways in India* (London, 1911)
Stracey, P.D. *Tigers* (Arthur Barker Ltd., London, 1968)
Sukumar, R. *The Asian Elephant* (Cambridge University Press, Cambridge, 1989)
—*Elephant Days and Nights* (OUP, New Delhi, 1994)
Sunquist, Fiona and Mel. *Tiger Moon* (University of Chicago Press, Chicago, 1988)
Thapar, Valmik. *With Tigers in the Wild* (Vikas Publishing, Delhi, 1983)
—*Tiger: Portrait of a Predator* (Collins, London, 1986)

—*Tigers: The Secret Life* (Hamish Hamilton, London, 1989)
—*The Secret Life of Tigers* (OUP, New Delhi, 1998)
—*The Tiger's Destiny* (Kyle Cathie, London, 1992)
—*The Land of the Tiger* (BBC Books, London, 1997)
—*Tiger: Habitats, Life Cycle, Food Chains, Threats* (Wayland Publishers, 1999)
—and Fateh Singh Rathore. *Wild Tigers of Ranthambhore* (OUP, New Delhi, 2000)
Tikader, B.M. *Threatened Animals of India* (ZSI, Calcutta, 1993)
Tilson, R.L. and V. Seal, *Tigers of the World: The Biology, Biopolitics, Management and Conservation of an Endangered Species* (Noyes Publications, New Jersey, 1987)
Toogood, C. 'Number of cubs in a tigress' litter' (*Journal of the Bombay Natural History Society* 39 (1): 158, 1936)
Toovey, J. (ed.) *Tigers of the Raj* (Alan Sutton, Gloucester, 1987)
Tyabji, Hashim. *Bandhovgarh National Park* (New Delhi, 1994)
Ward, Geoffrey C. *Tiger-Wallahs*, (HarperCollins, New York, 1993)
—*The Year of the Tiger* (National Geographic Society, Washington, 1998)
Zwaenepoel, Jean-Pierre. *Tigers* (Chronicle Books, San Francisco, 1992)

Copyright Statement

The editor and publishers have sought permission to reproduce material in this book from all traceable copyright holders, as shown below. Perceived omissions should be brought to the notice of the publishers for rectification before reprinting.

Sainthill Eardley-Wilmot, 'Of Forests and Foresters' (originally titled 'Conclusion'), *Forest Life and Sport in India*, Edward Arnold, London, 1911.

E.P. Stebbing, 'Game Sanctuaries and Game Protection in India', *The Dairy of a Sportsman Naturalist*, John Lane, London, 1920.

F.W. Champion, 'Preserving Wildlife in The United Provinces', *Journal of the Bombay Natural History Society*, xxxvii.

Colonel A.I.R. Glasfurd, 'Various Musings', *Musings of an Old Shikari*, John Lane, London, 1928.

Jim Corbett, 'Why Tigers Become Man-Eaters', from the Author's Note in Martin Booth, *Carpet Sahib*, Constable, London, 1986.

Jim Corbett, 'Wildlife in the Village', *Review of the Week*, Naini Tal, 1932.

Stanley Jepson, 'An Appeal for the Preservation of Wild Life,' *Big Game Encounters,* ed. Stanley Jepson, London, 1936.

S.H. Prater, 'The Wild Animals of the Indian Empire', *Journal of the Bombay Natural History Society*, xxxvi, No. 4, 1933.

E.P. Gee, 'The Wild Life of India', *The Wild Life of India*, Fontana, 1964.

Richard Perry, 'The World of the Tiger' (originally titled 'Tigers Past and Present'), *The World of the Tiger*, Cassell, London, 1964.

George Schaller, 'The Deer and the Tiger' (retitled), *The Deer and the Tiger,* © 1967 by The University of Chicago Press. Reprinted by permission of the University of Chicago Press and the Author.

P.D. Stracey, 'The Future of the Tiger', *Tigers*, Arthur Barker, London, 1968.

B. Seshadri, 'The Twilight of the Animals', *The Twilight of India's Wildlife*, John Baker, London, 1969.

Kailash Sankhala, 'The Skin Trade', *Tiger!*, Collins, 1977. © Pradeep Sankhala, Reprinted by permission of Pradeep Sankhala and Tiger Trust.

Billy Arjan Singh, 'The Lost Cause?', *Tiger Haven,* Macmillan, London, 1973. © Billy Arjan Singh. Reprinted by permission of the Author.

Charles McDougal, 'Tigers and Man', *The Face of the Tiger,* Rivington Books, London, 1977. © Charles McDougal. Reprinted with permission.

M.E. Sunquist, 'Radiotracking the Tiger' (originally titled 'Radio Tracking and its Application to the Study and Conservation of Tigers'), paper presented at the International Symposium on Tiger Conservation in India, 1979.

S.P. Shahi, 'Battling for Wildlife in Bihar', *Backs to the Wall*, The Affiliated East West Press, Chennai, 1977.

M. Krishnan, 'Looking Back on Project Tiger', *The Times of India Annual 1977*, reprinted by permission of Dr Meenakshi Harikrishnan, © Meenakshi Harikrishnan.

John Seidensticker, 'Bearing Witness', in *Tigers of the World*, ed. Tilson and Seal, Noyes Publications, New Jersey, 1987.

Guy Mountfort, 'Back from the Brink', *Saving the Tiger*, Michael Joseph Ltd. London, 1981.

Nicholas Courtney, 'If all the Beasts were Gone', *The Tiger*, Quartet Books, London, 1980. © Nicholas Courtney.

Peter Jackson, 'Problems and Solutions', from *Tigers*, The Apple Press, London, 1990. By permission of the author.

Alan Rabinowitz, 'Wildlife Abuse', *Chasing the Dragon's Tail*, © Alan Rabinowitz 1991. Reprinted by permission of William Morris Agency, Inc, on behalf of the author.

Geoffrey Ward, 'Massacre', *Tigerwallahs*, HarperCollins, NY, 1993, © Geoffrey Ward. Reprinted by permission of the author.

John Seidensticker, 'Why Save Tigers' (retitled), in *Tigers*, 1996, Text © John Seidensticker, is reprinted with permission of the publisher, Voyageur Press, 123 North Second Street, PO BOX 338, Stillwater, MN 5508 USA, Fax: 612-430-2211, email books@voyageurpress.com.

Ullas Karanth, 'The Brutal Encounter: Man and Tiger', *In Danger*, ed. Paola Manfredi, © The Ranthambhore Foundation, Delhi, 1977.

Alan Rabinowitz, 'The Status of the Indochinese Tiger', *Riding the Tiger*, ed. John Seidensticker, Sarah Christie and Peter Jackson, Cambridge University Press, 1999, © The Zoological Society of London.

John Seidensticker *et al.*, 'Approaches to Tiger Conservation', ibid.

Steven Russel Galster and Karin Vaud Eliot, 'Roaring Back', ibid.

Sarah Christie *et al.*, 'Vision and process in Securing a Future for Wild Tigers', ibid.

R.S. Chundawat and Neel Gogate, 'Saving Wild Tigers in a Sub-Optimal Dry Forest Habitat', unpublished. © The Authors.

'The Big Cat Massacre' and 'Introduction' © Valmik Thapar.

